Hot Gimmick

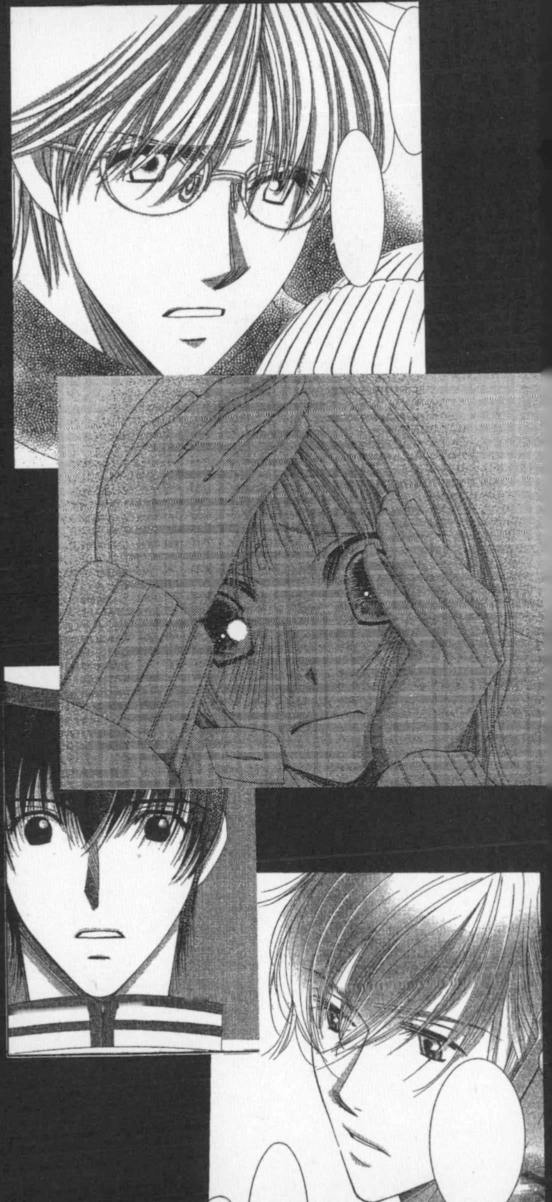

vol.6

MIKI AIHARA

HOT GIMMICK
CONTENTS

Chapter 24

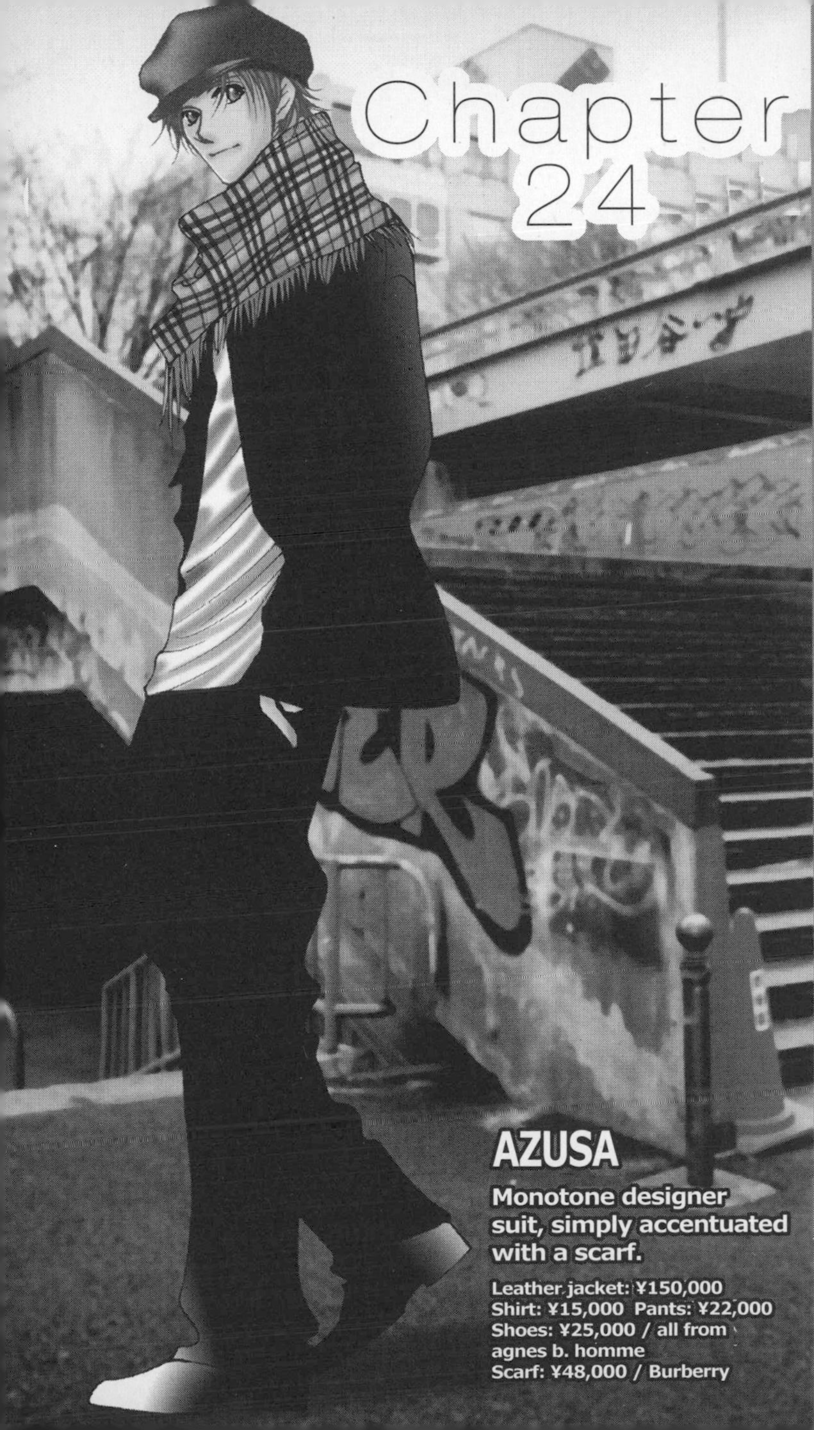
AZUSA
Monotone designer suit, simply accentuated with a scarf.
Leather jacket: ¥150,000
Shirt: ¥15,000 Pants: ¥22,000
Shoes: ¥25,000 / all from agnes b. homme
Scarf: ¥48,000 / Burberry

hotgimmick

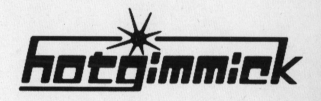

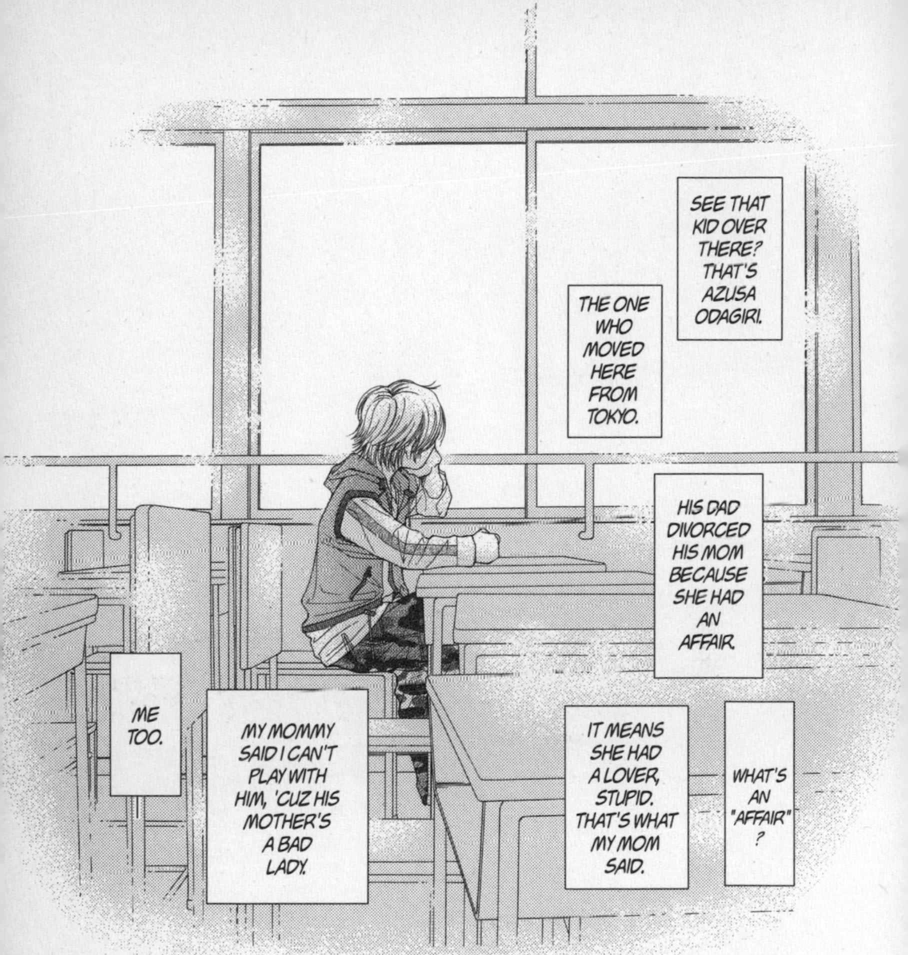
SEE THAT KID OVER THERE? THAT'S AZUSA ODAGIRI.
THE ONE WHO MOVED HERE FROM TOKYO.
HIS DAD DIVORCED HIS MOM BECAUSE SHE HAD AN AFFAIR.
WHAT'S AN "AFFAIR"?
IT MEANS SHE HAD A LOVER, STUPID. THAT'S WHAT MY MOM SAID.
MY MOMMY SAID I CAN'T PLAY WITH HIM, 'CUZ HIS MOTHER'S A BAD LADY.
ME TOO.

hot gimmick

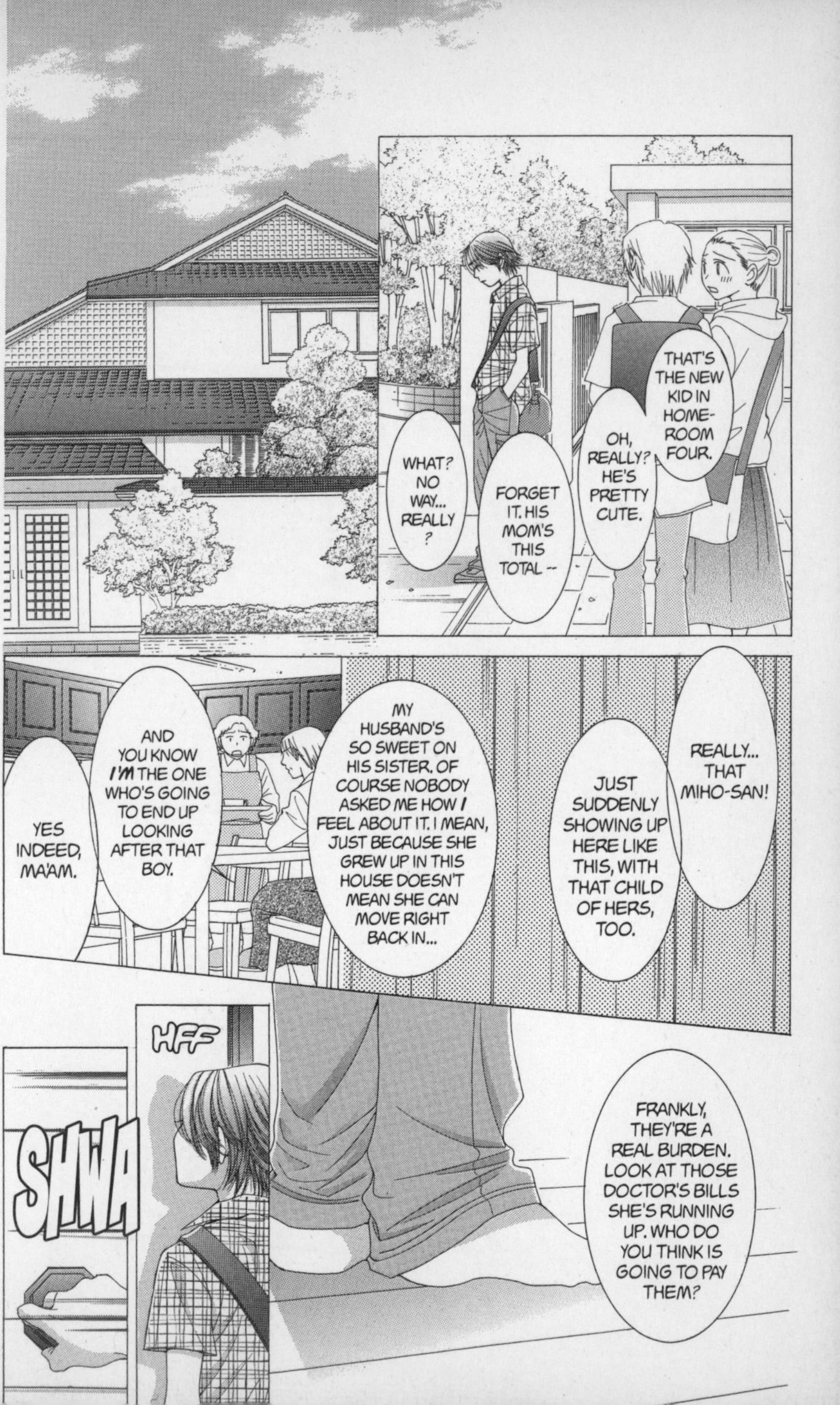
THAT'S THE NEW KID IN HOME-ROOM FOUR.
OH, REALLY? HE'S PRETTY CUTE.
FORGET IT. HIS MOM'S THIS TOTAL --
WHAT? NO WAY... REALLY?
REALLY... THAT MIHO-SAN!
JUST SUDDENLY SHOWING UP HERE LIKE THIS, WITH THAT CHILD OF HERS, TOO.
MY HUSBAND'S SO SWEET ON HIS SISTER. OF COURSE NOBODY ASKED ME HOW *I* FEEL ABOUT IT. I MEAN, JUST BECAUSE SHE GREW UP IN THIS HOUSE DOESN'T MEAN SHE CAN MOVE RIGHT BACK IN...
AND YOU KNOW *I'M* THE ONE WHO'S GOING TO END UP LOOKING AFTER THAT BOY.
YES INDEED, MA'AM.
FRANKLY, THEY'RE A REAL BURDEN. LOOK AT THOSE DOCTOR'S BILLS SHE'S RUNNING UP. WHO DO YOU THINK IS GOING TO PAY THEM?
HFF
SHWA

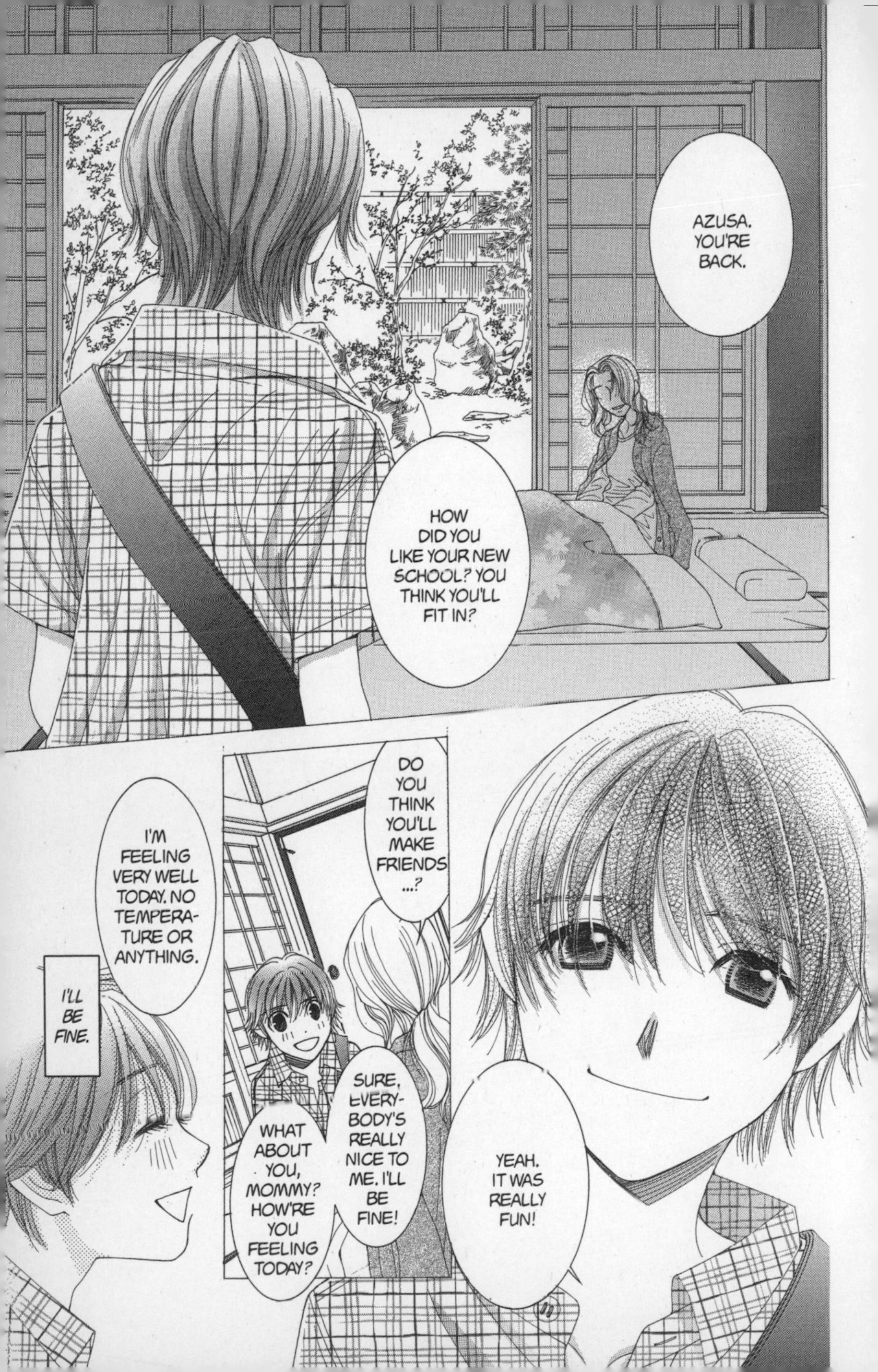
AZUSA. YOU'RE BACK.
HOW DID YOU LIKE YOUR NEW SCHOOL? YOU THINK YOU'LL FIT IN?
YEAH. IT WAS REALLY FUN!
DO YOU THINK YOU'LL MAKE FRIENDS ...?
SURE, EVERYBODY'S REALLY NICE TO ME. I'LL BE FINE!
WHAT ABOUT YOU, MOMMY? HOW'RE YOU FEELING TODAY?
I'M FEELING VERY WELL TODAY. NO TEMPERATURE OR ANYTHING.
I'LL BE FINE.

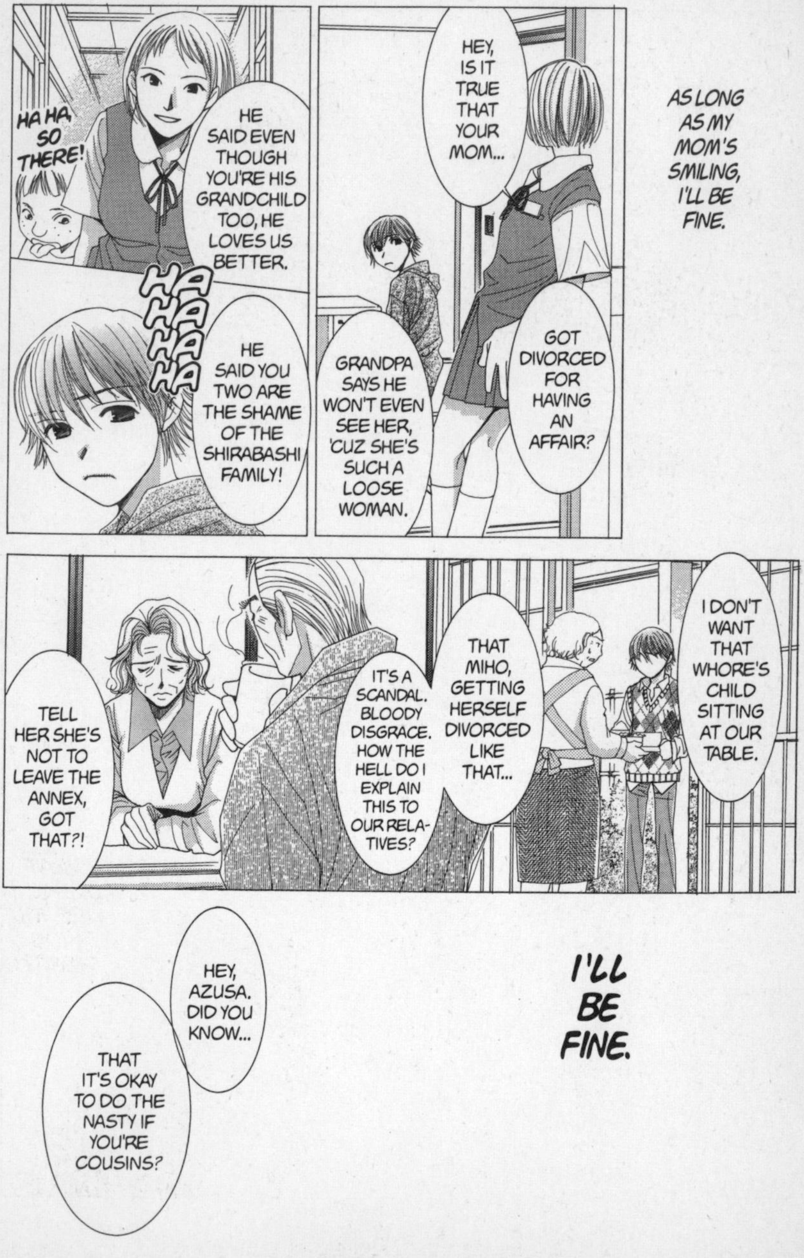
AS LONG AS MY MOM'S SMILING, I'LL BE FINE.
HEY, IS IT TRUE THAT YOUR MOM...
GOT DIVORCED FOR HAVING AN AFFAIR?
GRANDPA SAYS HE WON'T EVEN SEE HER, 'CUZ SHE'S SUCH A LOOSE WOMAN.
HE SAID EVEN THOUGH YOU'RE HIS GRANDCHILD TOO, HE LOVES US BETTER.
HA HA, SO THERE!
HAHAHAHA
HE SAID YOU TWO ARE THE SHAME OF THE SHIRABASHI FAMILY!
I DON'T WANT THAT WHORE'S CHILD SITTING AT OUR TABLE.
THAT MIHO, GETTING HERSELF DIVORCED LIKE THAT...
IT'S A SCANDAL. BLOODY DISGRACE. HOW THE HELL DO I EXPLAIN THIS TO OUR RELATIVES?
TELL HER SHE'S NOT TO LEAVE THE ANNEX, GOT THAT?!
I'LL BE FINE.
HEY, AZUSA. DID YOU KNOW...
THAT IT'S OKAY TO DO THE NASTY IF YOU'RE COUSINS?

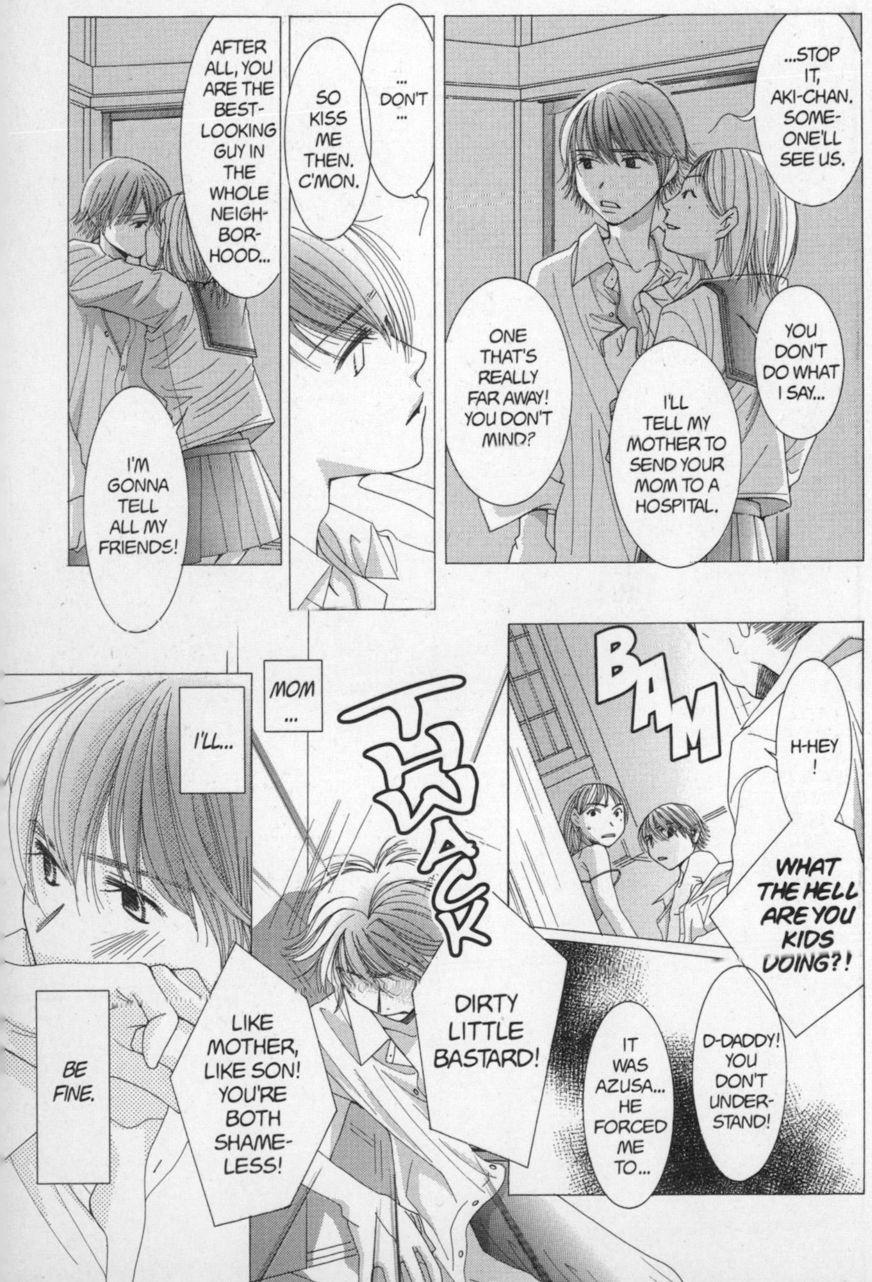
...STOP IT, AKI-CHAN. SOME-ONE'LL SEE US.
YOU DON'T DO WHAT I SAY...
I'LL TELL MY MOTHER TO SEND YOUR MOM TO A HOSPITAL.
ONE THAT'S REALLY FAR AWAY! YOU DON'T MIND?
... DON'T ...
SO KISS ME THEN. C'MON.
AFTER ALL, YOU ARE THE BEST-LOOKING GUY IN THE WHOLE NEIGH-BOR-HOOD...
I'M GONNA TELL ALL MY FRIENDS!
BAM
H-HEY!
WHAT THE HELL ARE YOU KIDS DOING?!
D-DADDY! YOU DON'T UNDER-STAND!
IT WAS AZUSA... HE FORCED ME TO...
THWACK
DIRTY LITTLE BASTARD!
LIKE MOTHER, LIKE SON! YOU'RE BOTH SHAME-LESS!
MOM ...
I'LL...
BE FINE.

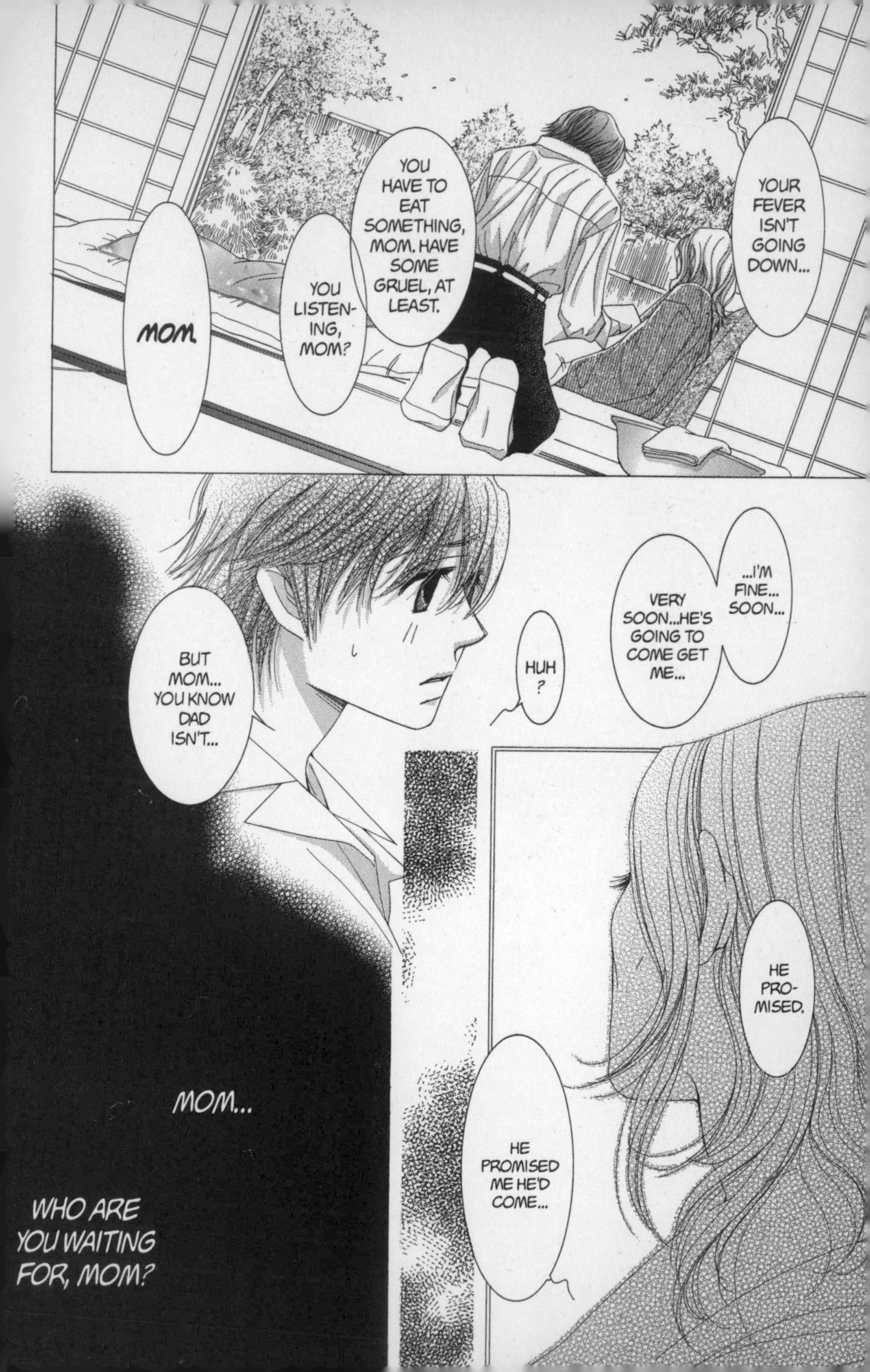
YOUR FEVER ISN'T GOING DOWN...
YOU HAVE TO EAT SOMETHING, MOM. HAVE SOME GRUEL, AT LEAST.
YOU LISTENING, MOM?
MOM.
...I'M FINE... SOON...
VERY SOON...HE'S GOING TO COME GET ME...
HUH?
BUT MOM... YOU KNOW DAD ISN'T...
HE PROMISED.
HE PROMISED ME HE'D COME...
MOM...
WHO ARE YOU WAITING FOR, MOM?

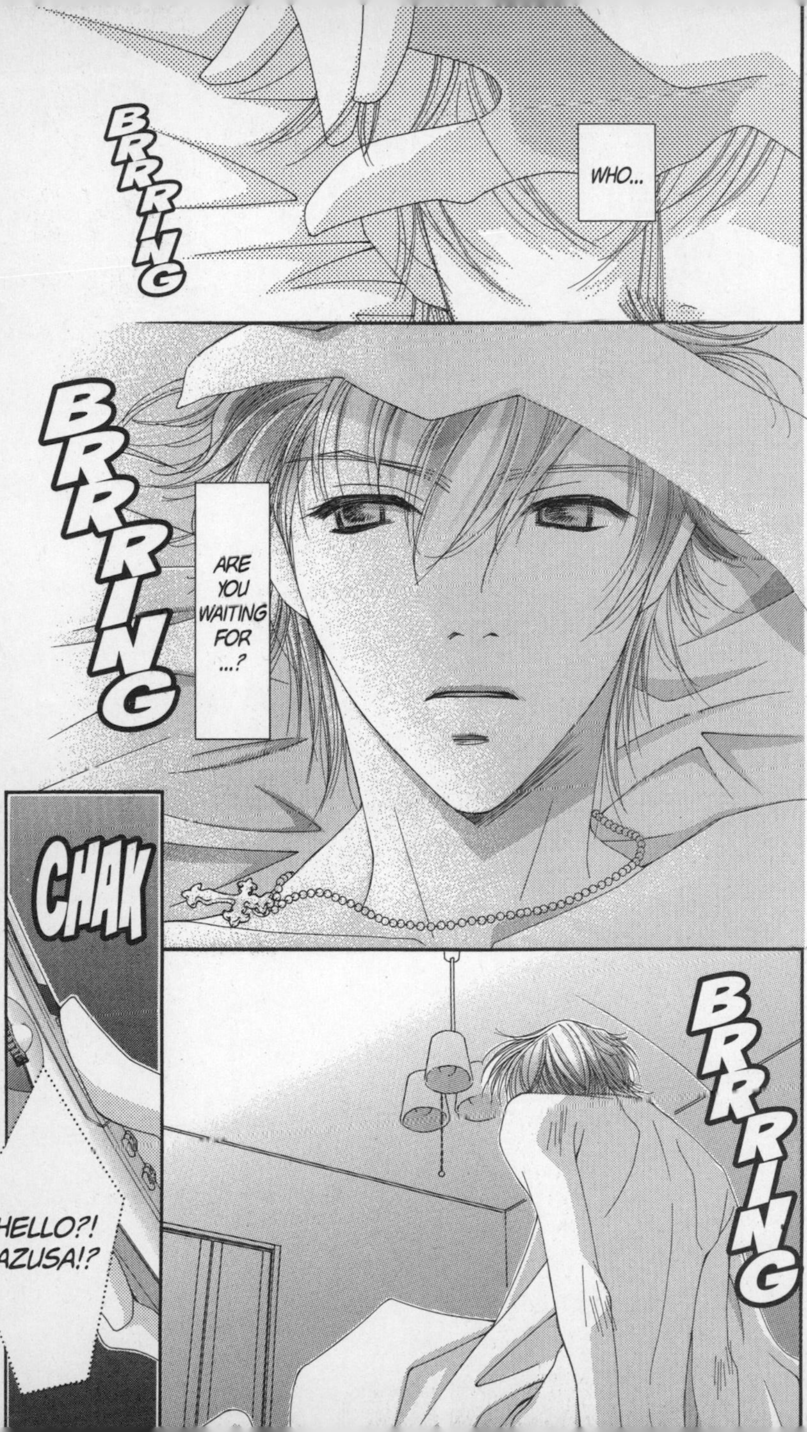
WHO...
BRRRING
ARE YOU WAITING FOR ...?
BRRRING
BRRRING
CHAK
HELLO?! AZUSA!?

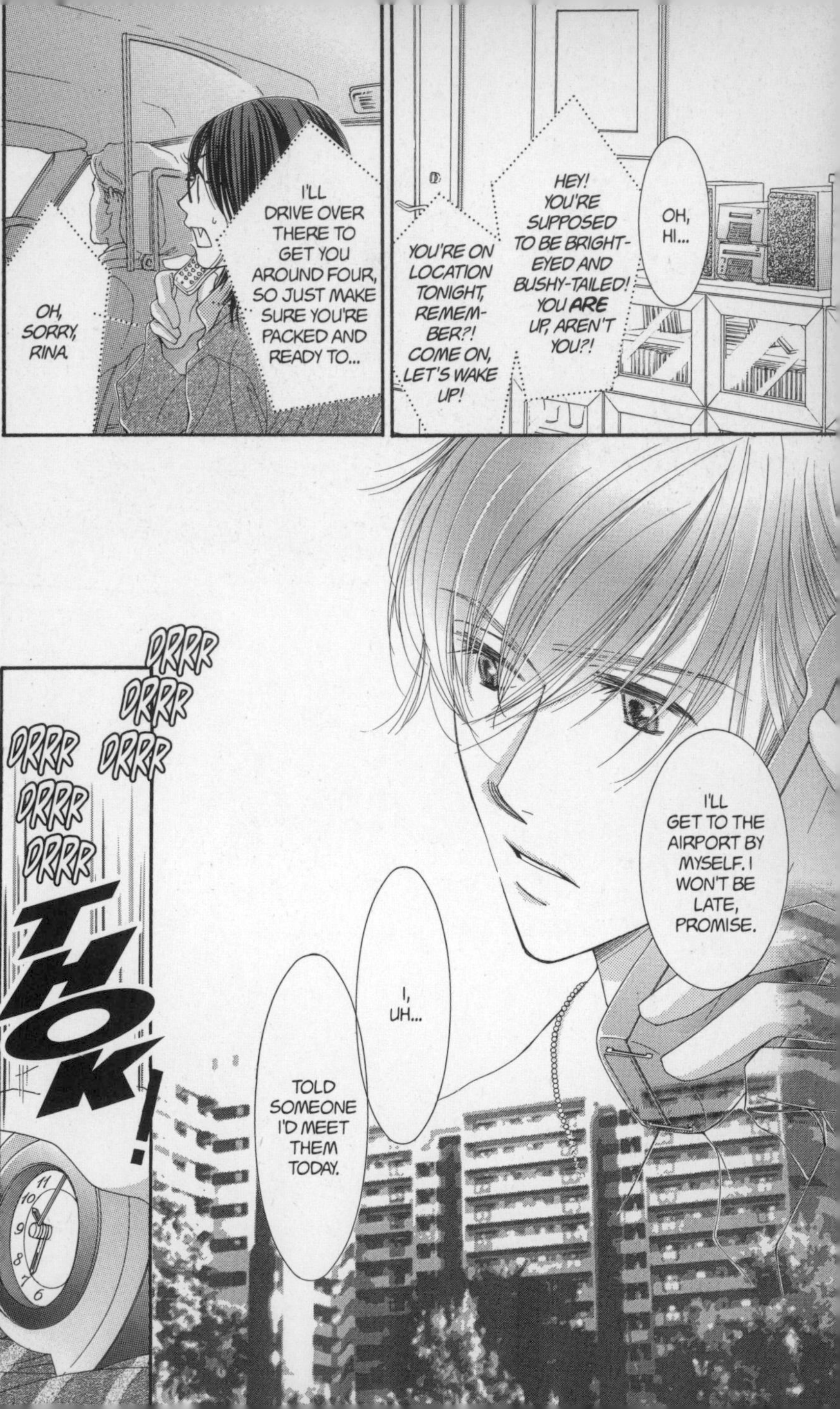
OH, HI...
HEY! YOU'RE SUPPOSED TO BE BRIGHT-EYED AND BUSHY-TAILED! YOU **ARE** UP, AREN'T YOU?!
YOU'RE ON LOCATION TONIGHT, REMEMBER?! COME ON, LET'S WAKE UP!
I'LL DRIVE OVER THERE TO GET YOU AROUND FOUR, SO JUST MAKE SURE YOU'RE PACKED AND READY TO...
OH, SORRY, RINA.
I'LL GET TO THE AIRPORT BY MYSELF. I WON'T BE LATE, PROMISE.
I, UH...
TOLD SOMEONE I'D MEET THEM TODAY.
DRRR DRRR DRRR DRRR DRRR DRRR
THOK!

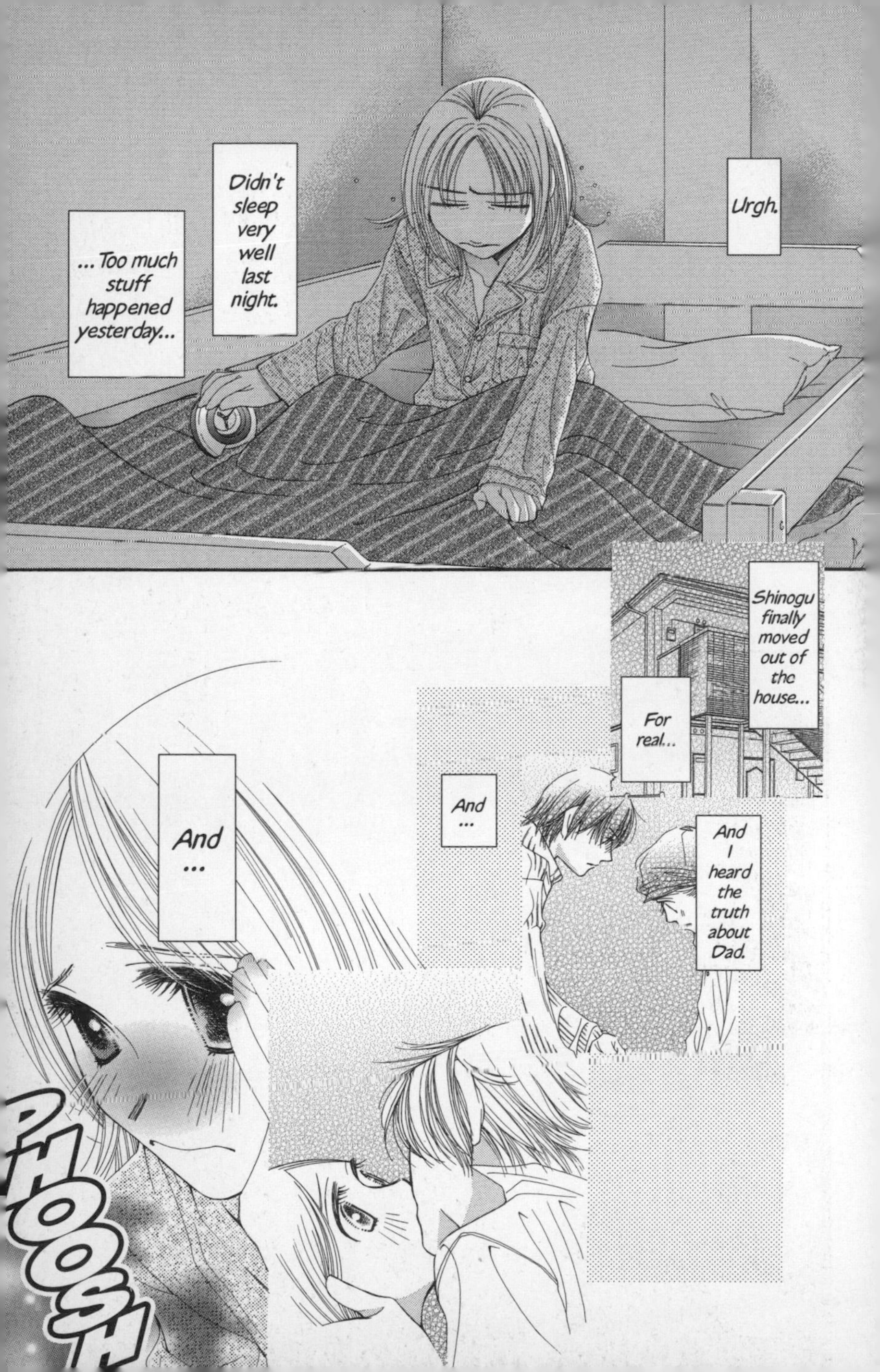
Urgh.
Didn't sleep very well last night.
...Too much stuff happened yesterday...
Shinogu finally moved out of the house...
For real...
And I heard the truth about Dad.
And ...
And ...
PHOOSH

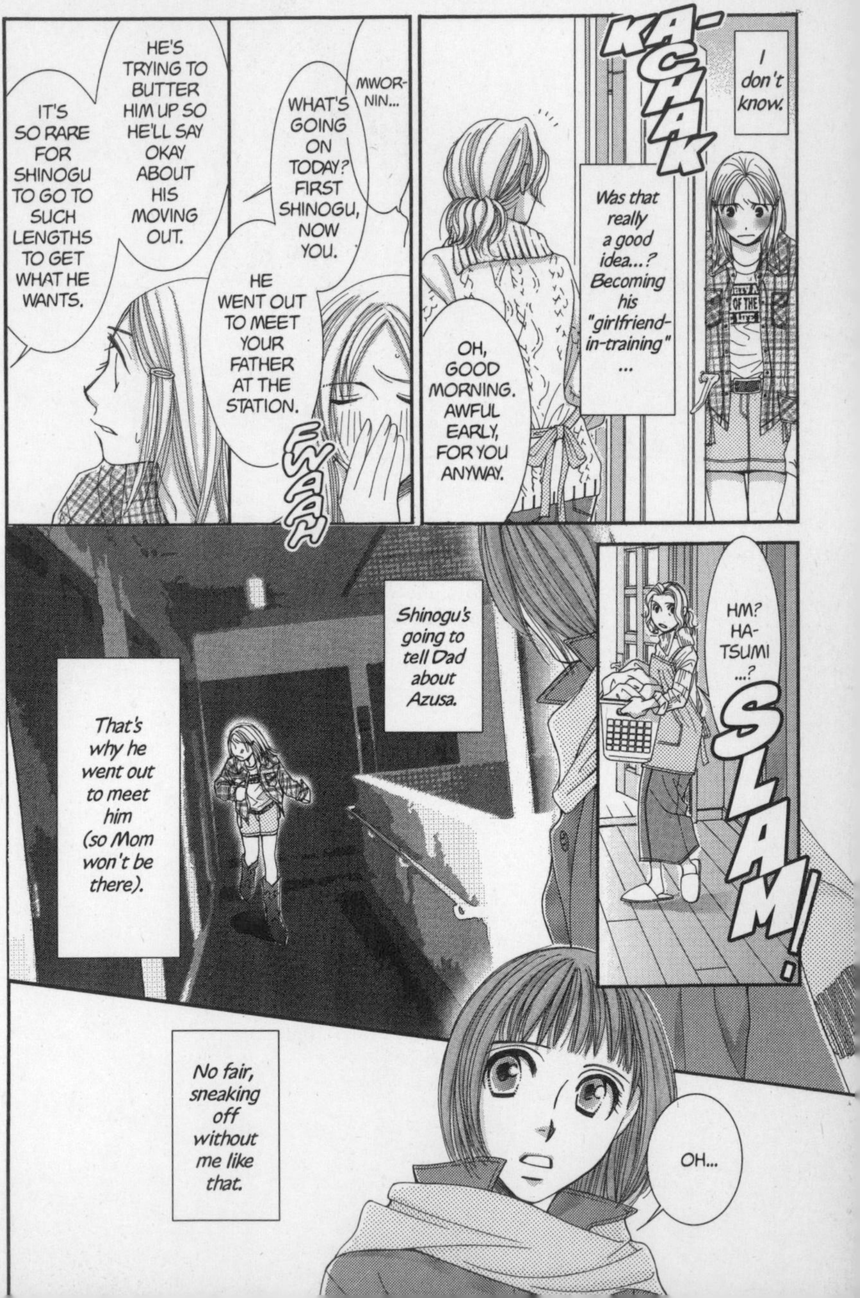
I don't know.
KA-CHAK
Was that really a good idea...? Becoming his "girlfriend-in-training"...
OH, GOOD MORNING. AWFUL EARLY, FOR YOU ANYWAY.
MWOR-NIN...
WHAT'S GOING ON TODAY? FIRST SHINOGU, NOW YOU.
HE WENT OUT TO MEET YOUR FATHER AT THE STATION.
FWAAH
HE'S TRYING TO BUTTER HIM UP SO HE'LL SAY OKAY ABOUT HIS MOVING OUT.
IT'S SO RARE FOR SHINOGU TO GO TO SUCH LENGTHS TO GET WHAT HE WANTS.
HM? HA-TSUMI...?
SLAM!
Shinogu's going to tell Dad about Azusa.
That's why he went out to meet him (so Mom won't be there).
OH...
No fair, sneaking off without me like that.

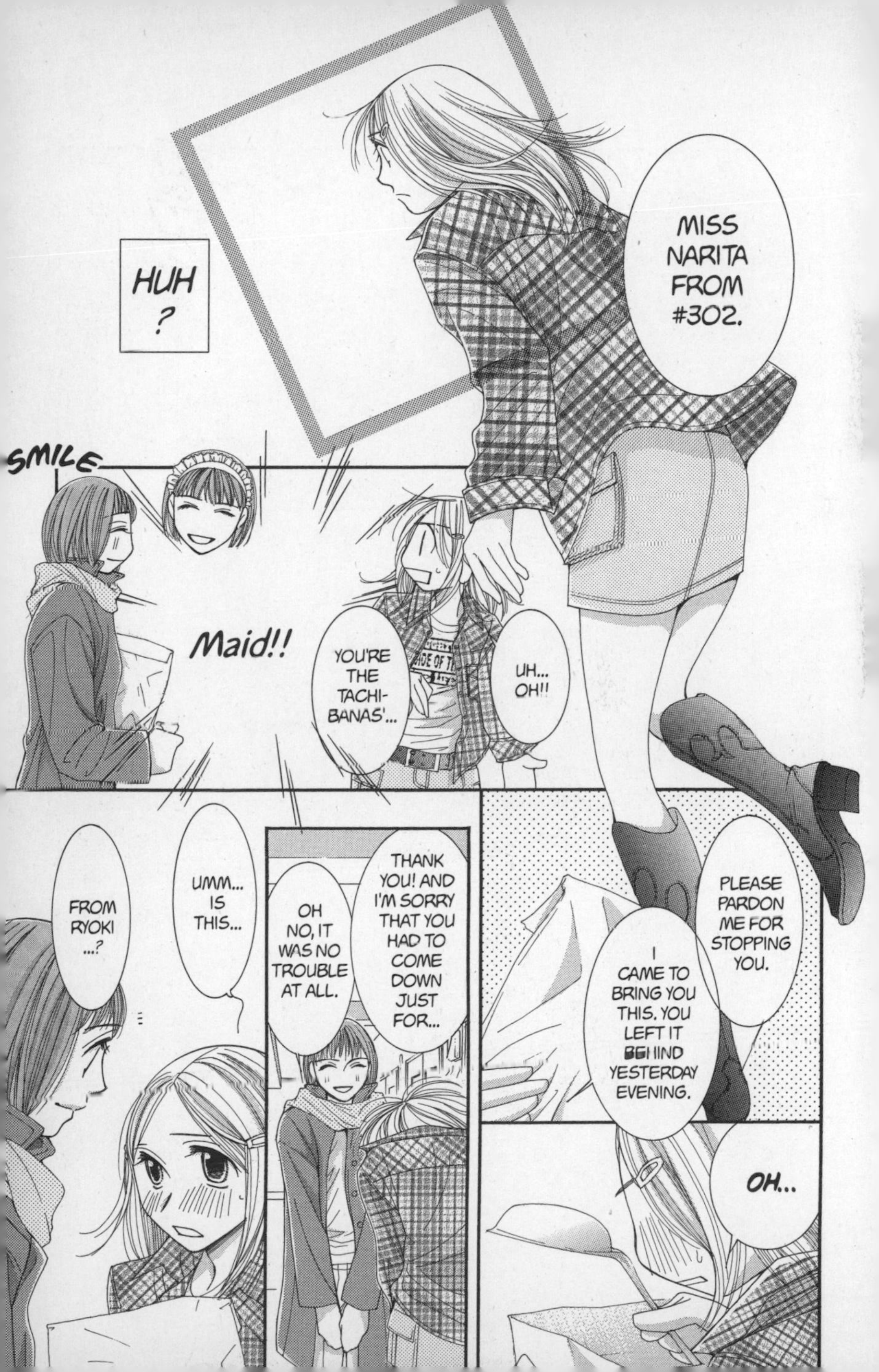
MISS NARITA FROM #302.
HUH ?
UH... OH!!
YOU'RE THE TACHIBANAS'...
Maid!!
SMILE
PLEASE PARDON ME FOR STOPPING YOU.
I CAME TO BRING YOU THIS. YOU LEFT IT BEHIND YESTERDAY EVENING.
OH...
THANK YOU! AND I'M SORRY THAT YOU HAD TO COME DOWN JUST FOR...
OH NO, IT WAS NO TROUBLE AT ALL.
UMM... IS THIS...
FROM RYOKI ...?

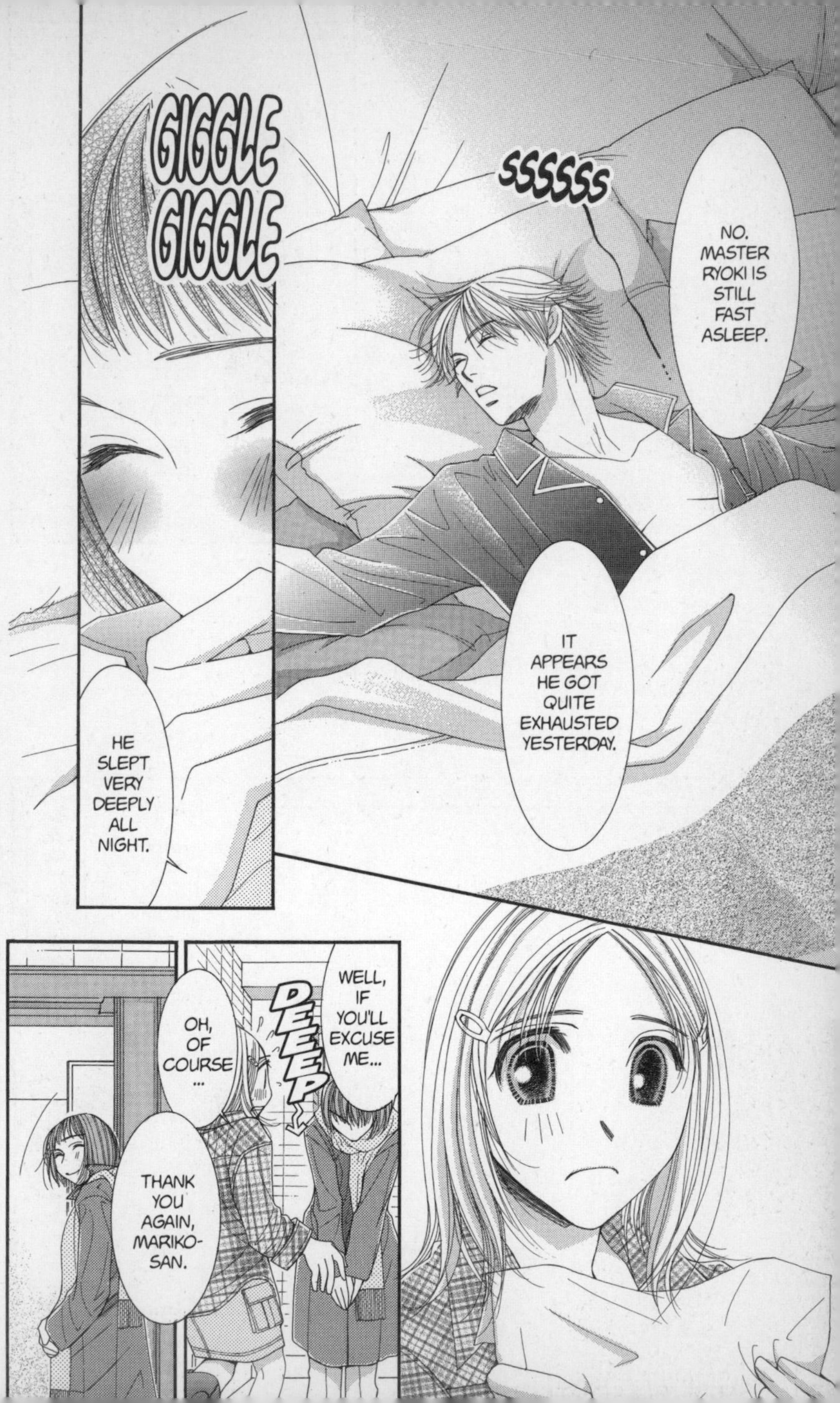
SSSSSS
NO. MASTER RYOKI IS STILL FAST ASLEEP.
IT APPEARS HE GOT QUITE EXHAUSTED YESTERDAY.
GIGGLE GIGGLE
HE SLEPT VERY DEEPLY ALL NIGHT.
WELL, IF YOU'LL EXCUSE ME...
DEEEP
OH, OF COURSE ...
THANK YOU AGAIN, MARIKO-SAN.

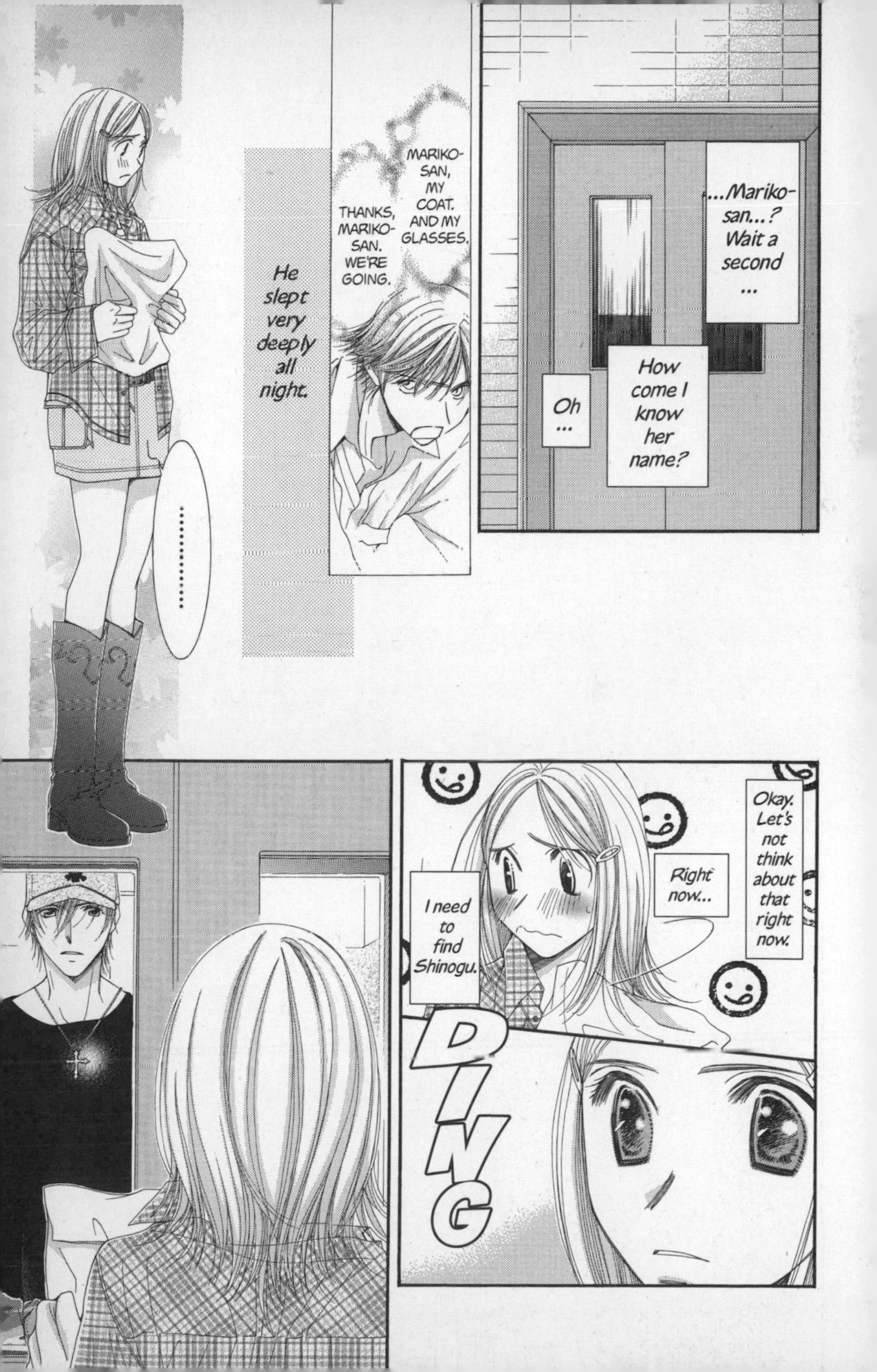
...Mariko-san...? Wait a second ...
How come I know her name?
Oh ...
MARIKO-SAN, MY COAT. AND MY GLASSES.
THANKS, MARIKO-SAN. WE'RE GOING.
He slept very deeply all night.
......
Okay. Let's not think about that right now.
Right now...
I need to find Shinogu.
DING

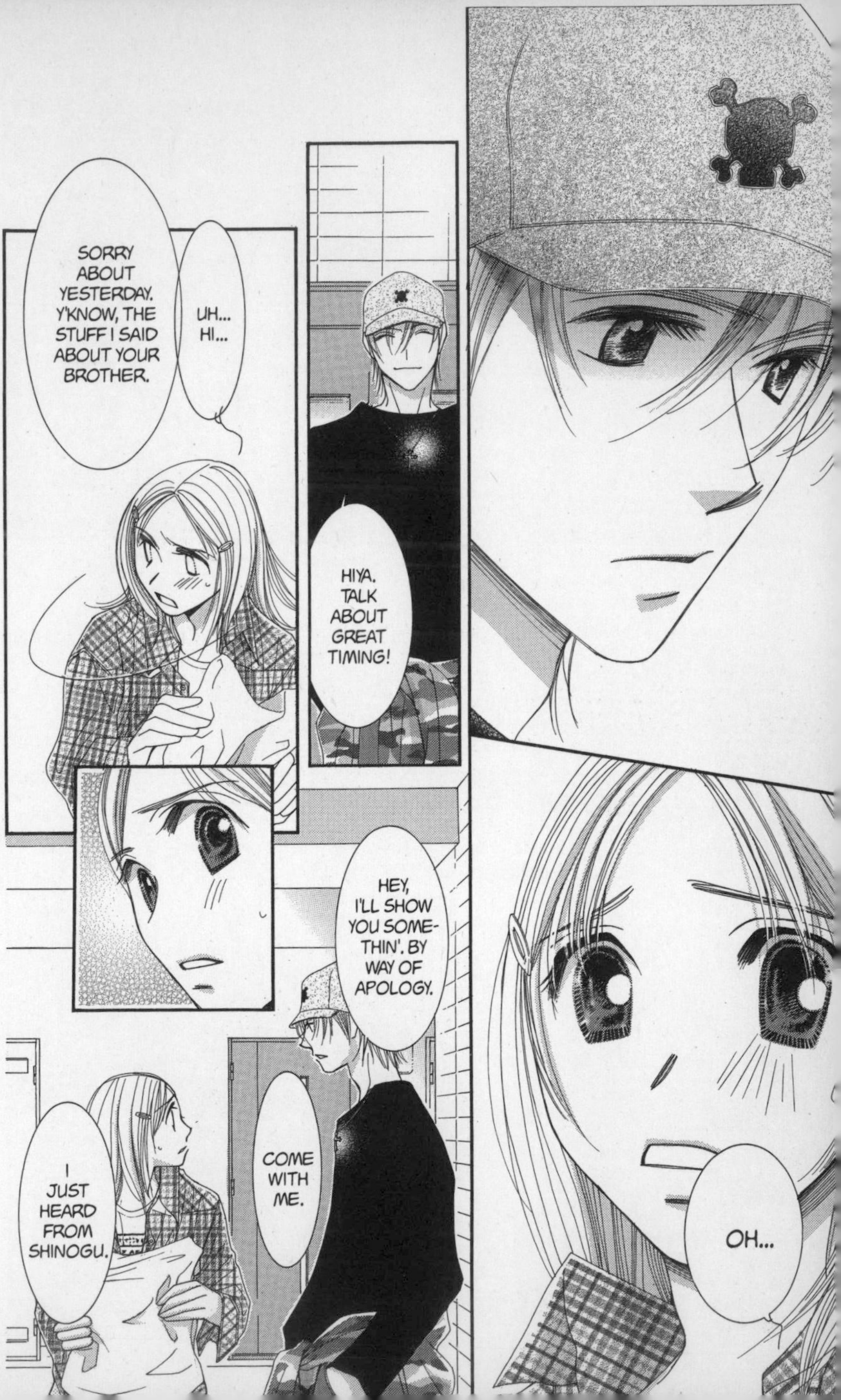
OH...
HIYA. TALK ABOUT GREAT TIMING!
UH... HI...
SORRY ABOUT YESTERDAY. Y'KNOW, THE STUFF I SAID ABOUT YOUR BROTHER.
HEY, I'LL SHOW YOU SOME-THIN'. BY WAY OF APOLOGY.
COME WITH ME.
I JUST HEARD FROM SHINOGU.

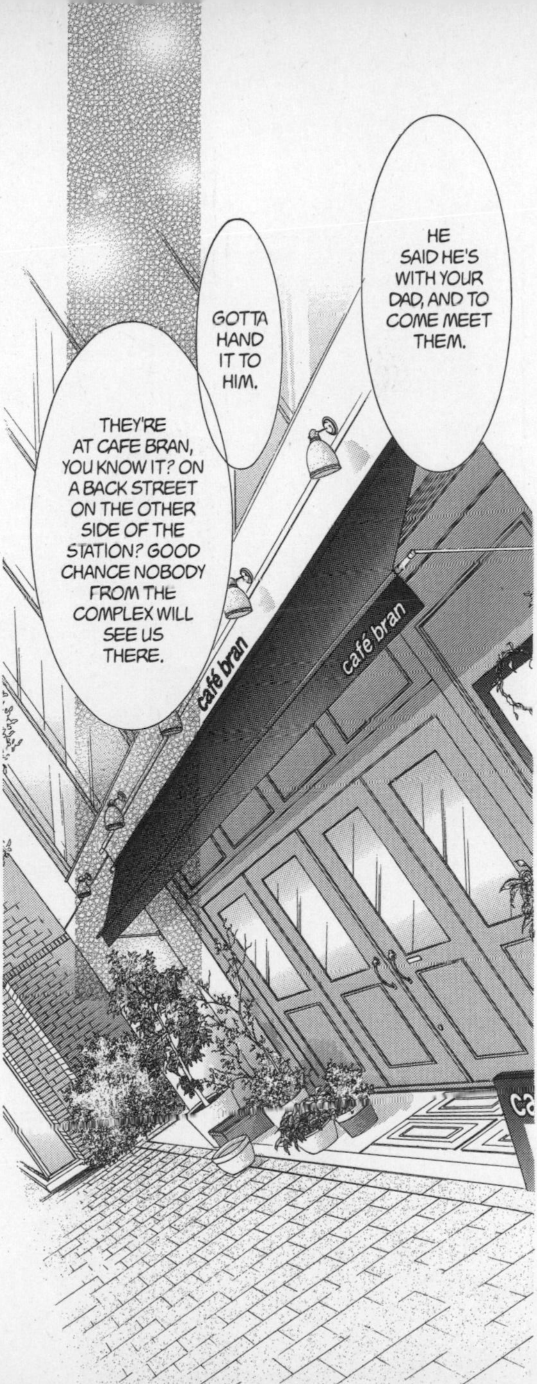
HE SAID HE'S WITH YOUR DAD, AND TO COME MEET THEM.
GOTTA HAND IT TO HIM.
THEY'RE AT CAFE BRAN, YOU KNOW IT? ON A BACK STREET ON THE OTHER SIDE OF THE STATION? GOOD CHANCE NOBODY FROM THE COMPLEX WILL SEE US THERE.
café bran
café bran

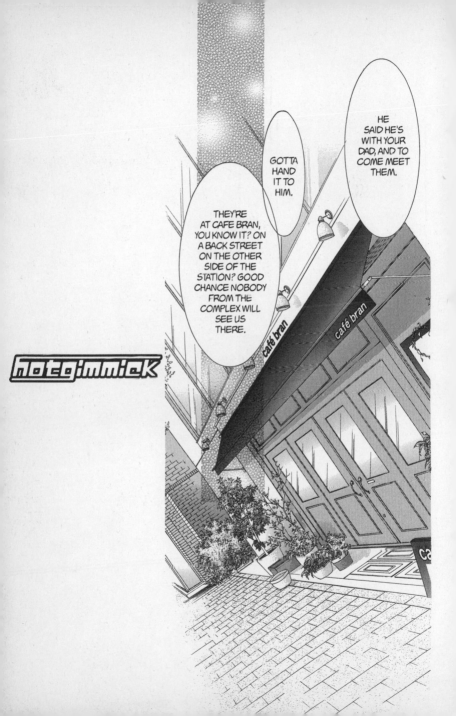

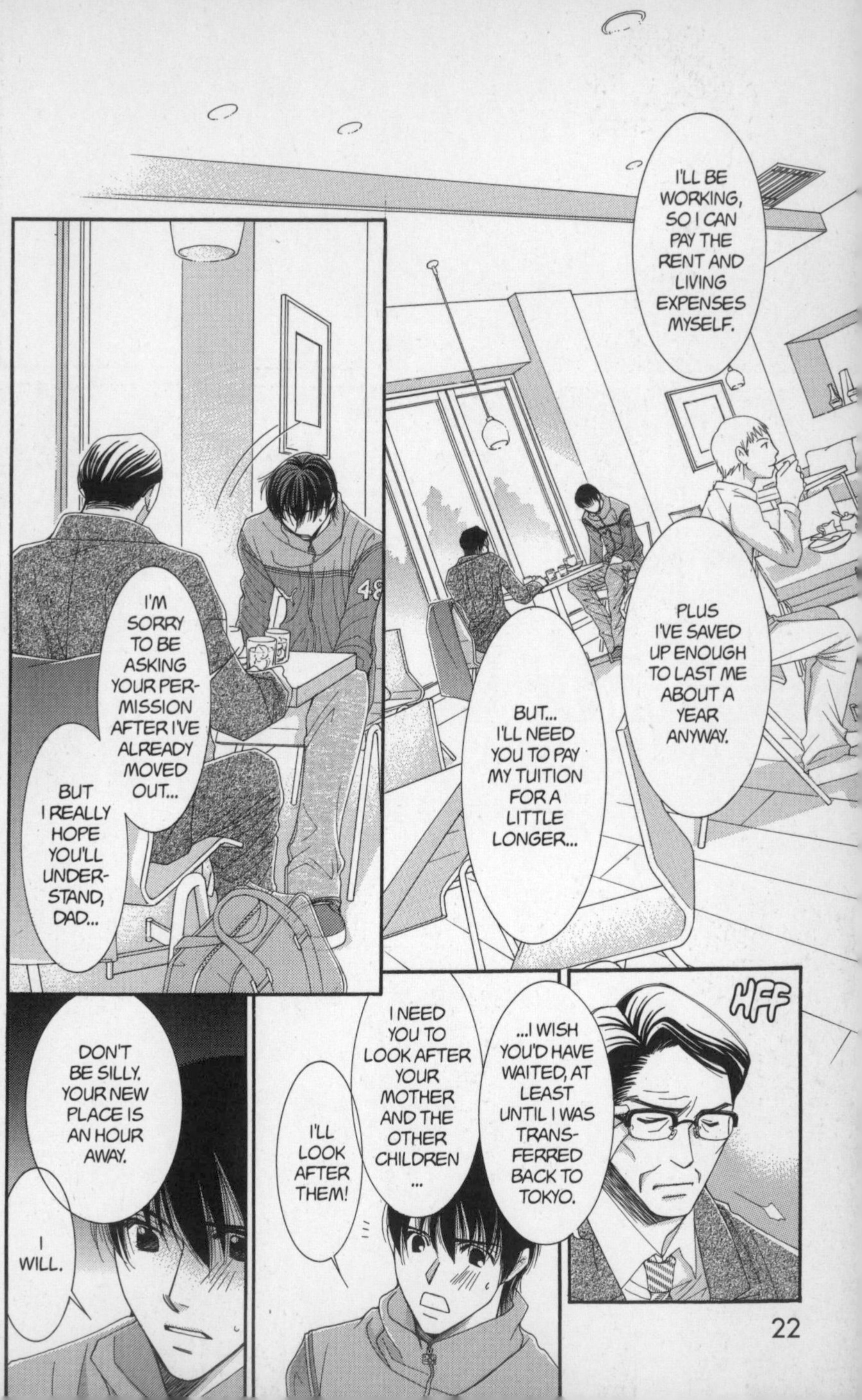
I'LL BE WORKING, SO I CAN PAY THE RENT AND LIVING EXPENSES MYSELF.
PLUS I'VE SAVED UP ENOUGH TO LAST ME ABOUT A YEAR ANYWAY.
BUT... I'LL NEED YOU TO PAY MY TUITION FOR A LITTLE LONGER...
I'M SORRY TO BE ASKING YOUR PER-MISSION AFTER I'VE ALREADY MOVED OUT...
BUT I REALLY HOPE YOU'LL UNDER-STAND, DAD...
HFF
...I WISH YOU'D HAVE WAITED, AT LEAST UNTIL I WAS TRANS-FERRED BACK TO TOKYO.
I NEED YOU TO LOOK AFTER YOUR MOTHER AND THE OTHER CHILDREN ...
I'LL LOOK AFTER THEM!
DON'T BE SILLY. YOUR NEW PLACE IS AN HOUR AWAY.
I WILL.

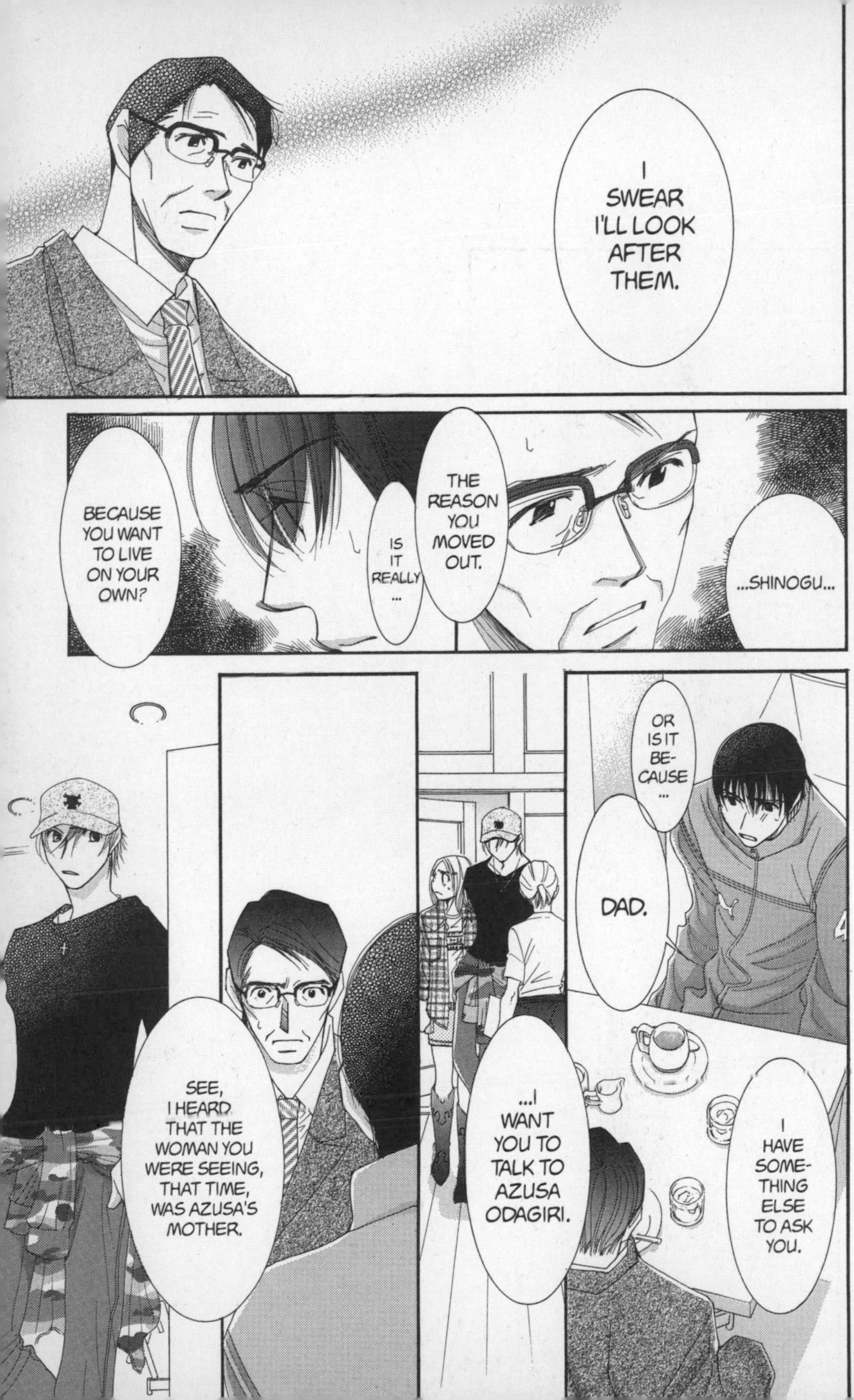
I SWEAR I'LL LOOK AFTER THEM.
...SHINOGU...
THE REASON YOU MOVED OUT.
IS IT REALLY ...
BECAUSE YOU WANT TO LIVE ON YOUR OWN?
OR IS IT BE-CAUSE ...
DAD.
I HAVE SOME-THING ELSE TO ASK YOU.
...I WANT YOU TO TALK TO AZUSA ODAGIRI.
SEE, I HEARD THAT THE WOMAN YOU WERE SEEING, THAT TIME, WAS AZUSA'S MOTHER.

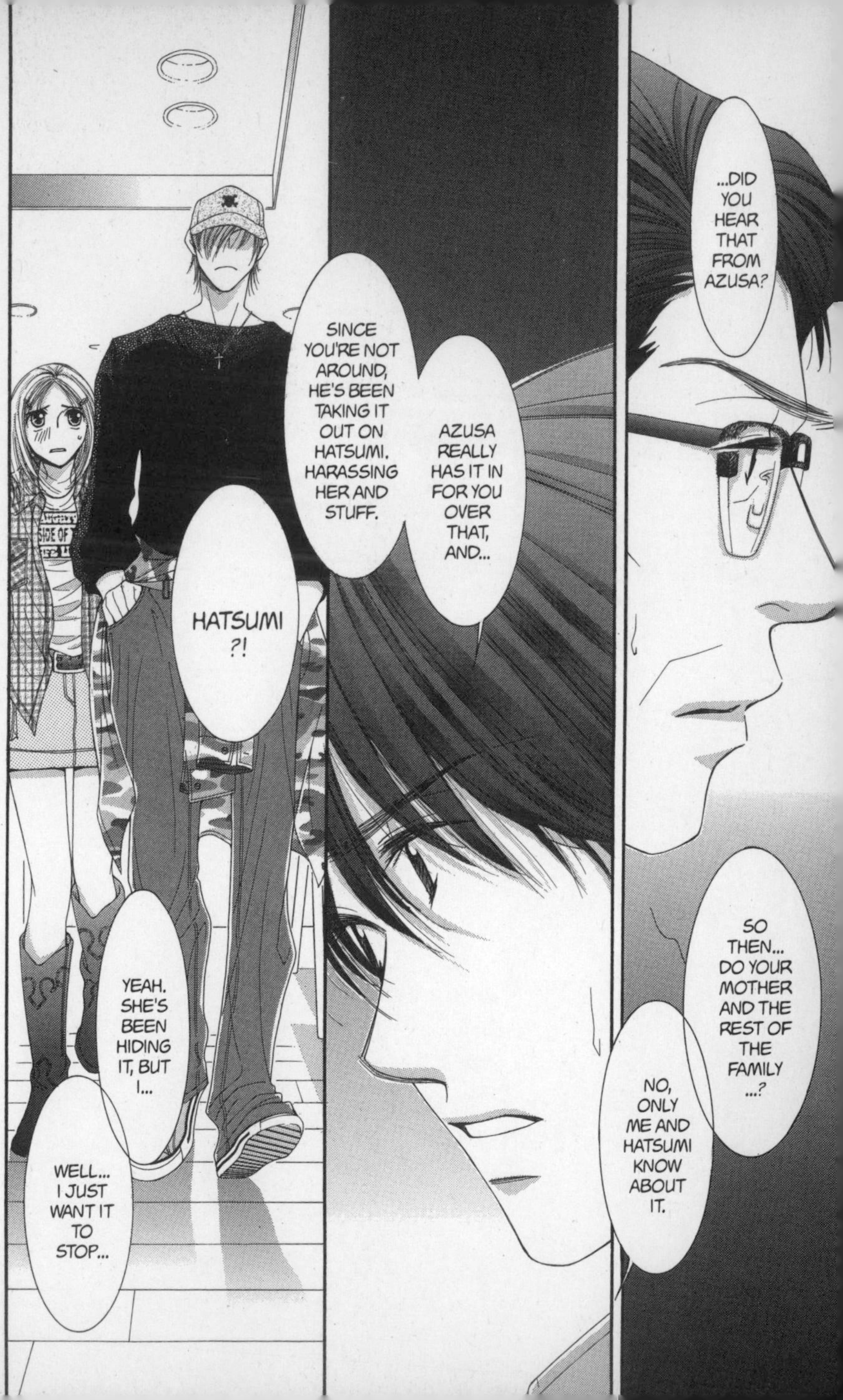
...DID YOU HEAR THAT FROM AZUSA?
SO THEN... DO YOUR MOTHER AND THE REST OF THE FAMILY ...?
NO, ONLY ME AND HATSUMI KNOW ABOUT IT.
AZUSA REALLY HAS IT IN FOR YOU OVER THAT, AND...
SINCE YOU'RE NOT AROUND, HE'S BEEN TAKING IT OUT ON HATSUMI. HARASSING HER AND STUFF.
HATSUMI ?!
YEAH. SHE'S BEEN HIDING IT, BUT I...
WELL... I JUST WANT IT TO STOP...

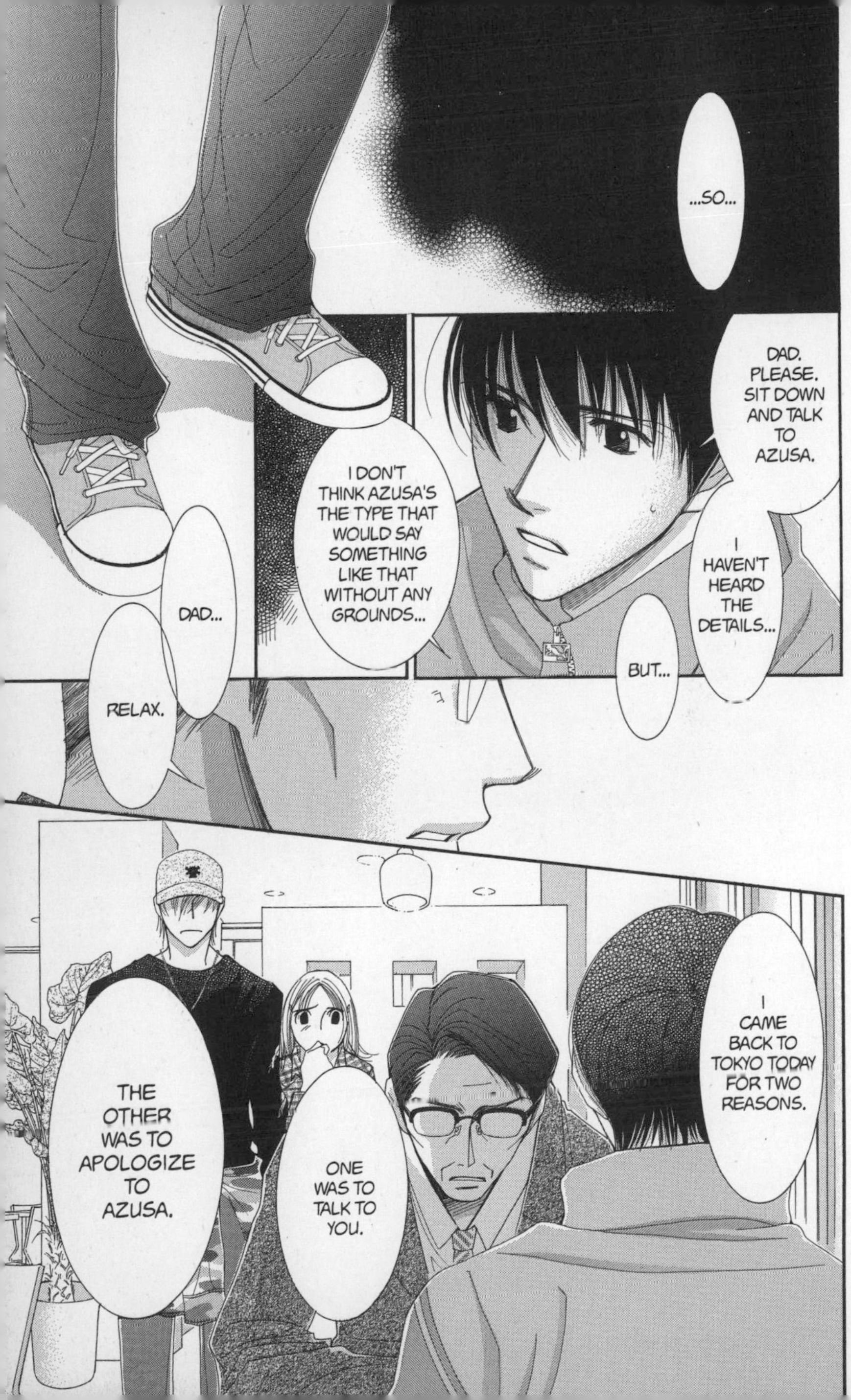
...SO...
DAD. PLEASE. SIT DOWN AND TALK TO AZUSA.
I HAVEN'T HEARD THE DETAILS...
BUT...
I DON'T THINK AZUSA'S THE TYPE THAT WOULD SAY SOMETHING LIKE THAT WITHOUT ANY GROUNDS...
DAD...
RELAX.
I CAME BACK TO TOKYO TODAY FOR TWO REASONS.
ONE WAS TO TALK TO YOU.
THE OTHER WAS TO APOLOGIZE TO AZUSA.

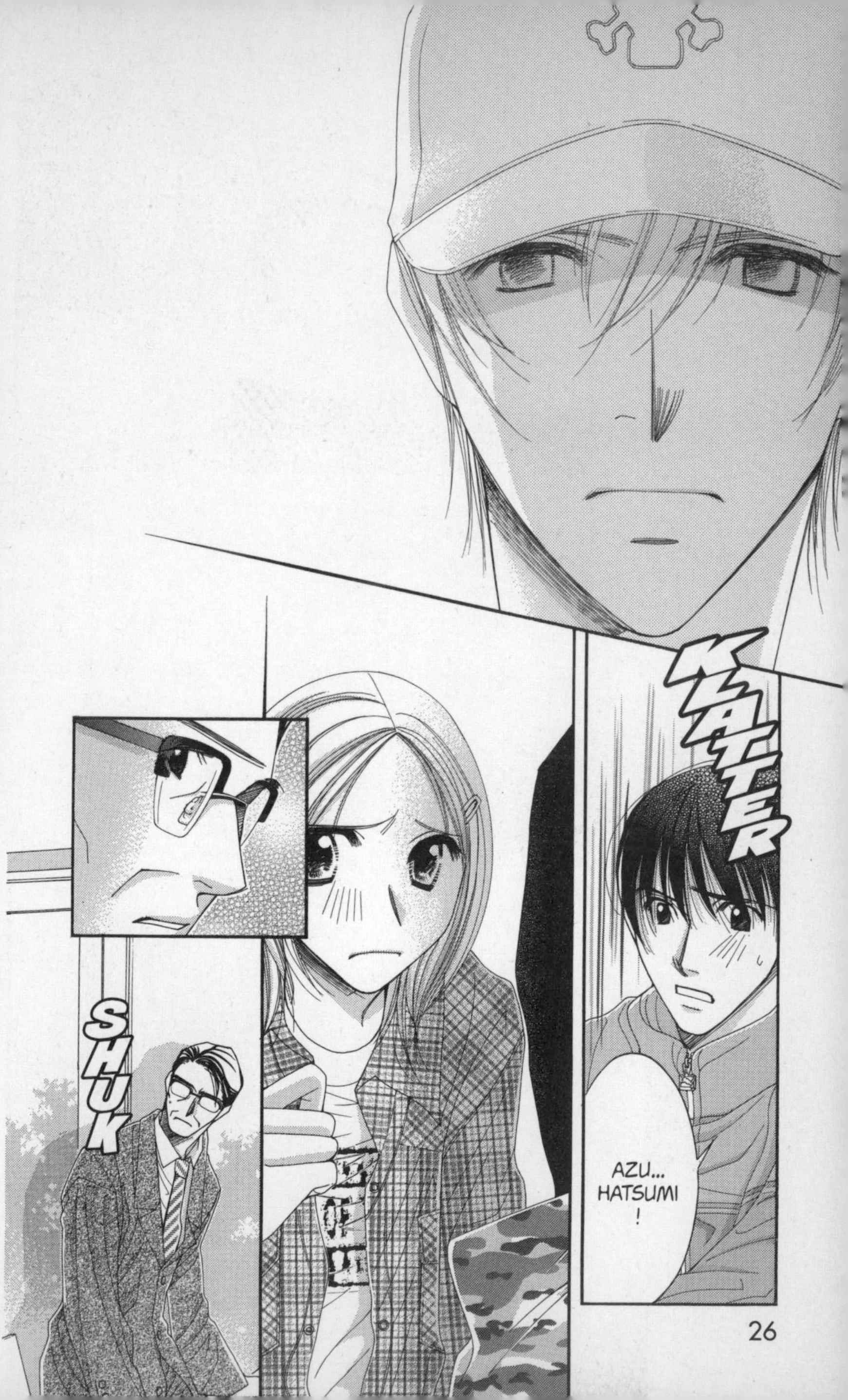
KLATTER
AZU... HATSUMI!
SHUK

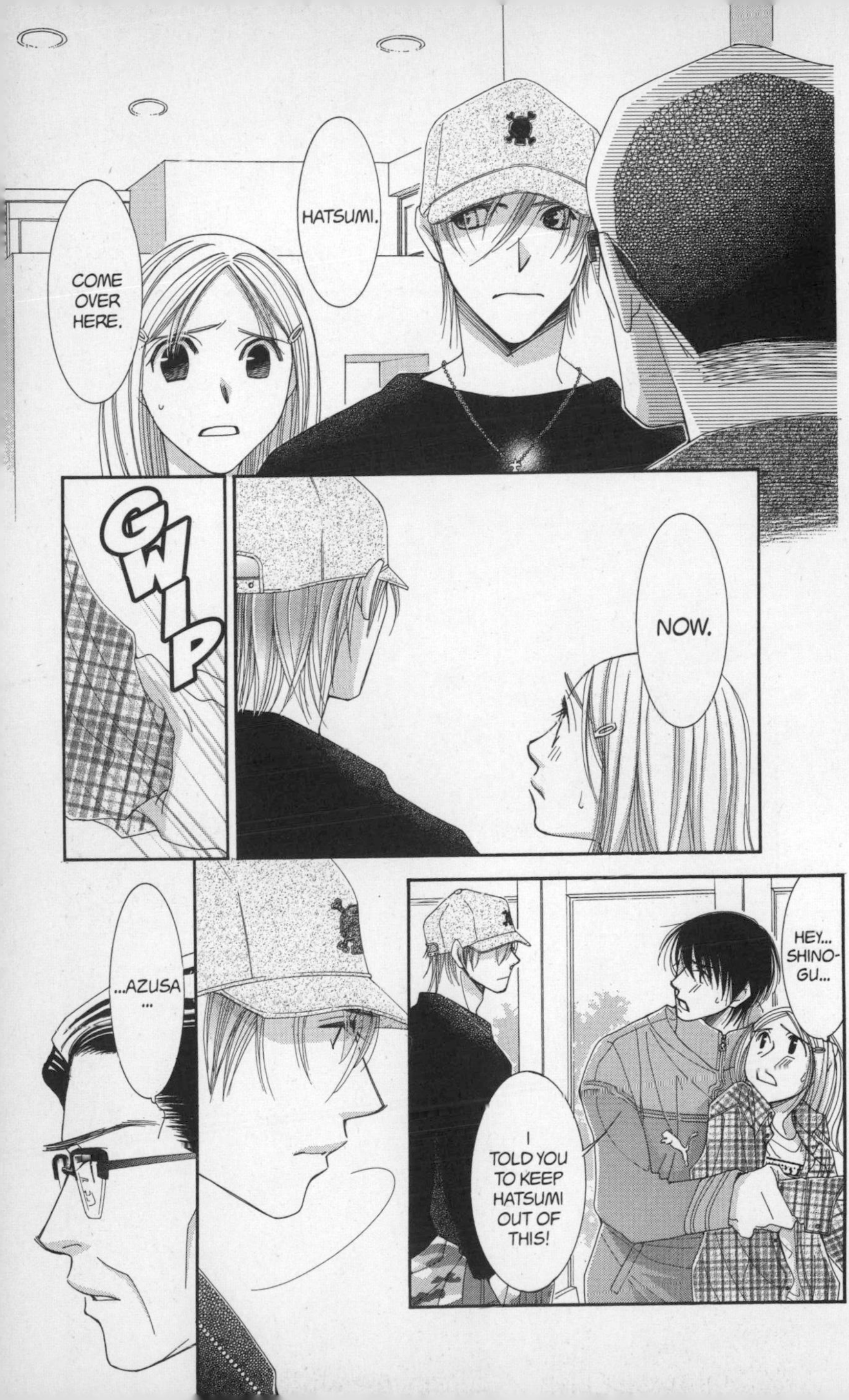
HATSUMI.
COME OVER HERE.
NOW.
GWIP
HEY... SHINO-GU...
I TOLD YOU TO KEEP HATSUMI OUT OF THIS!
...AZUSA ...

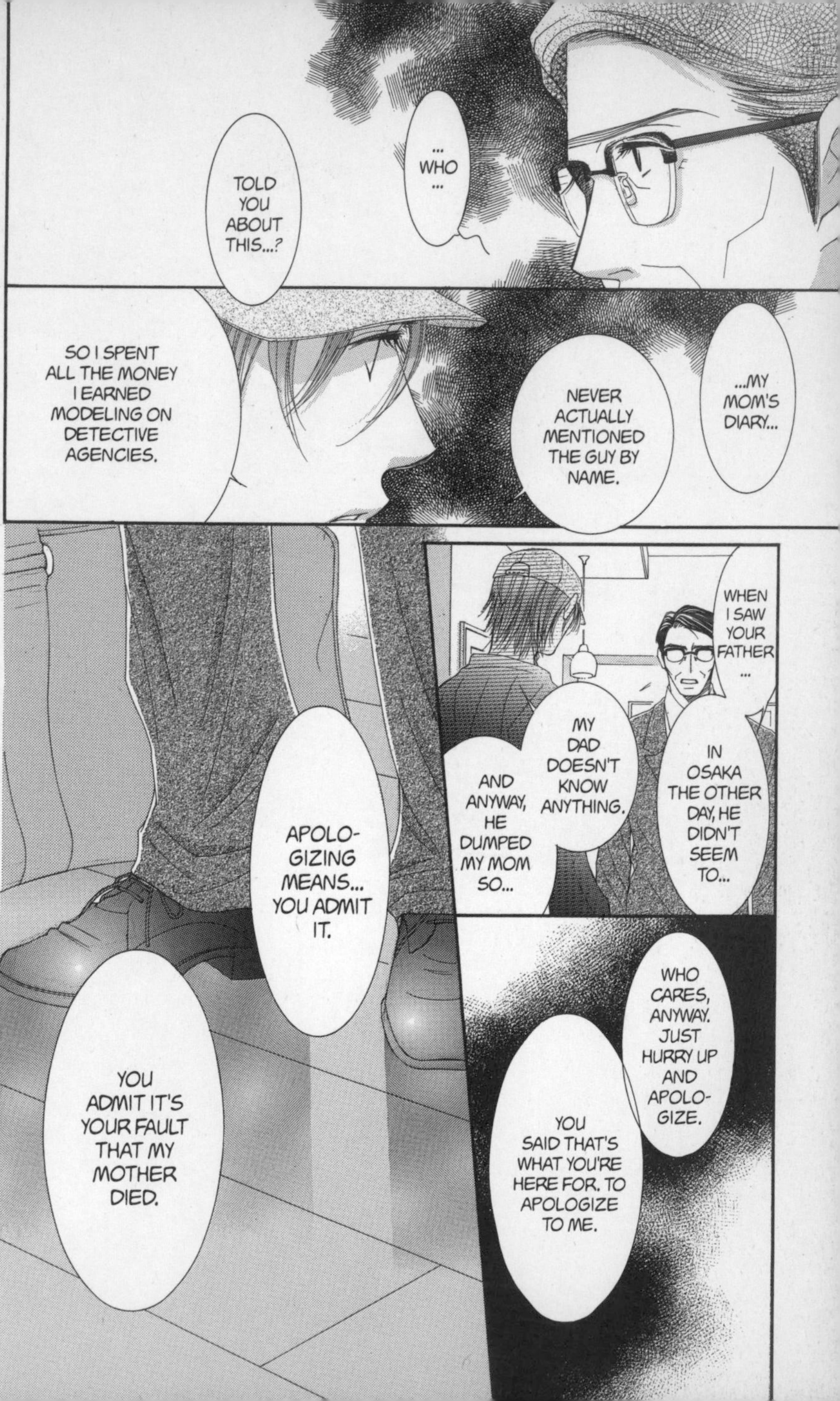
... WHO ...
TOLD YOU ABOUT THIS...?
...MY MOM'S DIARY...
NEVER ACTUALLY MENTIONED THE GUY BY NAME.
SO I SPENT ALL THE MONEY I EARNED MODELING ON DETECTIVE AGENCIES.
WHEN I SAW YOUR FATHER ...
IN OSAKA THE OTHER DAY, HE DIDN'T SEEM TO...
MY DAD DOESN'T KNOW ANYTHING.
AND ANYWAY, HE DUMPED MY MOM SO...
WHO CARES, ANYWAY. JUST HURRY UP AND APOLO-GIZE.
YOU SAID THAT'S WHAT YOU'RE HERE FOR. TO APOLOGIZE TO ME.
APOLO-GIZING MEANS... YOU ADMIT IT.
YOU ADMIT IT'S YOUR FAULT THAT MY MOTHER DIED.

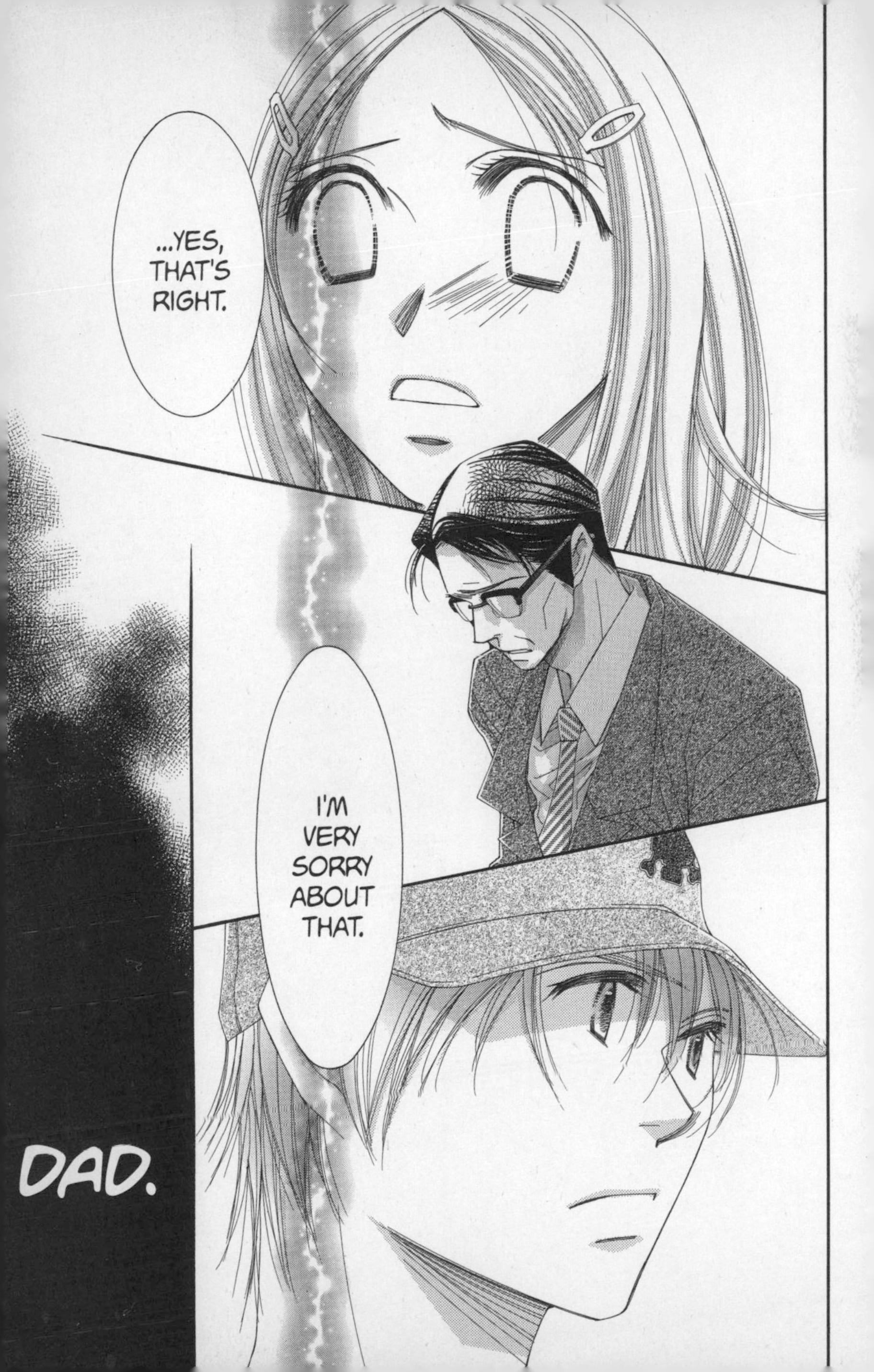
...YES, THAT'S RIGHT.
I'M VERY SORRY ABOUT THAT.
DAD.

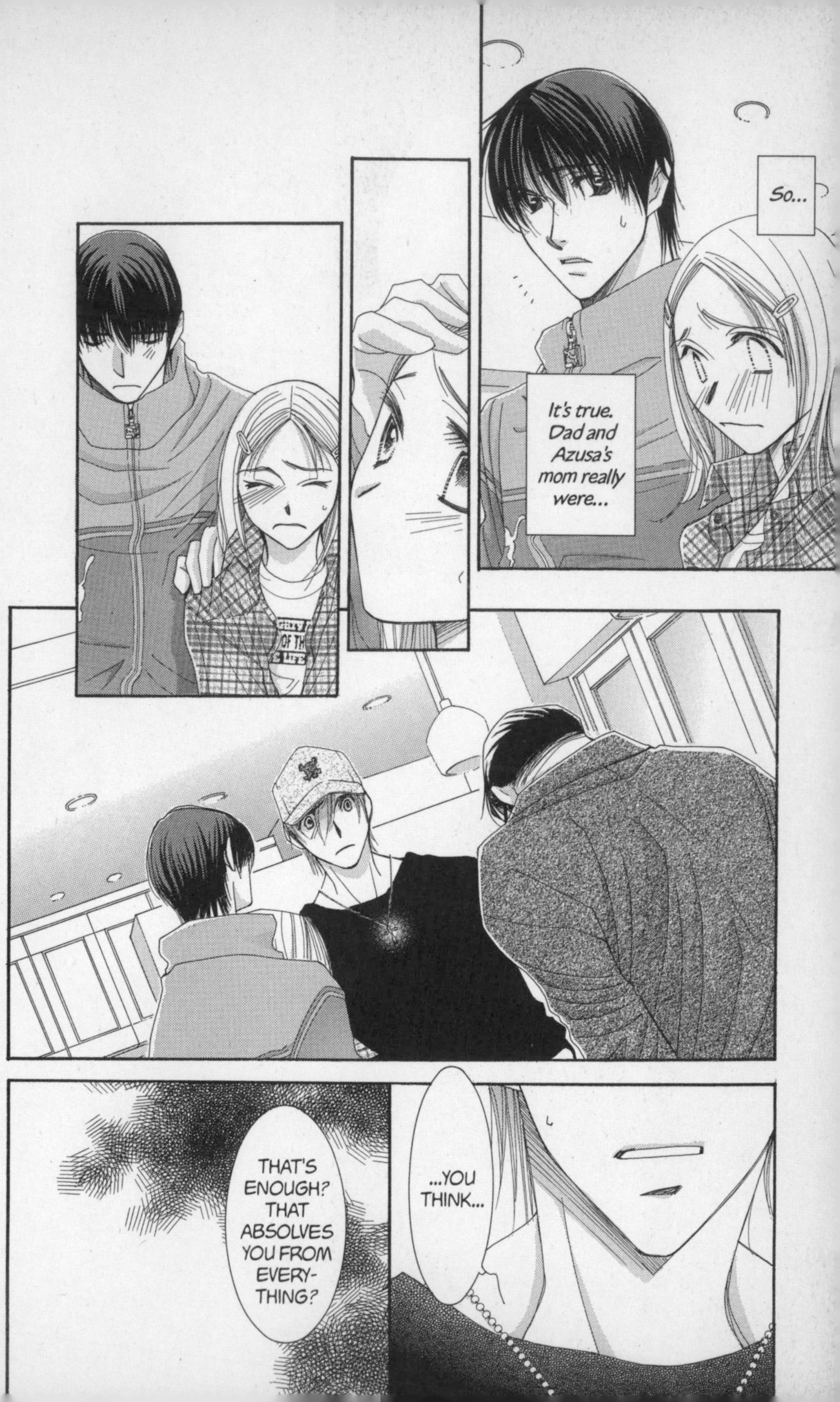
So...
It's true. Dad and Azusa's mom really were...
...YOU THINK...
THAT'S ENOUGH? THAT ABSOLVES YOU FROM EVERY-THING?

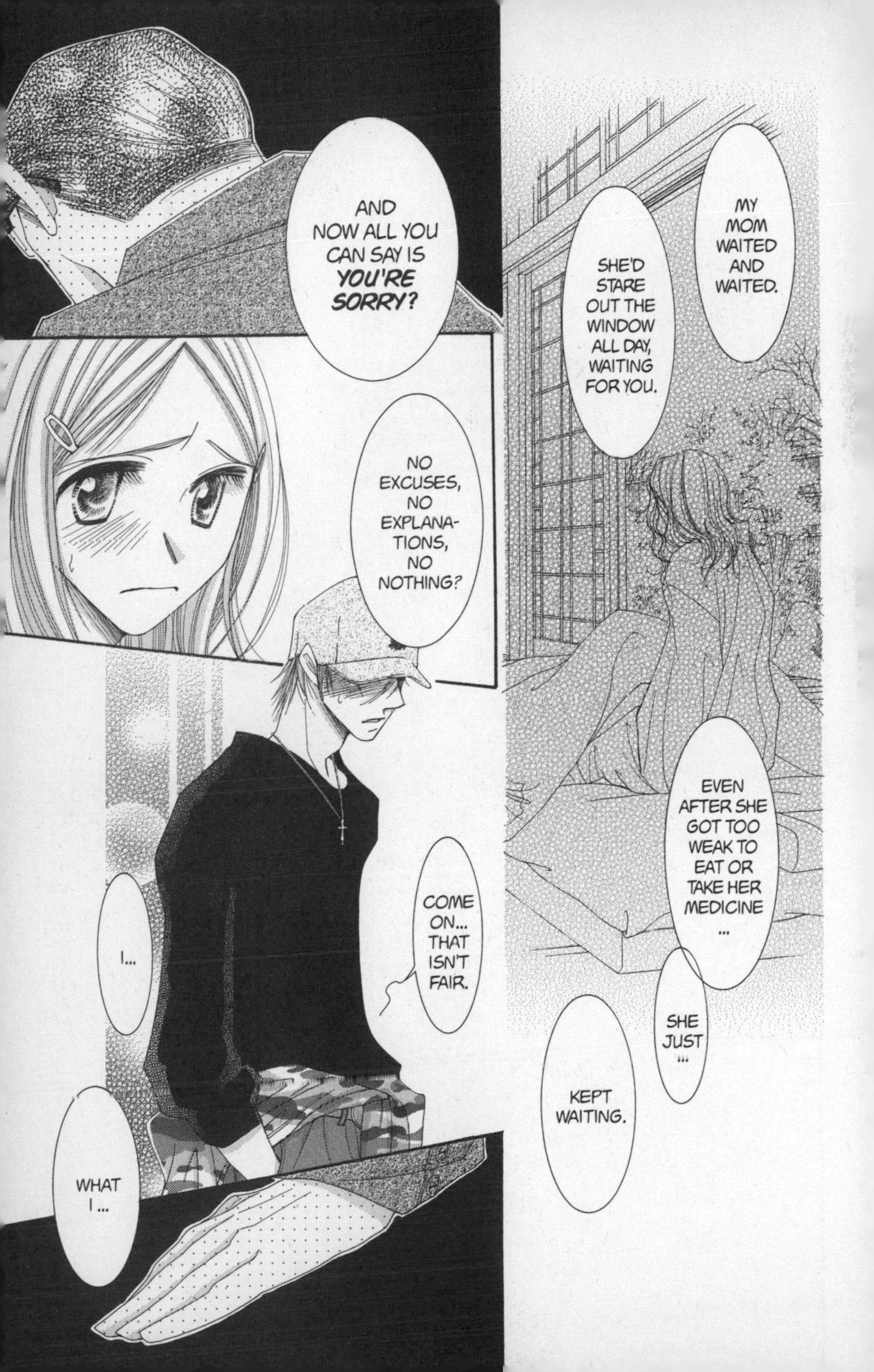
MY MOM WAITED AND WAITED.
SHE'D STARE OUT THE WINDOW ALL DAY, WAITING FOR YOU.
EVEN AFTER SHE GOT TOO WEAK TO EAT OR TAKE HER MEDICINE ...
SHE JUST ...
KEPT WAITING.
AND NOW ALL YOU CAN SAY IS ***YOU'RE SORRY***?
NO EXCUSES, NO EXPLANATIONS, NO NOTHING?
COME ON... THAT ISN'T FAIR.
I...
WHAT I ...

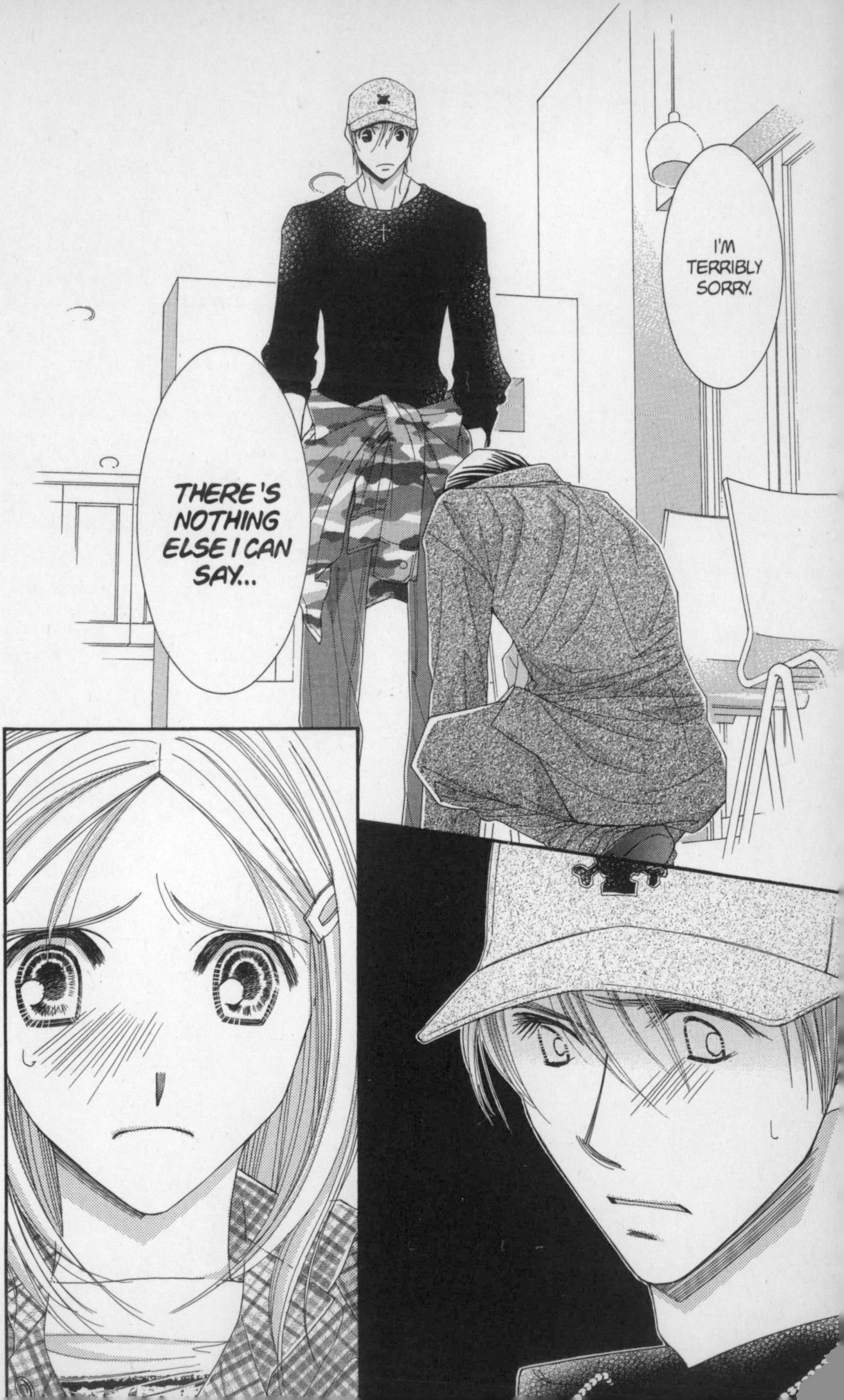
I'M TERRIBLY SORRY.
THERE'S NOTHING ELSE I CAN SAY...

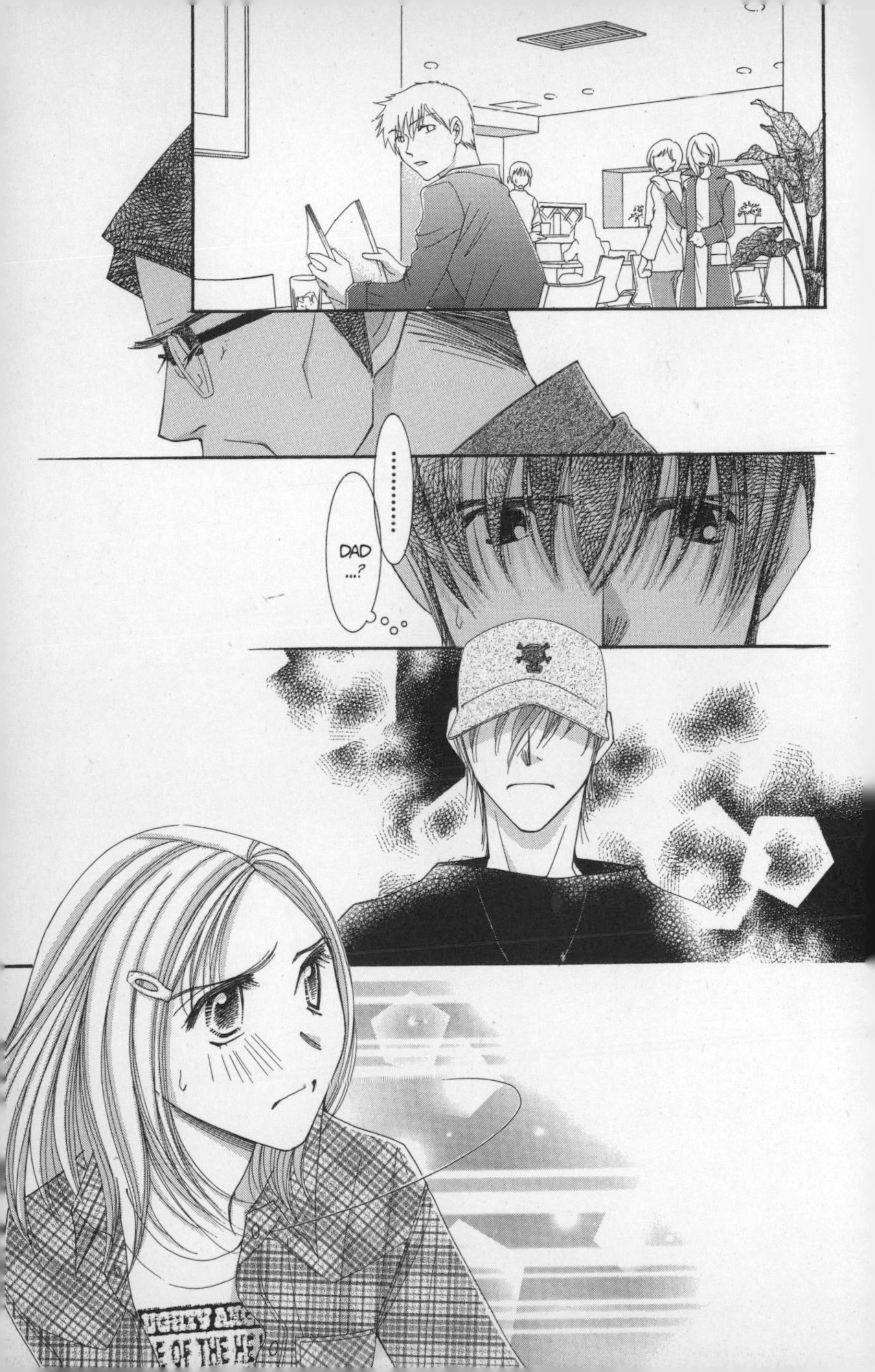

....
DAD ...?

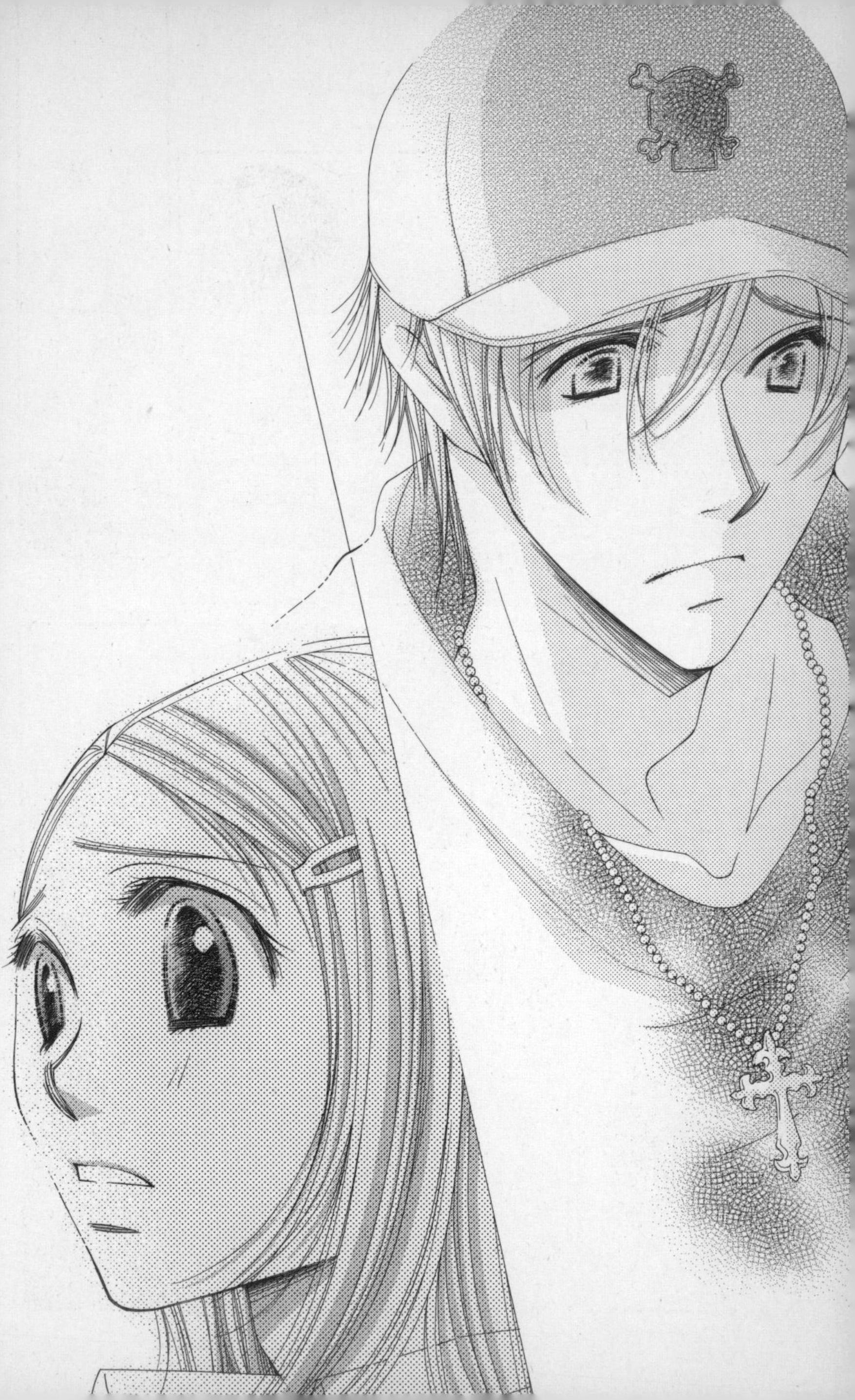

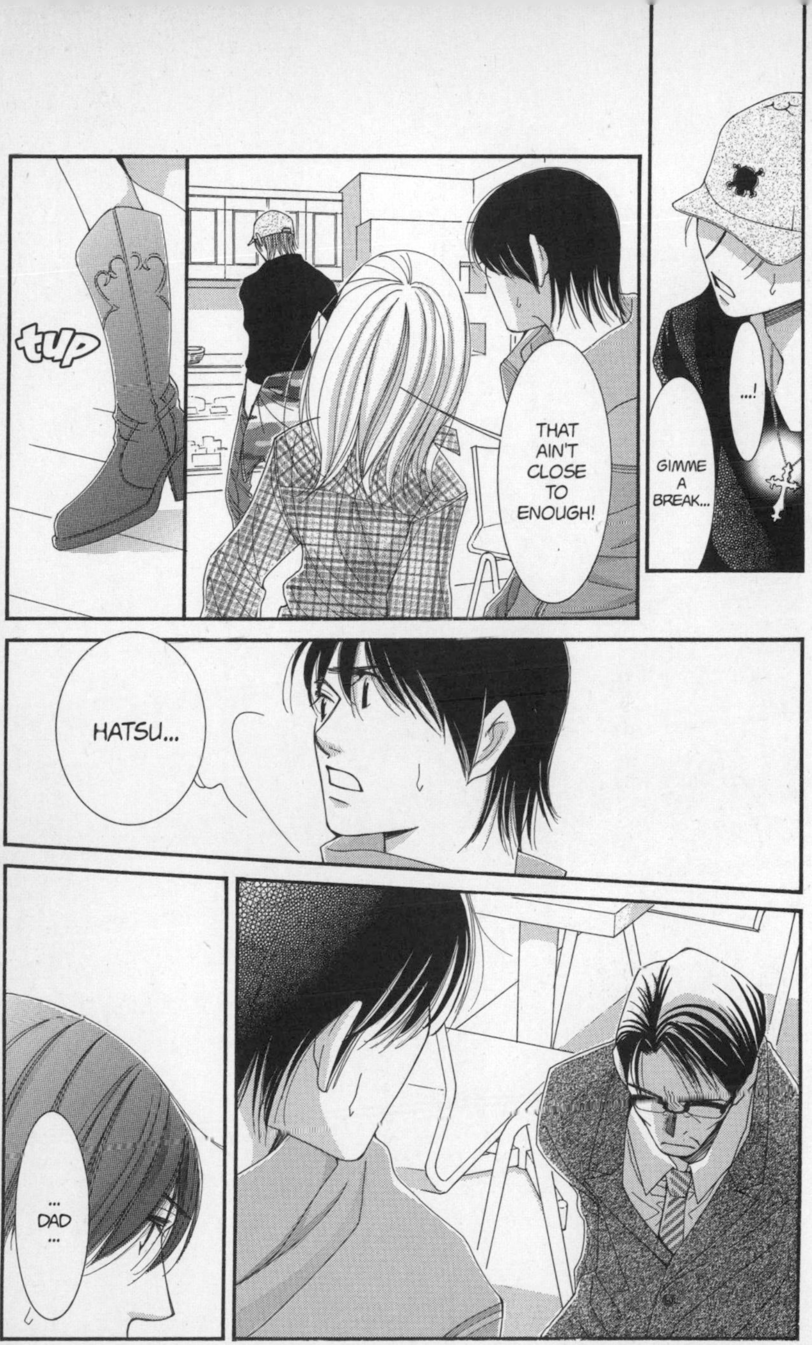
...!
GIMME A BREAK...
THAT AIN'T CLOSE TO ENOUGH!
tup
HATSU...
... DAD ...

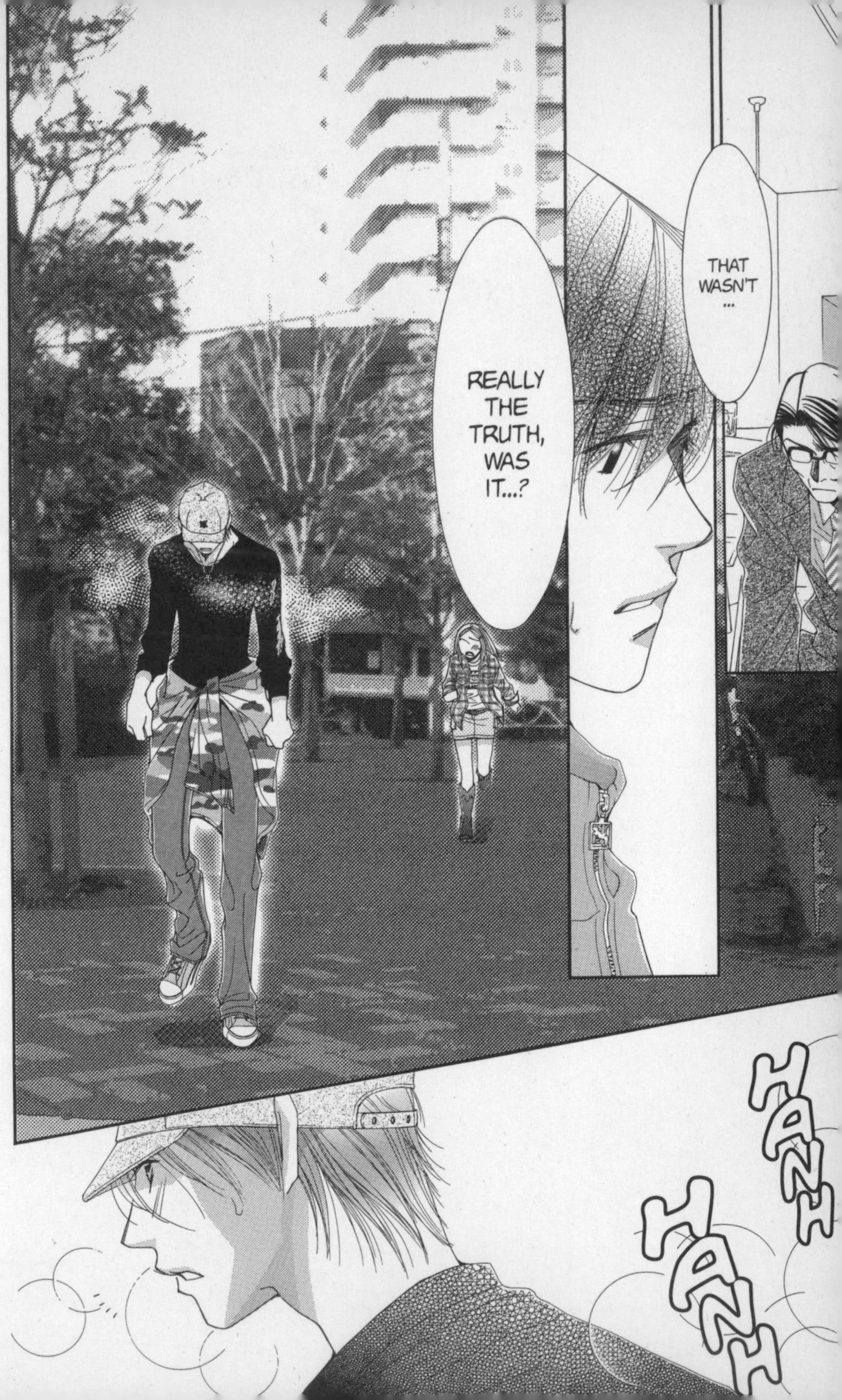
THAT WASN'T ...
REALLY THE TRUTH, WAS IT...?
HANH
HANH

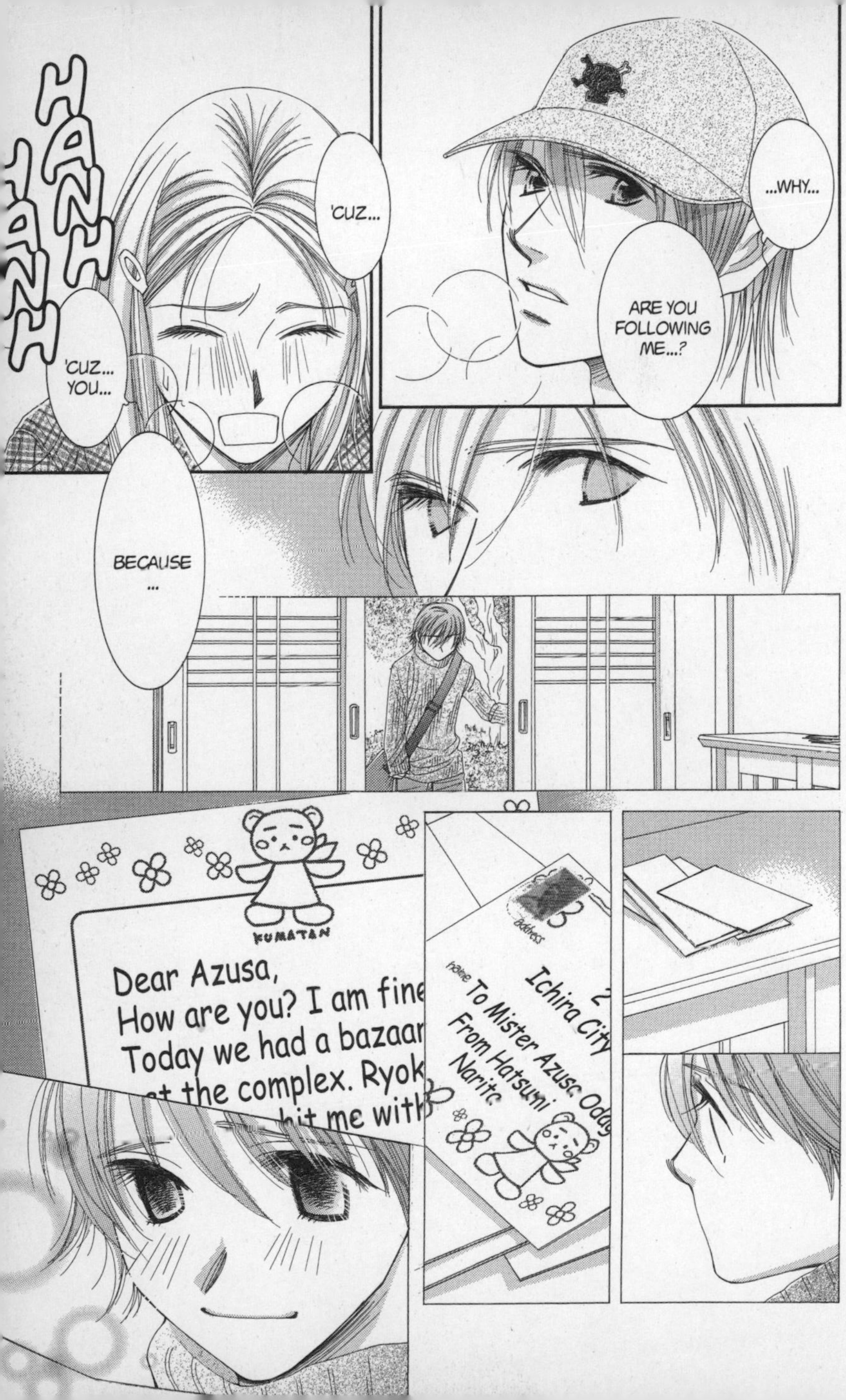
...WHY...
ARE YOU FOLLOWING ME...?
'CUZ...
HAH HAH HAH
'CUZ... YOU...
BECAUSE ...
Address
Ichira City
name To Mister Azusa Oday
From Hatsumi Narita
KUMATAN
Dear Azusa,
How are you? I am fine
Today we had a bazaar
the complex.
hit me with

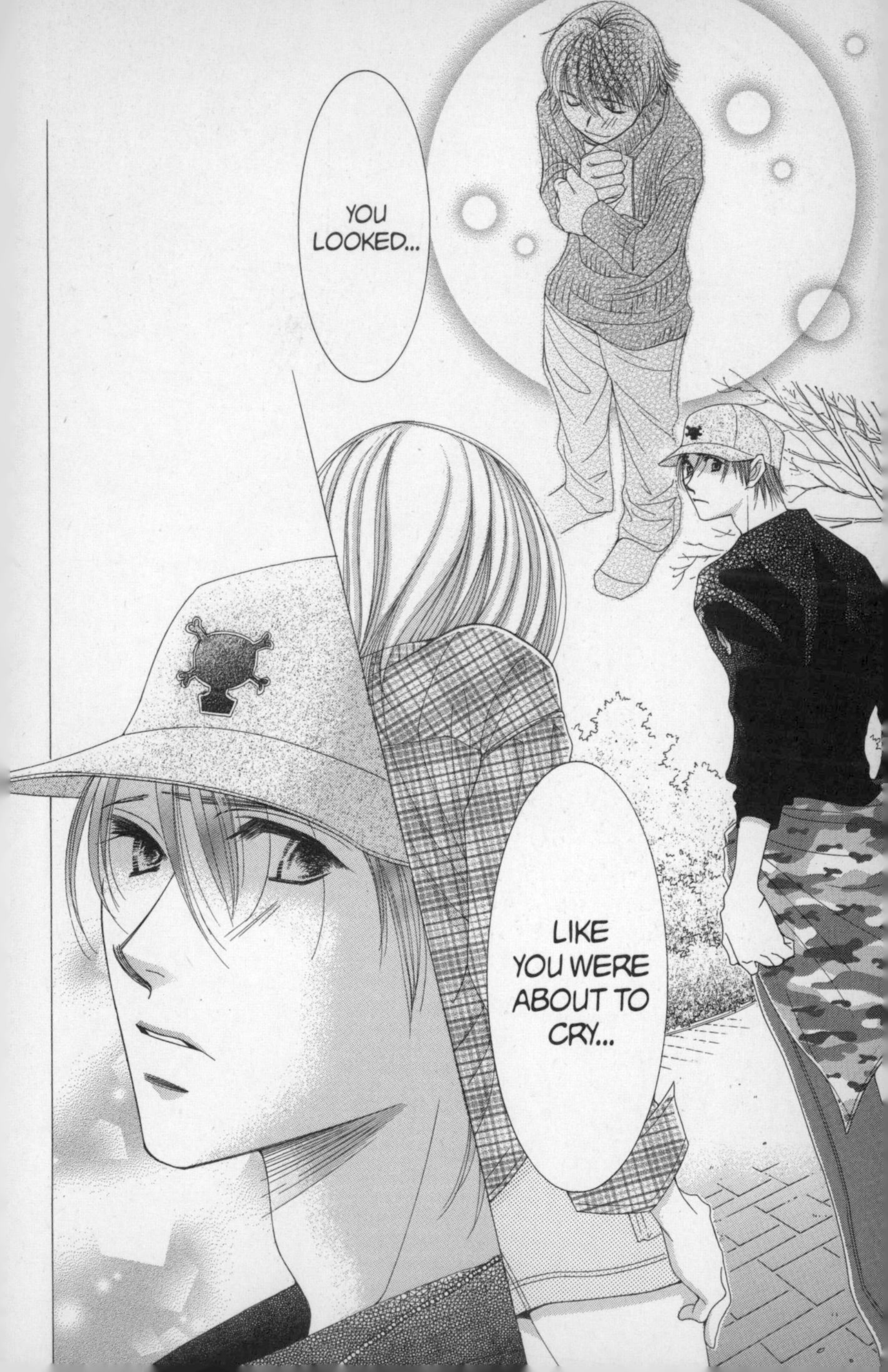
YOU LOOKED...
LIKE YOU WERE ABOUT TO CRY...

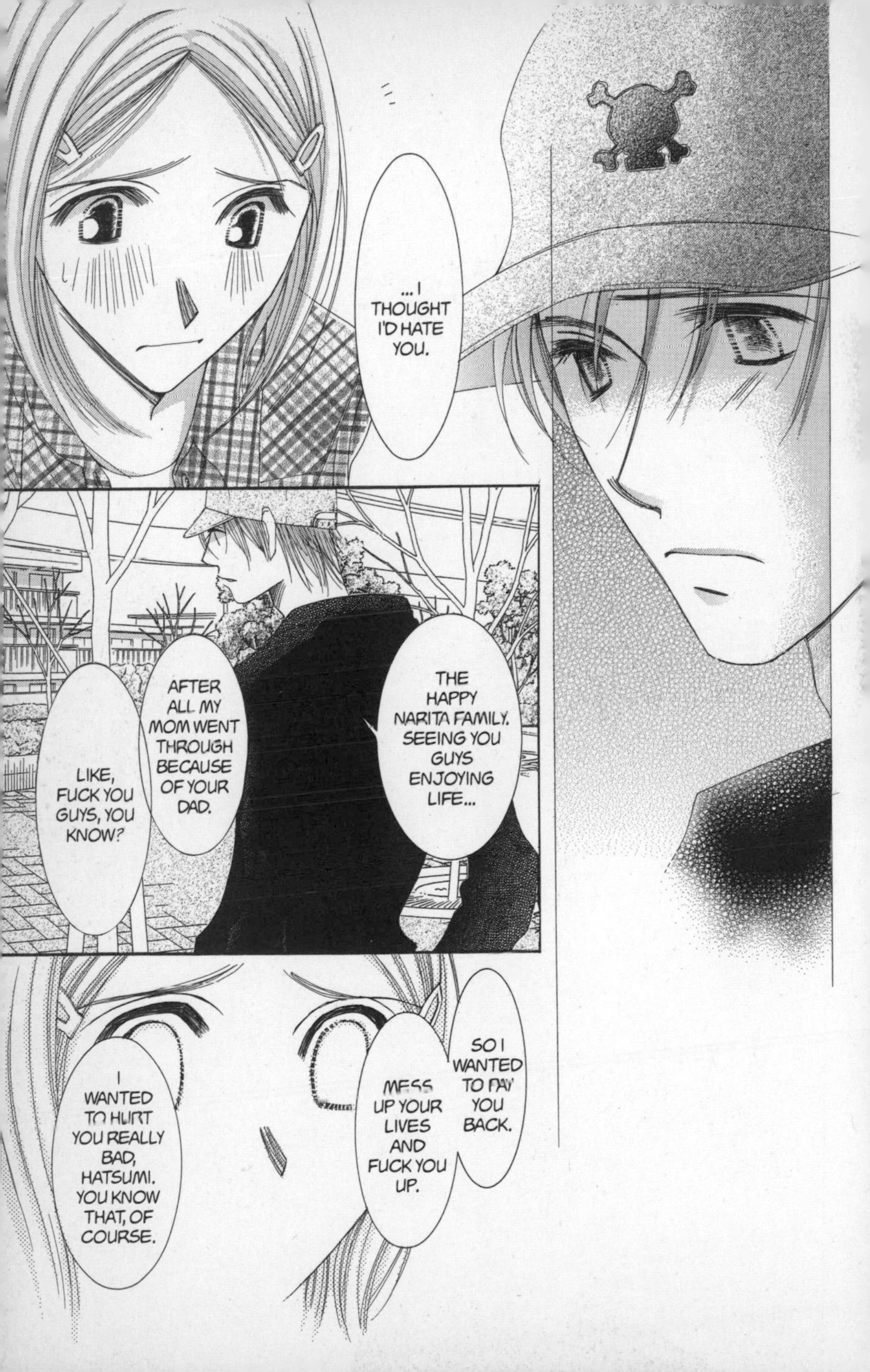
...I THOUGHT I'D HATE YOU.
THE HAPPY NARITA FAMILY. SEEING YOU GUYS ENJOYING LIFE...
AFTER ALL MY MOM WENT THROUGH BECAUSE OF YOUR DAD.
LIKE, FUCK YOU GUYS, YOU KNOW?
SO I WANTED TO PAY YOU BACK.
MESS UP YOUR LIVES AND FUCK YOU UP.
I WANTED TO HURT YOU REALLY BAD, HATSUMI. YOU KNOW THAT, OF COURSE.

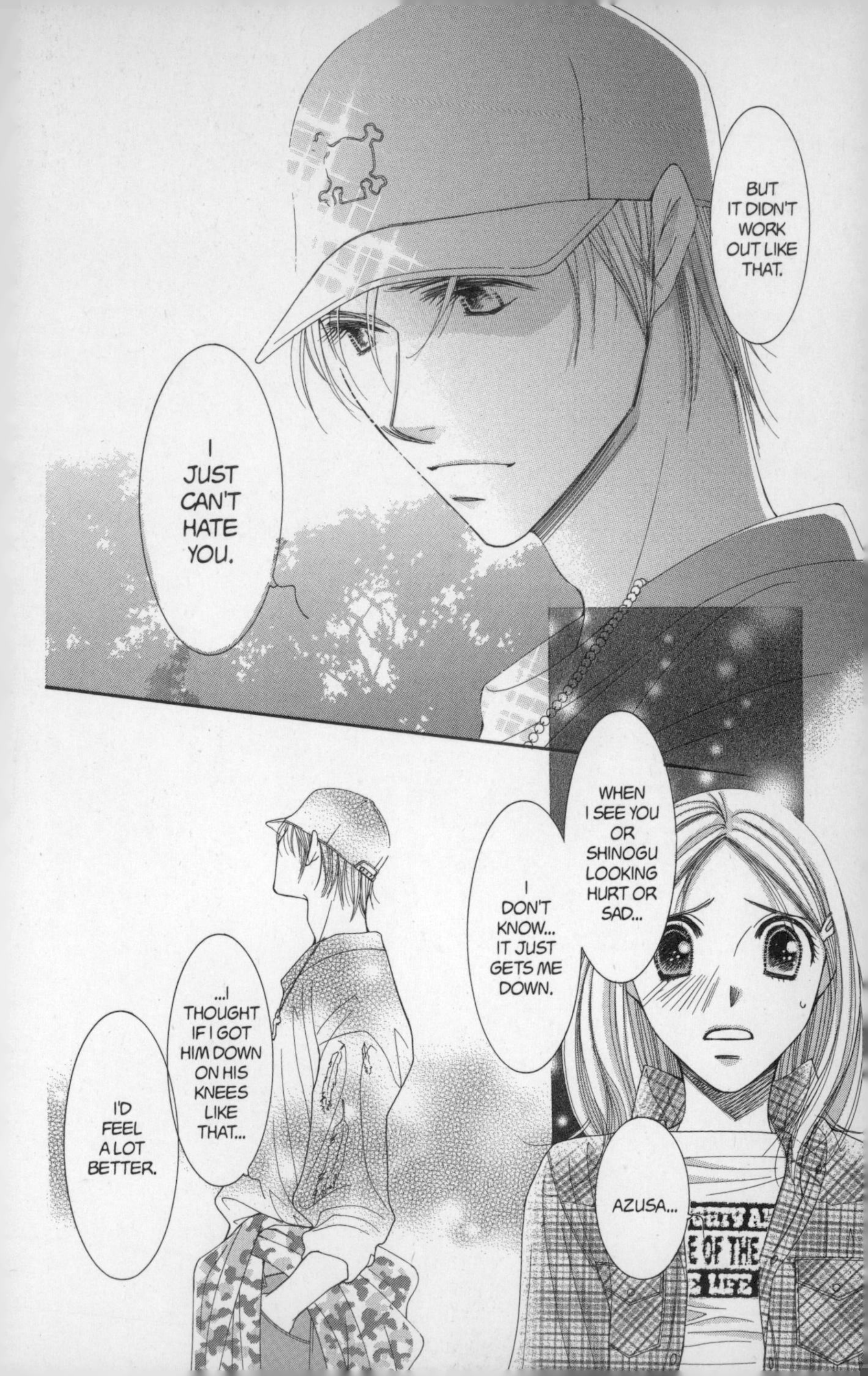
BUT IT DIDN'T WORK OUT LIKE THAT.
I JUST CAN'T HATE YOU.
WHEN I SEE YOU OR SHINOGU LOOKING HURT OR SAD...
I DON'T KNOW... IT JUST GETS ME DOWN.
...I THOUGHT IF I GOT HIM DOWN ON HIS KNEES LIKE THAT...
I'D FEEL A LOT BETTER.
AZUSA...

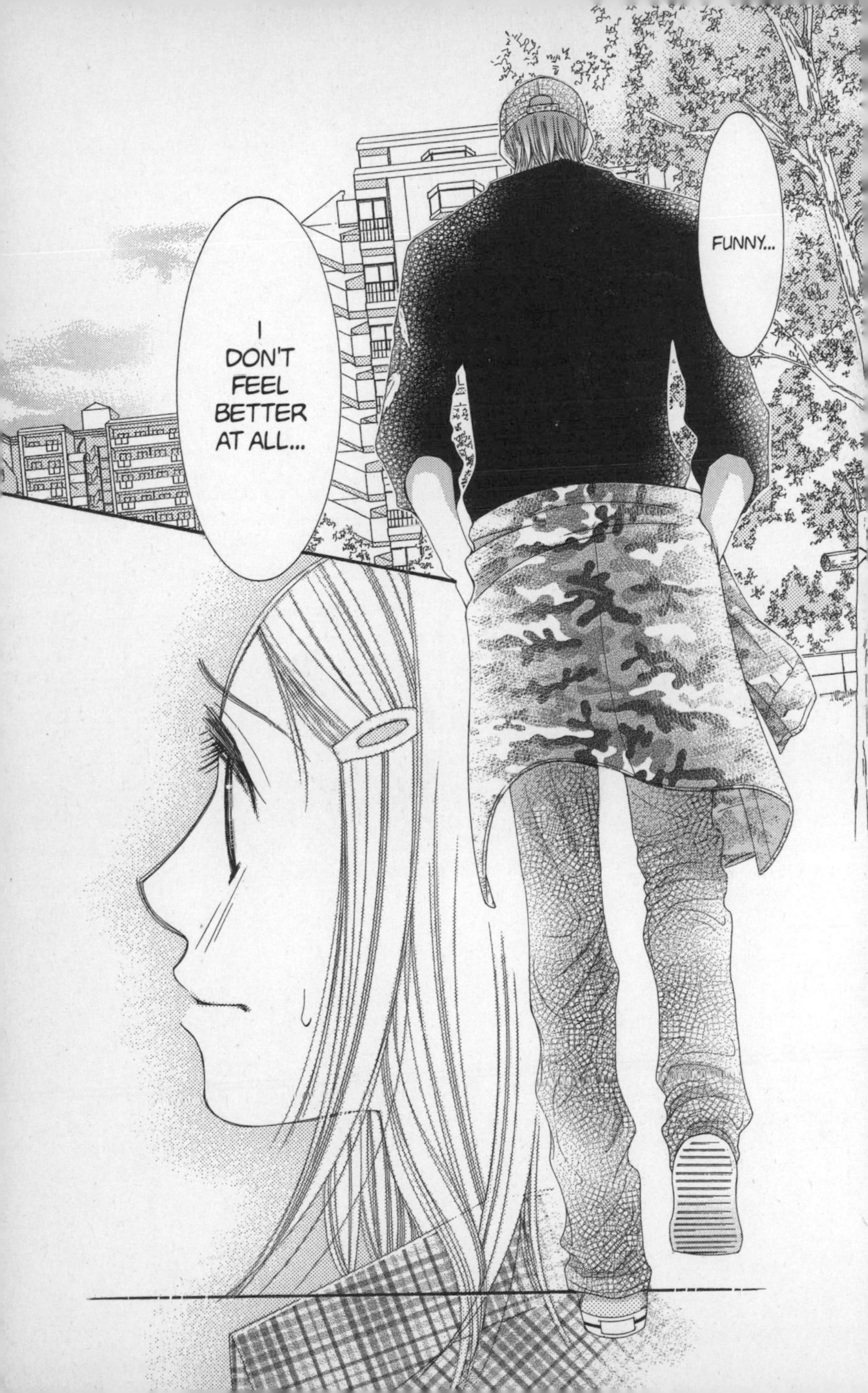
FUNNY...
I DON'T FEEL BETTER AT ALL...

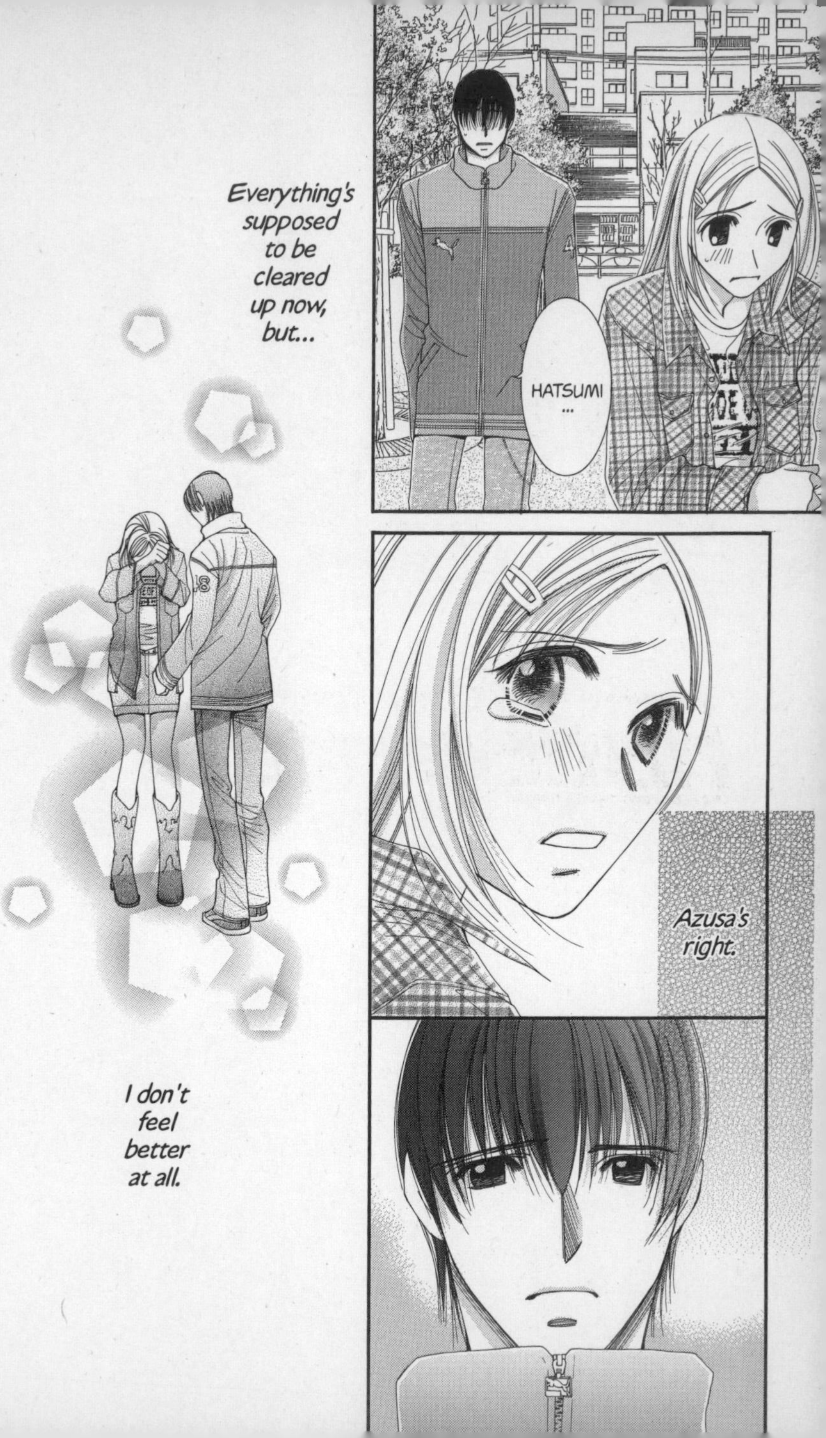
HATSUMI ...
Azusa's right.
Everything's supposed to be cleared up now, but...
I don't feel better at all.

hotgimmick

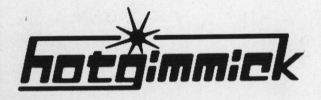

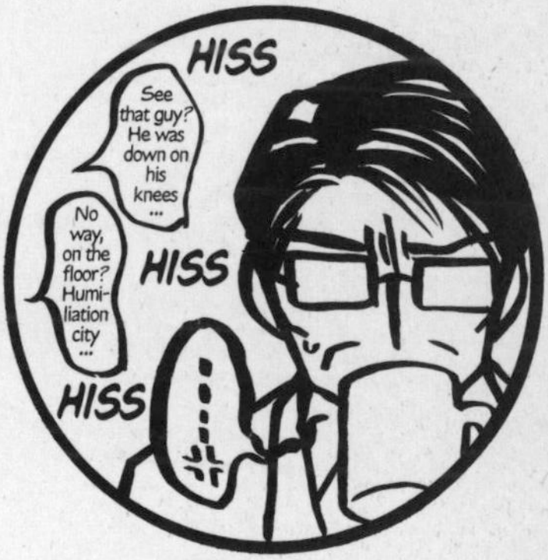
HISS
See that guy? He was down on his knees ...
HISS
No way, on the floor? Humi-liation city ...
HISS

LEFT BEHIND AT THE CAFE...

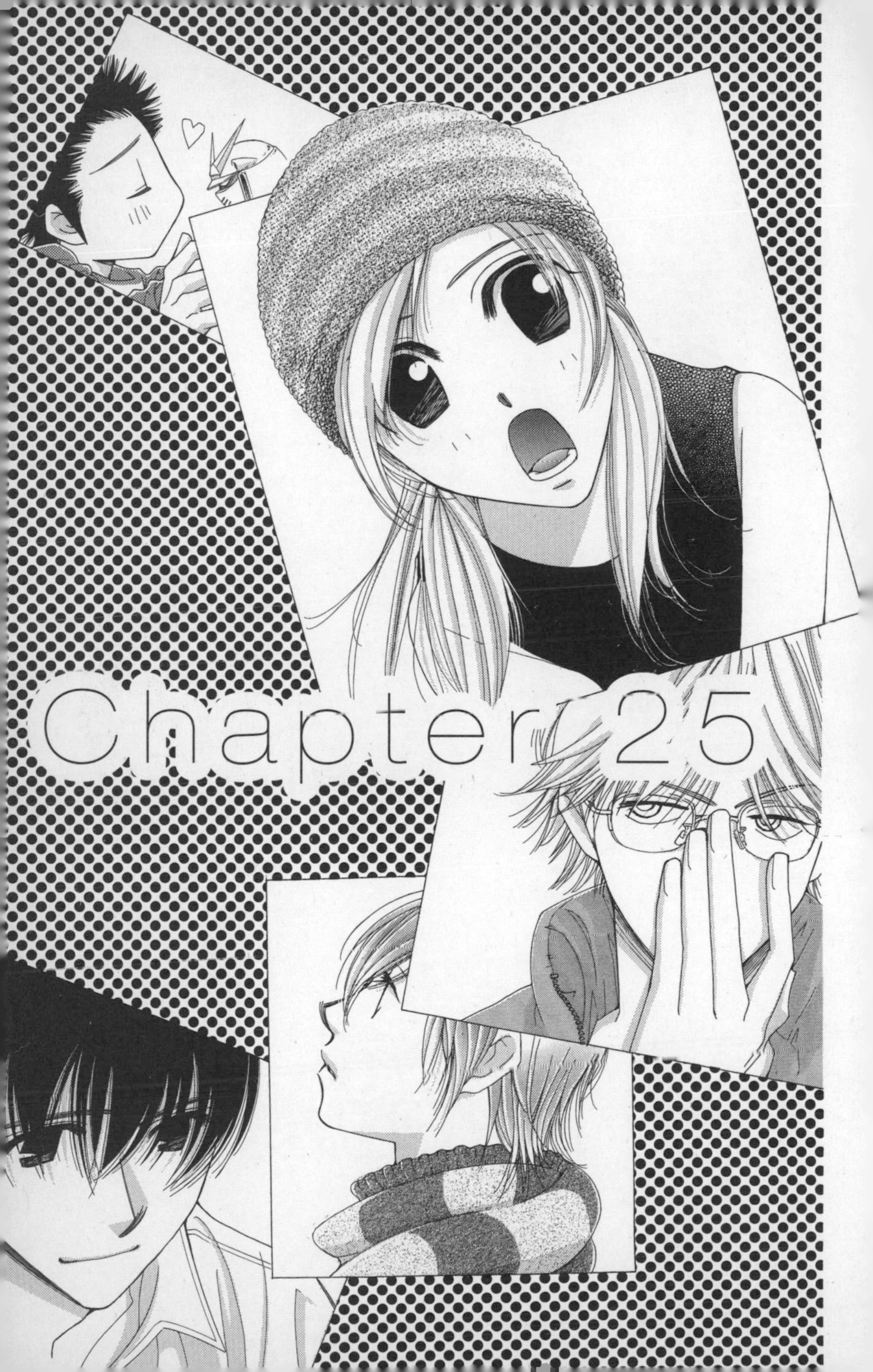
Chapter 25

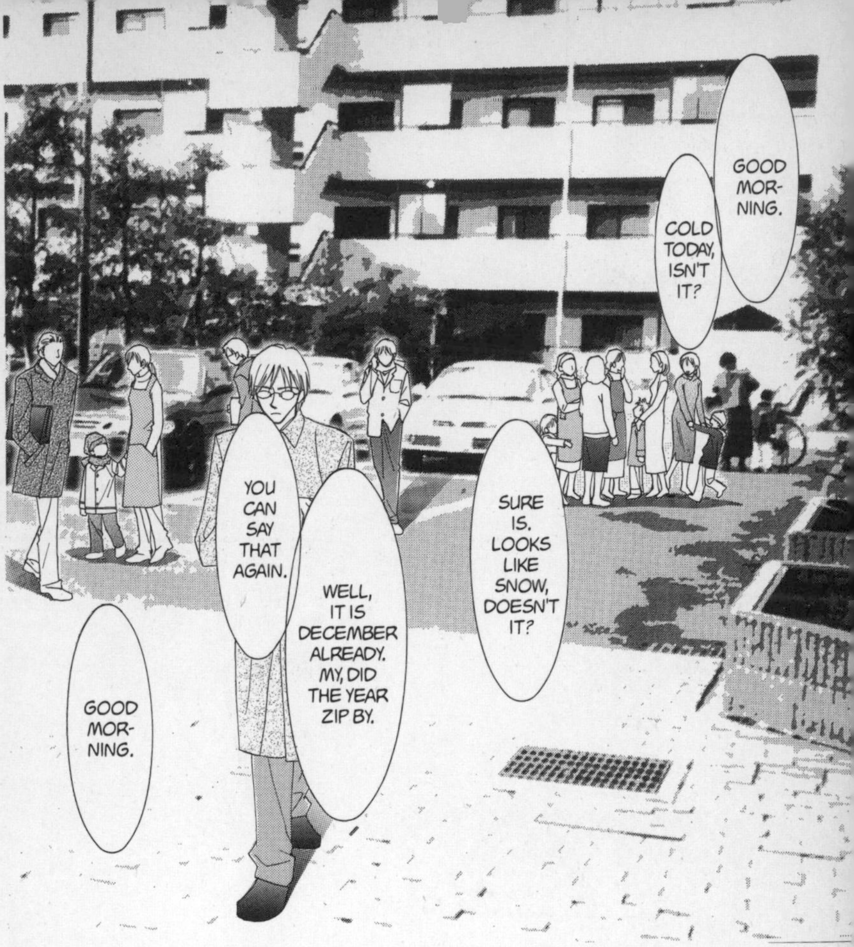
GOOD MORNING.
COLD TODAY, ISN'T IT?
SURE IS. LOOKS LIKE SNOW, DOESN'T IT?
WELL, IT IS DECEMBER ALREADY. MY, DID THE YEAR ZIP BY.
YOU CAN SAY THAT AGAIN.
GOOD MORNING.

hot gimmick

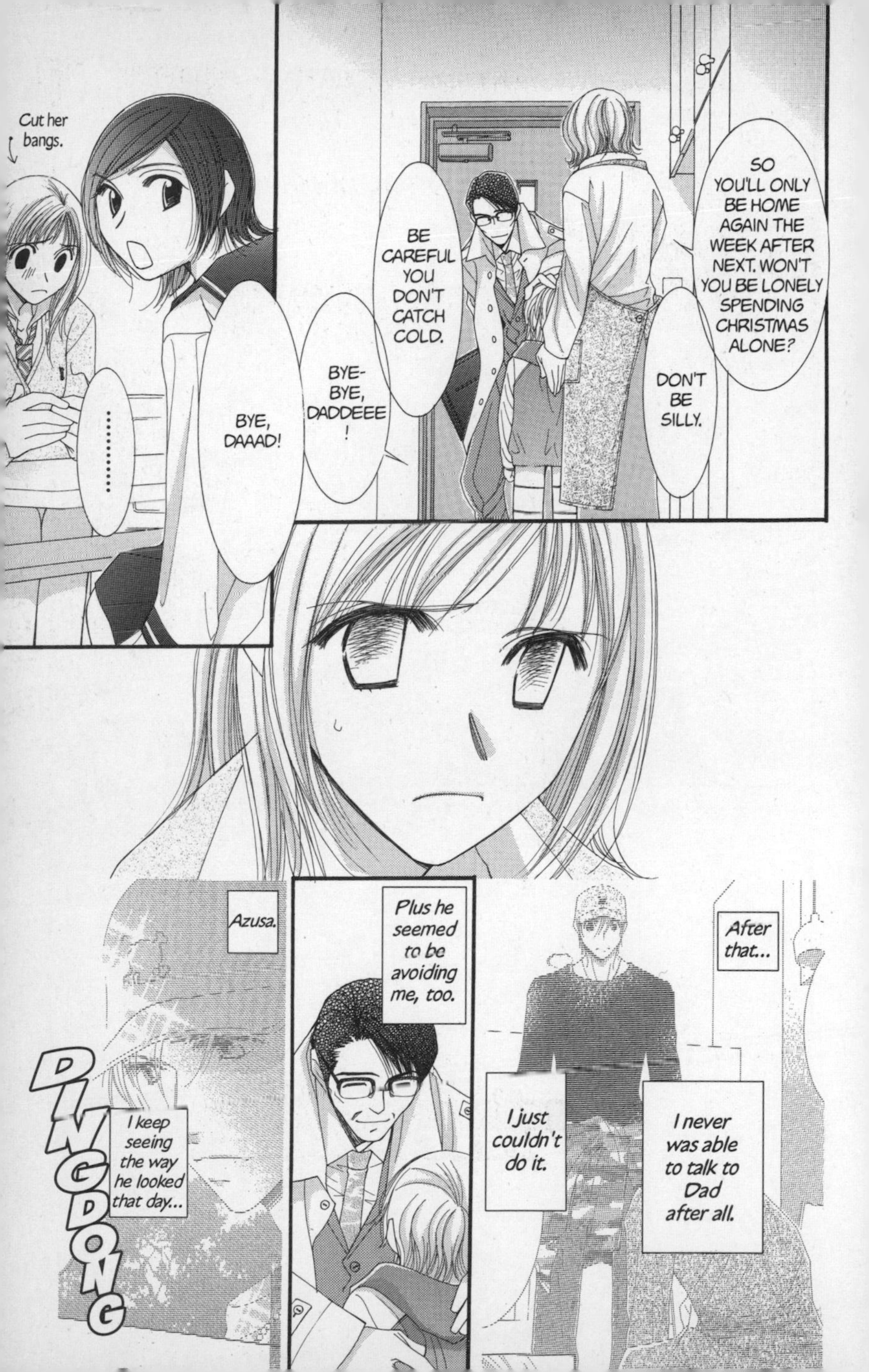
SO YOU'LL ONLY BE HOME AGAIN THE WEEK AFTER NEXT. WON'T YOU BE LONELY SPENDING CHRISTMAS ALONE?
DON'T BE SILLY.
BE CAREFUL YOU DON'T CATCH COLD.
BYE-BYE, DADDEEE!
BYE, DAAAD!
Cut her bangs.
....
After that...
I never was able to talk to Dad after all.
I just couldn't do it.
Plus he seemed to be avoiding me, too.
Azusa.
DING DONG
I keep seeing the way he looked that day...

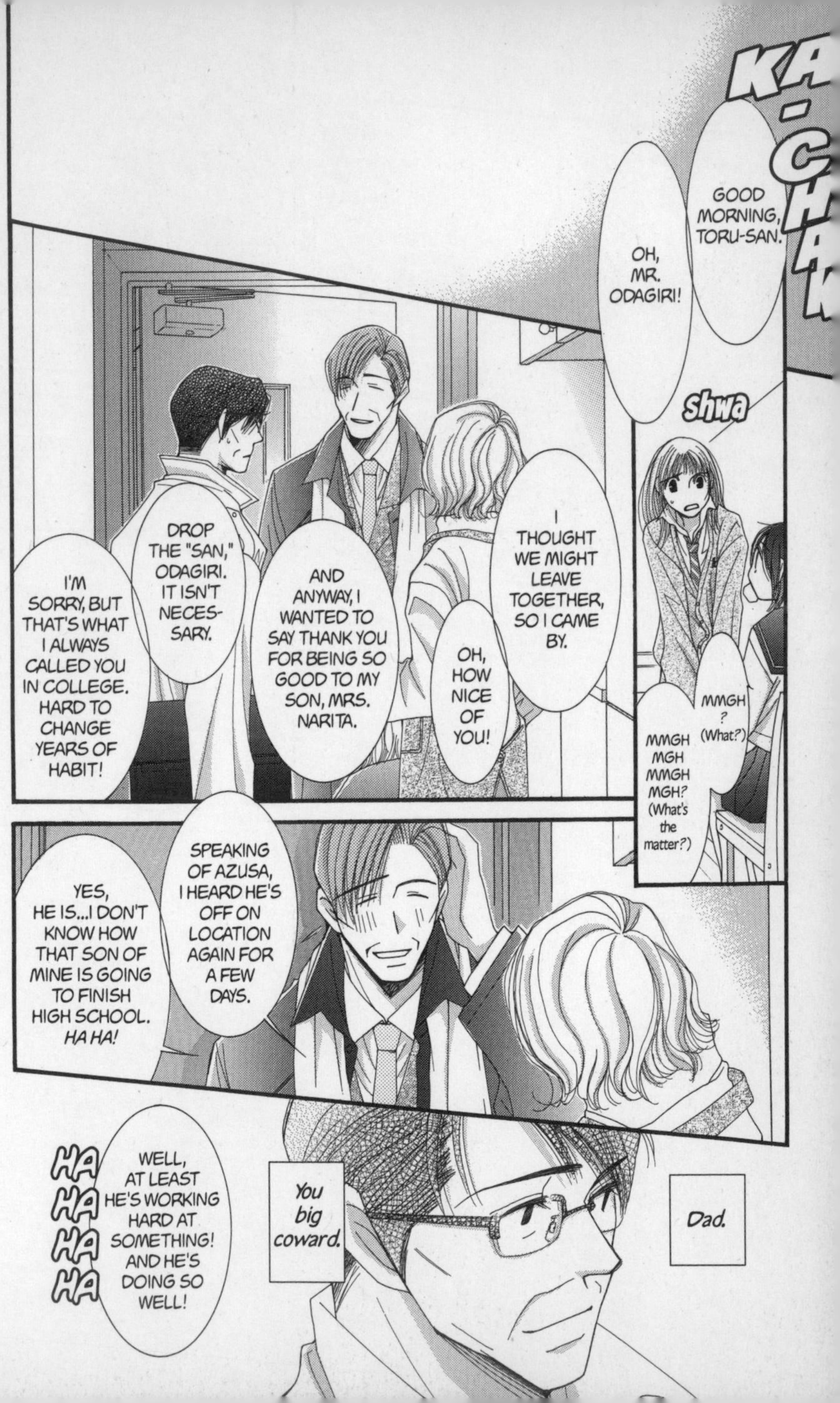
KA-CHAK
GOOD MORNING, TORU-SAN.
OH, MR. ODAGIRI!
shwa
MMGH? (What?)
MMGH MGH MMGH MGH? (What's the matter?)
I THOUGHT WE MIGHT LEAVE TOGETHER, SO I CAME BY.
OH, HOW NICE OF YOU!
AND ANYWAY, I WANTED TO SAY THANK YOU FOR BEING SO GOOD TO MY SON, MRS. NARITA.
DROP THE "SAN," ODAGIRI. IT ISN'T NECES-SARY.
I'M SORRY, BUT THAT'S WHAT I ALWAYS CALLED YOU IN COLLEGE. HARD TO CHANGE YEARS OF HABIT!
SPEAKING OF AZUSA, I HEARD HE'S OFF ON LOCATION AGAIN FOR A FEW DAYS.
YES, HE IS...I DON'T KNOW HOW THAT SON OF MINE IS GOING TO FINISH HIGH SCHOOL. HA HA!
Dad.
You big coward.
WELL, AT LEAST HE'S WORKING HARD AT SOMETHING! AND HE'S DOING SO WELL!
HA HA HA HA

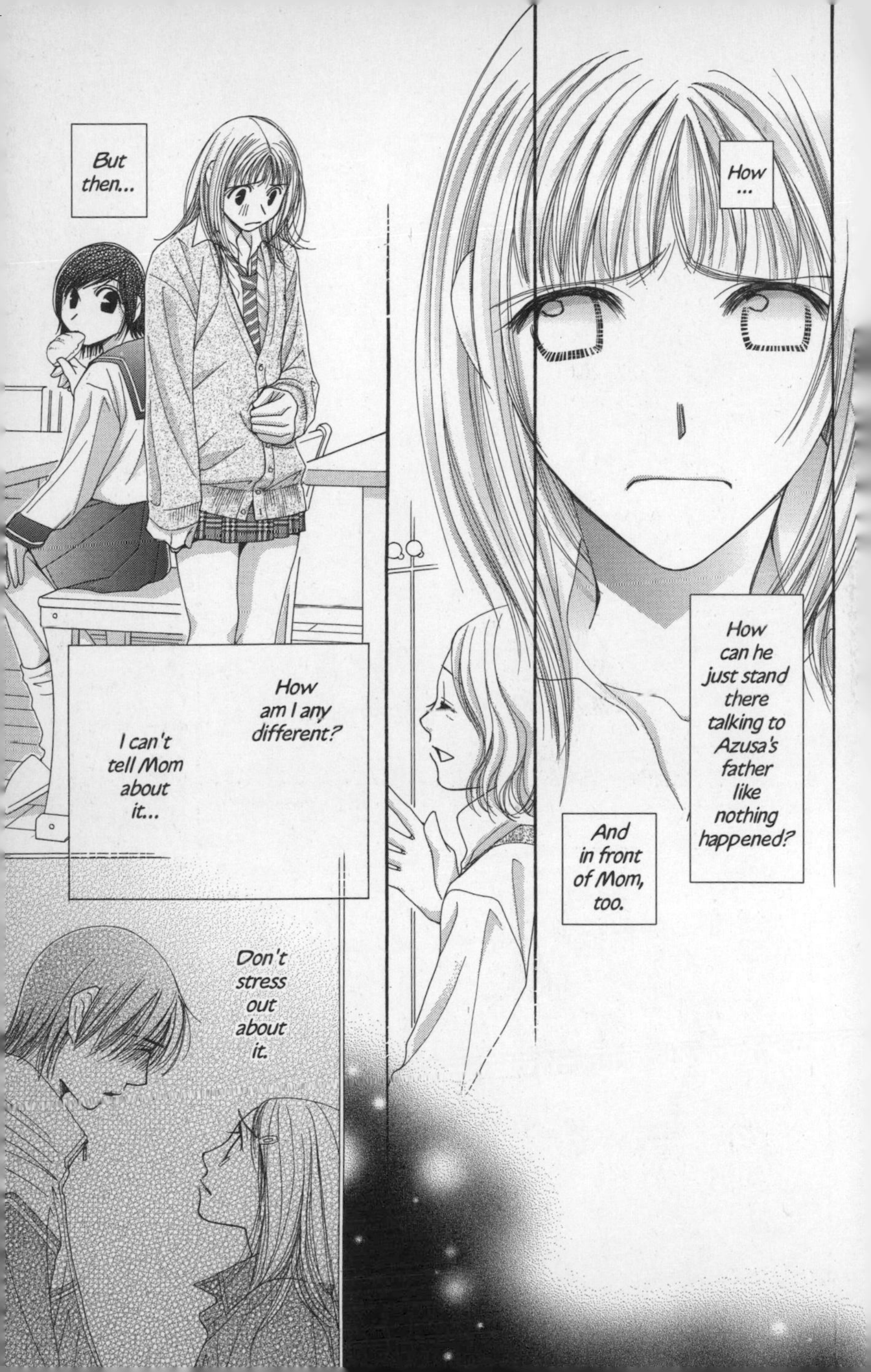
How...
How can he just stand there talking to Azusa's father like nothing happened?
And in front of Mom, too.
But then...
How am I any different?
I can't tell Mom about it...
Don't stress out about it.

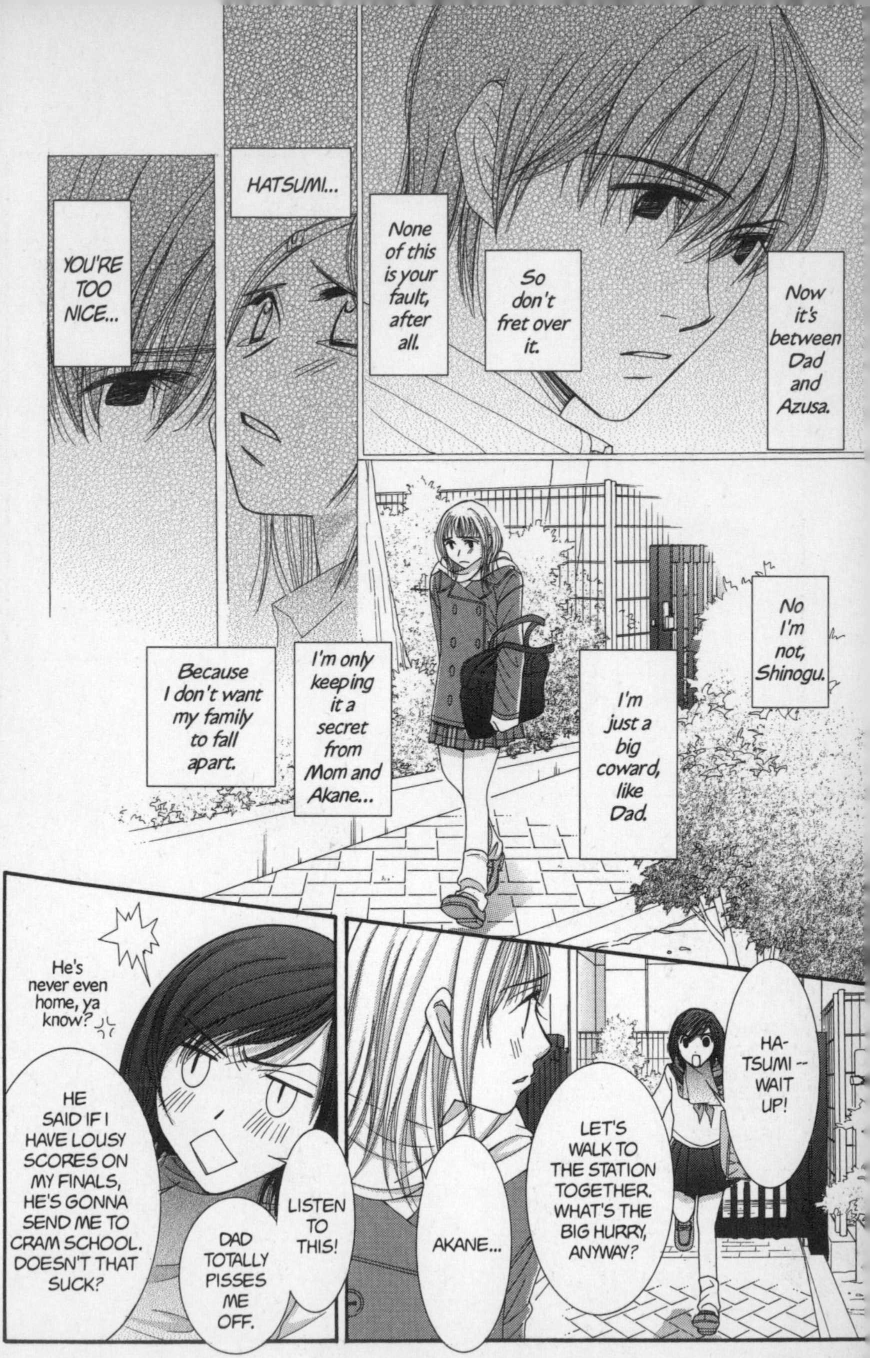
Now it's between Dad and Azusa.
So don't fret over it.
None of this is your fault, after all.
HATSUMI...
YOU'RE TOO NICE...
No I'm not, Shinogu.
I'm just a big coward, like Dad.
I'm only keeping it a secret from Mom and Akane...
Because I don't want my family to fall apart.
HA-TSUMI -- WAIT UP!
LET'S WALK TO THE STATION TOGETHER. WHAT'S THE BIG HURRY, ANYWAY?
AKANE...
LISTEN TO THIS!
DAD TOTALLY PISSES ME OFF.
HE SAID IF I HAVE LOUSY SCORES ON MY FINALS, HE'S GONNA SEND ME TO CRAM SCHOOL. DOESN'T THAT SUCK?
He's never even home, ya know?

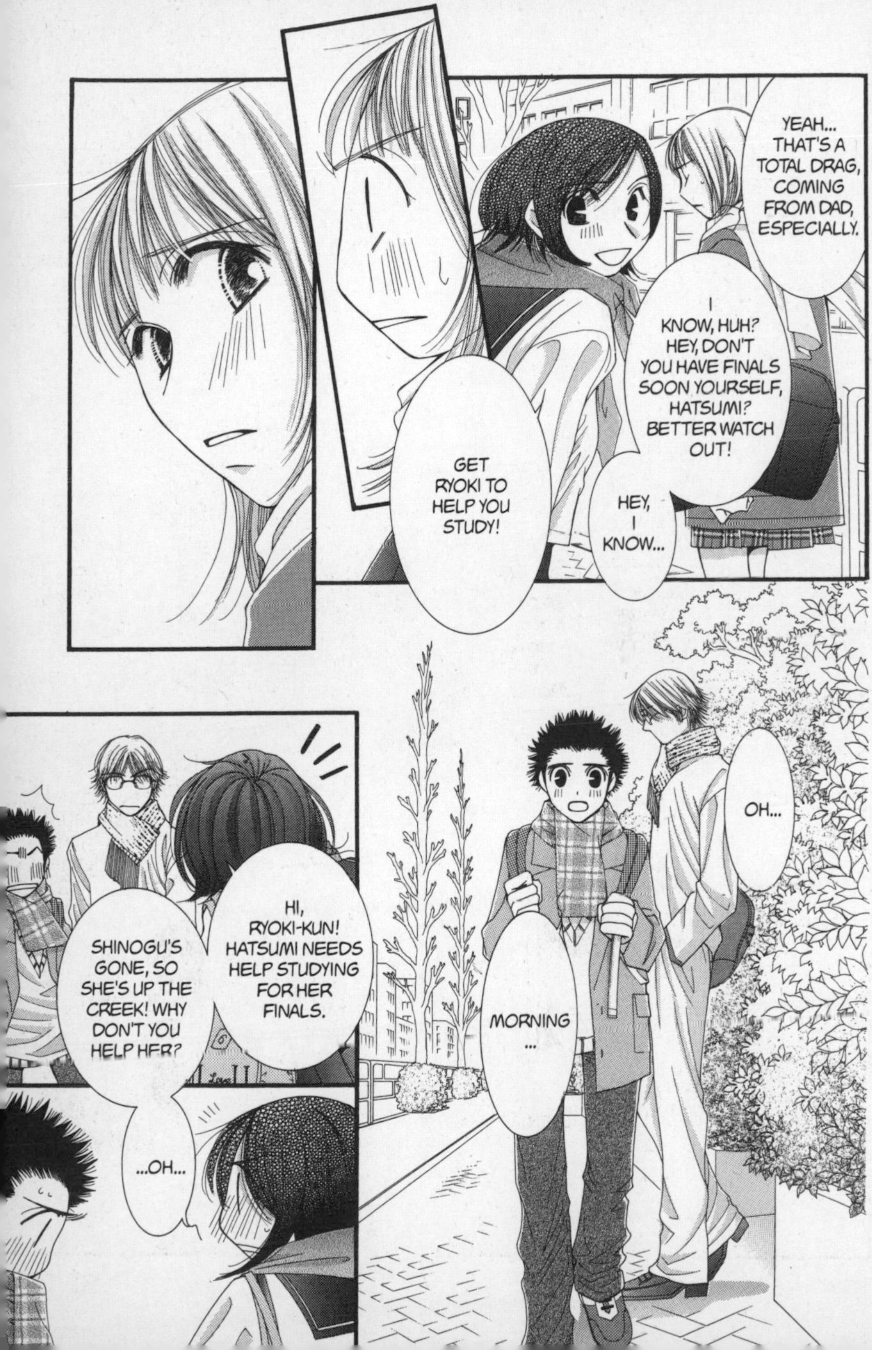
YEAH... THAT'S A TOTAL DRAG, COMING FROM DAD, ESPECIALLY.
I KNOW, HUH? HEY, DON'T YOU HAVE FINALS SOON YOURSELF, HATSUMI? BETTER WATCH OUT!
HEY, I KNOW...
GET RYOKI TO HELP YOU STUDY!
OH...
MORNING...
HI, RYOKI-KUN! HATSUMI NEEDS HELP STUDYING FOR HER FINALS.
SHINOGU'S GONE, SO SHE'S UP THE CREEK! WHY DON'T YOU HELP HER?
...OH...

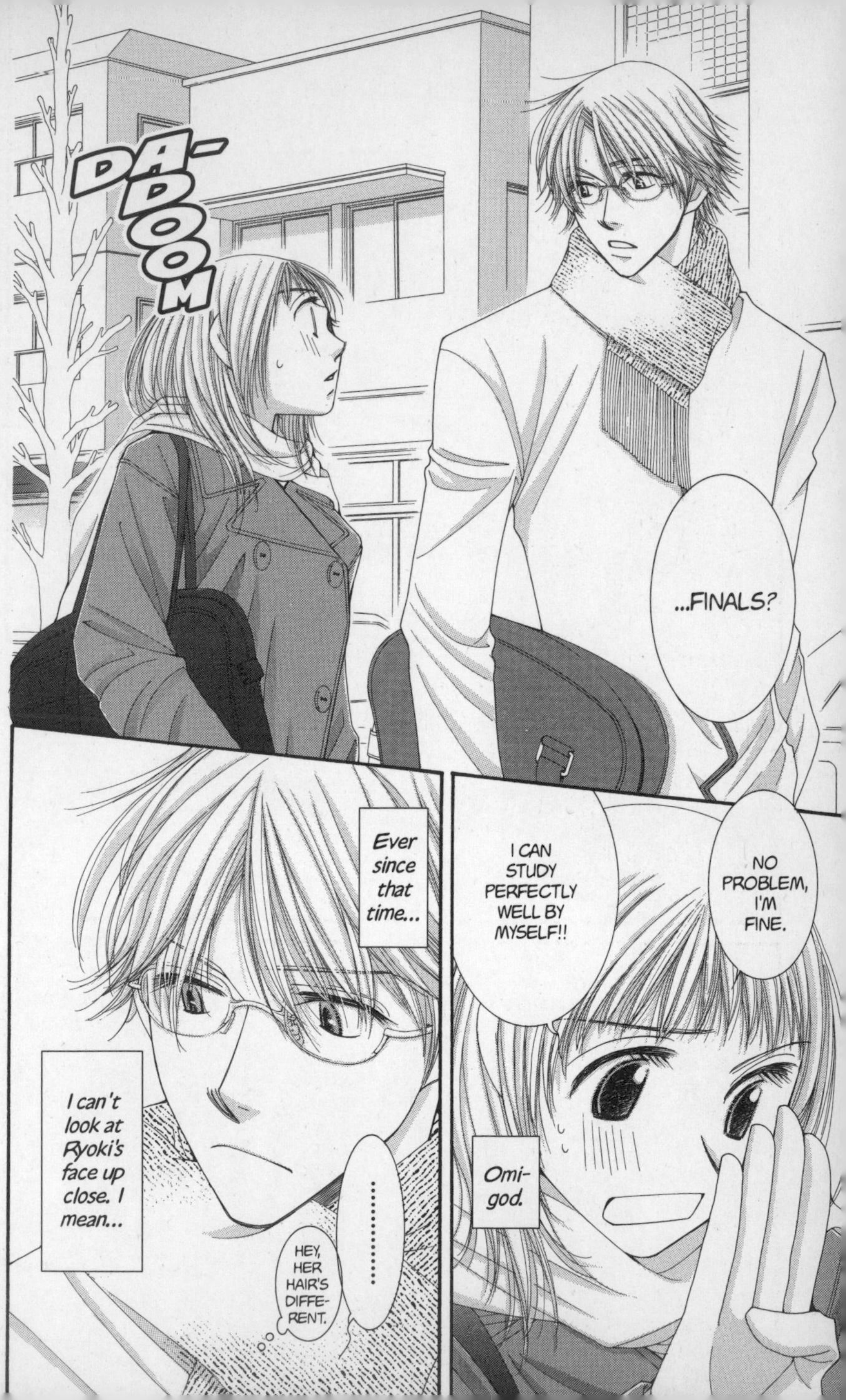
DA-DOOM
...FINALS?
NO PROBLEM, I'M FINE.
I CAN STUDY PERFECTLY WELL BY MYSELF!!
Omi-god.
Ever since that time...
I can't look at Ryoki's face up close. I mean...
....
HEY, HER HAIR'S DIFFERENT.

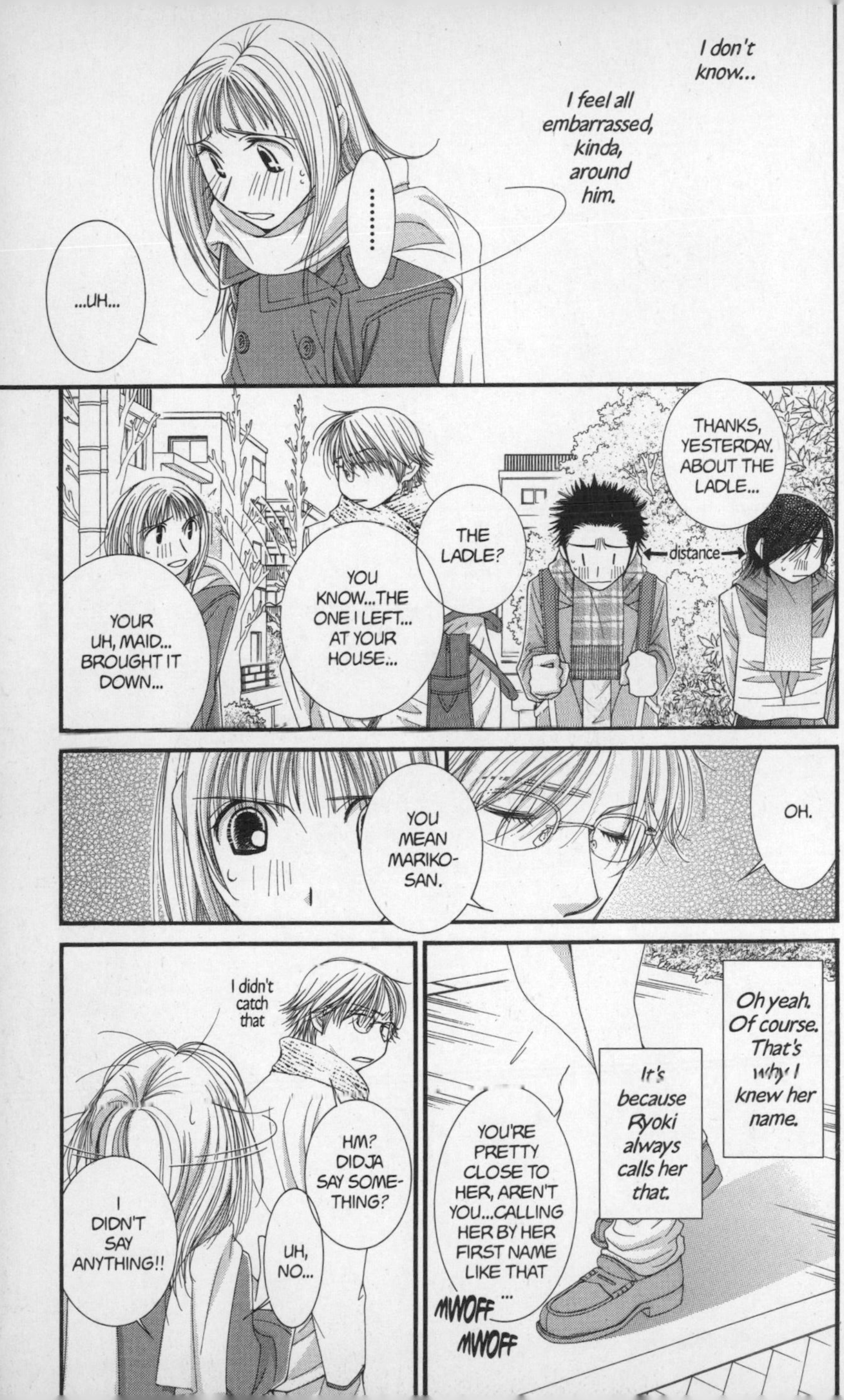
I don't know...
I feel all embarrassed, kinda, around him.
......
...UH...
THANKS, YESTERDAY. ABOUT THE LADLE...
distance
THE LADLE?
YOU KNOW...THE ONE I LEFT... AT YOUR HOUSE...
YOUR UH, MAID... BROUGHT IT DOWN...
OH.
YOU MEAN MARIKO-SAN.
Oh yeah. Of course. That's why I knew her name.
It's because Ryoki always calls her that.
YOU'RE PRETTY CLOSE TO HER, AREN'T YOU...CALLING HER BY HER FIRST NAME LIKE THAT ...
MWOFF MWOFF
I didn't catch that
HM? DIDJA SAY SOME-THING?
UH, NO...
I DIDN'T SAY ANYTHING!!

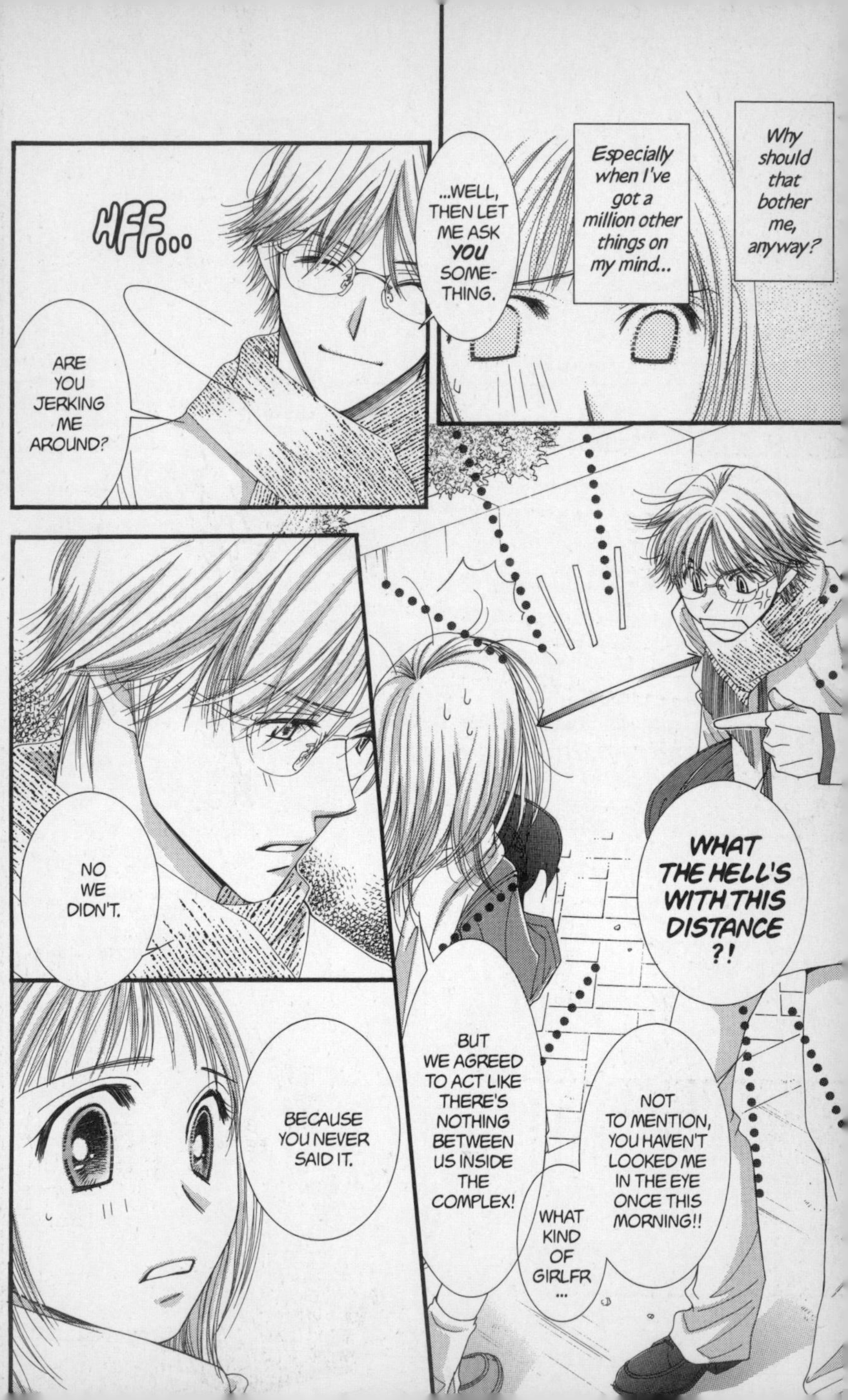
Why should that bother me, anyway?
Especially when I've got a million other things on my mind...
...WELL, THEN LET ME ASK YOU SOMETHING.
HFFooo
ARE YOU JERKING ME AROUND?
WHAT THE HELL'S WITH THIS DISTANCE?!
NOT TO MENTION, YOU HAVEN'T LOOKED ME IN THE EYE ONCE THIS MORNING!!
WHAT KIND OF GIRLFR...
BUT WE AGREED TO ACT LIKE THERE'S NOTHING BETWEEN US INSIDE THE COMPLEX!
NO WE DIDN'T.
BECAUSE YOU NEVER SAID IT.

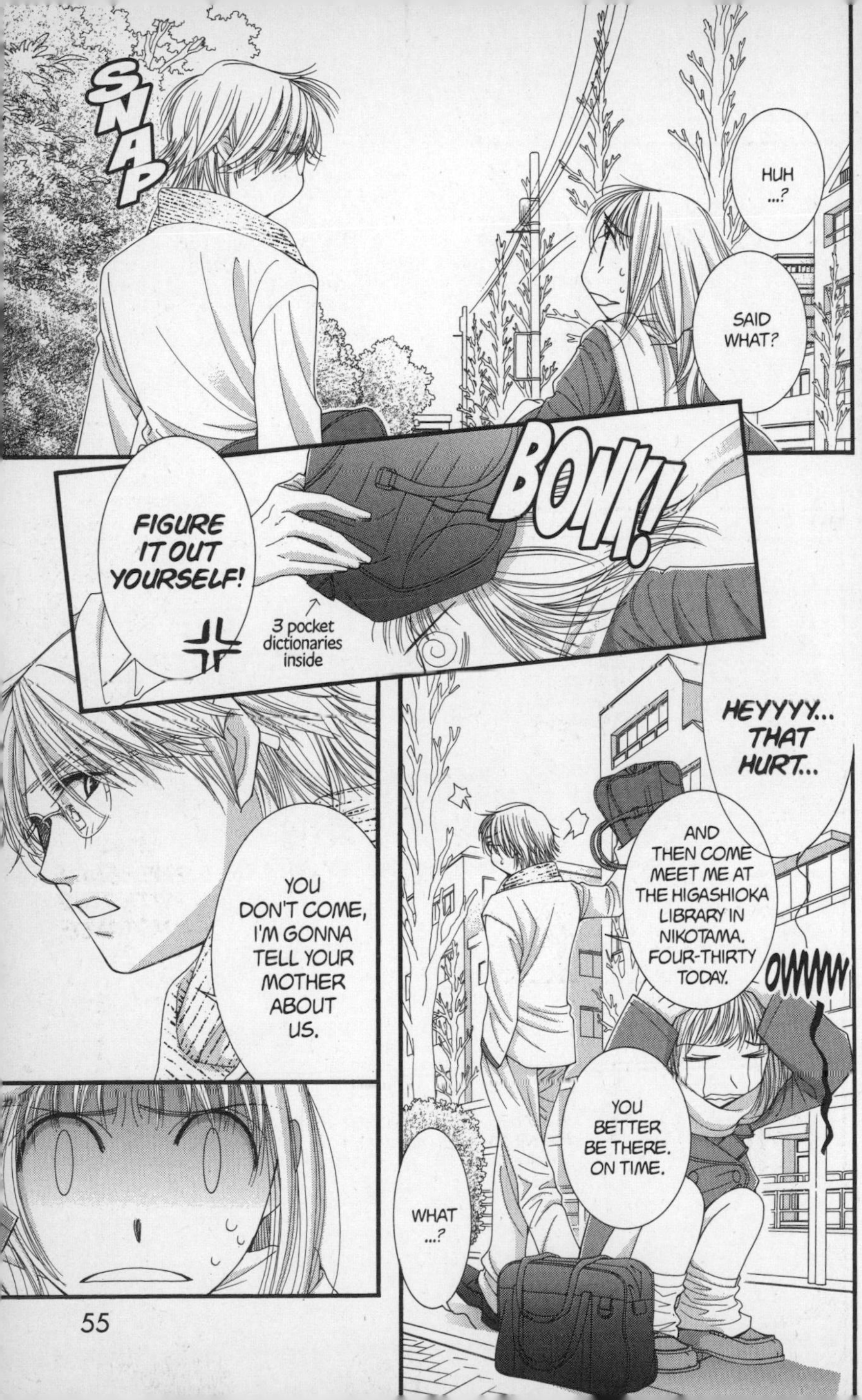
HUH ...?
SAID WHAT?
SNAP
BONK!
FIGURE IT OUT YOURSELF!
3 pocket dictionaries inside
HEYYYY... THAT HURT...
AND THEN COME MEET ME AT THE HIGASHIOKA LIBRARY IN NIKOTAMA. FOUR-THIRTY TODAY.
OWWW
YOU BETTER BE THERE. ON TIME.
WHAT ...?
YOU DON'T COME, I'M GONNA TELL YOUR MOTHER ABOUT US.

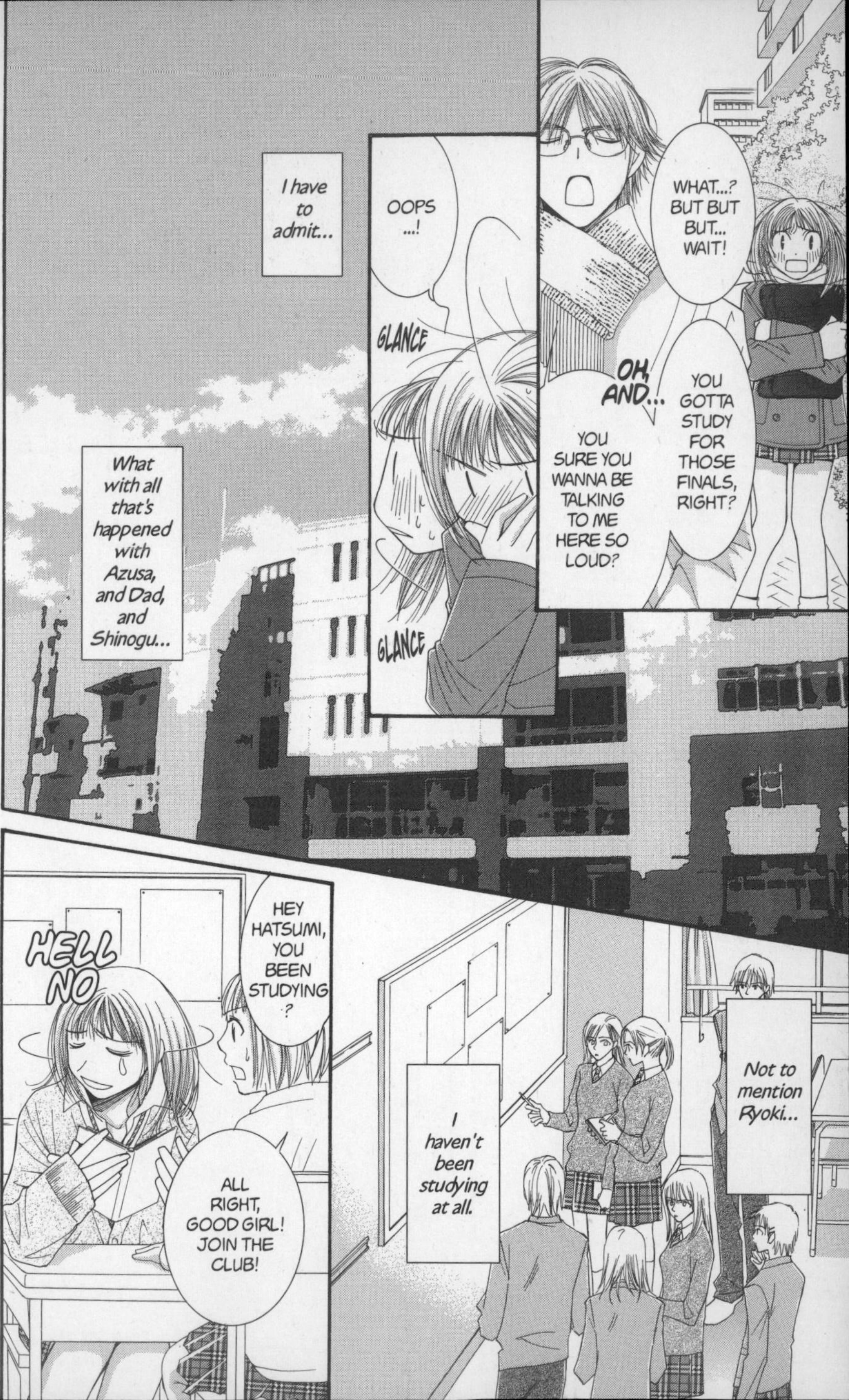
WHAT...? BUT BUT BUT... WAIT!
YOU GOTTA STUDY FOR THOSE FINALS, RIGHT?
OH, AND...
YOU SURE YOU WANNA BE TALKING TO ME HERE SO LOUD?
OOPS ...!
GLANCE
GLANCE
I have to admit...
What with all that's happened with Azusa, and Dad, and Shinogu...
Not to mention Ryoki...
I haven't been studying at all.
HEY HATSUMI, YOU BEEN STUDYING?
HELL NO
ALL RIGHT, GOOD GIRL! JOIN THE CLUB!

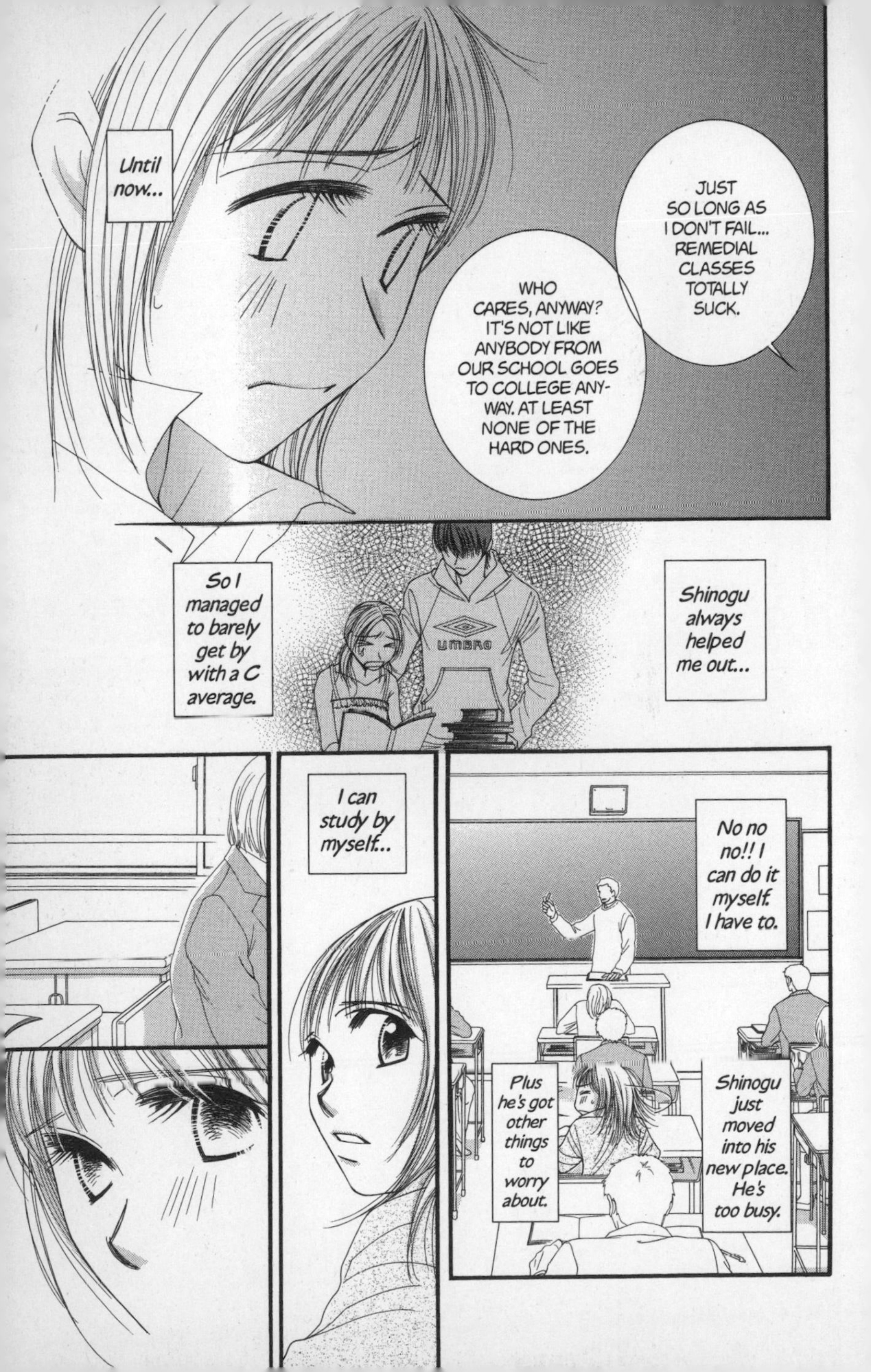
JUST SO LONG AS I DON'T FAIL... REMEDIAL CLASSES TOTALLY SUCK.
WHO CARES, ANYWAY? IT'S NOT LIKE ANYBODY FROM OUR SCHOOL GOES TO COLLEGE ANY-WAY. AT LEAST NONE OF THE HARD ONES.
Until now...
Shinogu always helped me out...
So I managed to barely get by with a C average.
No no no!! I can do it myself. I have to.
Shinogu just moved into his new place. He's too busy.
Plus he's got other things to worry about.
I can study by myself...

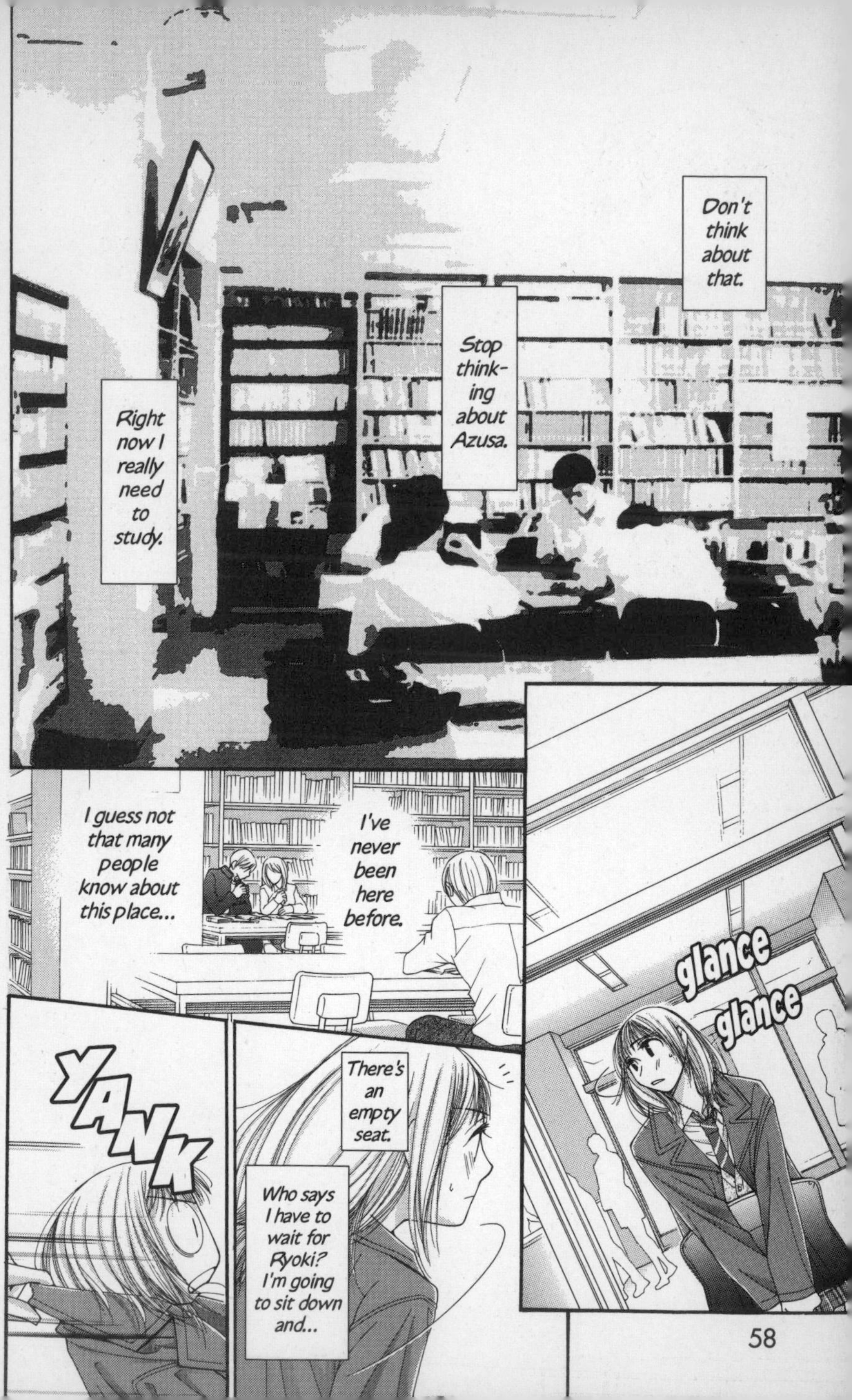

Don't think about that.
Stop thinking about Azusa.
Right now I really need to study.
glance glance
I've never been here before.
I guess not that many people know about this place...
There's an empty seat.
Who says I have to wait for Ryoki? I'm going to sit down and...
YANK

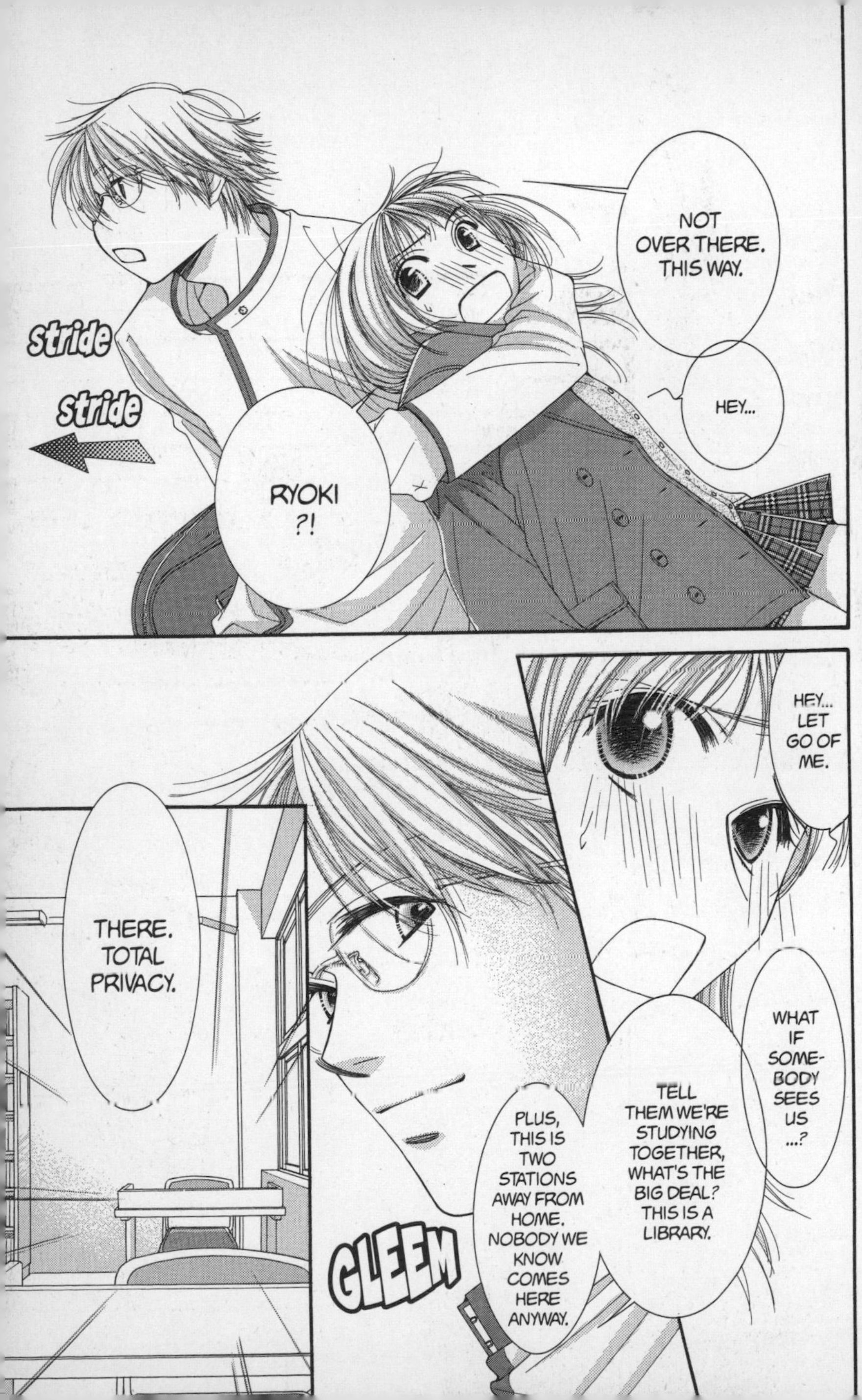
NOT OVER THERE. THIS WAY.
HEY...
stride
stride
RYOKI ?!
HEY... LET GO OF ME.
WHAT IF SOMEBODY SEES US ...?
TELL THEM WE'RE STUDYING TOGETHER, WHAT'S THE BIG DEAL? THIS IS A LIBRARY.
PLUS, THIS IS TWO STATIONS AWAY FROM HOME. NOBODY WE KNOW COMES HERE ANYWAY.
GLEEM
THERE. TOTAL PRIVACY.

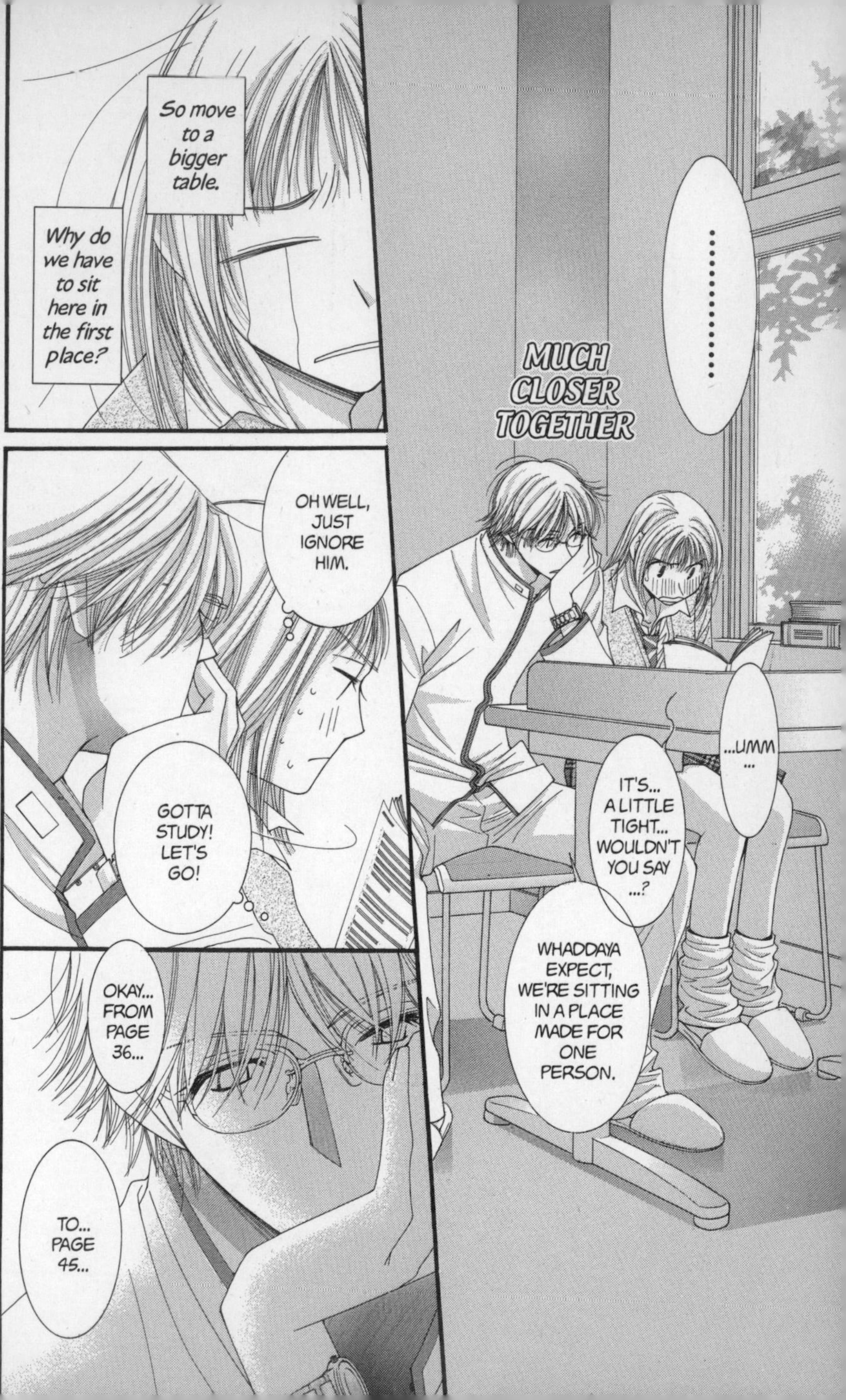

......
MUCH CLOSER TOGETHER
...UMM ...
IT'S... A LITTLE TIGHT... WOULDN'T YOU SAY ...?
WHADDAYA EXPECT, WE'RE SITTING IN A PLACE MADE FOR ONE PERSON.
So move to a bigger table.
Why do we have to sit here in the first place?
OH WELL, JUST IGNORE HIM.
GOTTA STUDY! LET'S GO!
OKAY... FROM PAGE 36...
TO... PAGE 45...

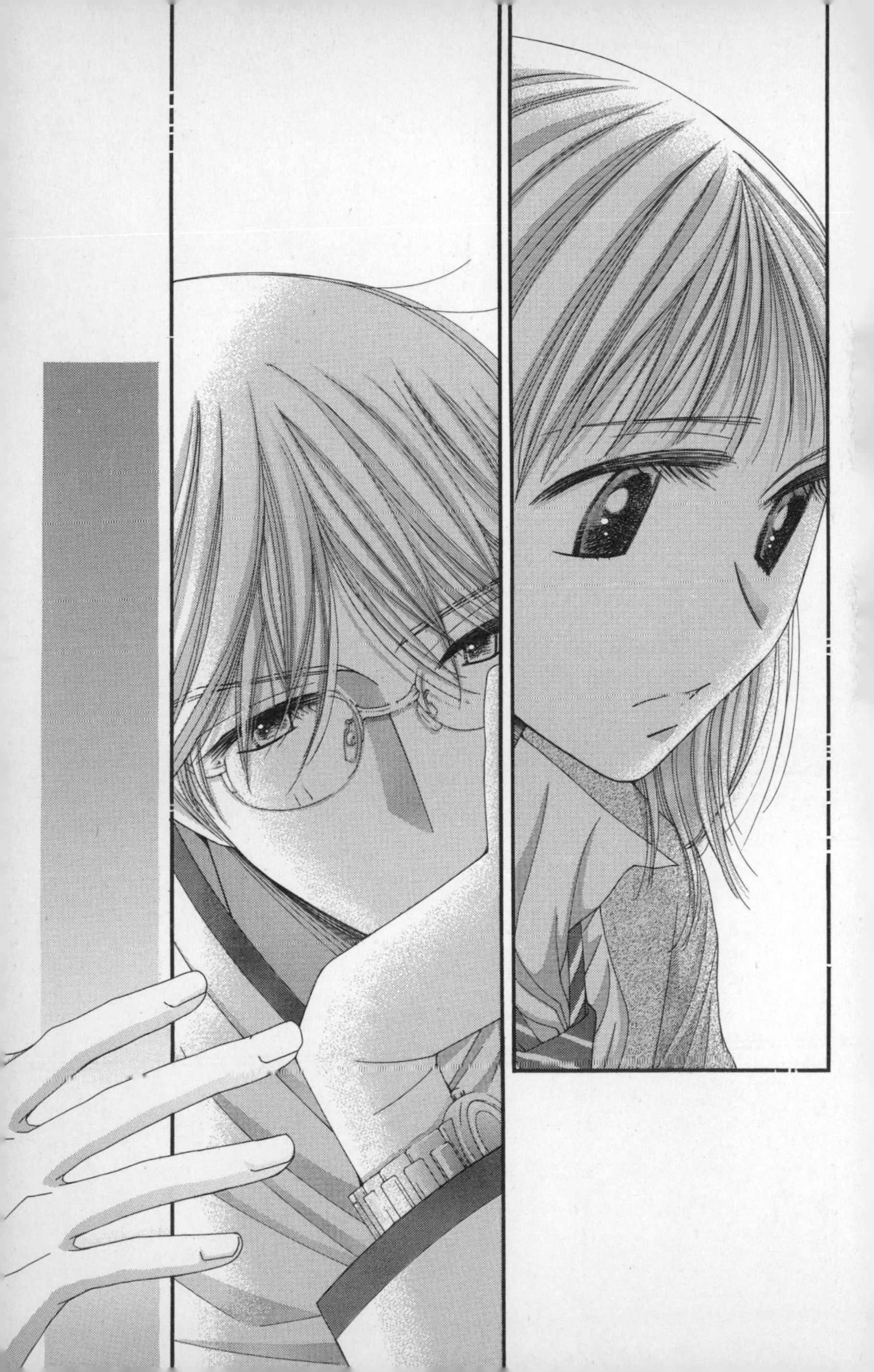

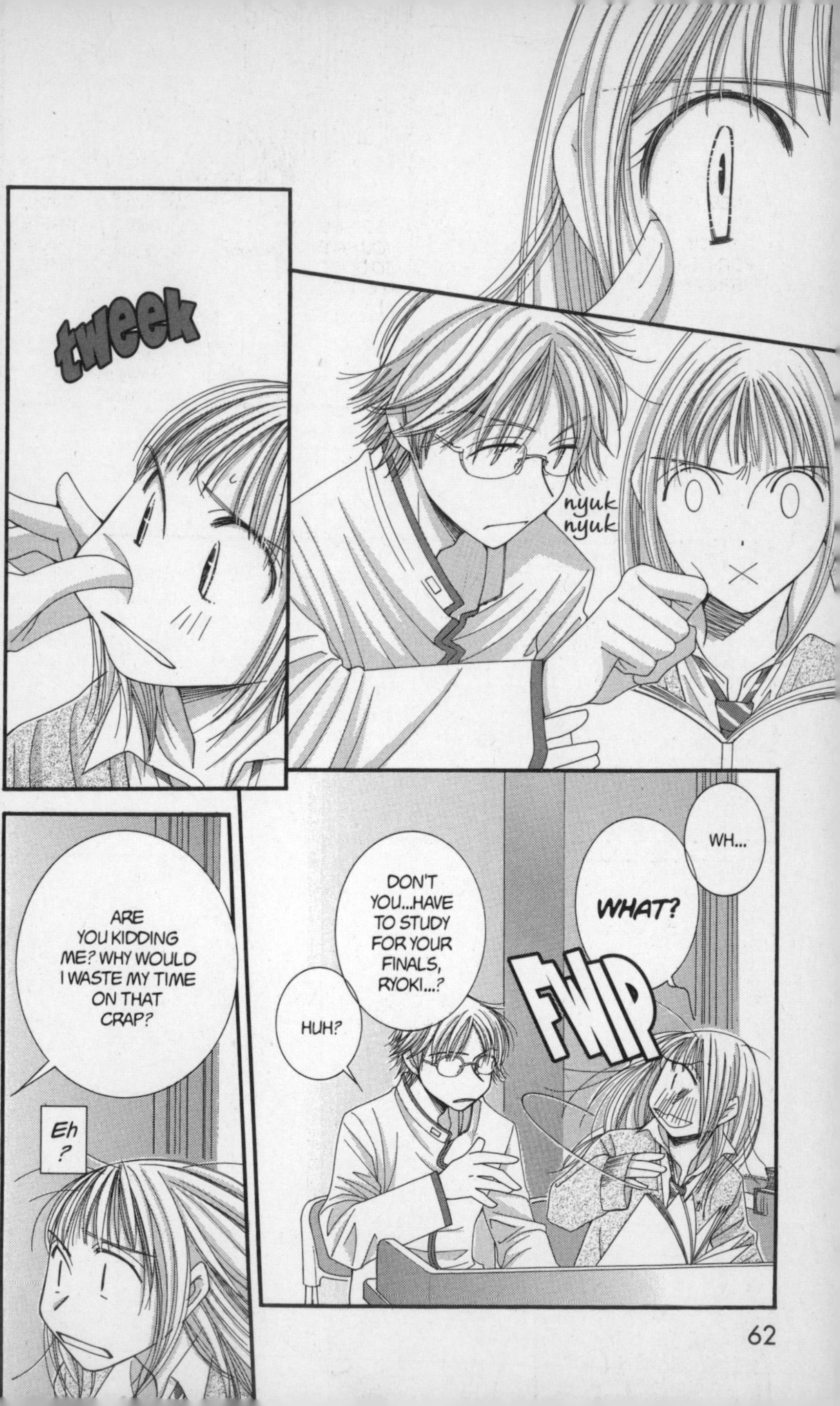

nyuk nyuk
tweek
WH...
WHAT?
FWIP
DON'T YOU...HAVE TO STUDY FOR YOUR FINALS, RYOKI...?
HUH?
ARE YOU KIDDING ME? WHY WOULD I WASTE MY TIME ON THAT CRAP?
Eh?

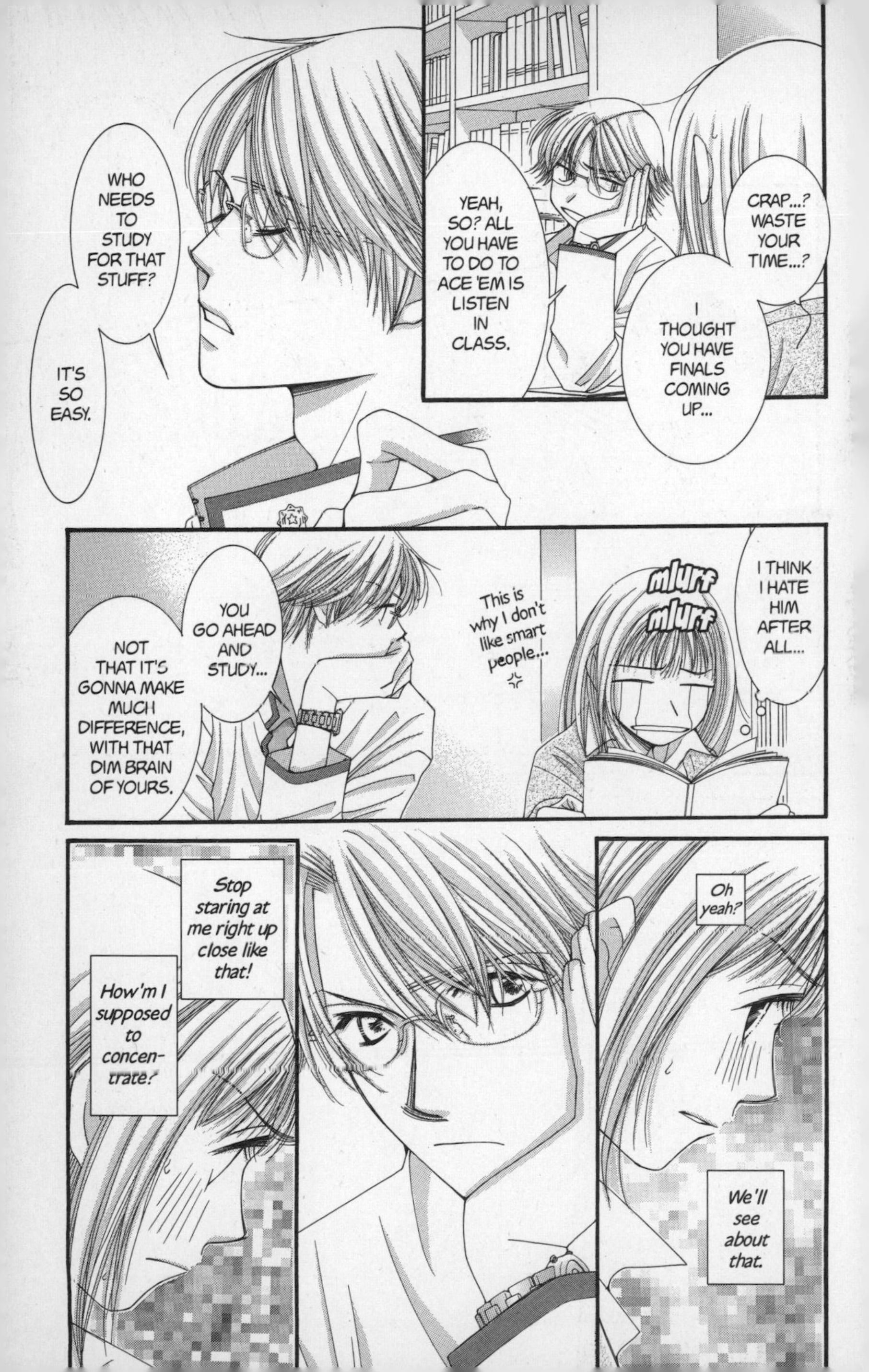
CRAP...? WASTE YOUR TIME...?
I THOUGHT YOU HAVE FINALS COMING UP...
YEAH, SO? ALL YOU HAVE TO DO TO ACE 'EM IS LISTEN IN CLASS.
WHO NEEDS TO STUDY FOR THAT STUFF?
IT'S SO EASY.
I THINK I HATE HIM AFTER ALL...
mlurf mlurf
This is why I don't like smart people...
YOU GO AHEAD AND STUDY...
NOT THAT IT'S GONNA MAKE MUCH DIFFERENCE, WITH THAT DIM BRAIN OF YOURS.
Oh yeah?
We'll see about that.
Stop staring at me right up close like that!
How'm I supposed to concentrate?

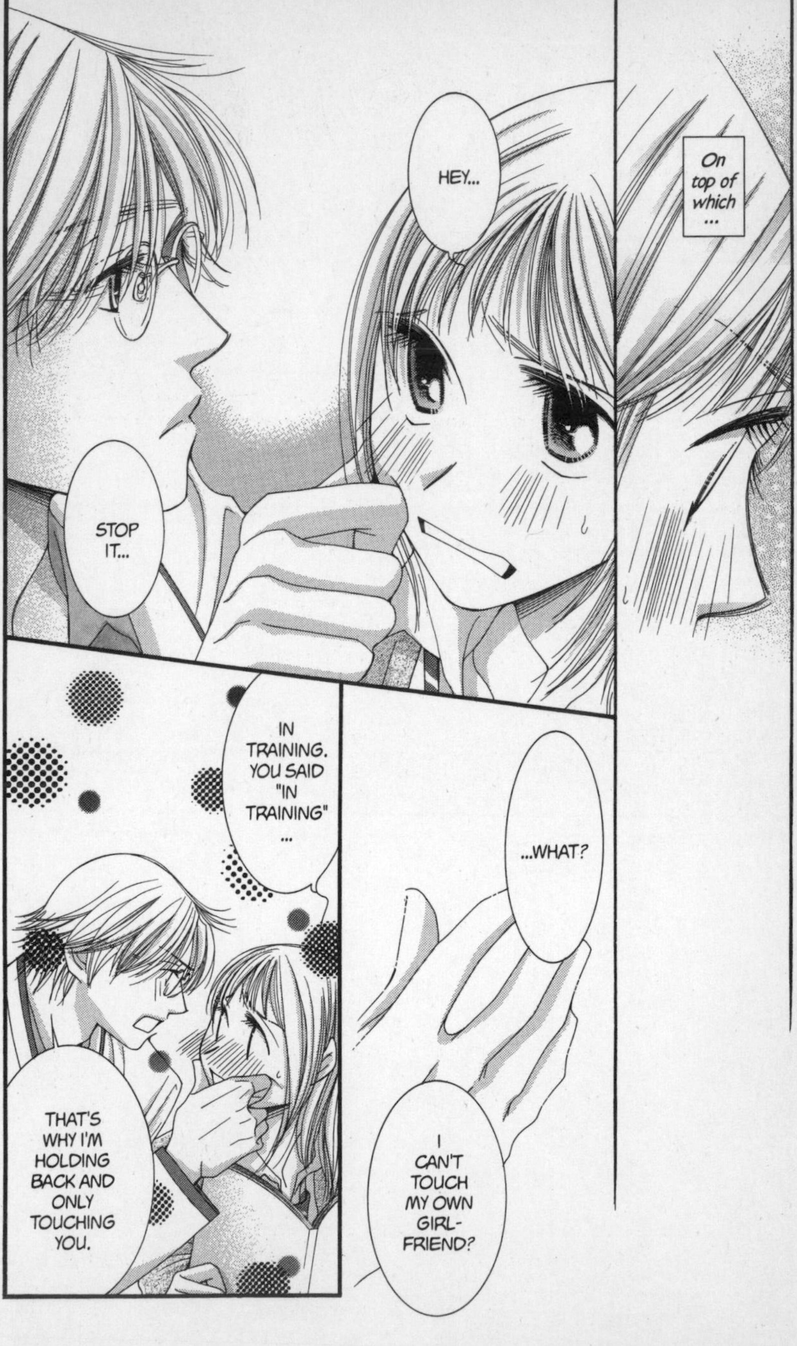
On top of which ...
HEY...
STOP IT...
...WHAT?
I CAN'T TOUCH MY OWN GIRL-FRIEND?
IN TRAINING. YOU SAID "IN TRAINING" ...
THAT'S WHY I'M HOLDING BACK AND ONLY TOUCHING YOU.

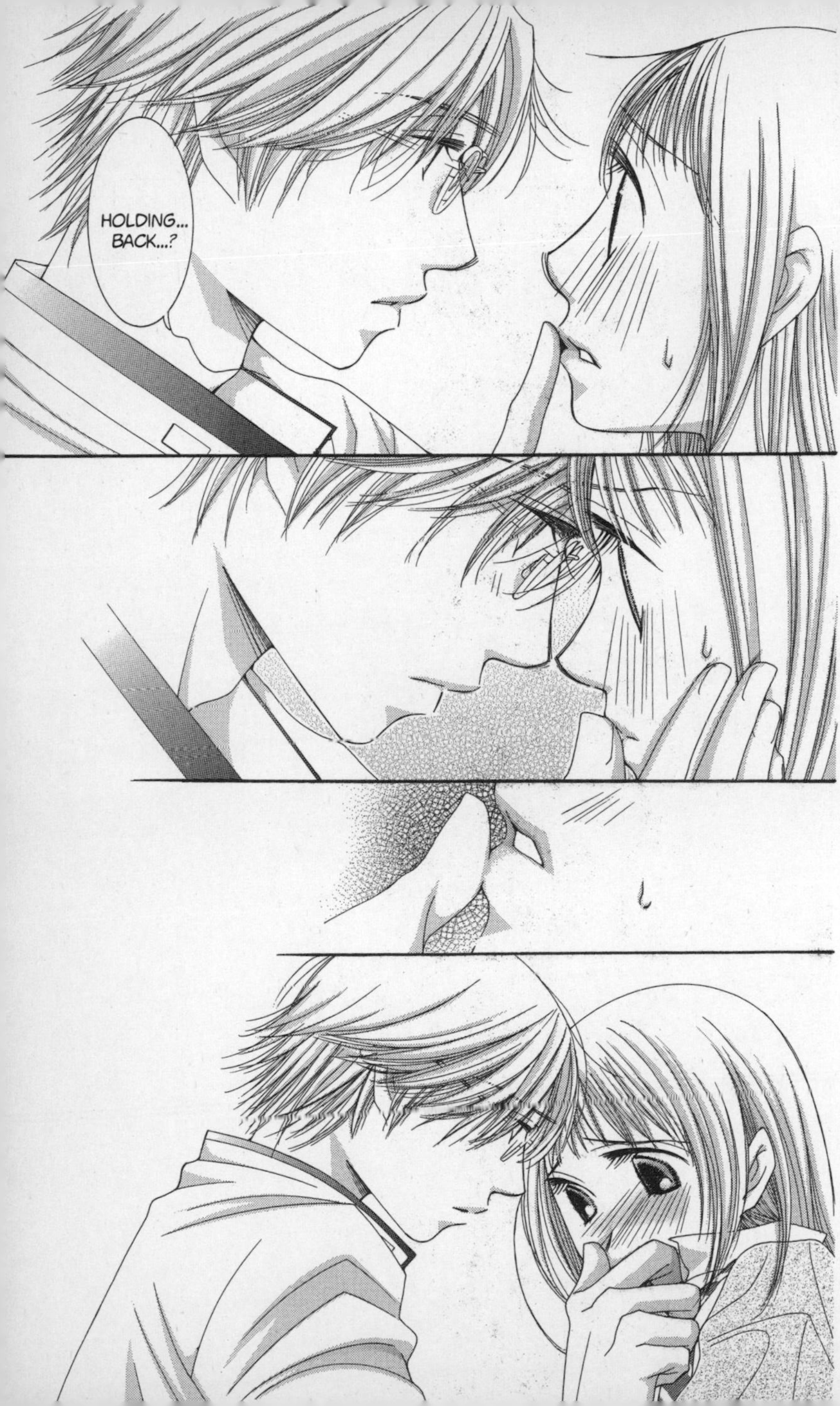
HOLDING... BACK...?

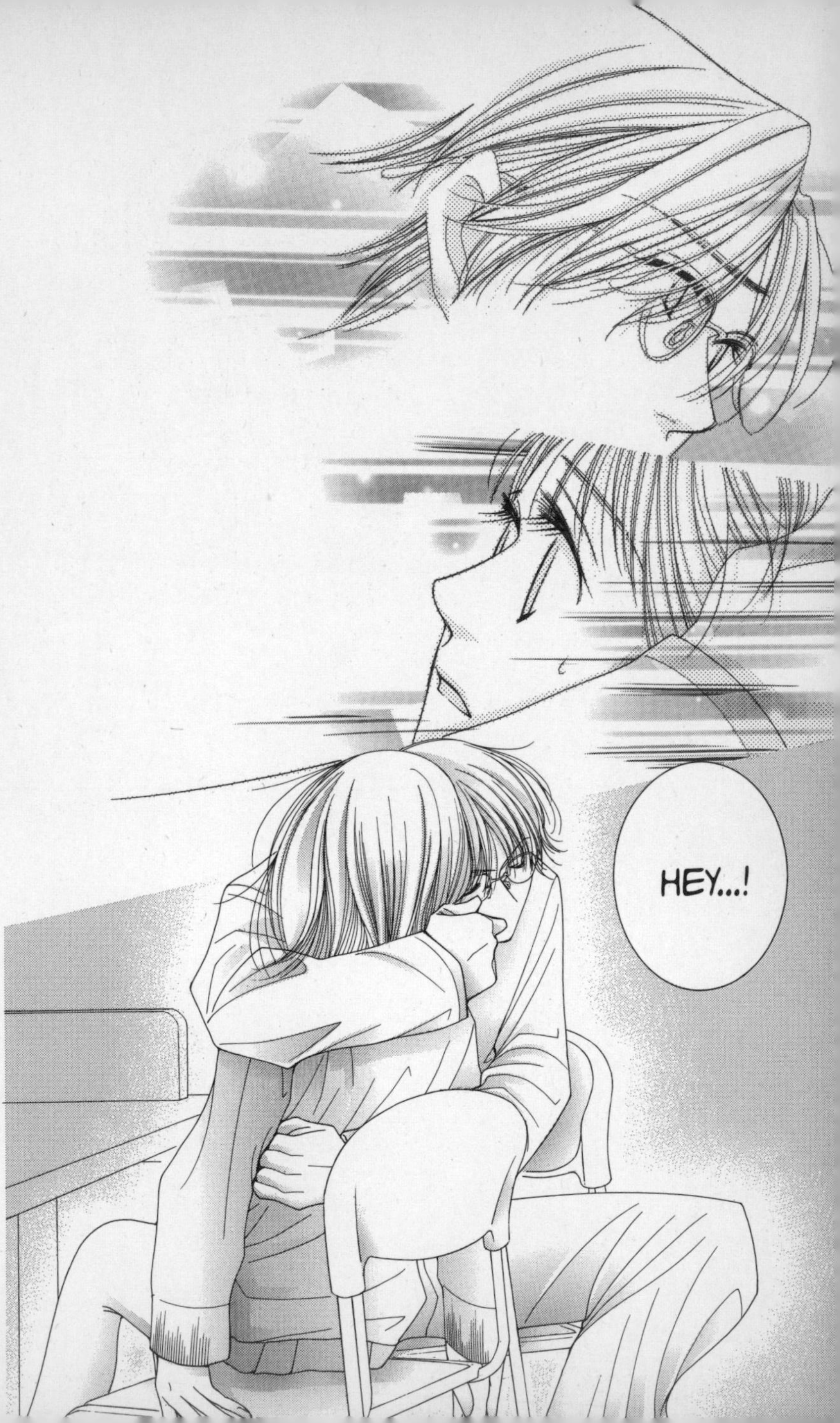
HEY...!

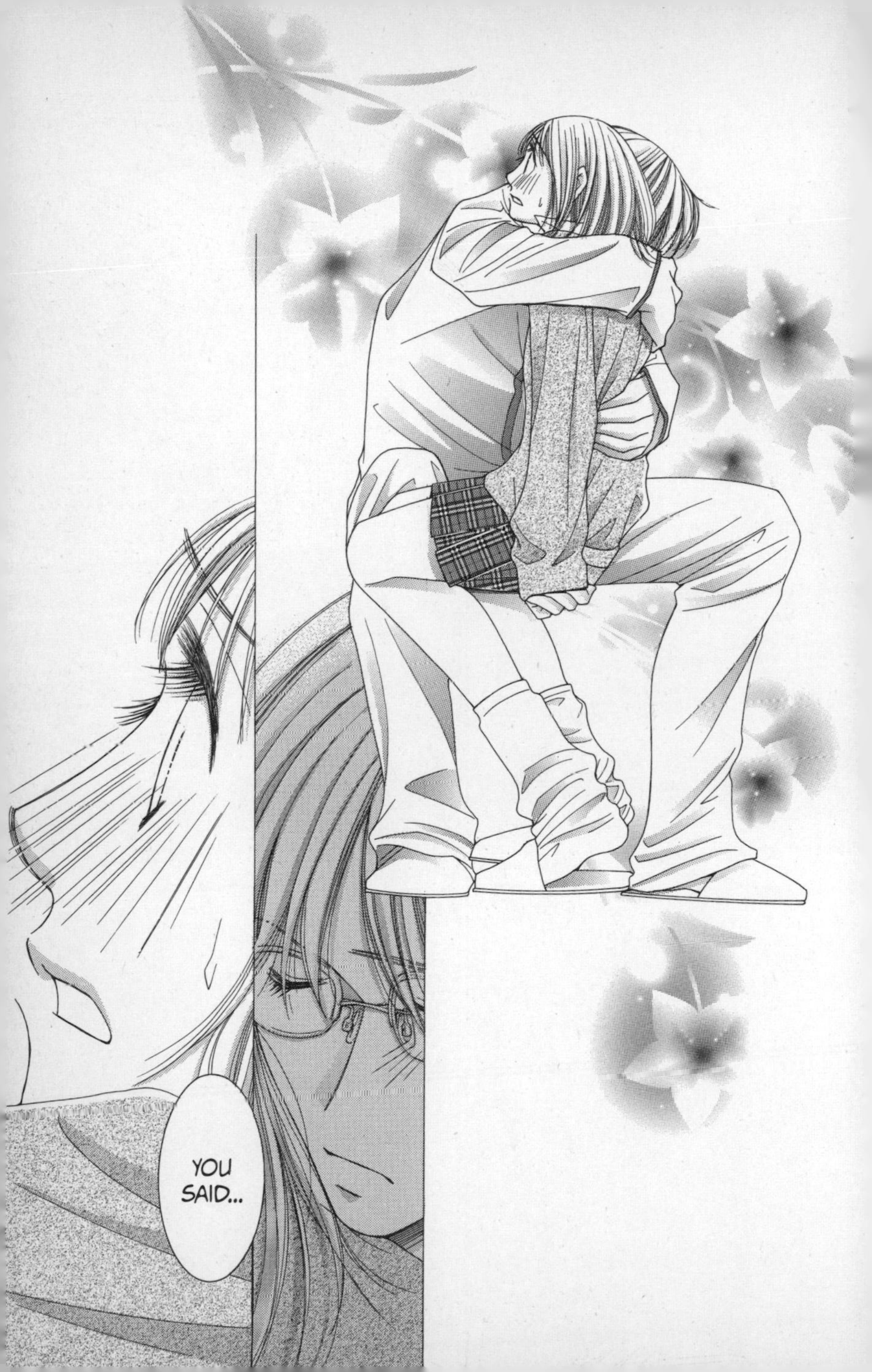
YOU SAID...

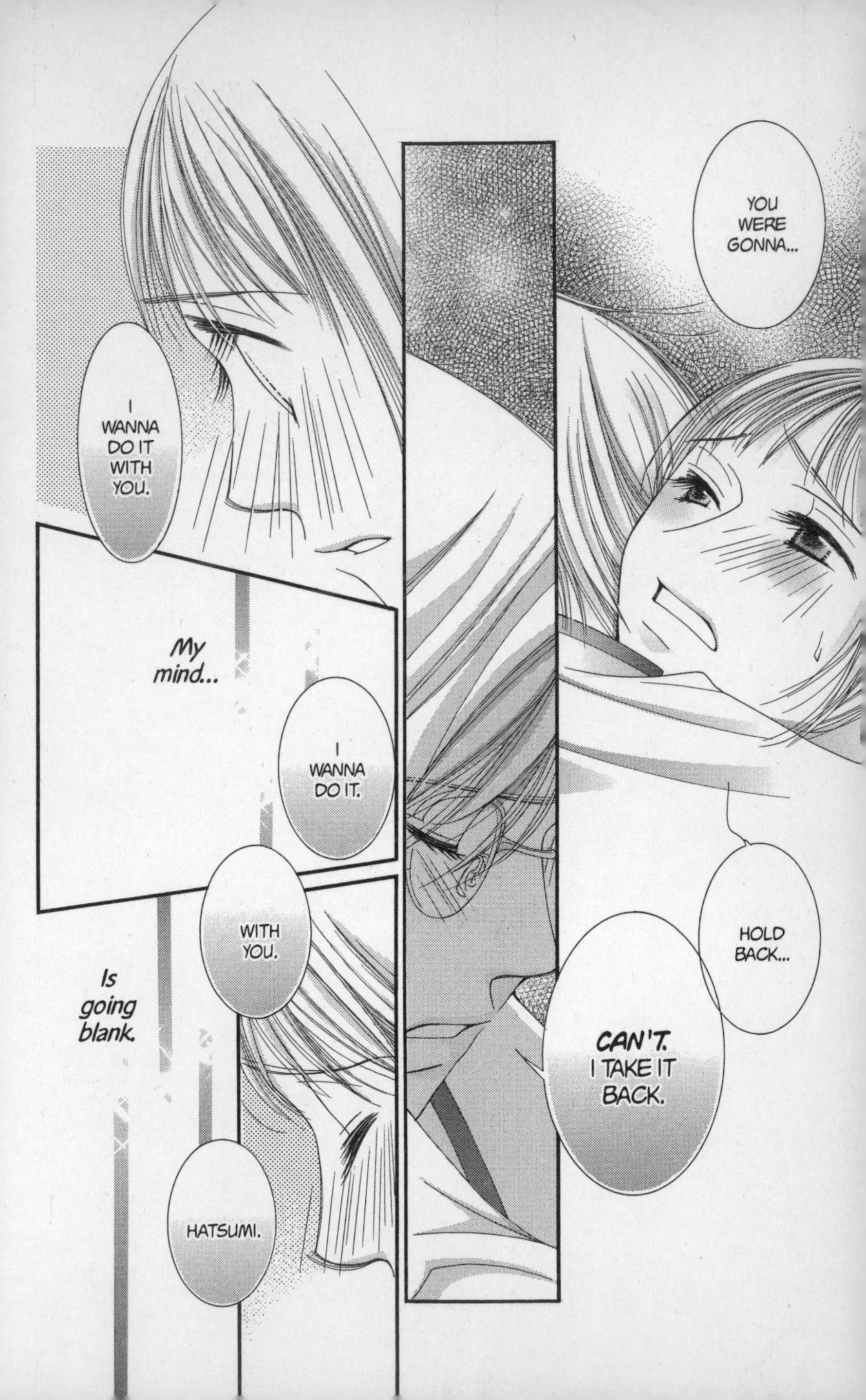
YOU WERE GONNA...
HOLD BACK...
CAN'T. I TAKE IT BACK.
I WANNA DO IT WITH YOU.
My mind...
I WANNA DO IT.
WITH YOU.
Is going blank.
HATSUMI.

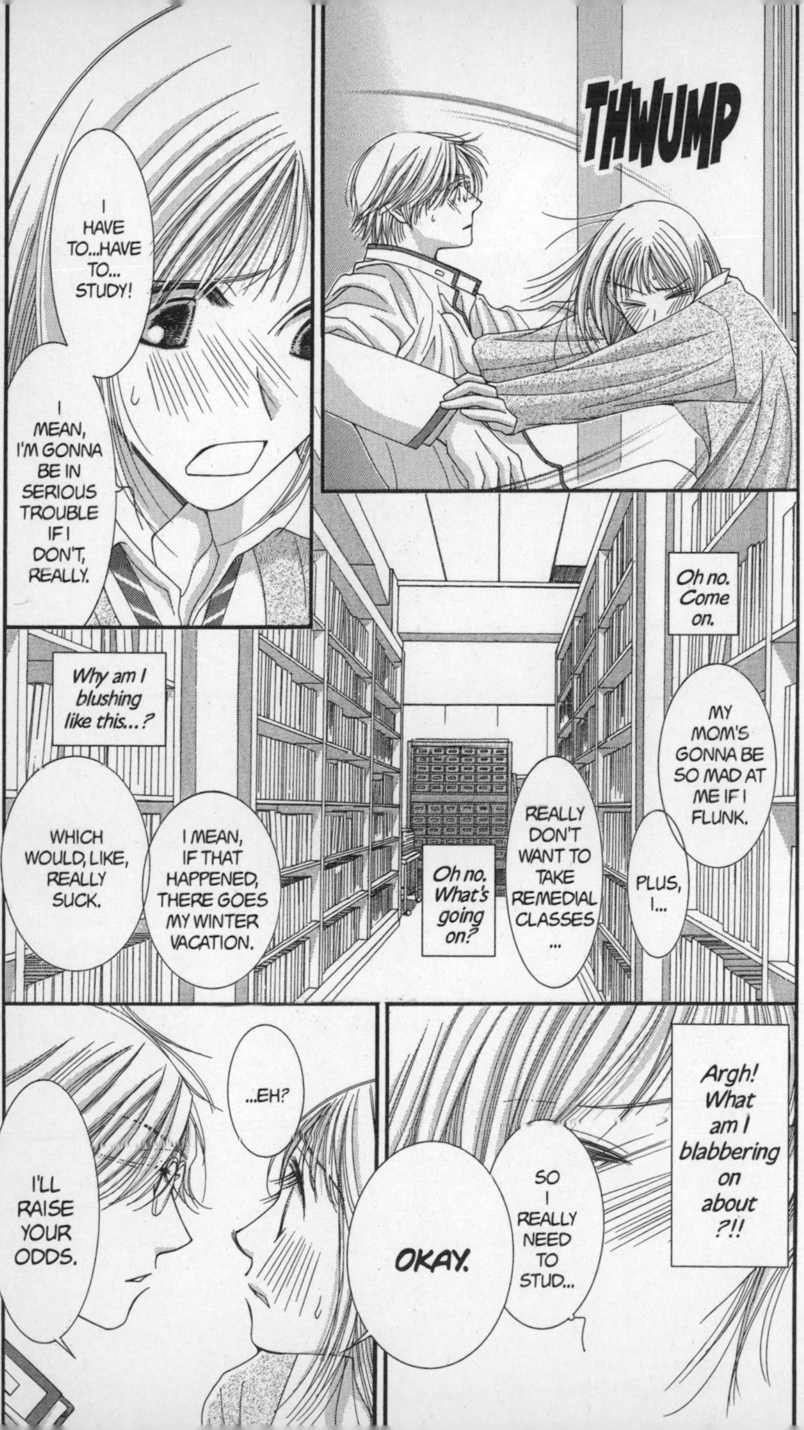
THWUMP
I HAVE TO...HAVE TO... STUDY!
I MEAN, I'M GONNA BE IN SERIOUS TROUBLE IF I DON'T, REALLY.
Oh no. Come on.
MY MOM'S GONNA BE SO MAD AT ME IF I FLUNK.
PLUS, I...
REALLY DON'T WANT TO TAKE REMEDIAL CLASSES ...
Oh no. What's going on?
I MEAN, IF THAT HAPPENED, THERE GOES MY WINTER VACATION.
WHICH WOULD, LIKE, REALLY SUCK.
Why am I blushing like this...?
Argh! What am I blabbering on about ?!!
SO I REALLY NEED TO STUD...
OKAY.
...EH?
I'LL RAISE YOUR ODDS.

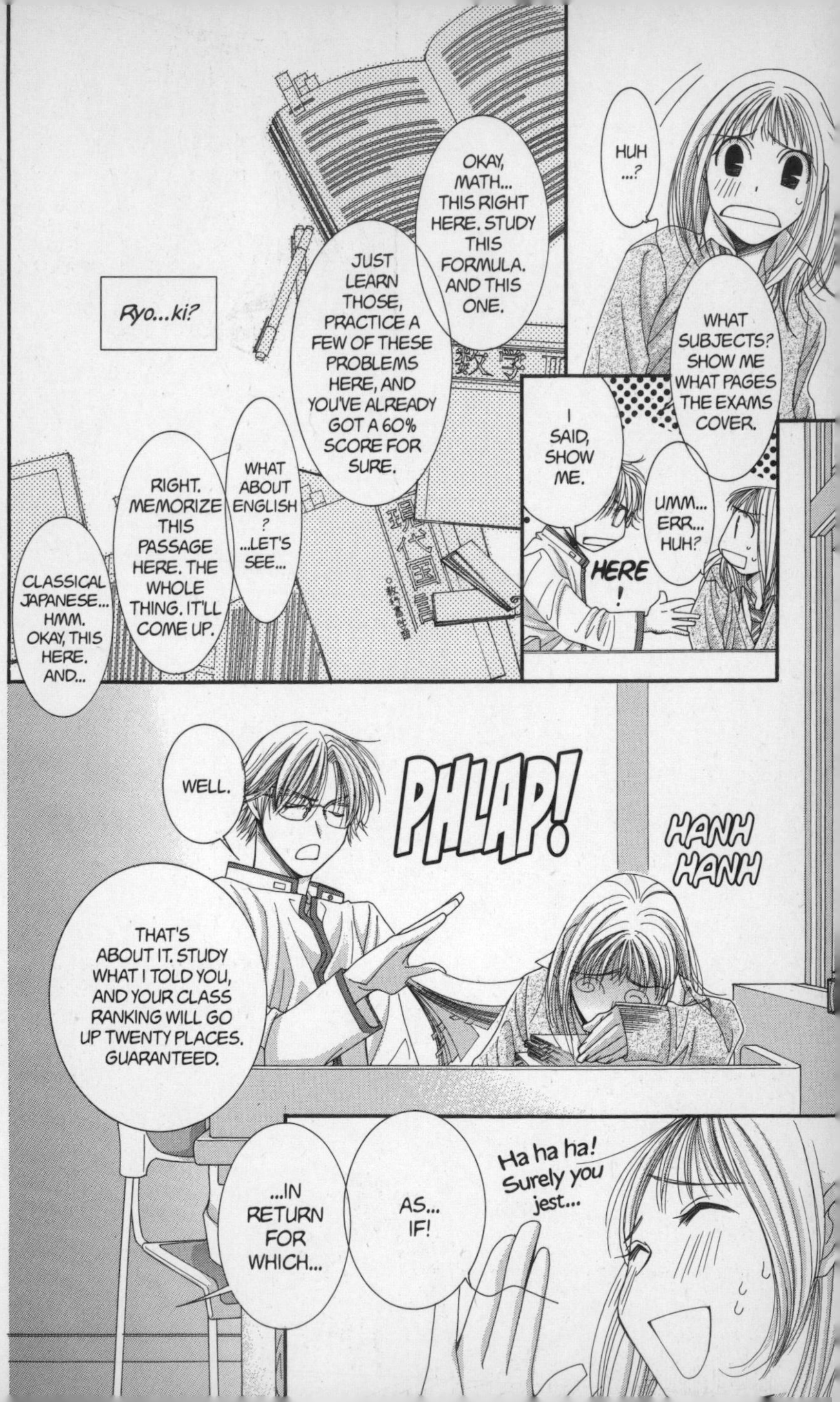

HUH ...?
WHAT SUBJECTS? SHOW ME WHAT PAGES THE EXAMS COVER.
UMM... ERR... HUH?
I SAID, SHOW ME.
HERE!
OKAY, MATH... THIS RIGHT HERE. STUDY THIS FORMULA. AND THIS ONE.
JUST LEARN THOSE, PRACTICE A FEW OF THESE PROBLEMS HERE, AND YOU'VE ALREADY GOT A 60% SCORE FOR SURE.
WHAT ABOUT ENGLISH? ...LET'S SEE...
RIGHT. MEMORIZE THIS PASSAGE HERE. THE WHOLE THING. IT'LL COME UP.
CLASSICAL JAPANESE... HMM. OKAY, THIS HERE. AND...
Ryo...ki?
HANH HANH
PHLAP!
WELL.
THAT'S ABOUT IT. STUDY WHAT I TOLD YOU, AND YOUR CLASS RANKING WILL GO UP TWENTY PLACES. GUARANTEED.
Ha ha ha! Surely you jest...
AS... IF!
...IN RETURN FOR WHICH...

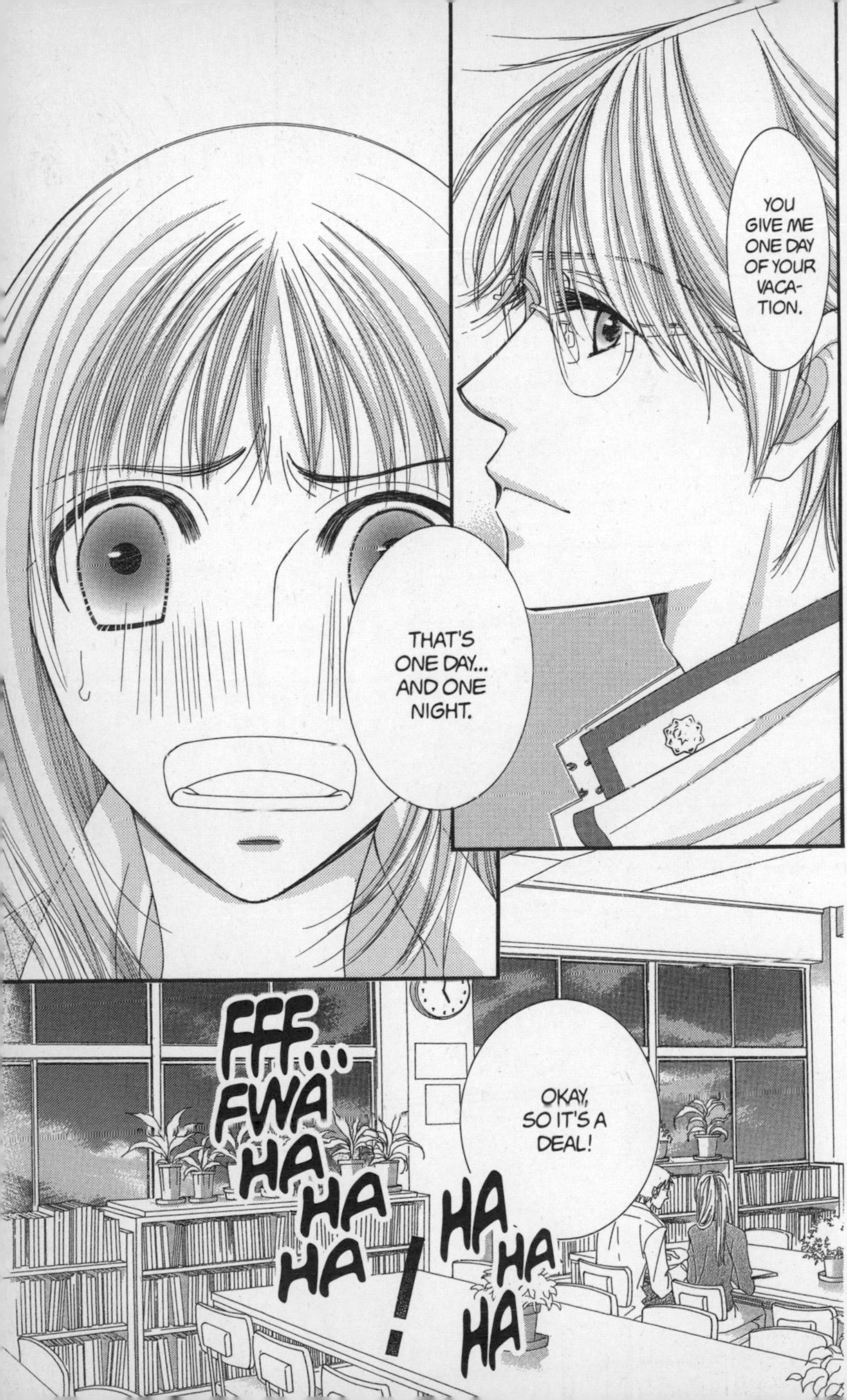
YOU GIVE ME ONE DAY OF YOUR VACATION.
THAT'S ONE DAY... AND ONE NIGHT.
OKAY, SO IT'S A DEAL!
FFF... FWA HA HA HA HA!
HA HA HA HA

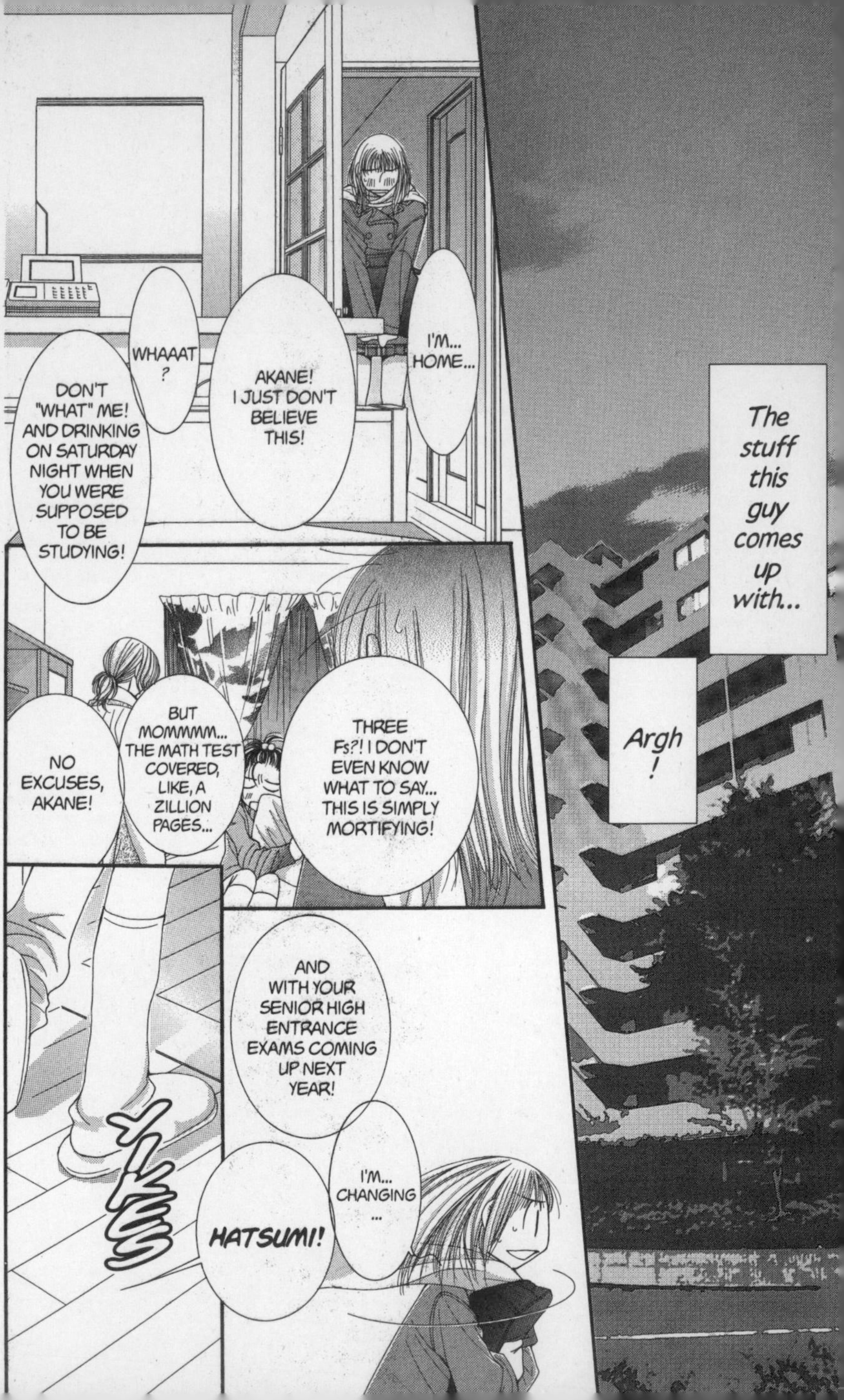
The stuff this guy comes up with...
Argh!
I'M... HOME...
AKANE! I JUST DON'T BELIEVE THIS!
WHAAAT?
DON'T "WHAT" ME! AND DRINKING ON SATURDAY NIGHT WHEN YOU WERE SUPPOSED TO BE STUDYING!
THREE Fs?! I DON'T EVEN KNOW WHAT TO SAY... THIS IS SIMPLY MORTIFYING!
BUT MOMMMM... THE MATH TEST COVERED, LIKE, A ZILLION PAGES...
NO EXCUSES, AKANE!
AND WITH YOUR SENIOR HIGH ENTRANCE EXAMS COMING UP NEXT YEAR!
I'M... CHANGING...
HATSUMI!

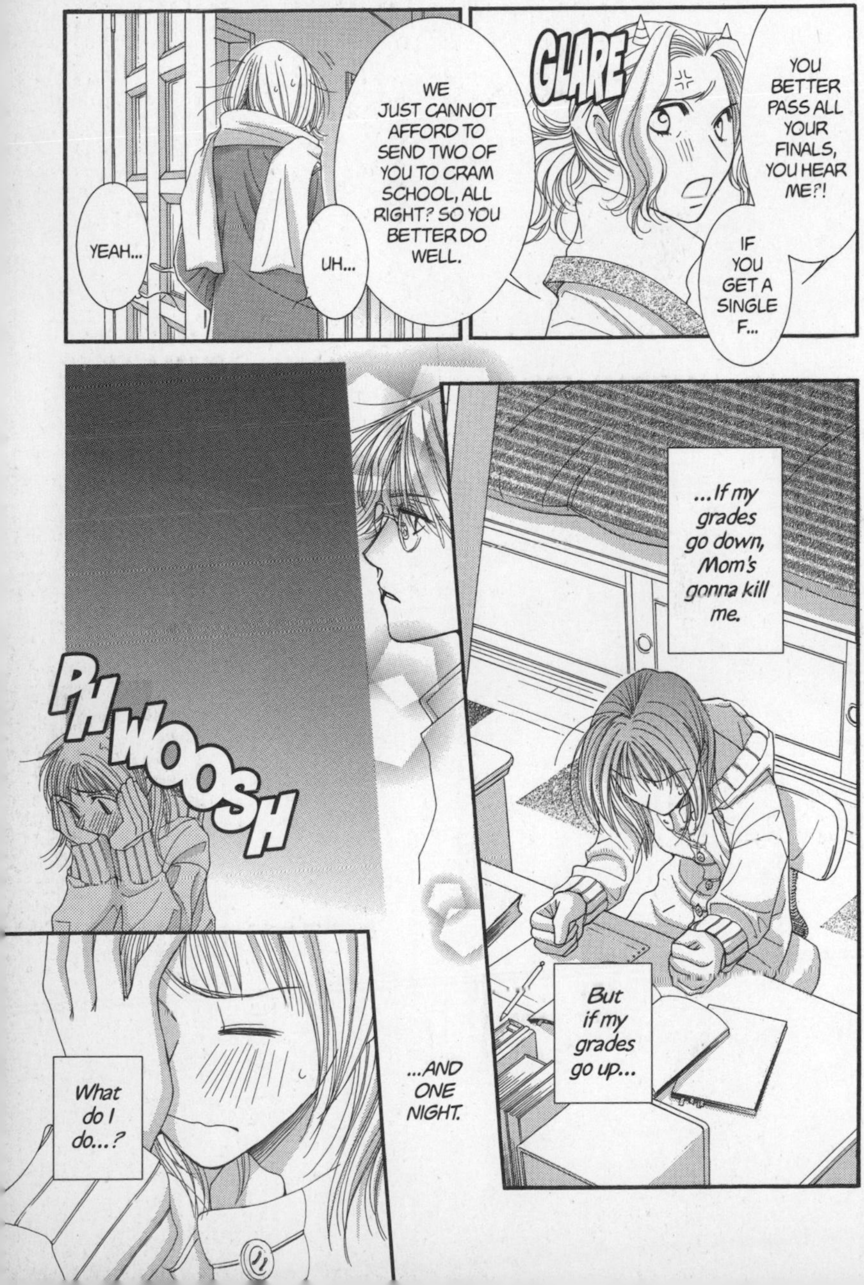
GLARE
YOU BETTER PASS ALL YOUR FINALS, YOU HEAR ME?!
IF YOU GET A SINGLE F...
WE JUST CANNOT AFFORD TO SEND TWO OF YOU TO CRAM SCHOOL, ALL RIGHT? SO YOU BETTER DO WELL.
UH...
YEAH...
...If my grades go down, Mom's gonna kill me.
But if my grades go up...
PHWOOSH
...AND ONE NIGHT.
What do I do...?

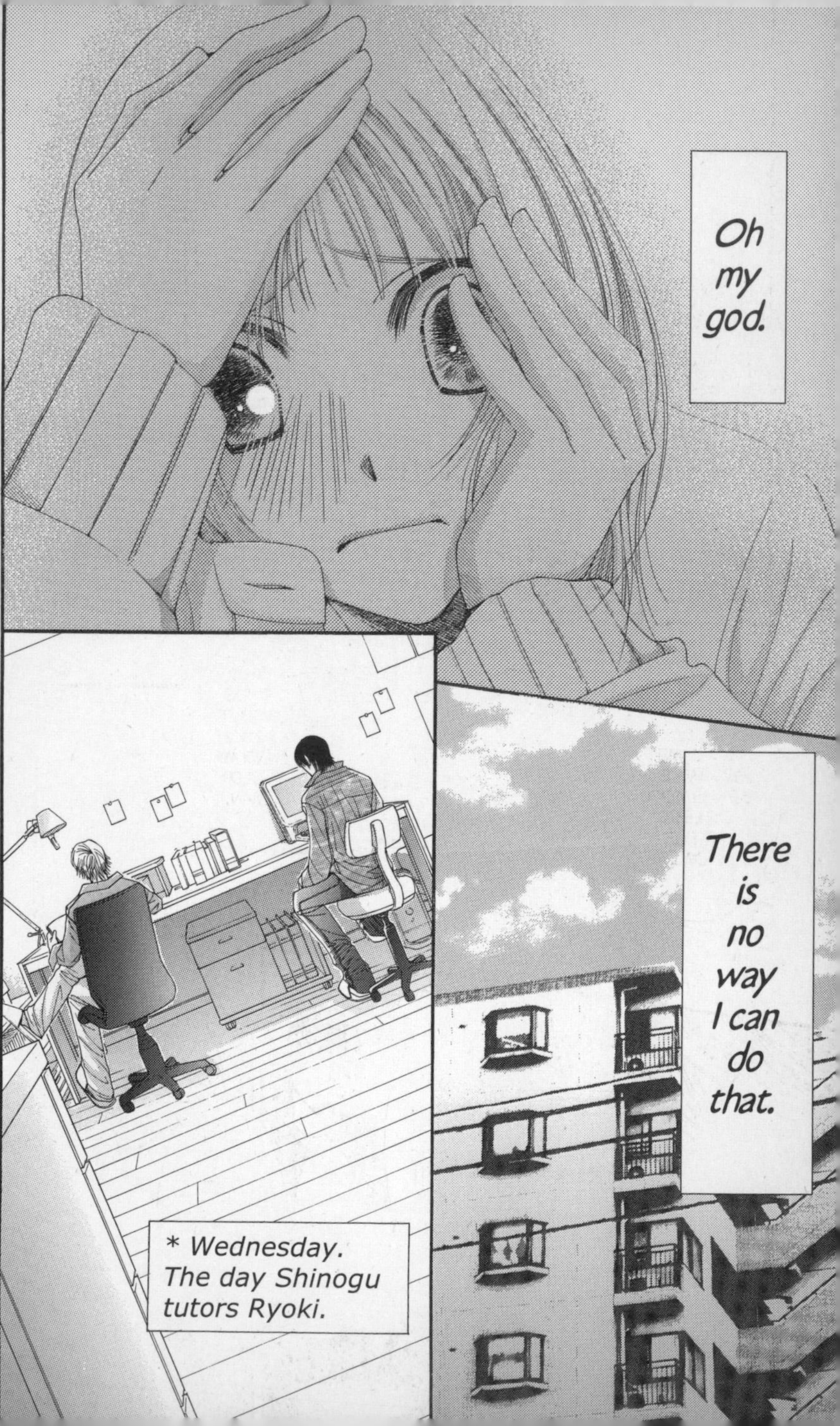
Oh my god.
There is no way I can do that.
* Wednesday. The day Shinogu tutors Ryoki.

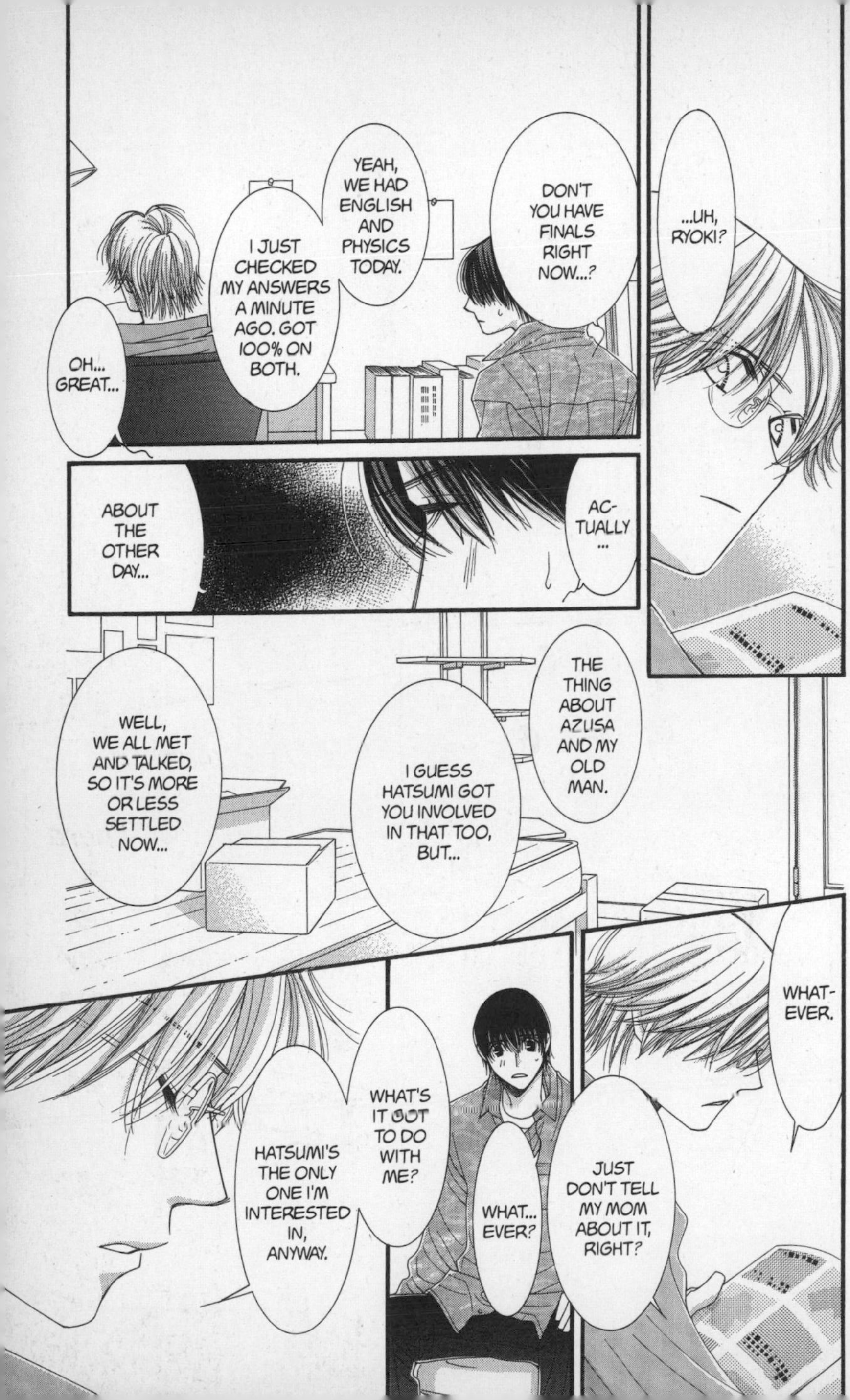
...UH, RYOKI?
DON'T YOU HAVE FINALS RIGHT NOW...?
YEAH, WE HAD ENGLISH AND PHYSICS TODAY.
I JUST CHECKED MY ANSWERS A MINUTE AGO. GOT 100% ON BOTH.
OH... GREAT...
AC-TUALLY...
ABOUT THE OTHER DAY...
THE THING ABOUT AZUSA AND MY OLD MAN.
I GUESS HATSUMI GOT YOU INVOLVED IN THAT TOO, BUT...
WELL, WE ALL MET AND TALKED, SO IT'S MORE OR LESS SETTLED NOW...
WHAT-EVER.
JUST DON'T TELL MY MOM ABOUT IT, RIGHT?
WHAT... EVER?
WHAT'S IT GOT TO DO WITH ME?
HATSUMI'S THE ONLY ONE I'M INTERESTED IN, ANYWAY.

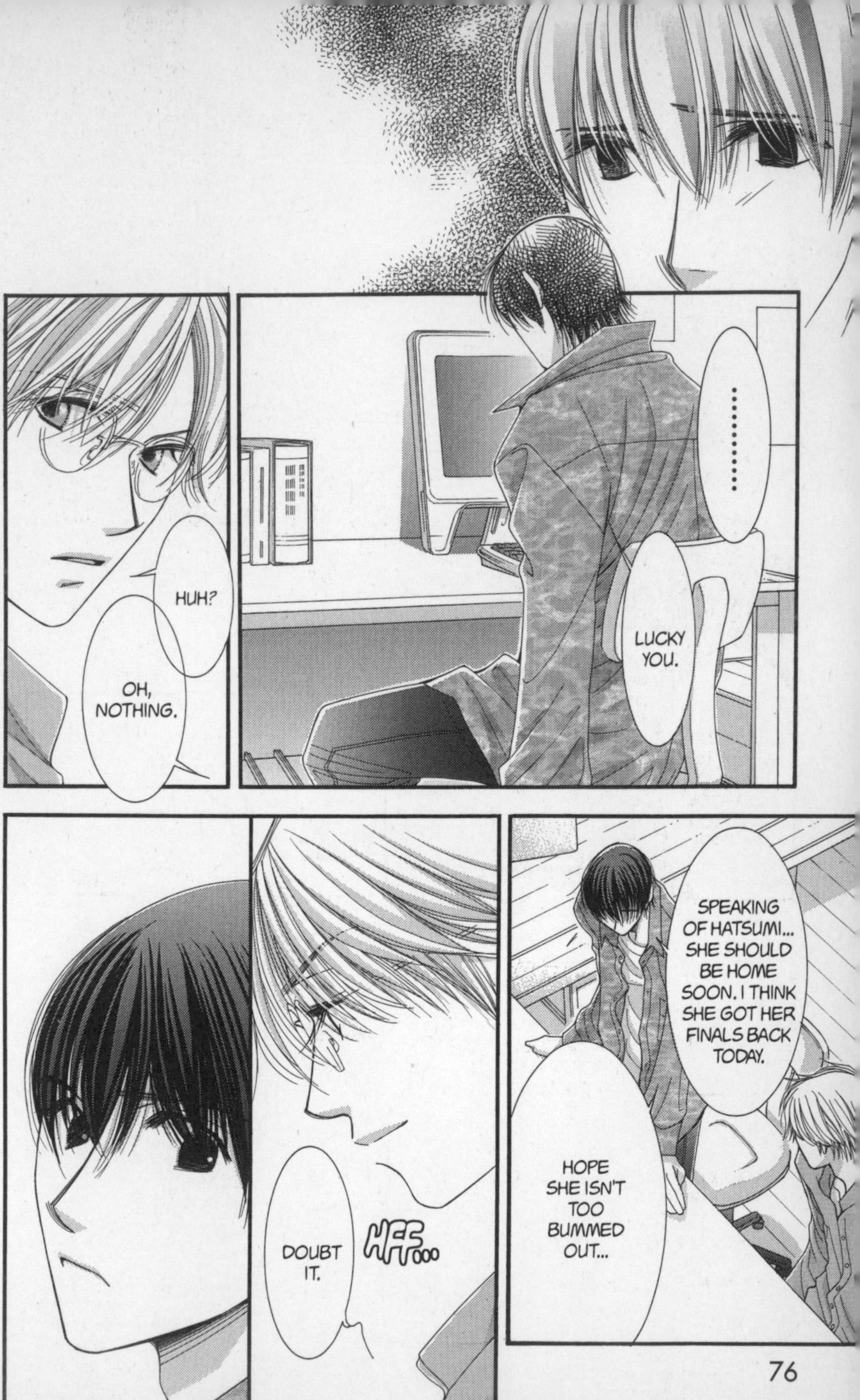
......
LUCKY YOU.
HUH?
OH, NOTHING.
SPEAKING OF HATSUMI... SHE SHOULD BE HOME SOON. I THINK SHE GOT HER FINALS BACK TODAY.
HOPE SHE ISN'T TOO BUMMED OUT...
HFF...
DOUBT IT.

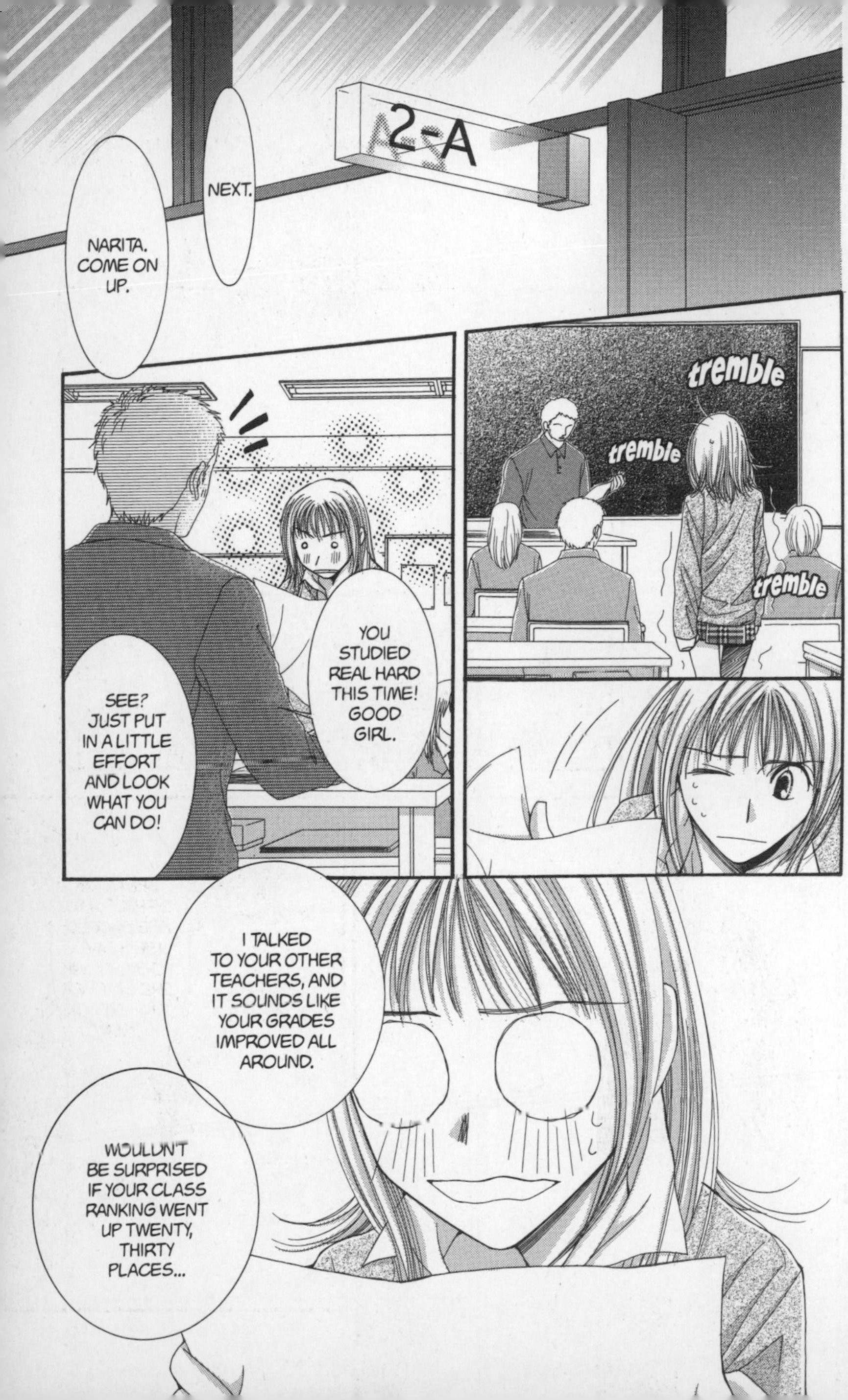
2-A
NEXT.
NARITA. COME ON UP.
tremble
tremble
tremble
YOU STUDIED REAL HARD THIS TIME! GOOD GIRL.
SEE? JUST PUT IN A LITTLE EFFORT AND LOOK WHAT YOU CAN DO!
I TALKED TO YOUR OTHER TEACHERS, AND IT SOUNDS LIKE YOUR GRADES IMPROVED ALL AROUND.
WOULDN'T BE SURPRISED IF YOUR CLASS RANKING WENT UP TWENTY, THIRTY PLACES...

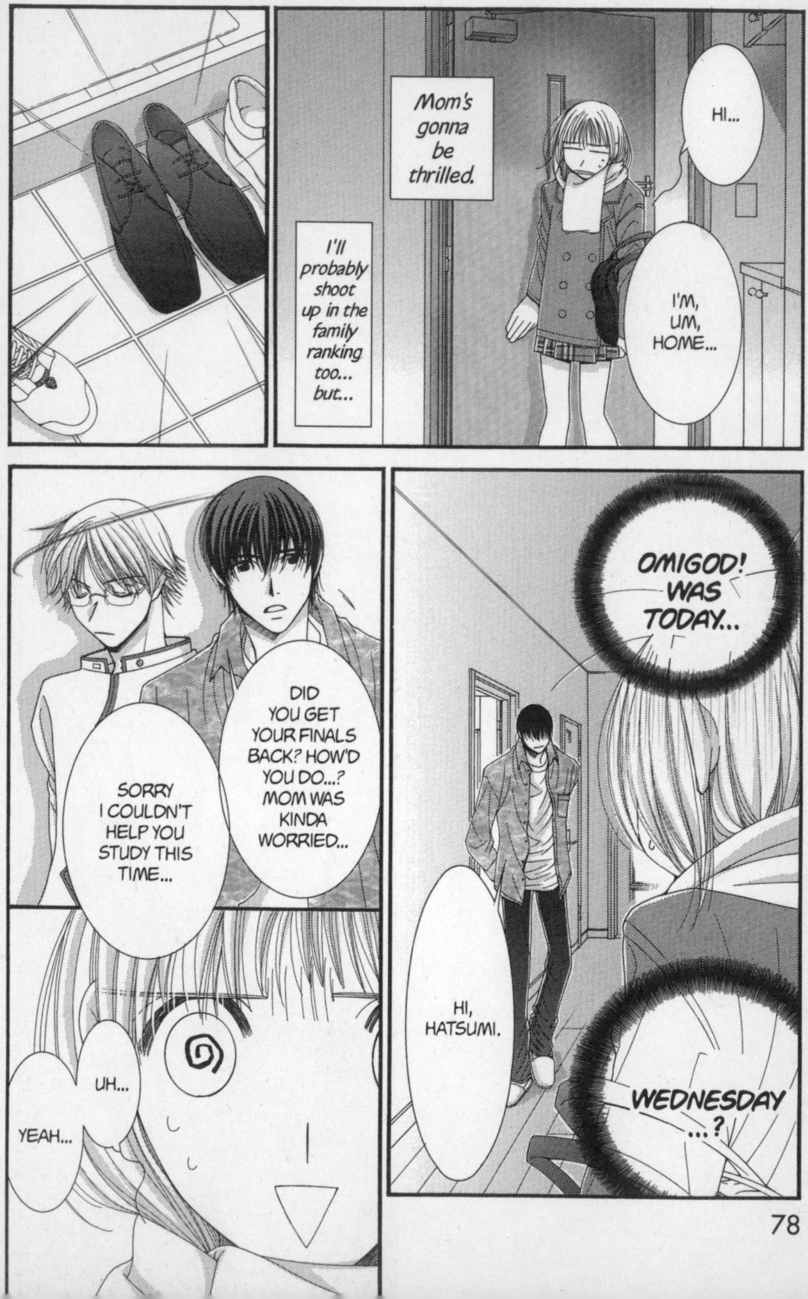
HI...
I'M, UM, HOME...
Mom's gonna be thrilled.
I'll probably shoot up in the family ranking too... but...
OMIGOD! WAS TODAY...
HI, HATSUMI.
WEDNESDAY ...?
DID YOU GET YOUR FINALS BACK? HOW'D YOU DO...? MOM WAS KINDA WORRIED...
SORRY I COULDN'T HELP YOU STUDY THIS TIME...
UH...
YEAH...

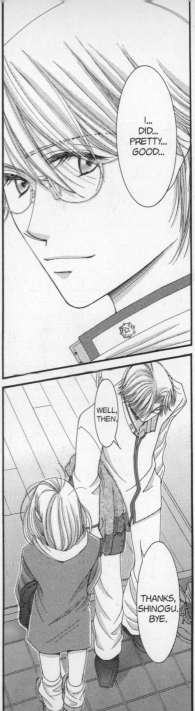

I... DID... PRETTY... GOOD...

WELL, THEN.

THANKS, SHINOGU. BYE.

murmur

...DON'T FORGET.

WE HAD A DEAL.

hotgimmick

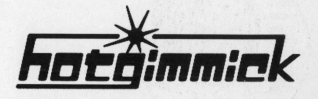

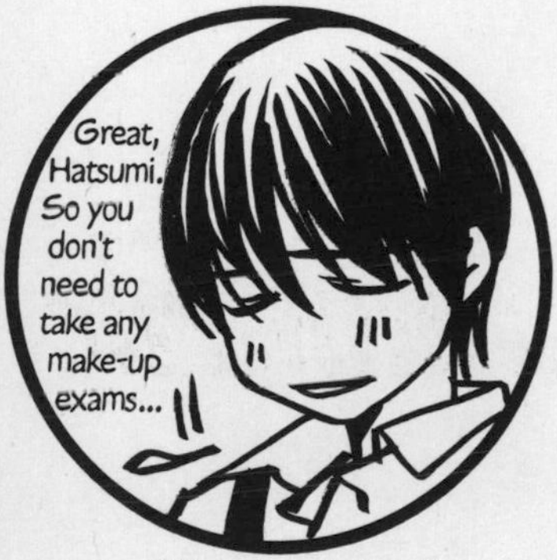
Great, Hatsumi. So you don't need to take any make-up exams...

Wait a minute! Should I be feeling relieved...?

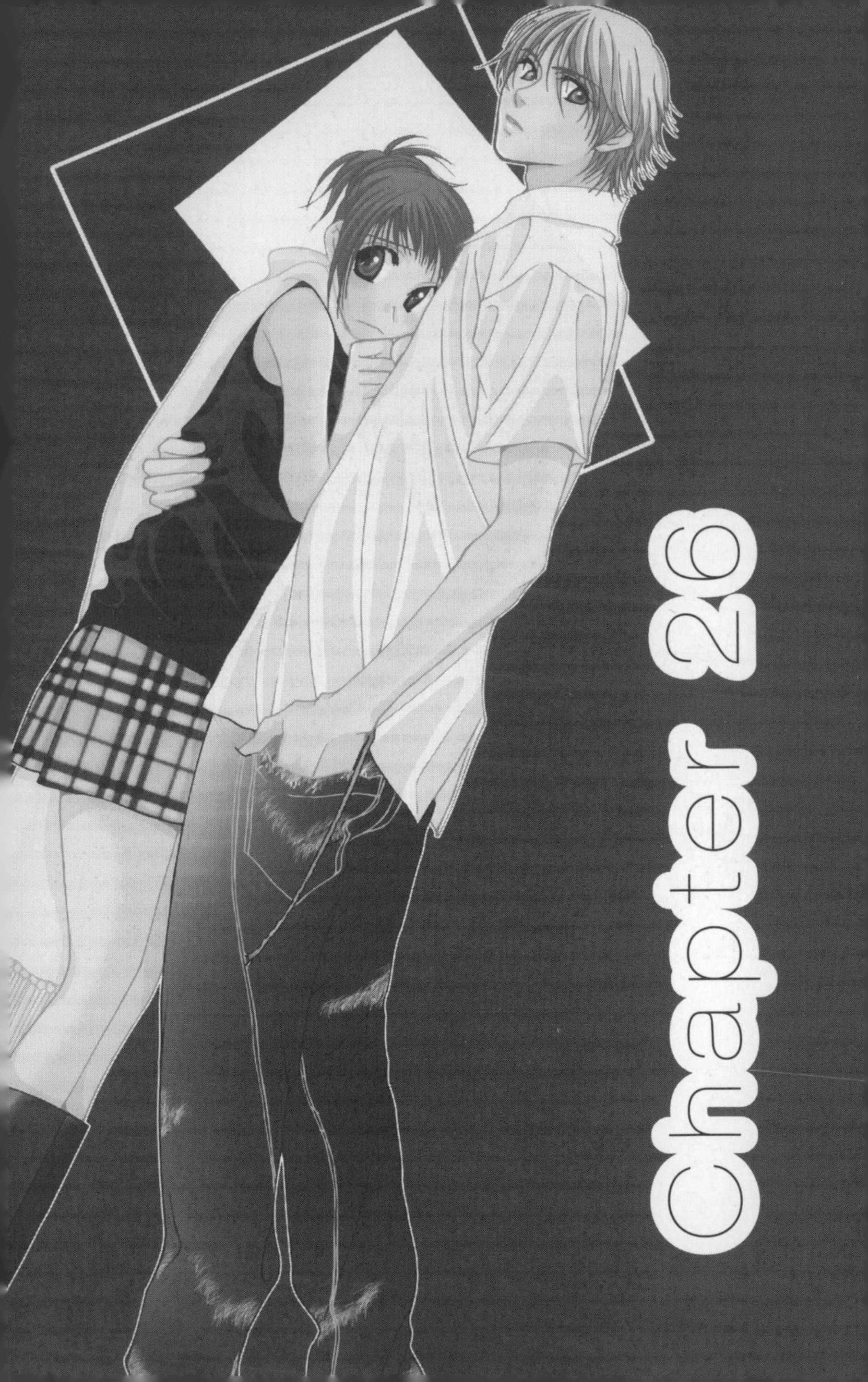
Chapter 26

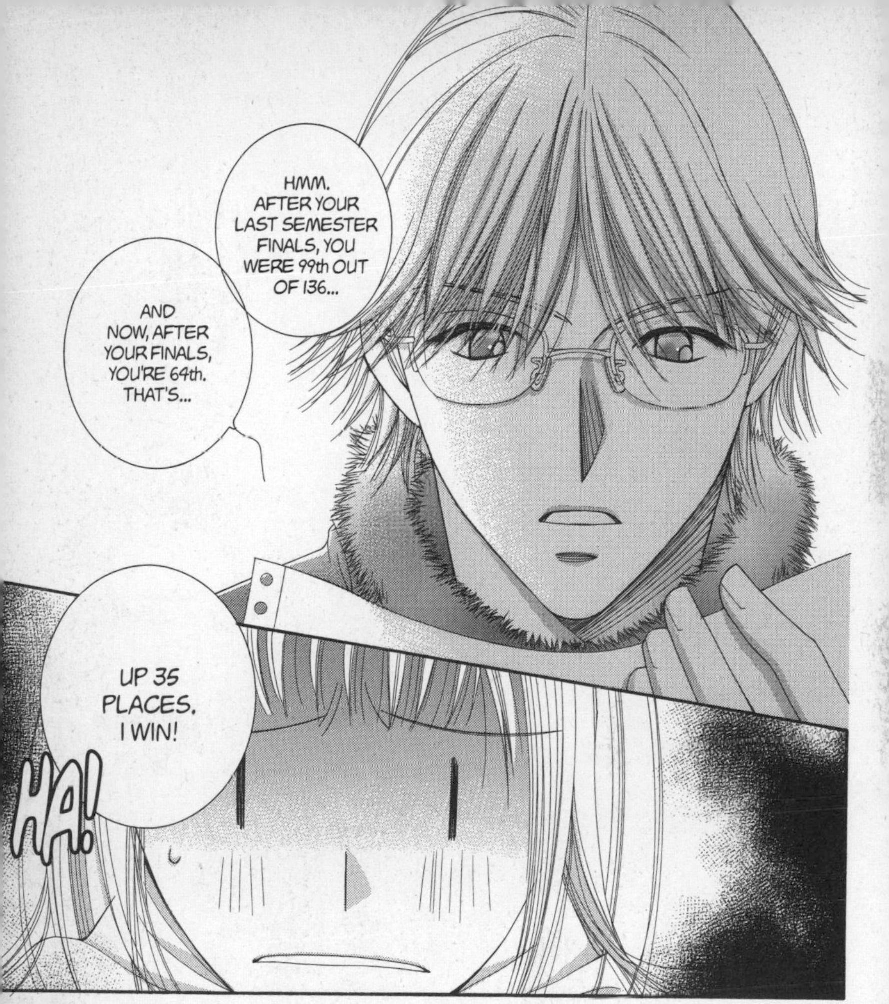
HMM. AFTER YOUR LAST SEMESTER FINALS, YOU WERE 99th OUT OF 136...
AND NOW, AFTER YOUR FINALS, YOU'RE 64th. THAT'S...
UP 35 PLACES. I WIN!
HA!

hot gimmick

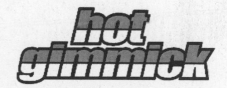

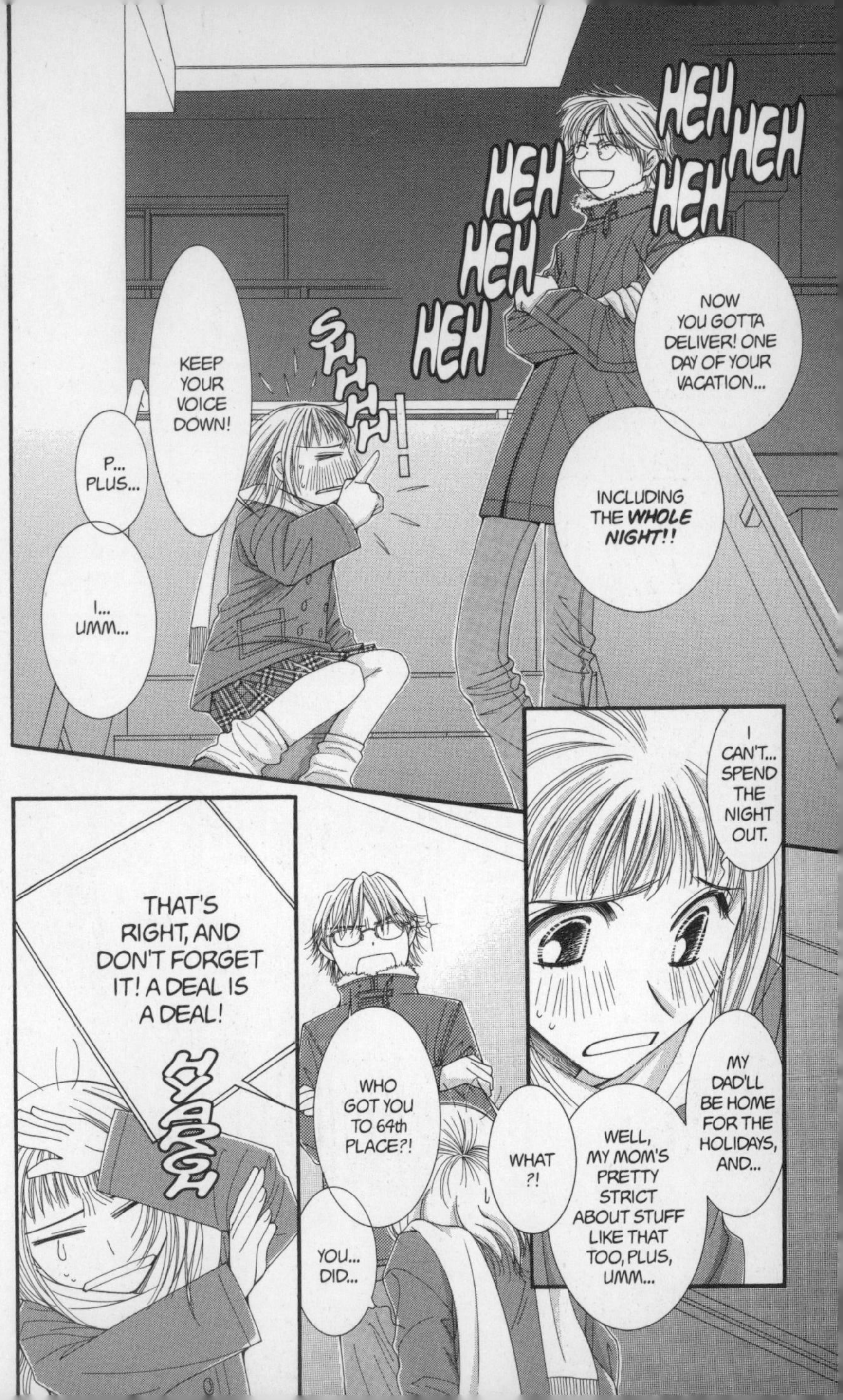
HEH HEH HEH HEH
HEH HEH HEH
NOW YOU GOTTA DELIVER! ONE DAY OF YOUR VACATION...
INCLUDING THE WHOLE NIGHT!!
SHHHH!!
KEEP YOUR VOICE DOWN!
P... PLUS...
I... UMM...
I CAN'T... SPEND THE NIGHT OUT.
MY DAD'LL BE HOME FOR THE HOLIDAYS, AND...
WELL, MY MOM'S PRETTY STRICT ABOUT STUFF LIKE THAT TOO, PLUS, UMM...
WHAT?!
WHO GOT YOU TO 64th PLACE?!
YOU... DID...
THAT'S RIGHT, AND DON'T FORGET IT! A DEAL IS A DEAL!

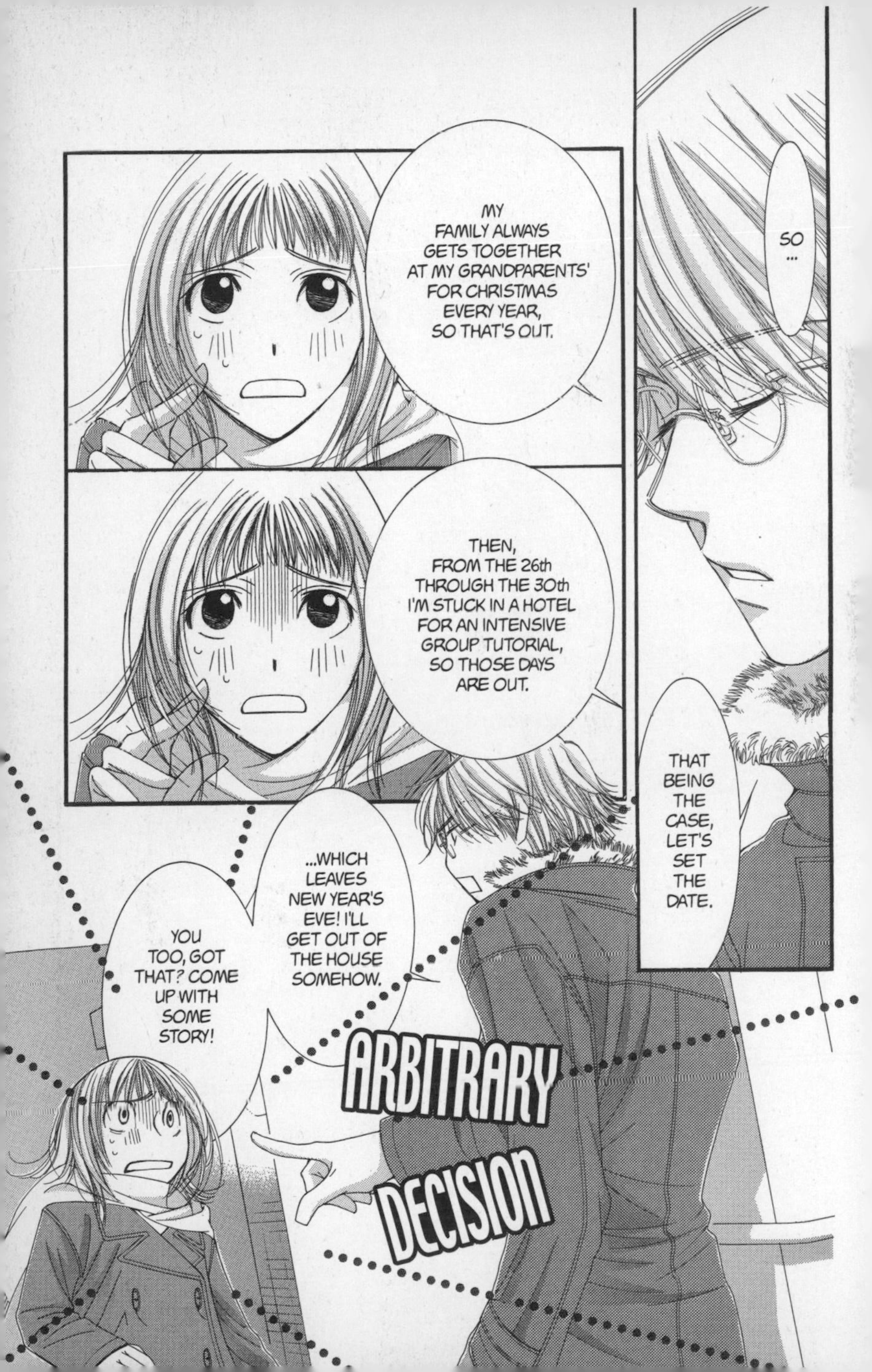
SO ...
THAT BEING THE CASE, LET'S SET THE DATE.
MY FAMILY ALWAYS GETS TOGETHER AT MY GRANDPARENTS' FOR CHRISTMAS EVERY YEAR, SO THAT'S OUT.
THEN, FROM THE 26th THROUGH THE 30th I'M STUCK IN A HOTEL FOR AN INTENSIVE GROUP TUTORIAL, SO THOSE DAYS ARE OUT.
...WHICH LEAVES NEW YEAR'S EVE! I'LL GET OUT OF THE HOUSE SOMEHOW.
YOU TOO, GOT THAT? COME UP WITH SOME STORY!
ARBITRARY DECISION

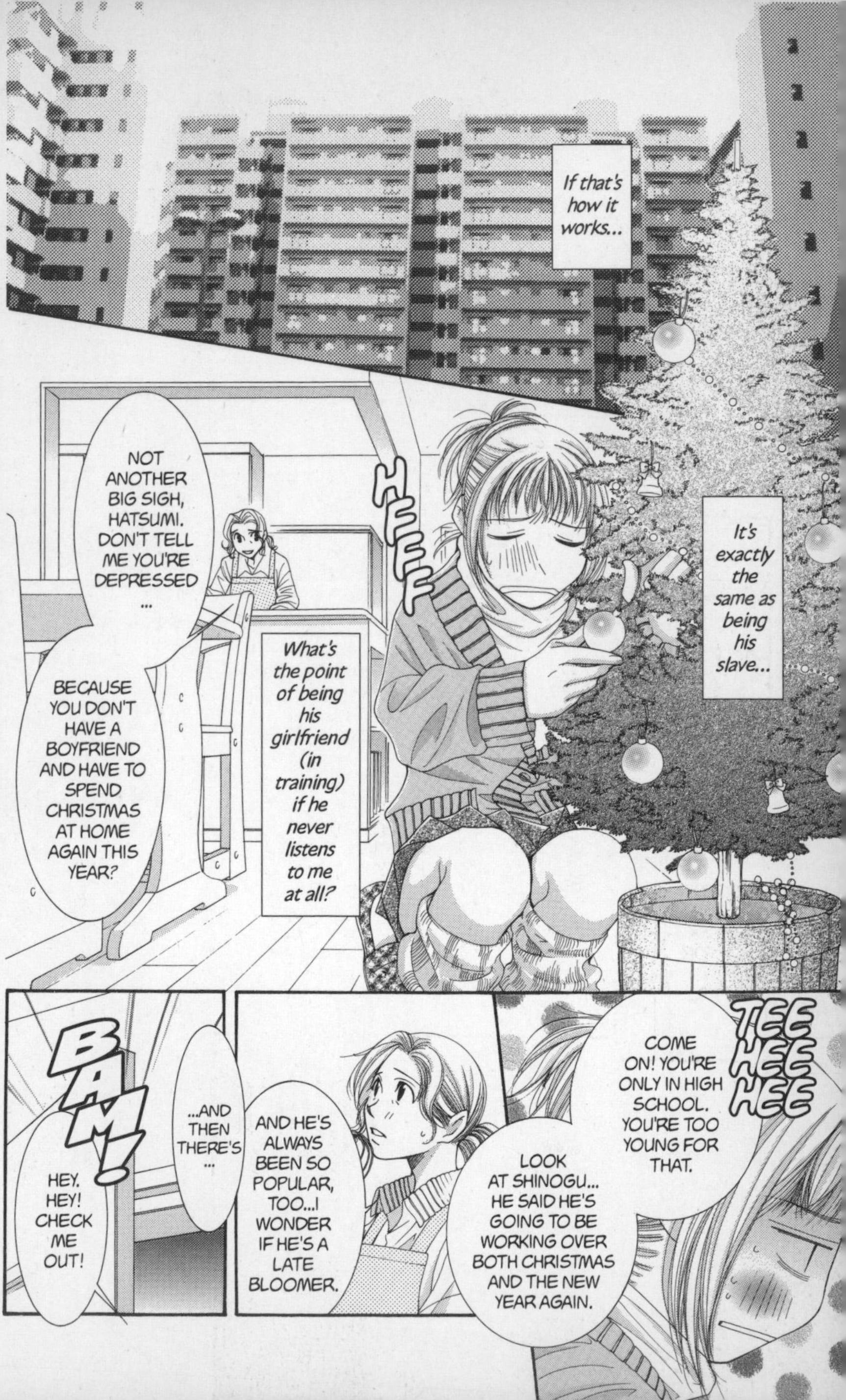
If that's how it works...
It's exactly the same as being his slave...
HEFF
NOT ANOTHER BIG SIGH, HATSUMI. DON'T TELL ME YOU'RE DEPRESSED ...
What's the point of being his girlfriend (in training) if he never listens to me at all?
BECAUSE YOU DON'T HAVE A BOYFRIEND AND HAVE TO SPEND CHRISTMAS AT HOME AGAIN THIS YEAR?
TEE HEE HEE
COME ON! YOU'RE ONLY IN HIGH SCHOOL. YOU'RE TOO YOUNG FOR THAT.
LOOK AT SHINOGU... HE SAID HE'S GOING TO BE WORKING OVER BOTH CHRISTMAS AND THE NEW YEAR AGAIN.
AND HE'S ALWAYS BEEN SO POPULAR, TOO...I WONDER IF HE'S A LATE BLOOMER.
...AND THEN THERE'S ...
BAM!
HEY. HEY! CHECK ME OUT!

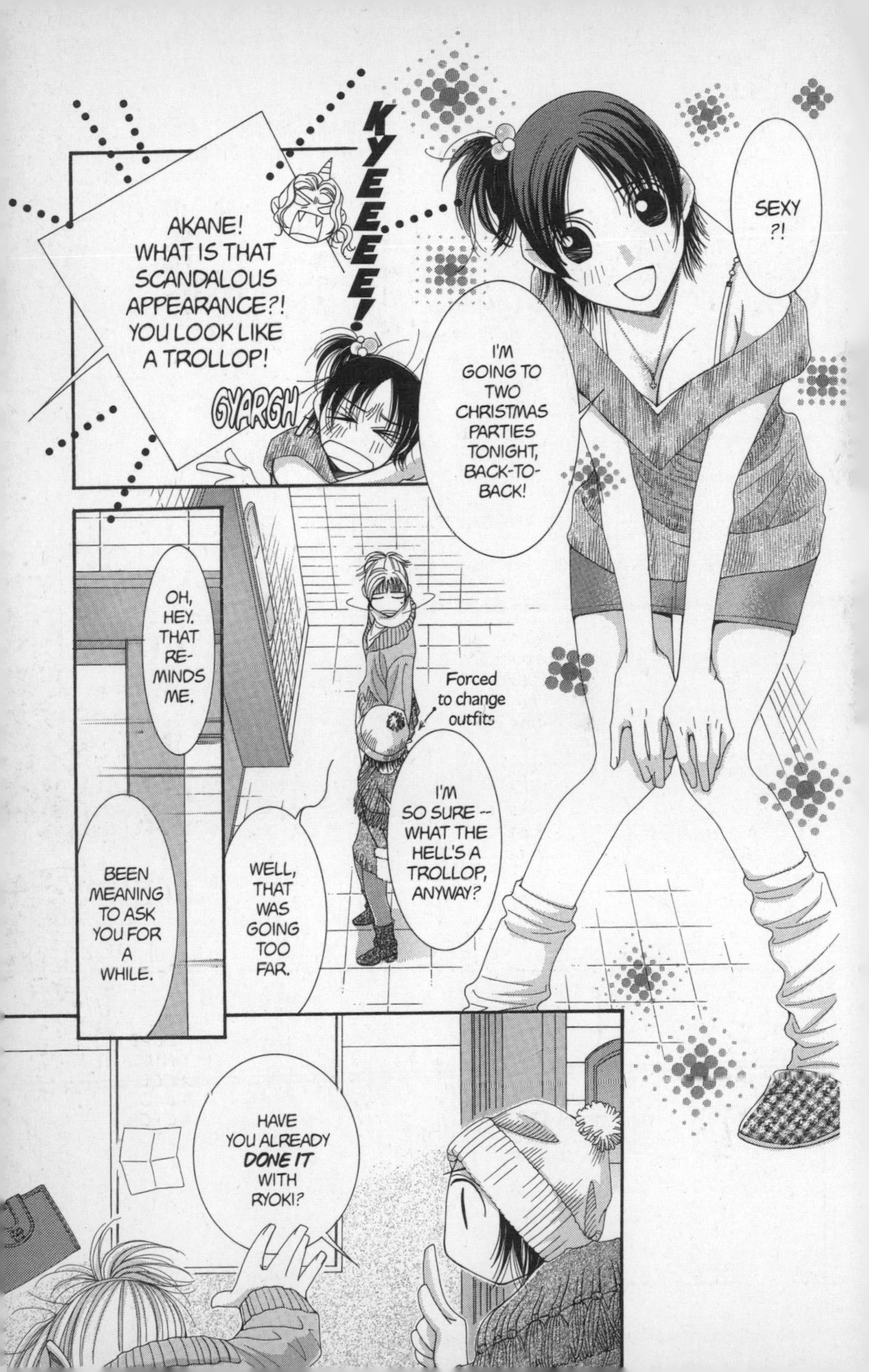
SEXY ?!
I'M GOING TO TWO CHRISTMAS PARTIES TONIGHT, BACK-TO-BACK!
KYEEEE!
AKANE! WHAT IS THAT SCANDALOUS APPEARANCE?! YOU LOOK LIKE A TROLLOP!
GYARGH
Forced to change outfits
I'M SO SURE -- WHAT THE HELL'S A TROLLOP, ANYWAY?
WELL, THAT WAS GOING TOO FAR.
OH, HEY. THAT RE-MINDS ME.
BEEN MEANING TO ASK YOU FOR A WHILE.
HAVE YOU ALREADY **DONE IT** WITH RYOKI?

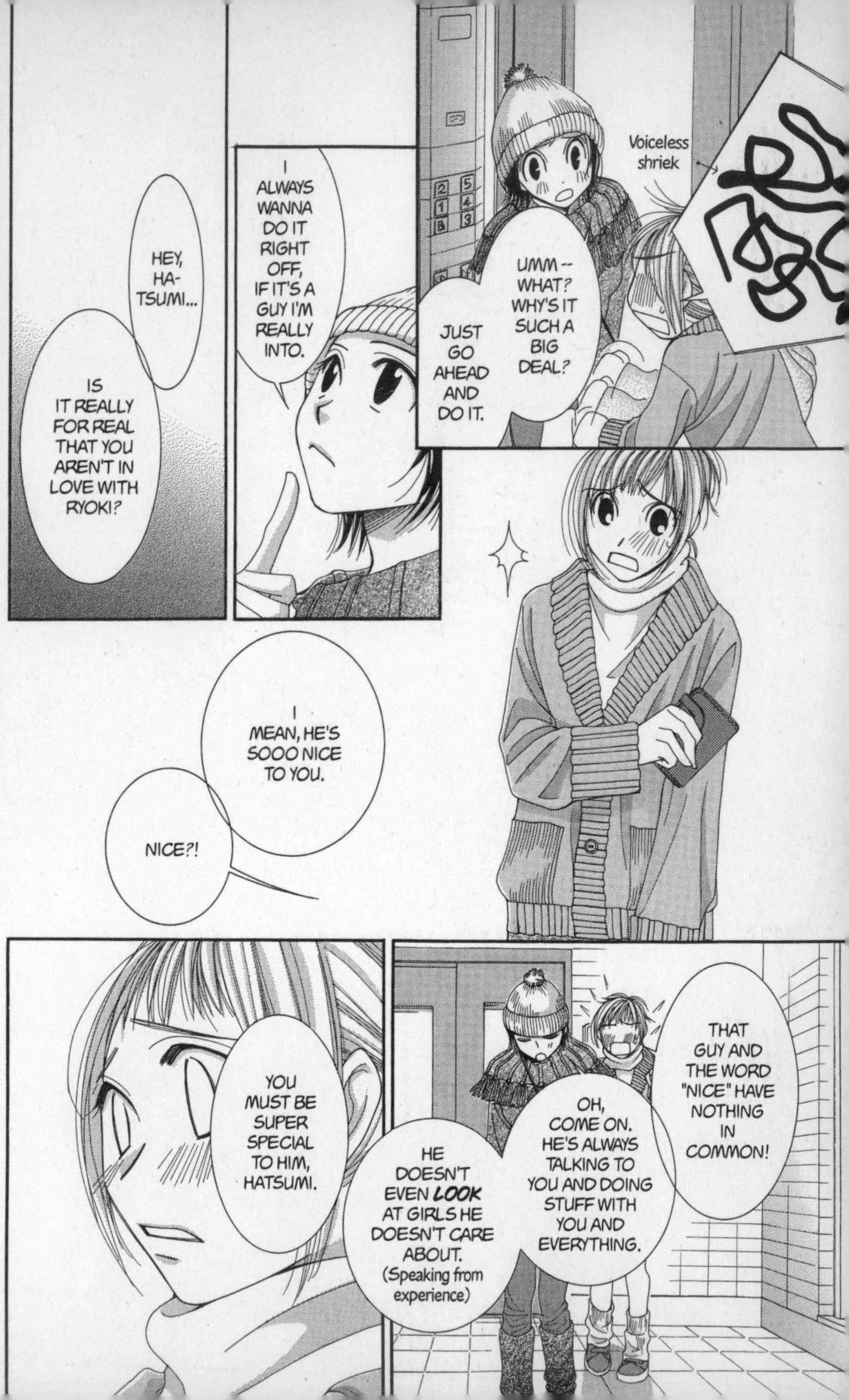
Voiceless shriek
UMM -- WHAT? WHY'S IT SUCH A BIG DEAL?
JUST GO AHEAD AND DO IT.
I ALWAYS WANNA DO IT RIGHT OFF, IF IT'S A GUY I'M REALLY INTO.
HEY, HA-TSUMI...
IS IT REALLY FOR REAL THAT YOU AREN'T IN LOVE WITH RYOKI?
I MEAN, HE'S SOOO NICE TO YOU.
NICE?!
THAT GUY AND THE WORD "NICE" HAVE NOTHING IN COMMON!
OH, COME ON. HE'S ALWAYS TALKING TO YOU AND DOING STUFF WITH YOU AND EVERYTHING.
HE DOESN'T EVEN ***LOOK*** AT GIRLS HE DOESN'T CARE ABOUT.
(Speaking from experience)
YOU MUST BE SUPER SPECIAL TO HIM, HATSUMI.

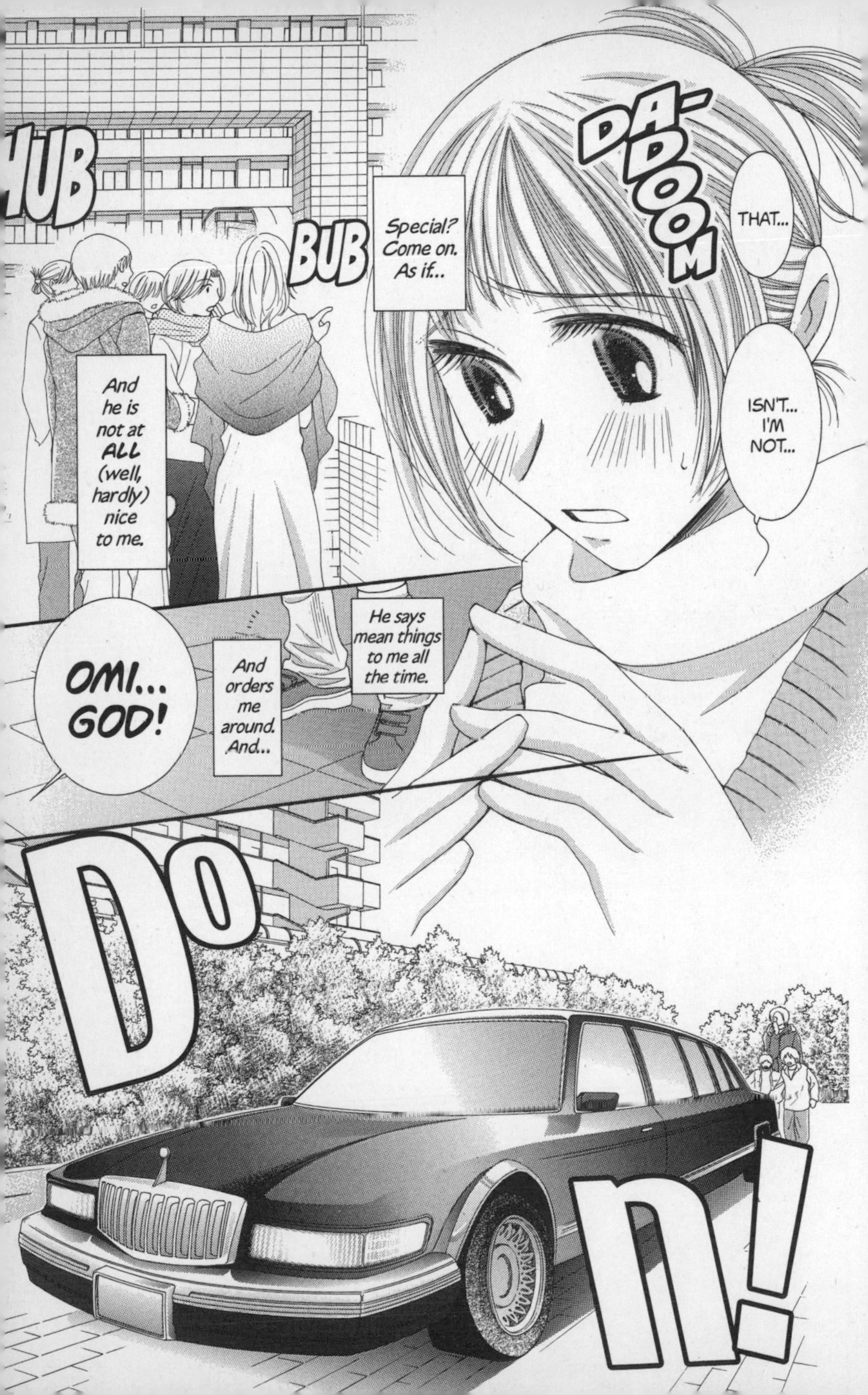
DA-DOOM
THAT...
ISN'T... I'M NOT...
Special? Come on. As if...
BUB
HUB
And he is not at ALL (well, hardly) nice to me.
He says mean things to me all the time.
And orders me around. And...
OMI... GOD!
Do
n!

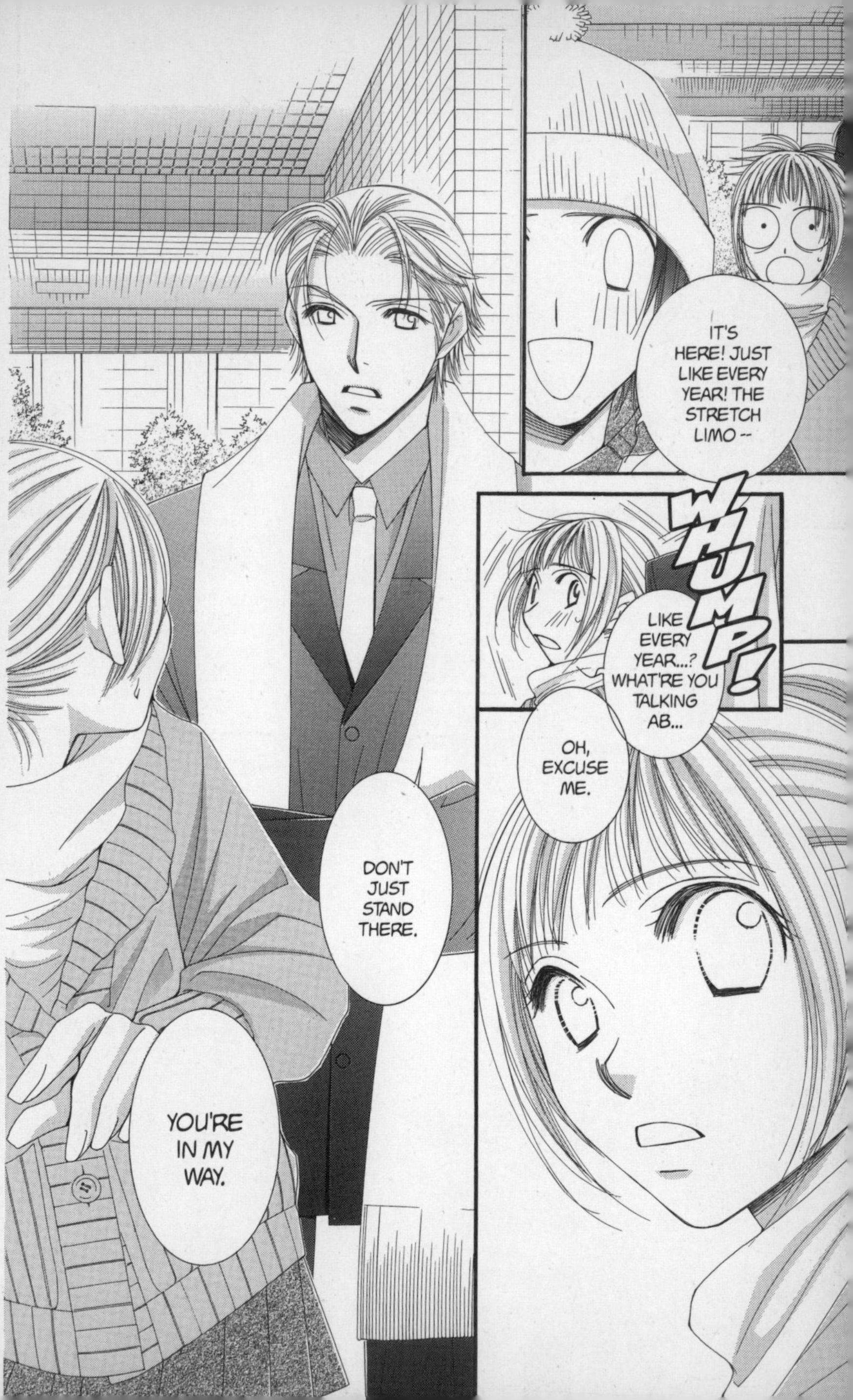
IT'S HERE! JUST LIKE EVERY YEAR! THE STRETCH LIMO --
WHUMP!
LIKE EVERY YEAR...? WHAT'RE YOU TALKING AB...
OH, EXCUSE ME.
DON'T JUST STAND THERE.
YOU'RE IN MY WAY.

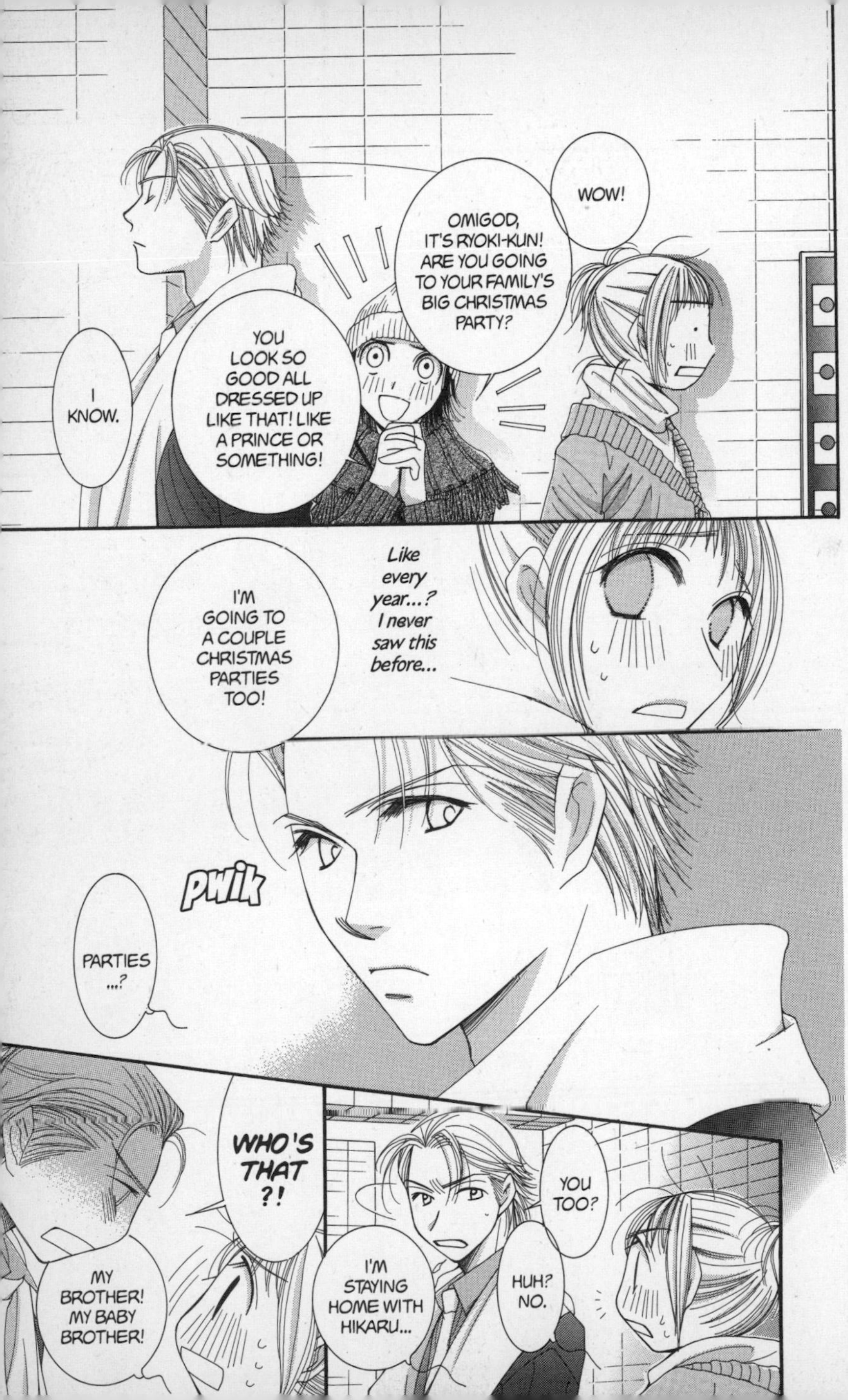
WOW!
OMIGOD, IT'S RYOKI-KUN! ARE YOU GOING TO YOUR FAMILY'S BIG CHRISTMAS PARTY?
YOU LOOK SO GOOD ALL DRESSED UP LIKE THAT! LIKE A PRINCE OR SOMETHING!
I KNOW.
Like every year...? I never saw this before...
I'M GOING TO A COUPLE CHRISTMAS PARTIES TOO!
pwik
PARTIES ...?
YOU TOO?
HUH? NO.
I'M STAYING HOME WITH HIKARU...
WHO'S THAT ?!
MY BROTHER! MY BABY BROTHER!

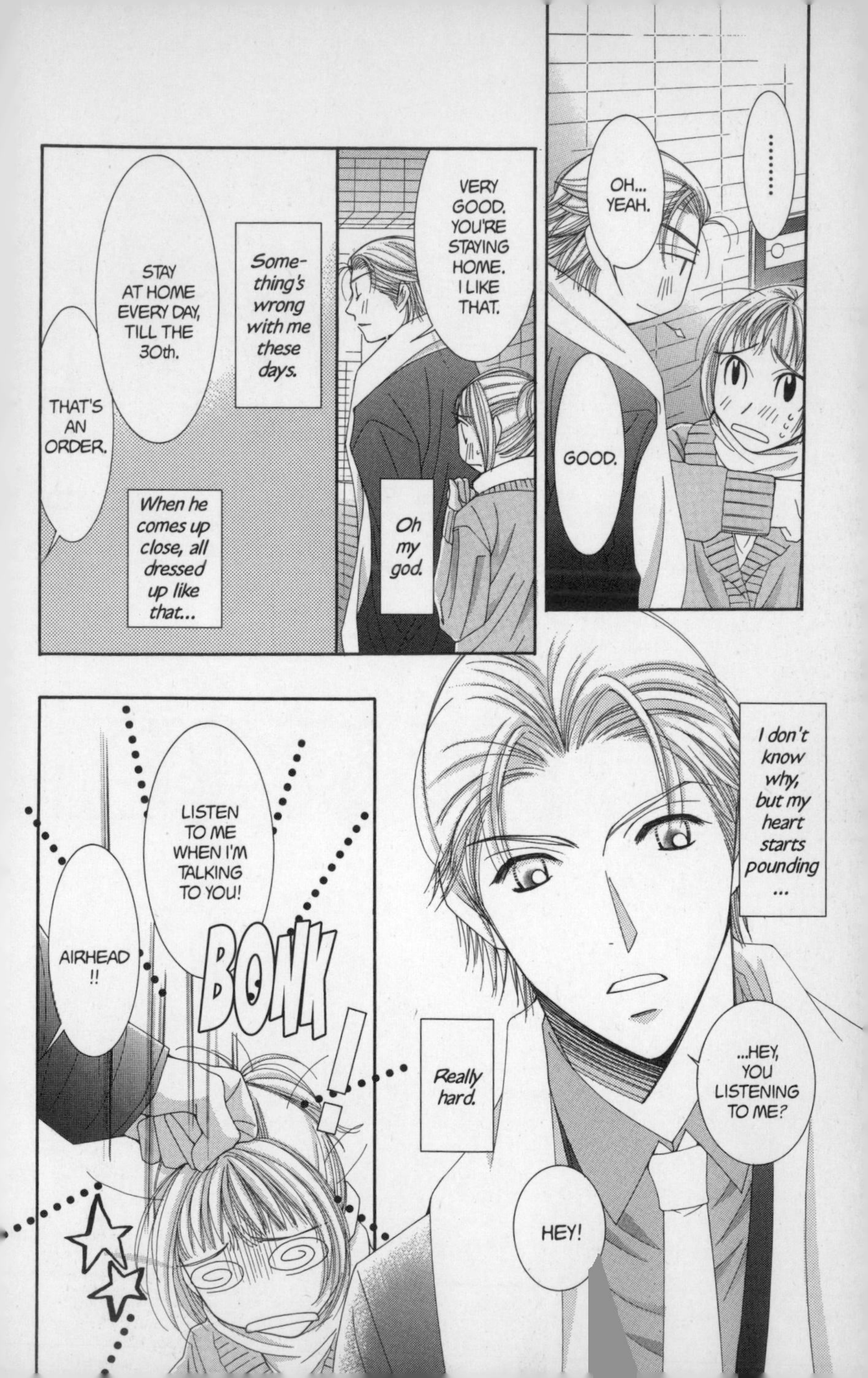
......
OH... YEAH.
GOOD.
VERY GOOD. YOU'RE STAYING HOME. I LIKE THAT.
Oh my god.
Something's wrong with me these days.
STAY AT HOME EVERY DAY, TILL THE 30th.
THAT'S AN ORDER.
When he comes up close, all dressed up like that...
I don't know why, but my heart starts pounding ...
...HEY, YOU LISTENING TO ME?
Really hard.
HEY!
LISTEN TO ME WHEN I'M TALKING TO YOU!
AIRHEAD !!
BONK
!

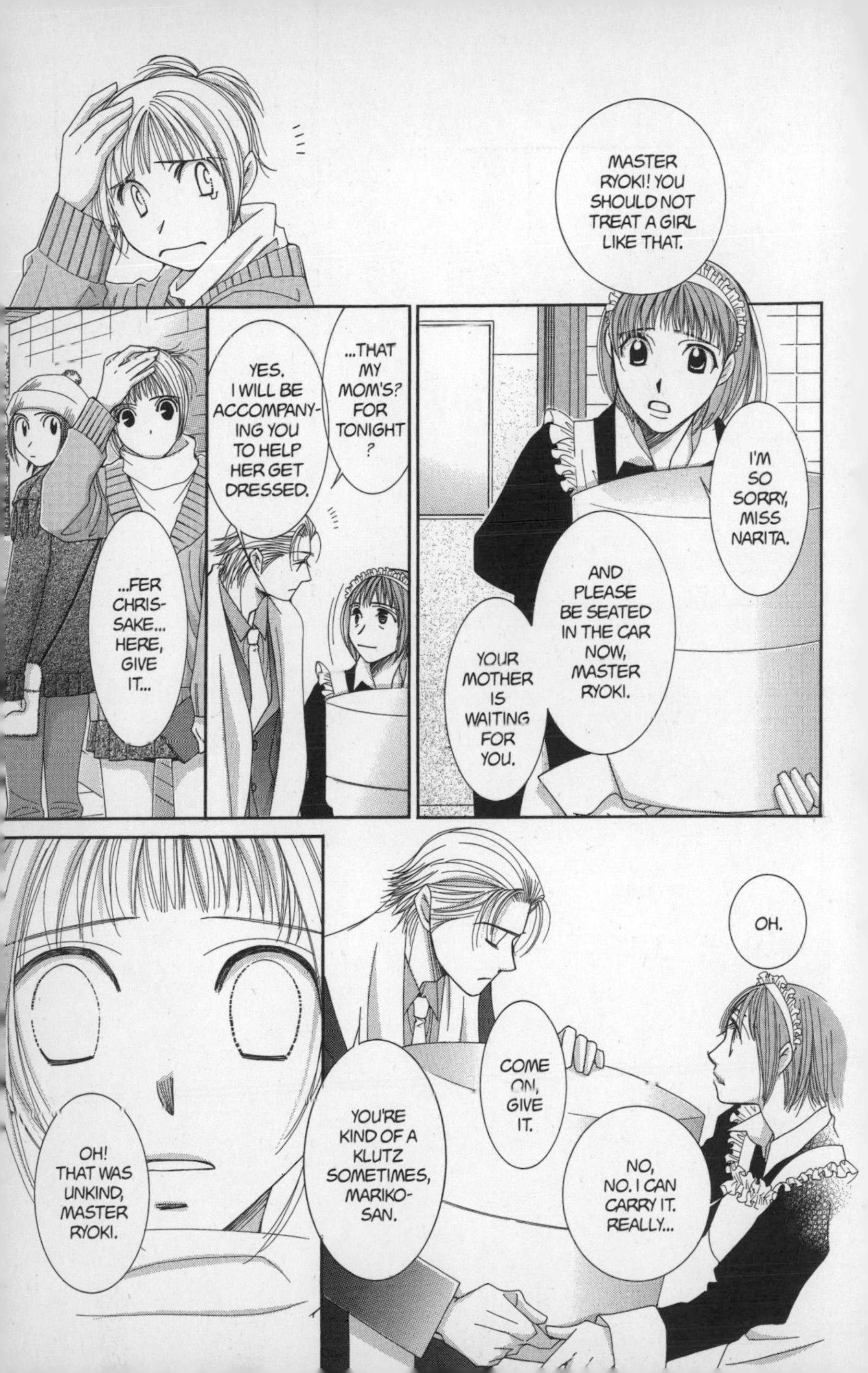
MASTER RYOKI! YOU SHOULD NOT TREAT A GIRL LIKE THAT.
I'M SO SORRY, MISS NARITA.
AND PLEASE BE SEATED IN THE CAR NOW, MASTER RYOKI.
YOUR MOTHER IS WAITING FOR YOU.
...THAT MY MOM'S? FOR TONIGHT?
YES. I WILL BE ACCOMPANY-ING YOU TO HELP HER GET DRESSED.
...FER CHRIS-SAKE... HERE, GIVE IT...
OH.
NO, NO. I CAN CARRY IT. REALLY...
COME ON, GIVE IT.
YOU'RE KIND OF A KLUTZ SOMETIMES, MARIKO-SAN.
OH! THAT WAS UNKIND, MASTER RYOKI.

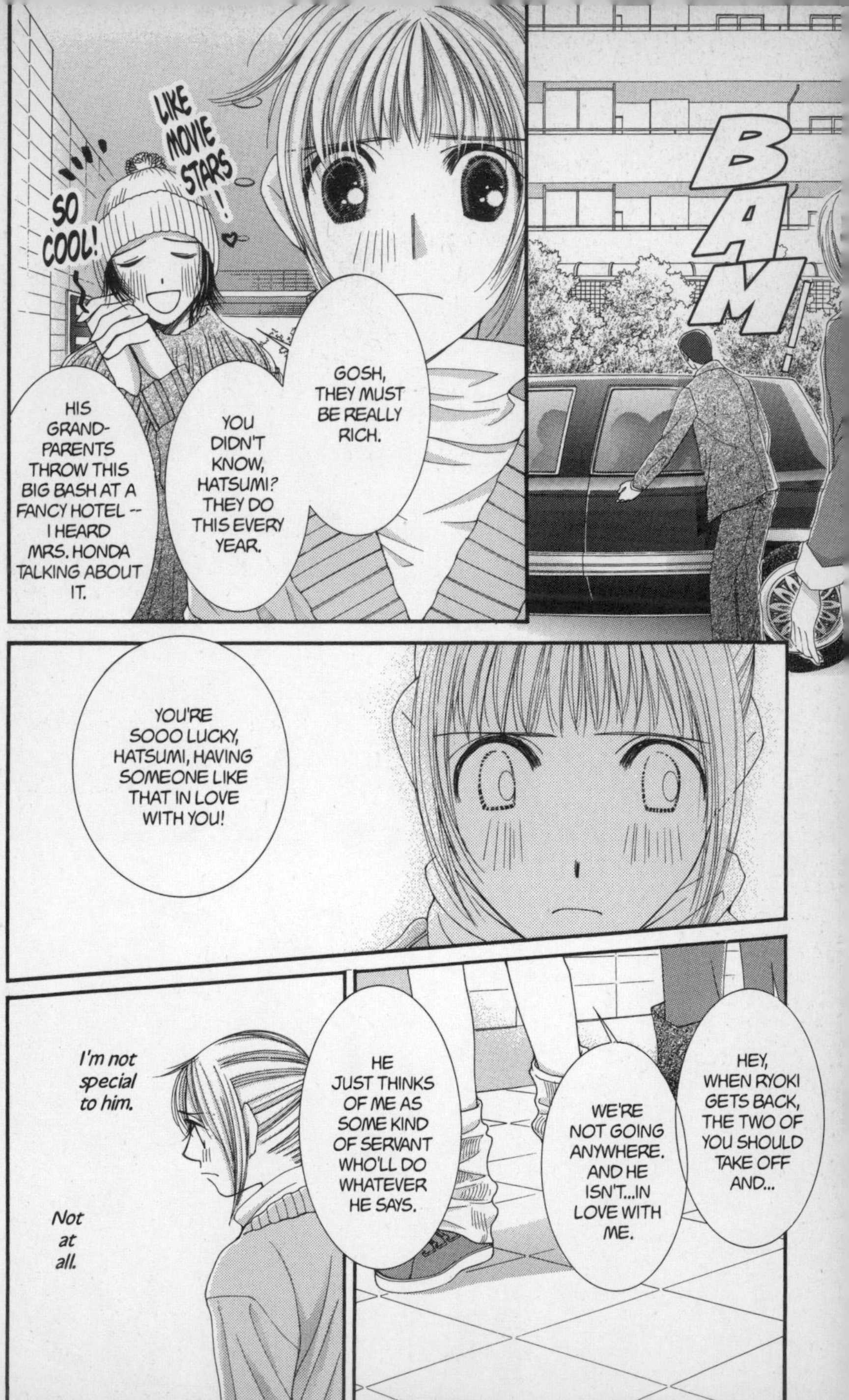
BAM!
LIKE MOVIE STARS!
SO COOL!
GOSH, THEY MUST BE REALLY RICH.
YOU DIDN'T KNOW, HATSUMI? THEY DO THIS EVERY YEAR.
HIS GRAND-PARENTS THROW THIS BIG BASH AT A FANCY HOTEL -- I HEARD MRS. HONDA TALKING ABOUT IT.
YOU'RE SOOO LUCKY, HATSUMI, HAVING SOMEONE LIKE THAT IN LOVE WITH YOU!
HEY, WHEN RYOKI GETS BACK, THE TWO OF YOU SHOULD TAKE OFF AND...
WE'RE NOT GOING ANYWHERE. AND HE ISN'T...IN LOVE WITH ME.
HE JUST THINKS OF ME AS SOME KIND OF SERVANT WHO'LL DO WHATEVER HE SAYS.
I'm not special to him.
Not at all.

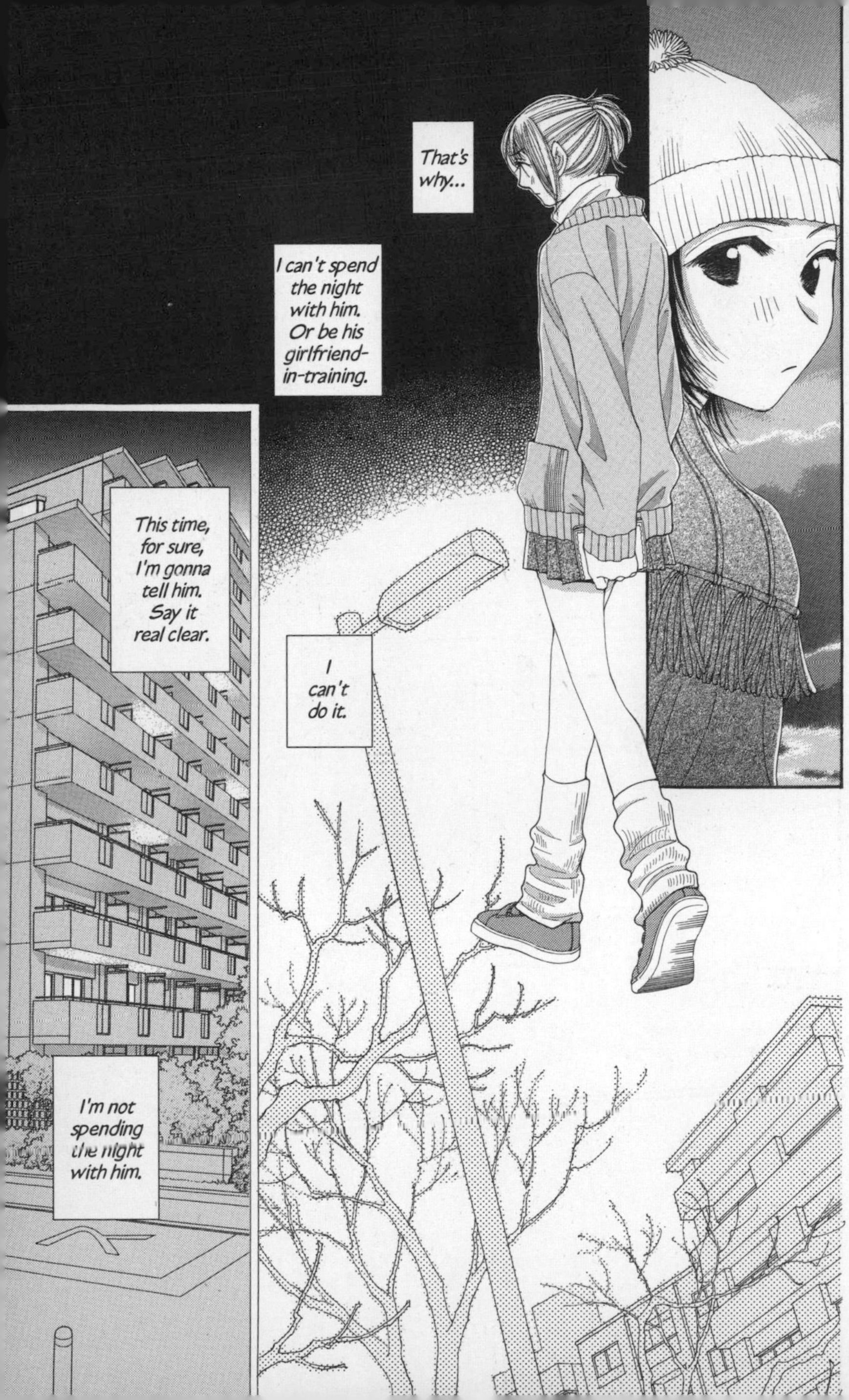
That's why...
I can't spend the night with him. Or be his girlfriend-in-training.
I can't do it.
This time, for sure, I'm gonna tell him. Say it real clear.
I'm not spending the night with him.

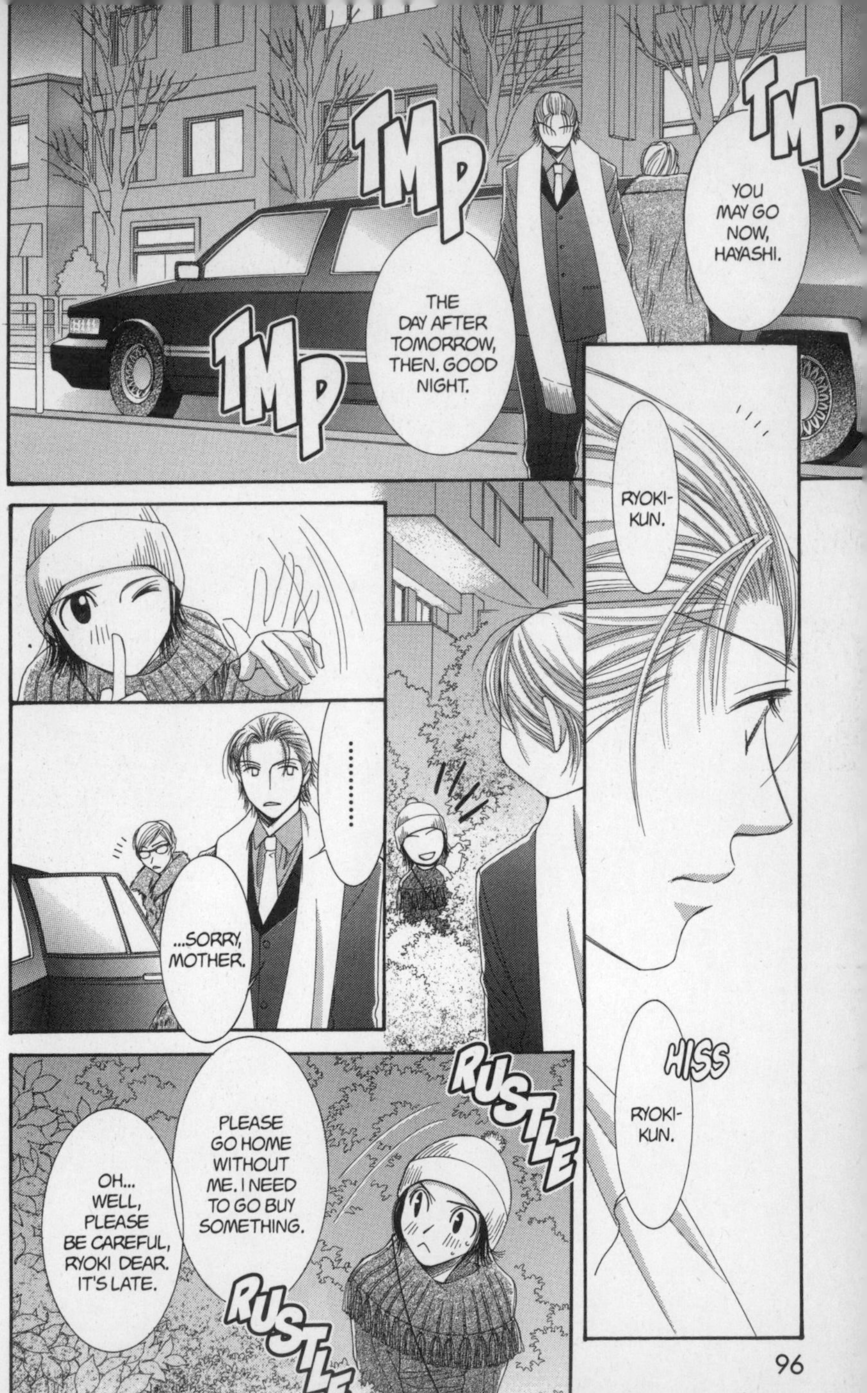

TMP
YOU MAY GO NOW, HAYASHI.
TMP
THE DAY AFTER TOMORROW, THEN. GOOD NIGHT.
TMP
RYOKI-KUN.
HISS
RYOKI-KUN.
......
...SORRY, MOTHER.
RUSTLE
PLEASE GO HOME WITHOUT ME. I NEED TO GO BUY SOMETHING.
OH... WELL, PLEASE BE CAREFUL, RYOKI DEAR. IT'S LATE.
RUSTLE

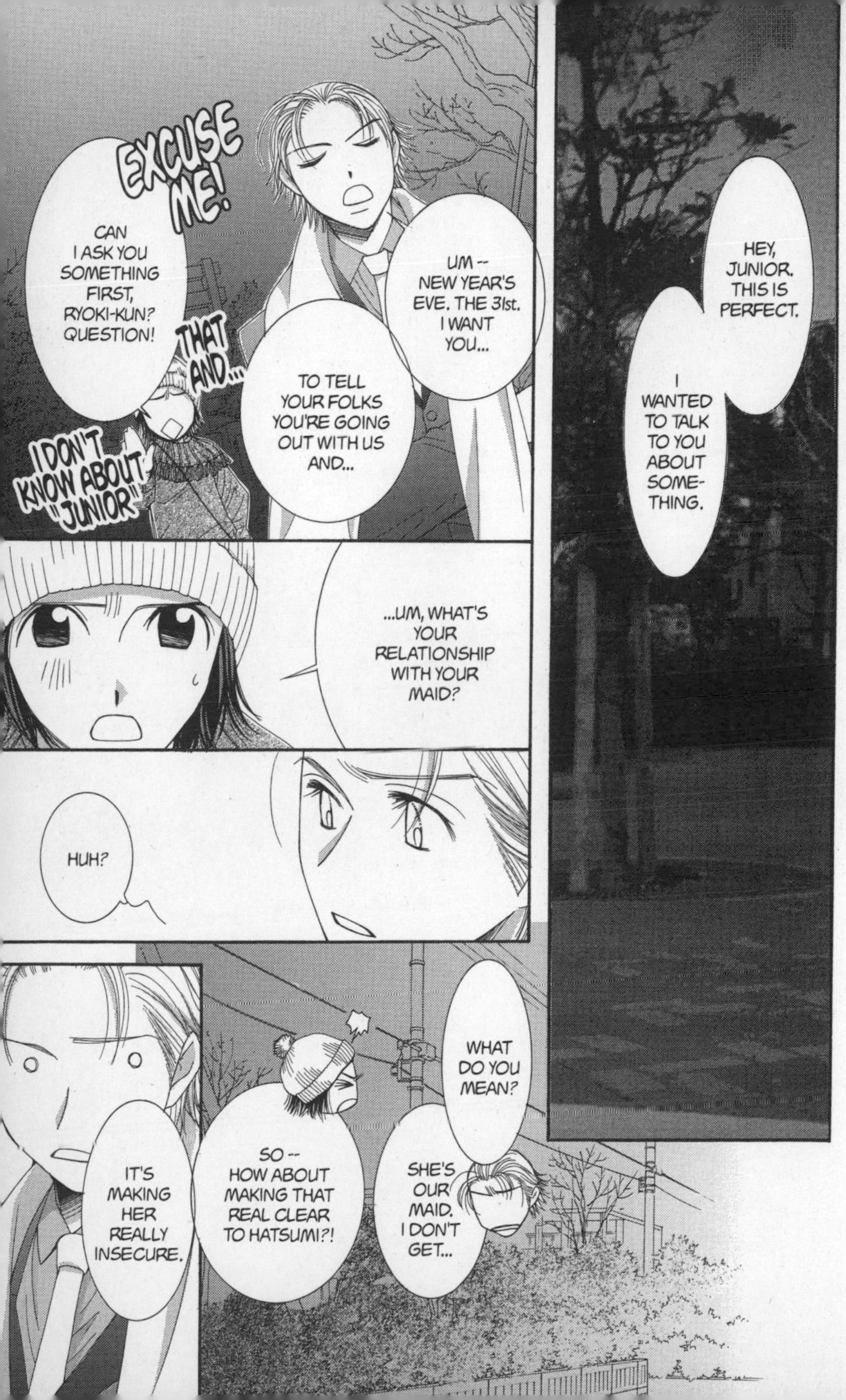
HEY, JUNIOR. THIS IS PERFECT.
I WANTED TO TALK TO YOU ABOUT SOME-THING.
UM -- NEW YEAR'S EVE. THE 31st. I WANT YOU...
TO TELL YOUR FOLKS YOU'RE GOING OUT WITH US AND...
EXCUSE ME!
CAN I ASK YOU SOMETHING FIRST, RYOKI-KUN? QUESTION!
THAT AND...
I DON'T KNOW ABOUT "JUNIOR"
...UM, WHAT'S YOUR RELATIONSHIP WITH YOUR MAID?
HUH?
WHAT DO YOU MEAN?
SHE'S OUR MAID. I DON'T GET...
SO -- HOW ABOUT MAKING THAT REAL CLEAR TO HATSUMI?!
IT'S MAKING HER REALLY INSECURE.

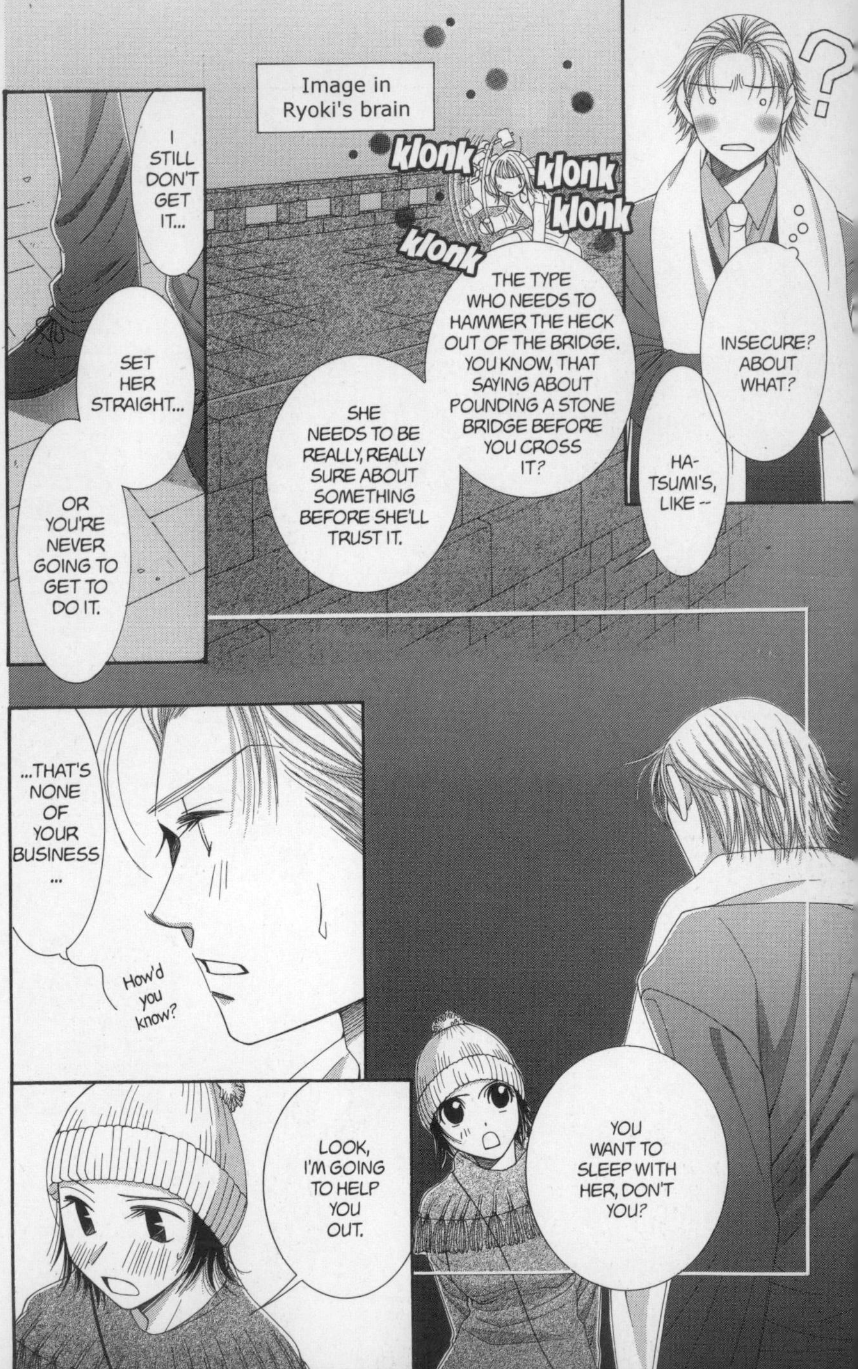
INSECURE? ABOUT WHAT?
HA-TSUMI'S, LIKE --
Image in Ryoki's brain
klonk
klonk
klonk
klonk
THE TYPE WHO NEEDS TO HAMMER THE HECK OUT OF THE BRIDGE. YOU KNOW, THAT SAYING ABOUT POUNDING A STONE BRIDGE BEFORE YOU CROSS IT?
SHE NEEDS TO BE REALLY, REALLY SURE ABOUT SOMETHING BEFORE SHE'LL TRUST IT.
I STILL DON'T GET IT...
SET HER STRAIGHT...
OR YOU'RE NEVER GOING TO GET TO DO IT.
YOU WANT TO SLEEP WITH HER, DON'T YOU?
...THAT'S NONE OF YOUR BUSINESS ...
How'd you know?
LOOK, I'M GOING TO HELP YOU OUT.

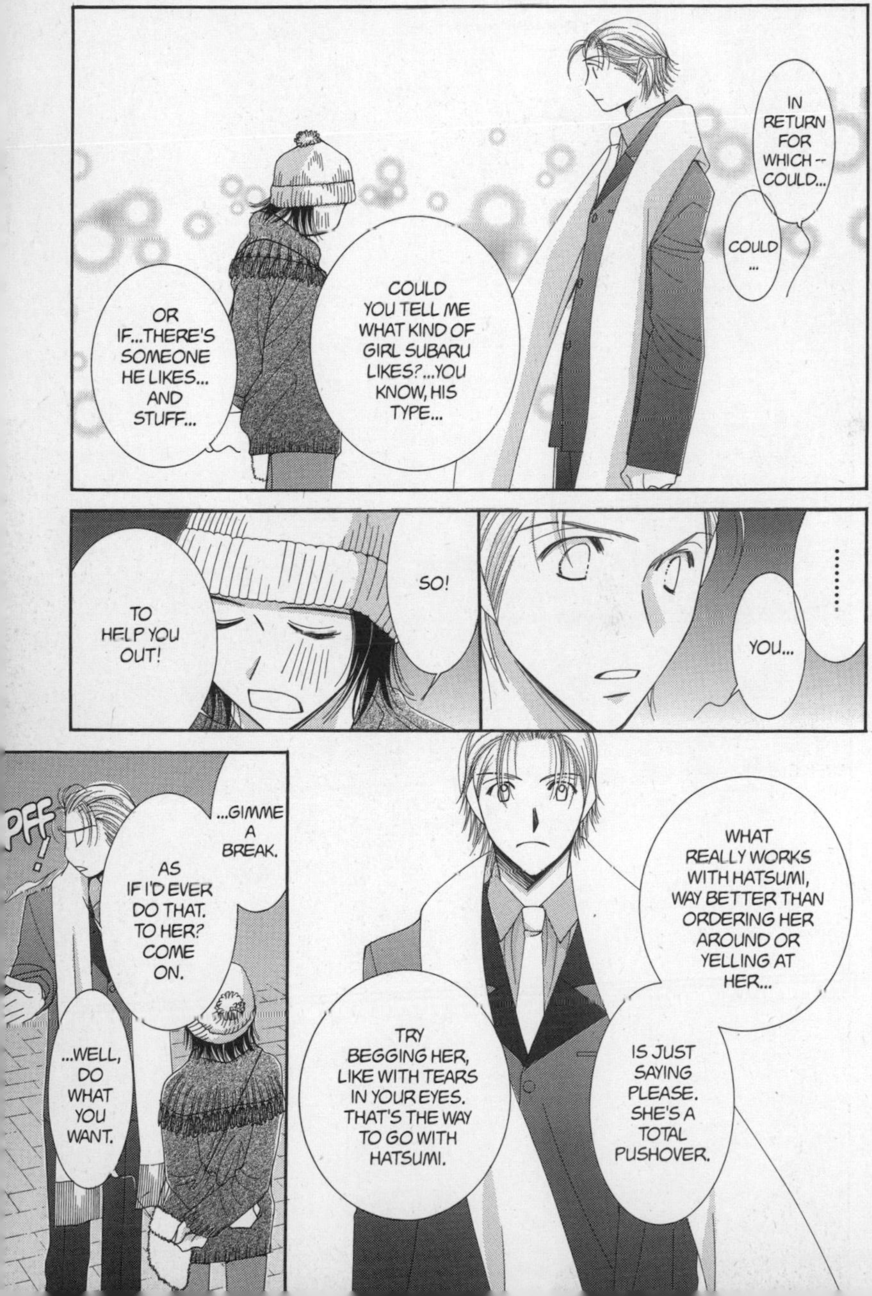
IN RETURN FOR WHICH -- COULD...
COULD ...
COULD YOU TELL ME WHAT KIND OF GIRL SUBARU LIKES?...YOU KNOW, HIS TYPE...
OR IF...THERE'S SOMEONE HE LIKES... AND STUFF...
....
YOU...
SO!
TO HELP YOU OUT!
WHAT REALLY WORKS WITH HATSUMI, WAY BETTER THAN ORDERING HER AROUND OR YELLING AT HER...
IS JUST SAYING PLEASE. SHE'S A TOTAL PUSHOVER.
TRY BEGGING HER, LIKE WITH TEARS IN YOUR EYES. THAT'S THE WAY TO GO WITH HATSUMI.
PFF!
...GIMME A BREAK.
AS IF I'D EVER DO THAT. TO HER? COME ON.
...WELL, DO WHAT YOU WANT.

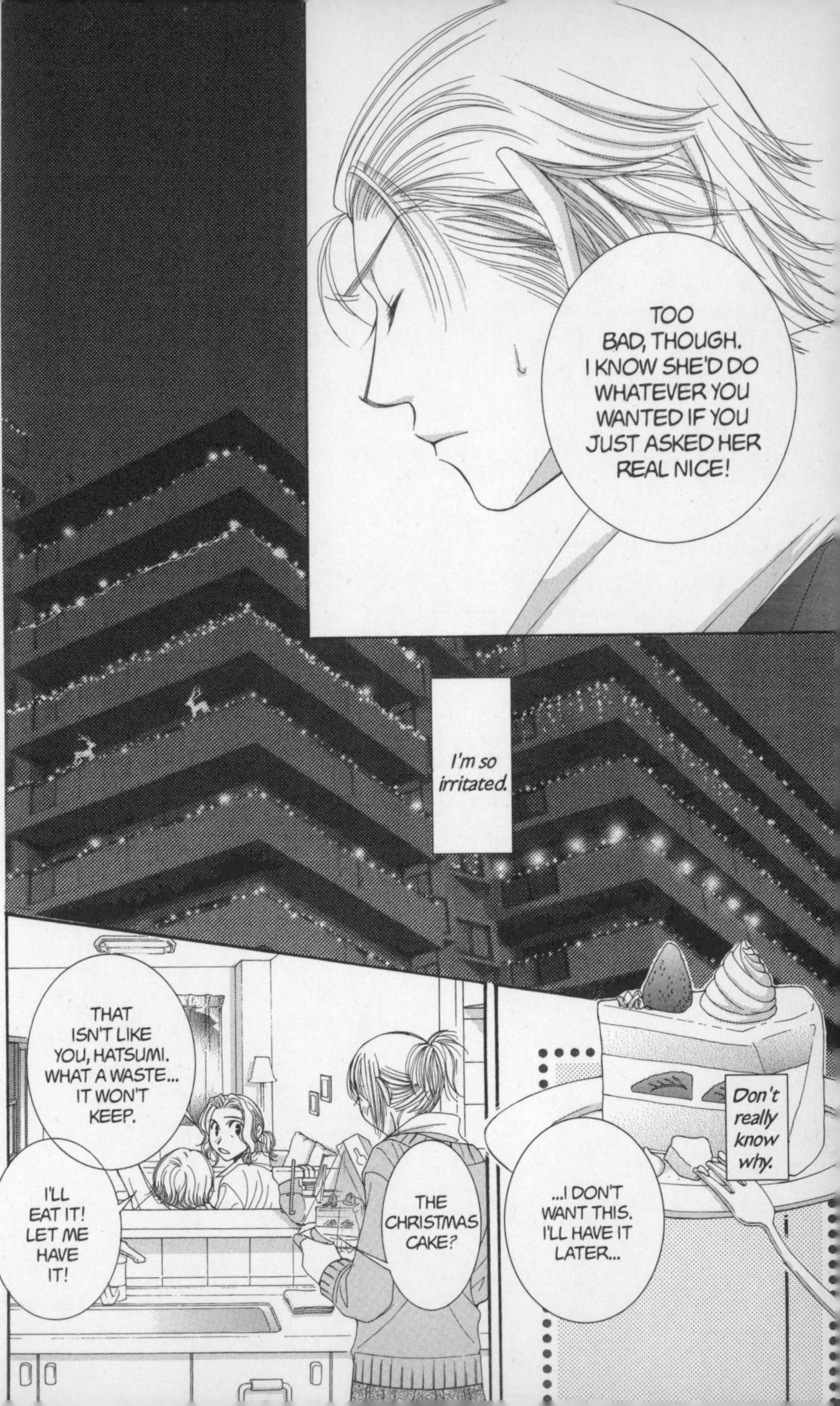
TOO BAD, THOUGH. I KNOW SHE'D DO WHATEVER YOU WANTED IF YOU JUST ASKED HER REAL NICE!
I'm so irritated.
Don't really know why.
...I DON'T WANT THIS. I'LL HAVE IT LATER...
THE CHRISTMAS CAKE?
THAT ISN'T LIKE YOU, HATSUMI. WHAT A WASTE... IT WON'T KEEP.
I'LL EAT IT! LET ME HAVE IT!

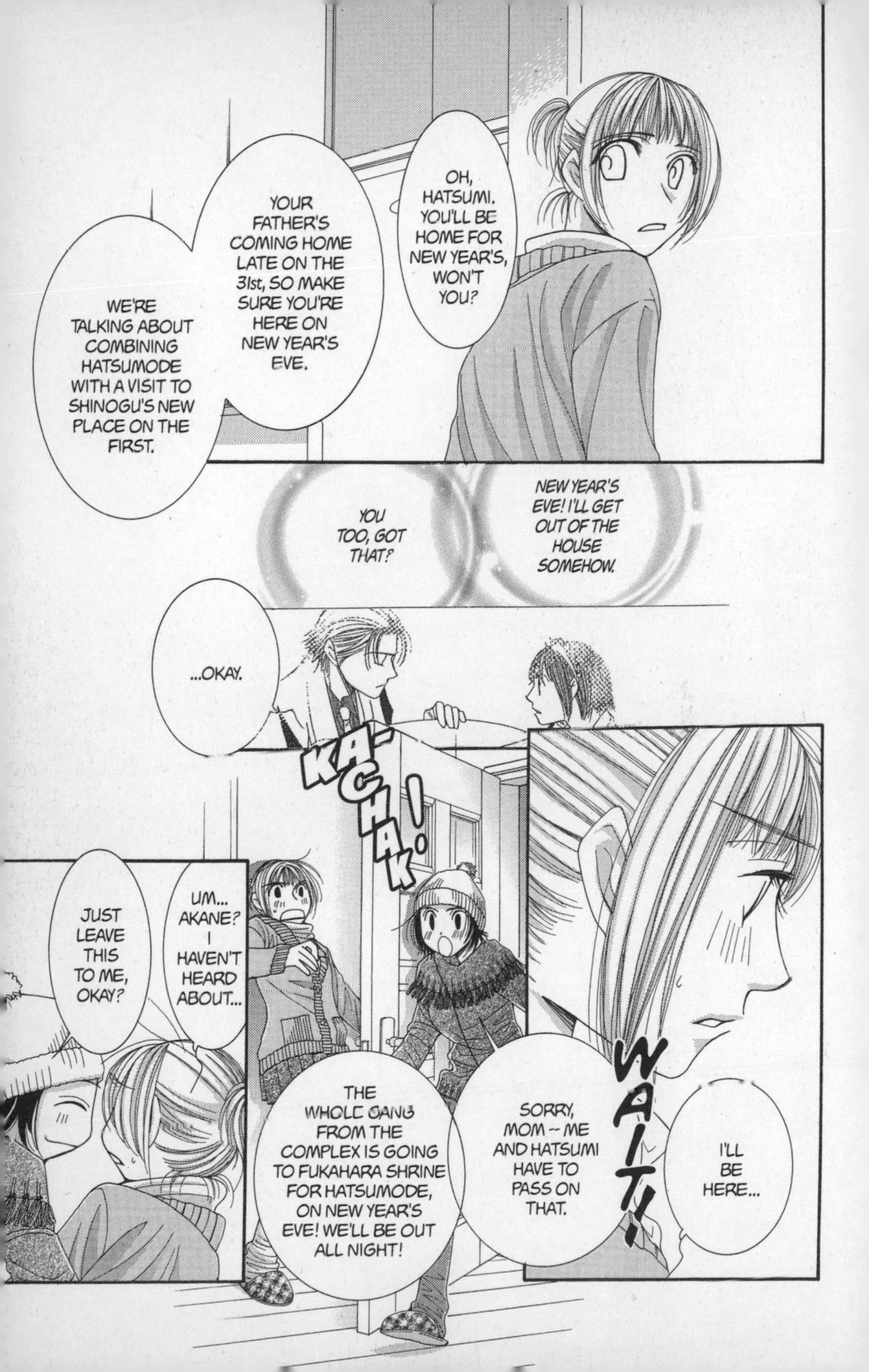
OH, HATSUMI. YOU'LL BE HOME FOR NEW YEAR'S, WON'T YOU?
YOUR FATHER'S COMING HOME LATE ON THE 31st, SO MAKE SURE YOU'RE HERE ON NEW YEAR'S EVE.
WE'RE TALKING ABOUT COMBINING HATSUMODE WITH A VISIT TO SHINOGU'S NEW PLACE ON THE FIRST.
NEW YEAR'S EVE! I'LL GET OUT OF THE HOUSE SOMEHOW.
YOU TOO, GOT THAT?
...OKAY.
I'LL BE HERE...
WAIT!
KA-CHAK!
SORRY, MOM -- ME AND HATSUMI HAVE TO PASS ON THAT.
THE WHOLE GANG FROM THE COMPLEX IS GOING TO FUKAHARA SHRINE FOR HATSUMODE, ON NEW YEAR'S EVE! WE'LL BE OUT ALL NIGHT!
UM... AKANE? I HAVEN'T HEARD ABOUT...
JUST LEAVE THIS TO ME, OKAY?

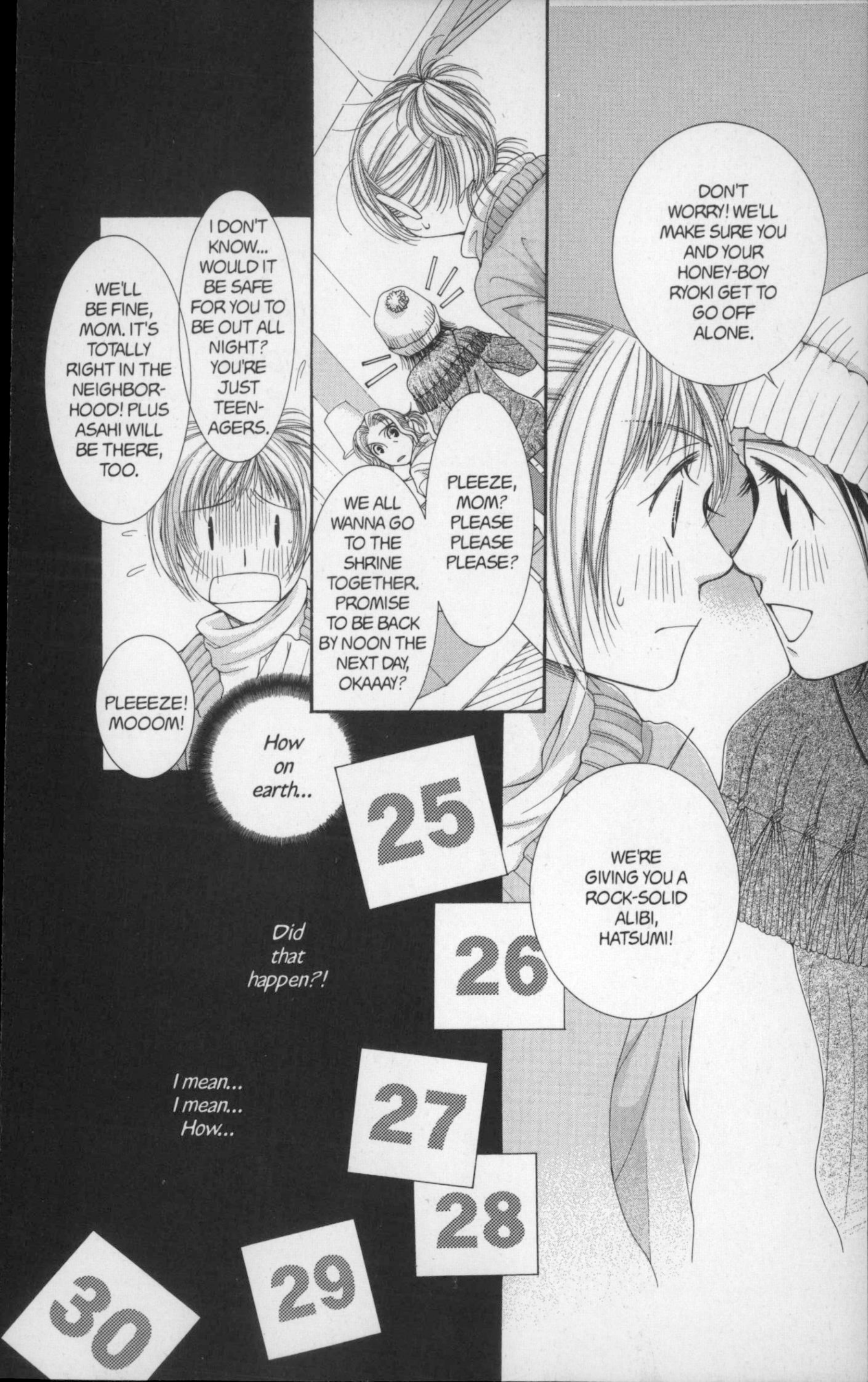
DON'T WORRY! WE'LL MAKE SURE YOU AND YOUR HONEY-BOY RYOKI GET TO GO OFF ALONE.
WE'RE GIVING YOU A ROCK-SOLID ALIBI, HATSUMI!
PLEEZE, MOM? PLEASE PLEASE PLEASE?
WE ALL WANNA GO TO THE SHRINE TOGETHER. PROMISE TO BE BACK BY NOON THE NEXT DAY, OKAAAY?
I DON'T KNOW... WOULD IT BE SAFE FOR YOU TO BE OUT ALL NIGHT? YOU'RE JUST TEEN-AGERS.
WE'LL BE FINE, MOM. IT'S TOTALLY RIGHT IN THE NEIGHBOR-HOOD! PLUS ASAHI WILL BE THERE, TOO.
PLEEEZE! MOOOM!
How on earth...
25
26
Did that happen?!
27
I mean... I mean... How...
28
29
30

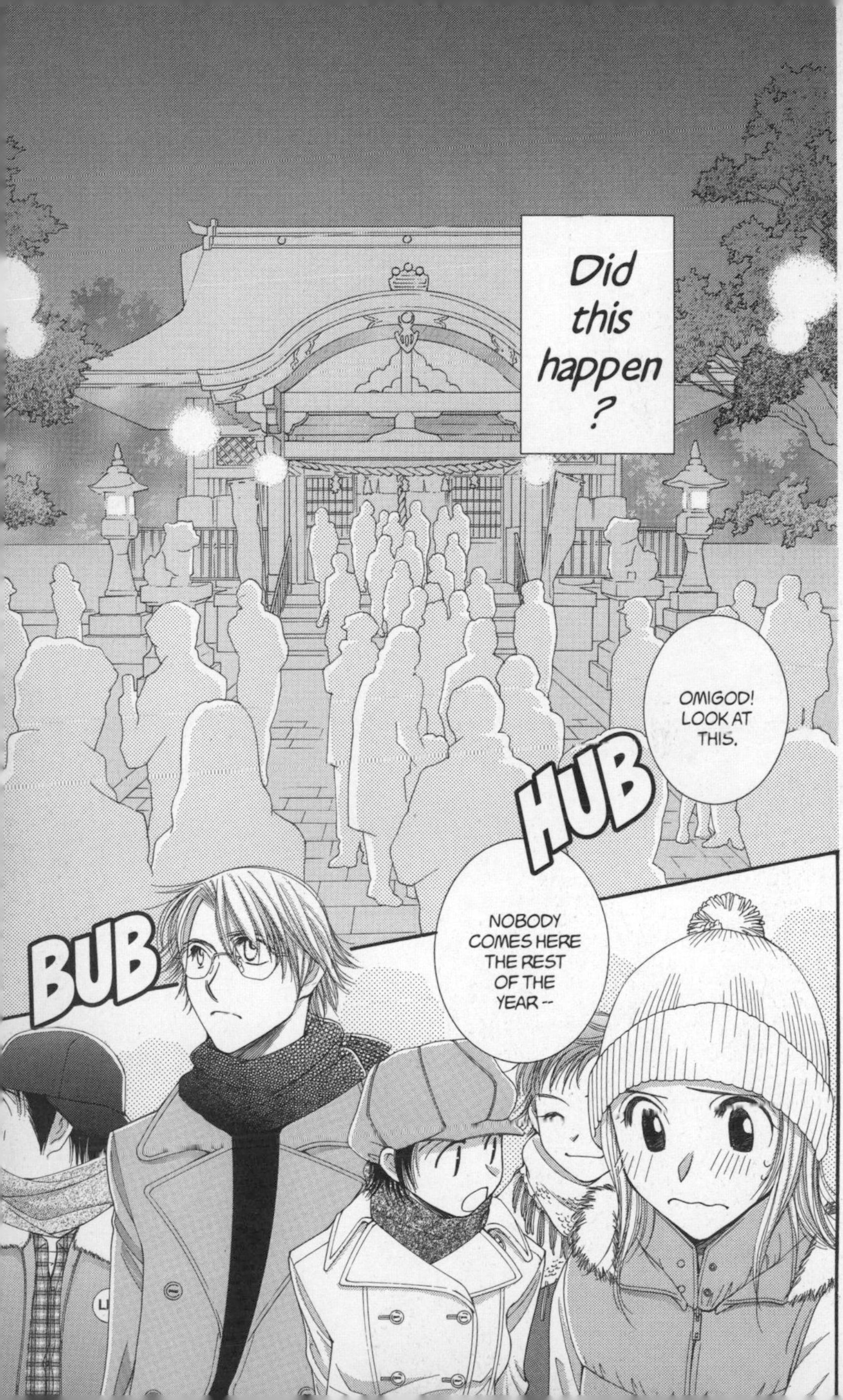
Did this happen?
OMIGOD! LOOK AT THIS.
HUB
NOBODY COMES HERE THE REST OF THE YEAR --
BUB

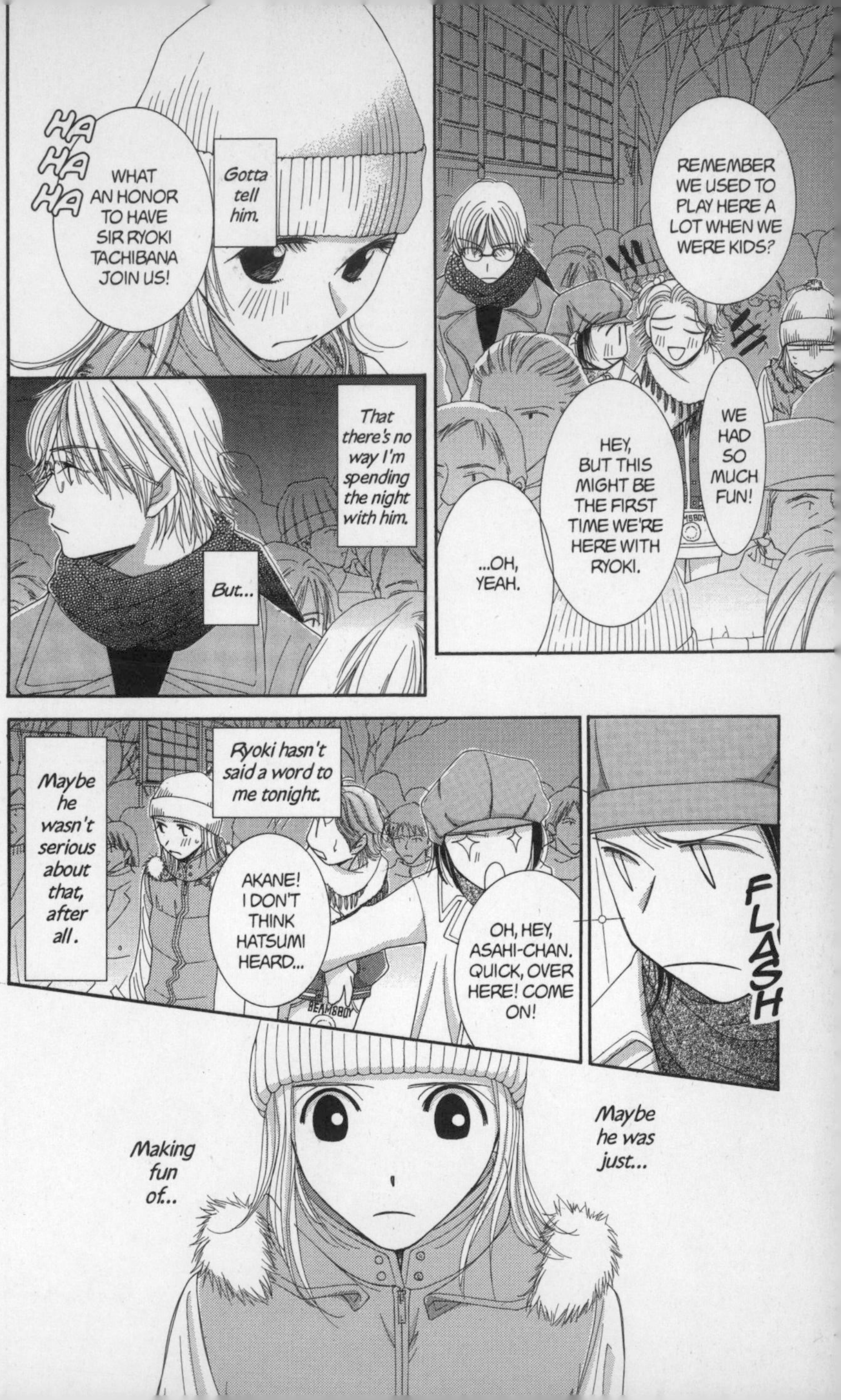
REMEMBER WE USED TO PLAY HERE A LOT WHEN WE WERE KIDS?
WE HAD SO MUCH FUN!
HEY, BUT THIS MIGHT BE THE FIRST TIME WE'RE HERE WITH RYOKI.
...OH, YEAH.
Gotta tell him.
WHAT AN HONOR TO HAVE SIR RYOKI TACHIBANA JOIN US!
HA HA HA
That there's no way I'm spending the night with him.
But...
FLASH
Ryoki hasn't said a word to me tonight.
Maybe he wasn't serious about that, after all.
OH, HEY, ASAHI-CHAN. QUICK, OVER HERE! COME ON!
AKANE! I DON'T THINK HATSUMI HEARD...
Maybe he was just...
Making fun of...

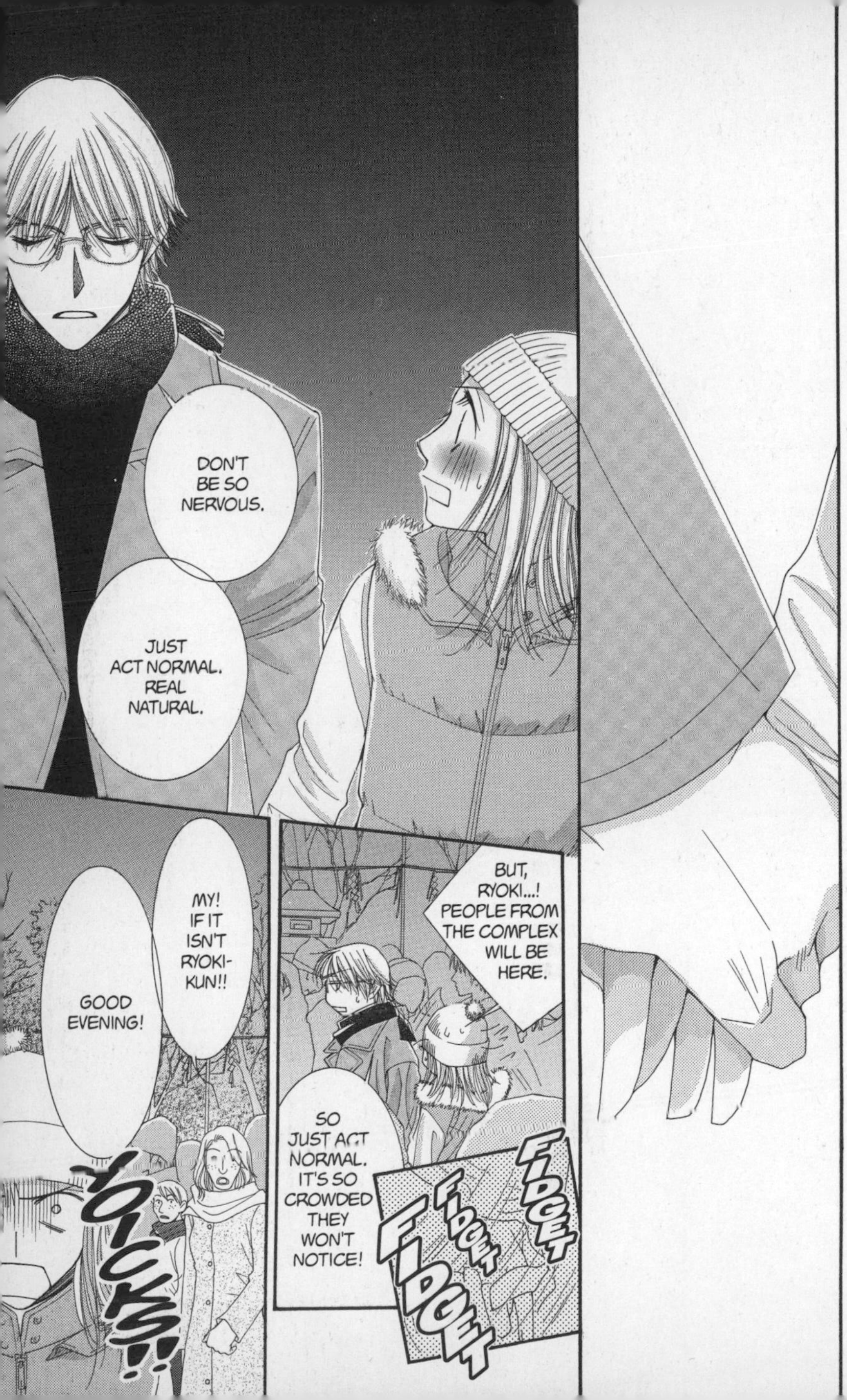
DON'T BE SO NERVOUS.
JUST ACT NORMAL. REAL NATURAL.
BUT, RYOKI...! PEOPLE FROM THE COMPLEX WILL BE HERE.
SO JUST ACT NORMAL. IT'S SO CROWDED THEY WON'T NOTICE!
FIDGET
FIDGET
FIDGET
MY! IF IT ISN'T RYOKI-KUN!!
GOOD EVENING!
ICKS!!

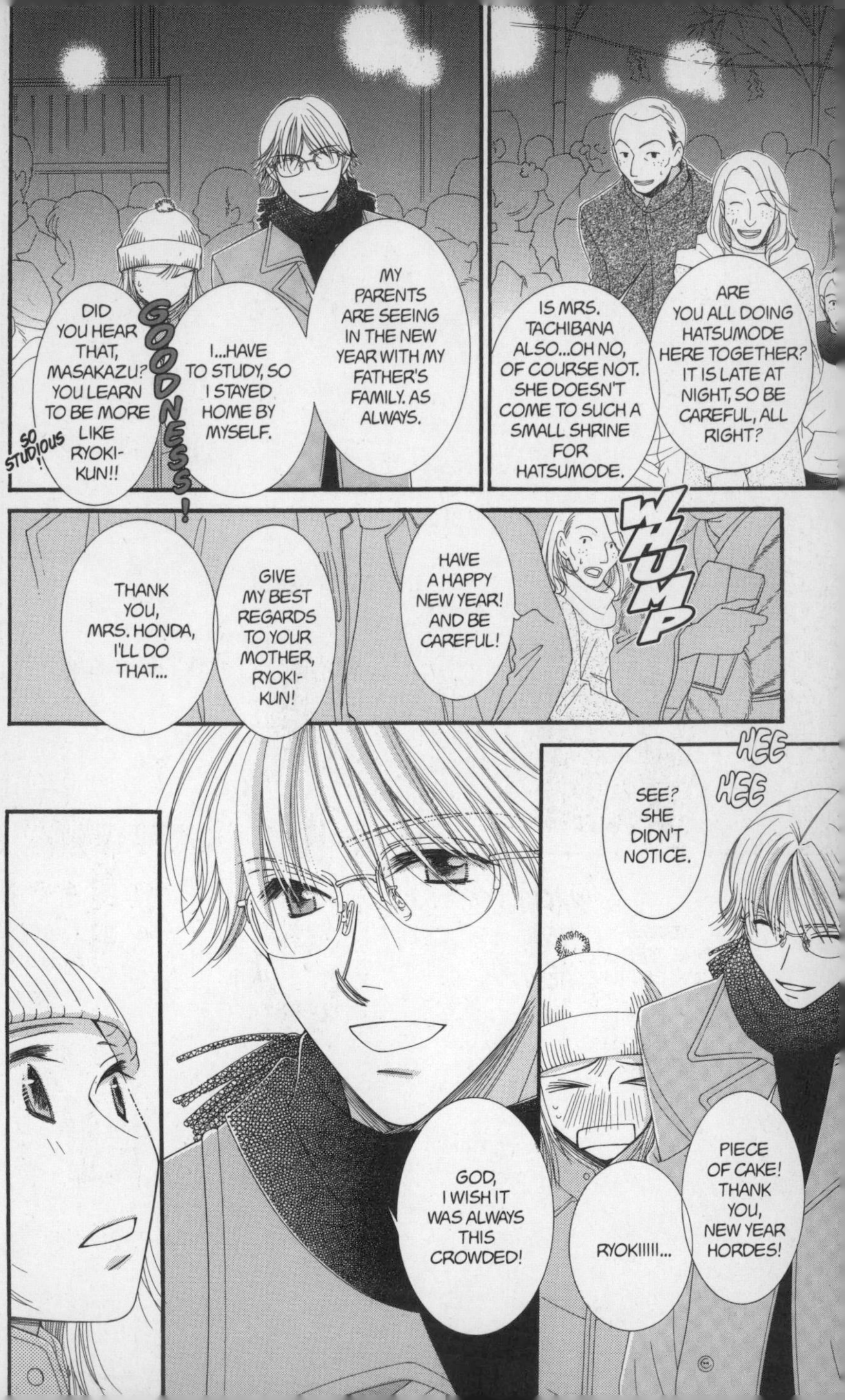
ARE YOU ALL DOING HATSUMODE HERE TOGETHER? IT IS LATE AT NIGHT, SO BE CAREFUL, ALL RIGHT?
IS MRS. TACHIBANA ALSO...OH NO, OF COURSE NOT. SHE DOESN'T COME TO SUCH A SMALL SHRINE FOR HATSUMODE.
MY PARENTS ARE SEEING IN THE NEW YEAR WITH MY FATHER'S FAMILY. AS ALWAYS.
I...HAVE TO STUDY, SO I STAYED HOME BY MYSELF.
GOODNESS!
DID YOU HEAR THAT, MASAKAZU? YOU LEARN TO BE MORE LIKE RYOKI-KUN!!
SO STUDIOUS!
WHUMP
HAVE A HAPPY NEW YEAR! AND BE CAREFUL!
GIVE MY BEST REGARDS TO YOUR MOTHER, RYOKI-KUN!
THANK YOU, MRS. HONDA, I'LL DO THAT...
HEE HEE
SEE? SHE DIDN'T NOTICE.
PIECE OF CAKE! THANK YOU, NEW YEAR HORDES!
RYOKIIIII...
GOD, I WISH IT WAS ALWAYS THIS CROWDED!

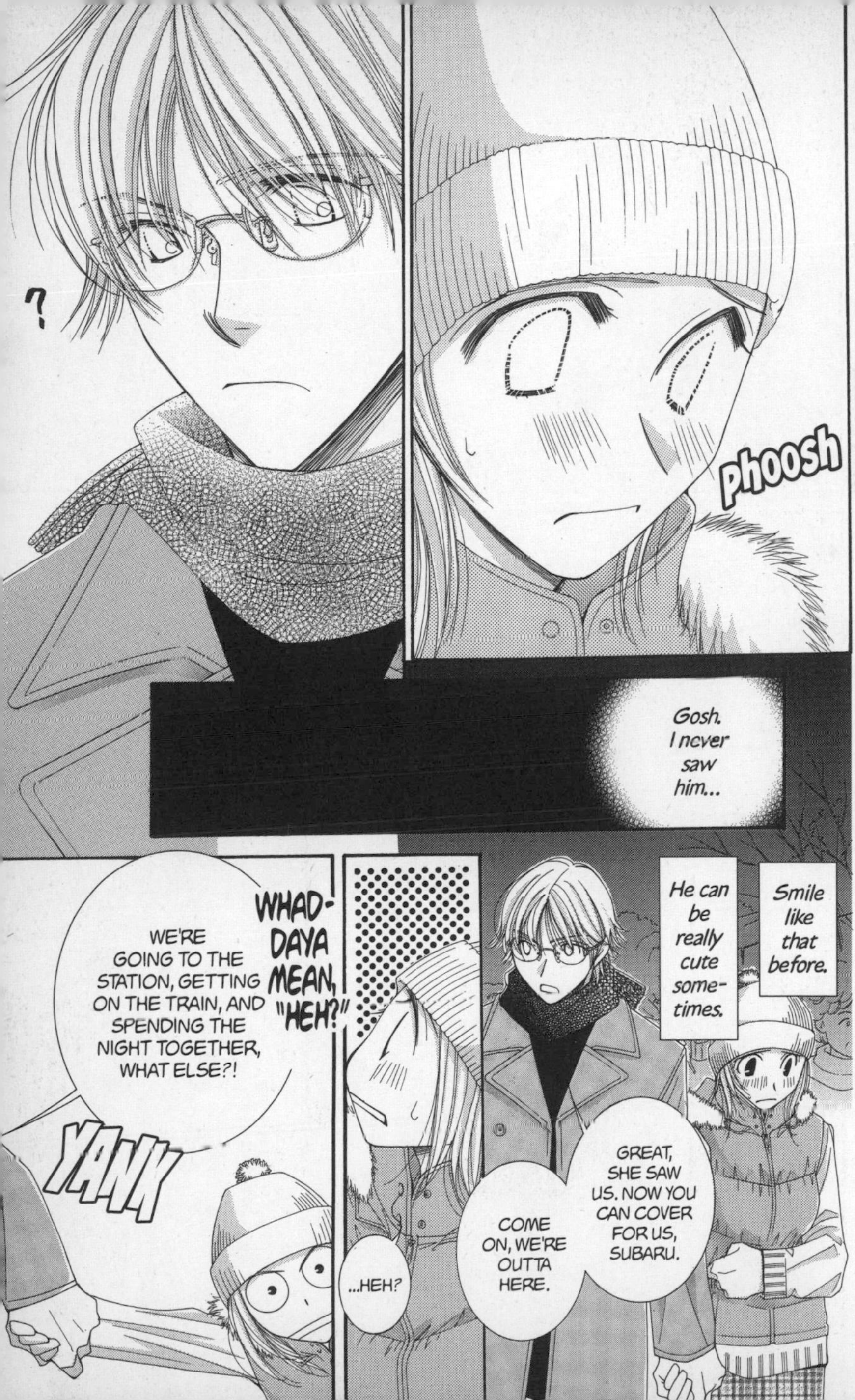

phoosh
?
Gosh. I never saw him...
Smile like that before.
He can be really cute some-times.
GREAT, SHE SAW US. NOW YOU CAN COVER FOR US, SUBARU.
COME ON, WE'RE OUTTA HERE.
...HEH?
WHAD-DAYA MEAN, "HEH?"
WE'RE GOING TO THE STATION, GETTING ON THE TRAIN, AND SPENDING THE NIGHT TOGETHER, WHAT ELSE?!
YANK

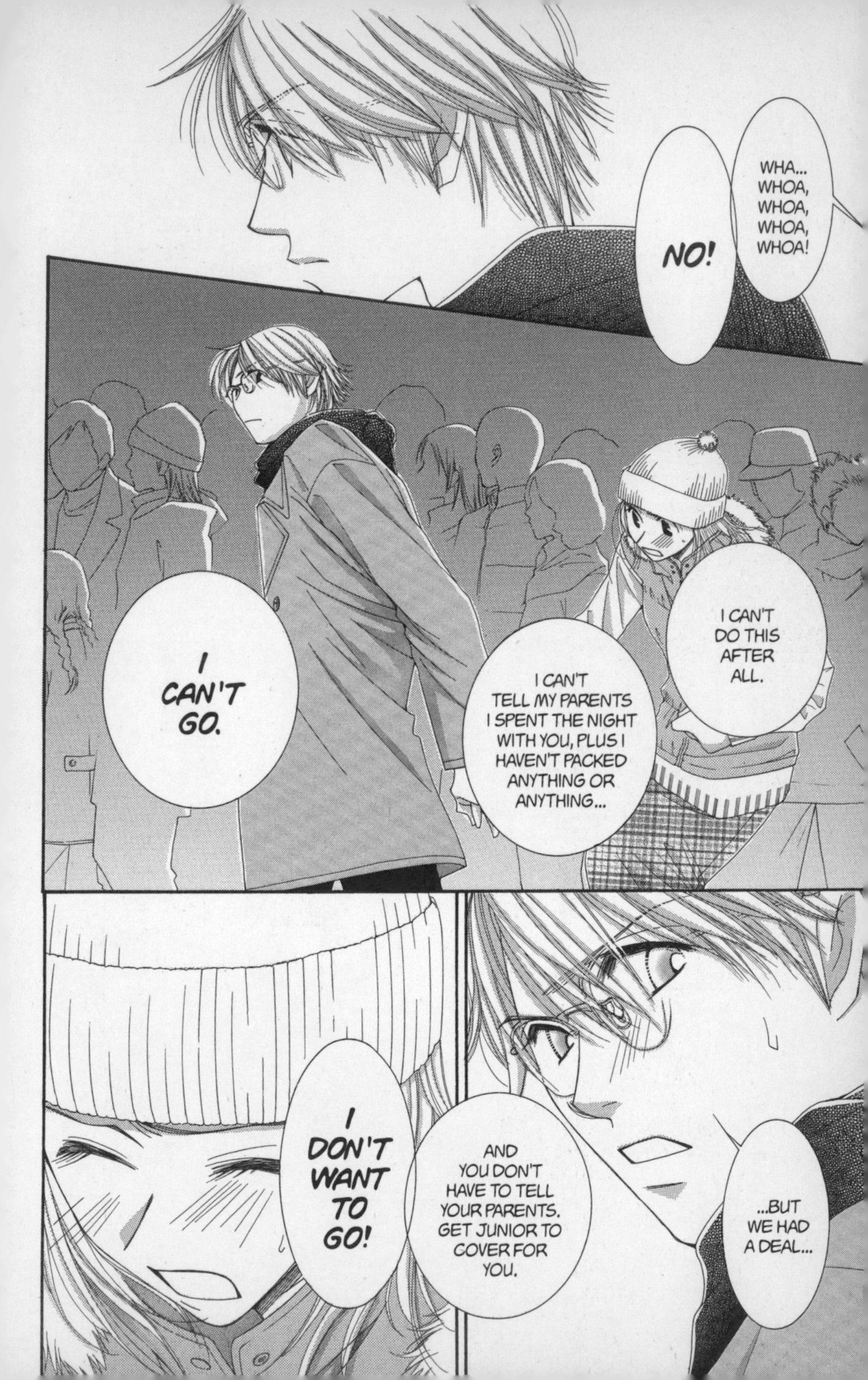
WHA... WHOA, WHOA, WHOA, WHOA!
NO!
I CAN'T DO THIS AFTER ALL.
I CAN'T TELL MY PARENTS I SPENT THE NIGHT WITH YOU, PLUS I HAVEN'T PACKED ANYTHING OR ANYTHING...
I CAN'T GO.
...BUT WE HAD A DEAL...
AND YOU DON'T HAVE TO TELL YOUR PARENTS. GET JUNIOR TO COVER FOR YOU.
I DON'T WANT TO GO!

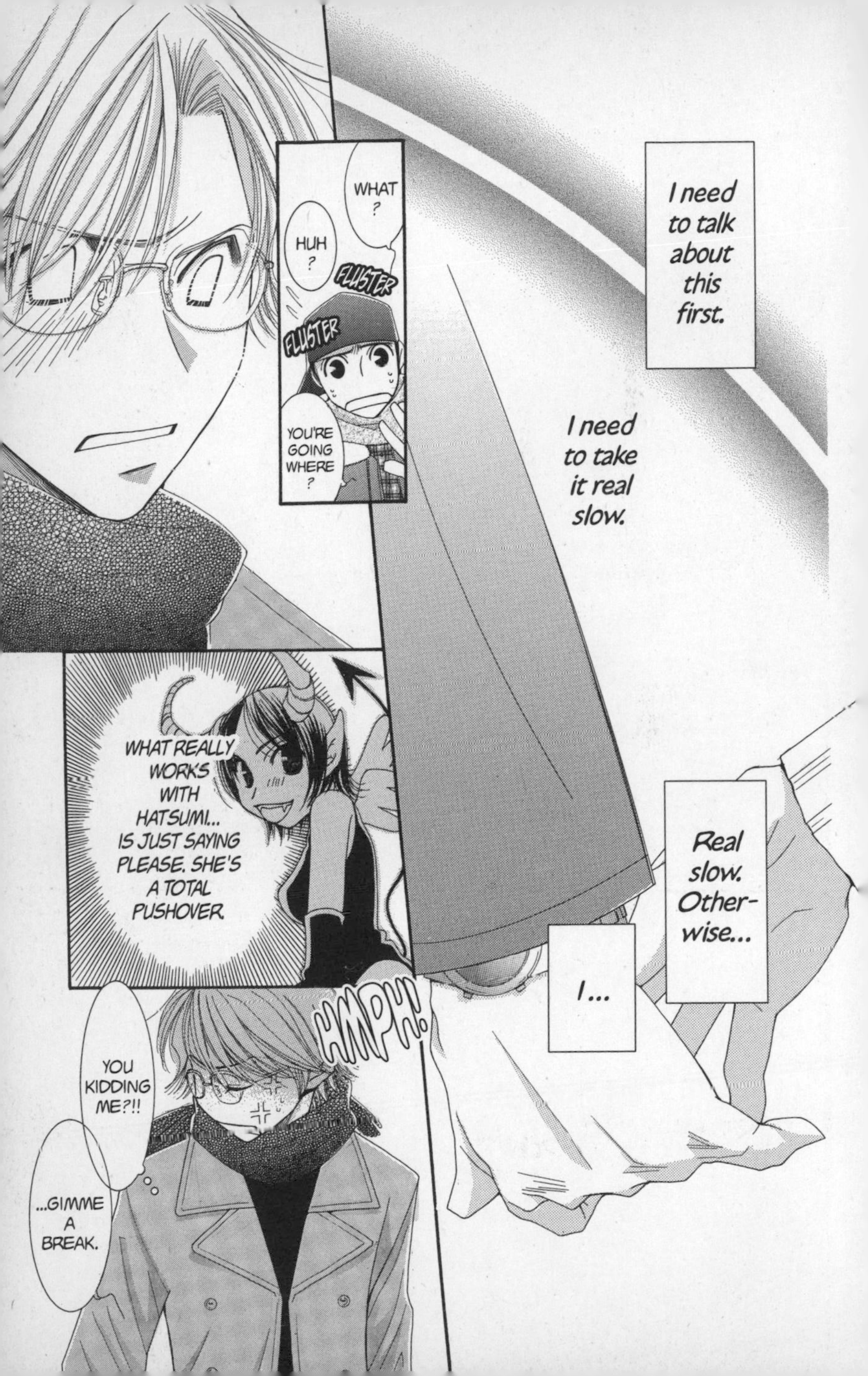
I need to talk about this first.
WHAT?
HUH?
FLUSTER
FLUSTER
YOU'RE GOING WHERE?
I need to take it real slow.
Real slow. Otherwise...
I...
WHAT REALLY WORKS WITH HATSUMI... IS JUST SAYING PLEASE. SHE'S A TOTAL PUSHOVER.
HMPH!
YOU KIDDING ME?!!
...GIMME A BREAK.

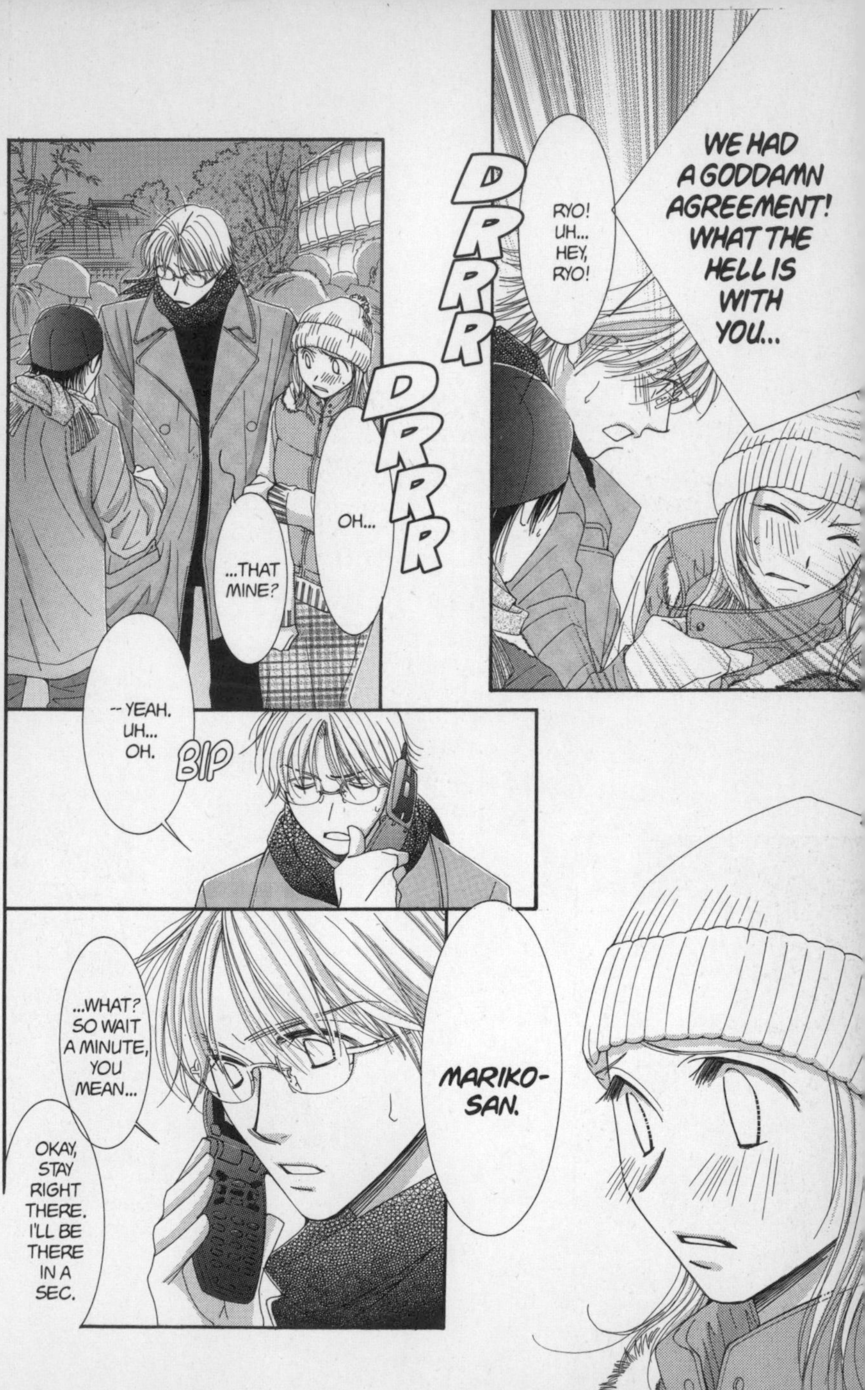
WE HAD A GODDAMN AGREEMENT! WHAT THE HELL IS WITH YOU...
RYO! UH... HEY, RYO!
DRRR
DRRR
OH...
...THAT MINE?
-- YEAH. UH... OH.
BIP
MARIKO-SAN.
...WHAT? SO WAIT A MINUTE, YOU MEAN...
OKAY, STAY RIGHT THERE. I'LL BE THERE IN A SEC.

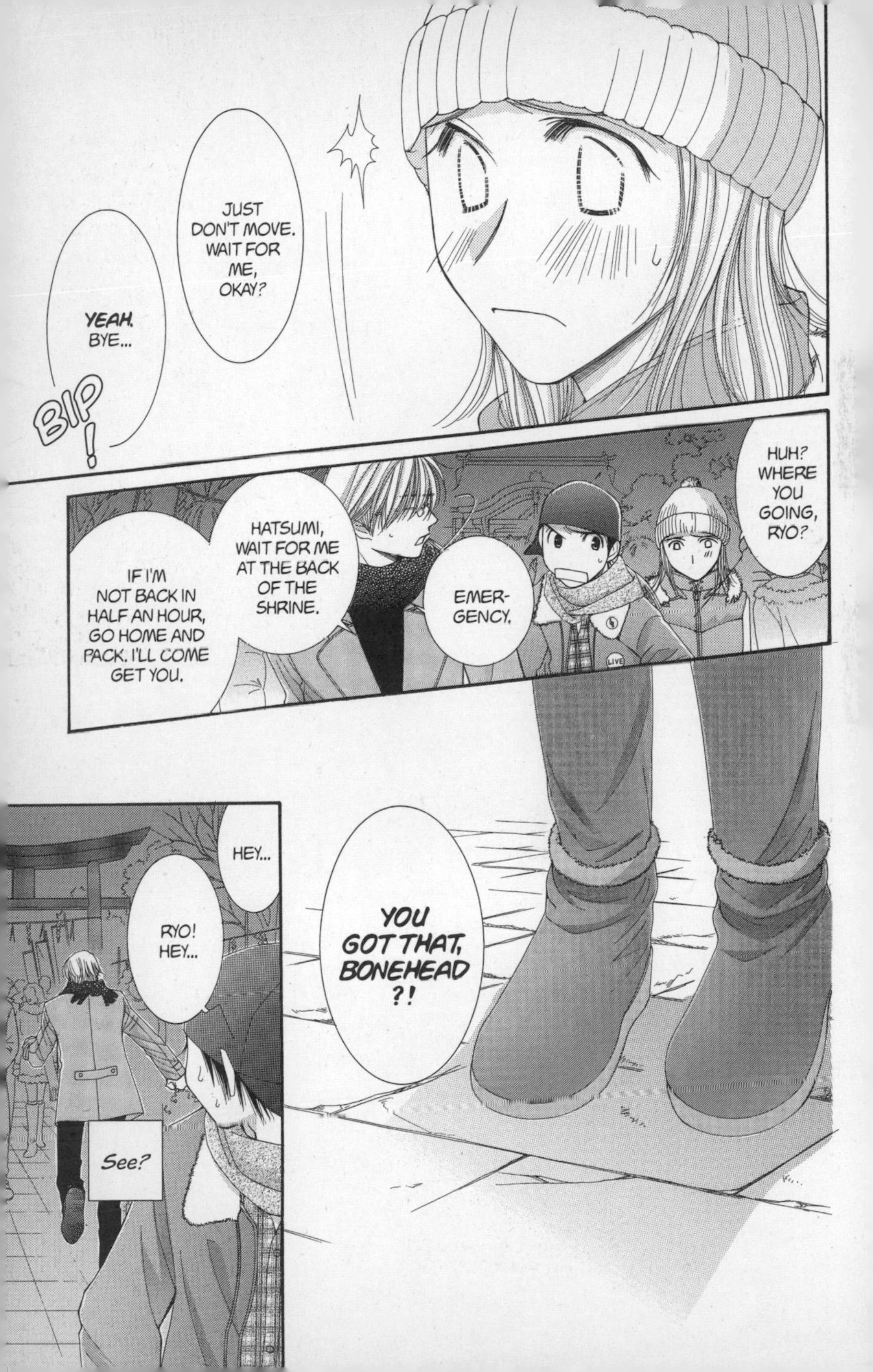
JUST DON'T MOVE. WAIT FOR ME, OKAY?
YEAH. BYE...
BIP!
HUH? WHERE YOU GOING, RYO?
EMERGENCY.
HATSUMI, WAIT FOR ME AT THE BACK OF THE SHRINE.
IF I'M NOT BACK IN HALF AN HOUR, GO HOME AND PACK. I'LL COME GET YOU.
YOU GOT THAT, BONEHEAD?!
HEY...
RYO! HEY...
See?

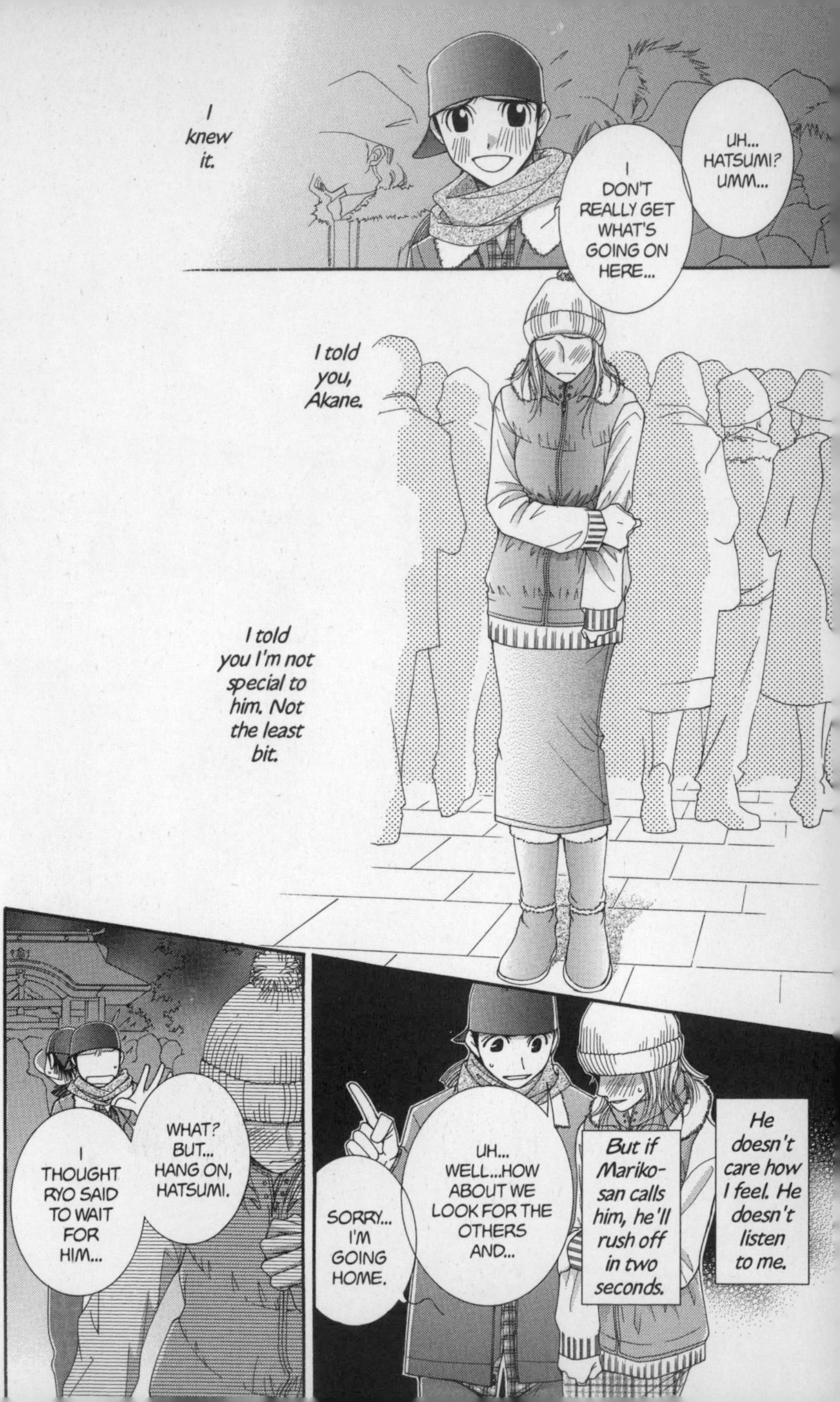
UH... HATSUMI? UMM...
I DON'T REALLY GET WHAT'S GOING ON HERE...
I knew it.
I told you, Akane.
I told you I'm not special to him. Not the least bit.
He doesn't care how I feel. He doesn't listen to me.
But if Mariko-san calls him, he'll rush off in two seconds.
UH... WELL...HOW ABOUT WE LOOK FOR THE OTHERS AND...
SORRY... I'M GOING HOME.
WHAT? BUT... HANG ON, HATSUMI.
I THOUGHT RYO SAID TO WAIT FOR HIM...

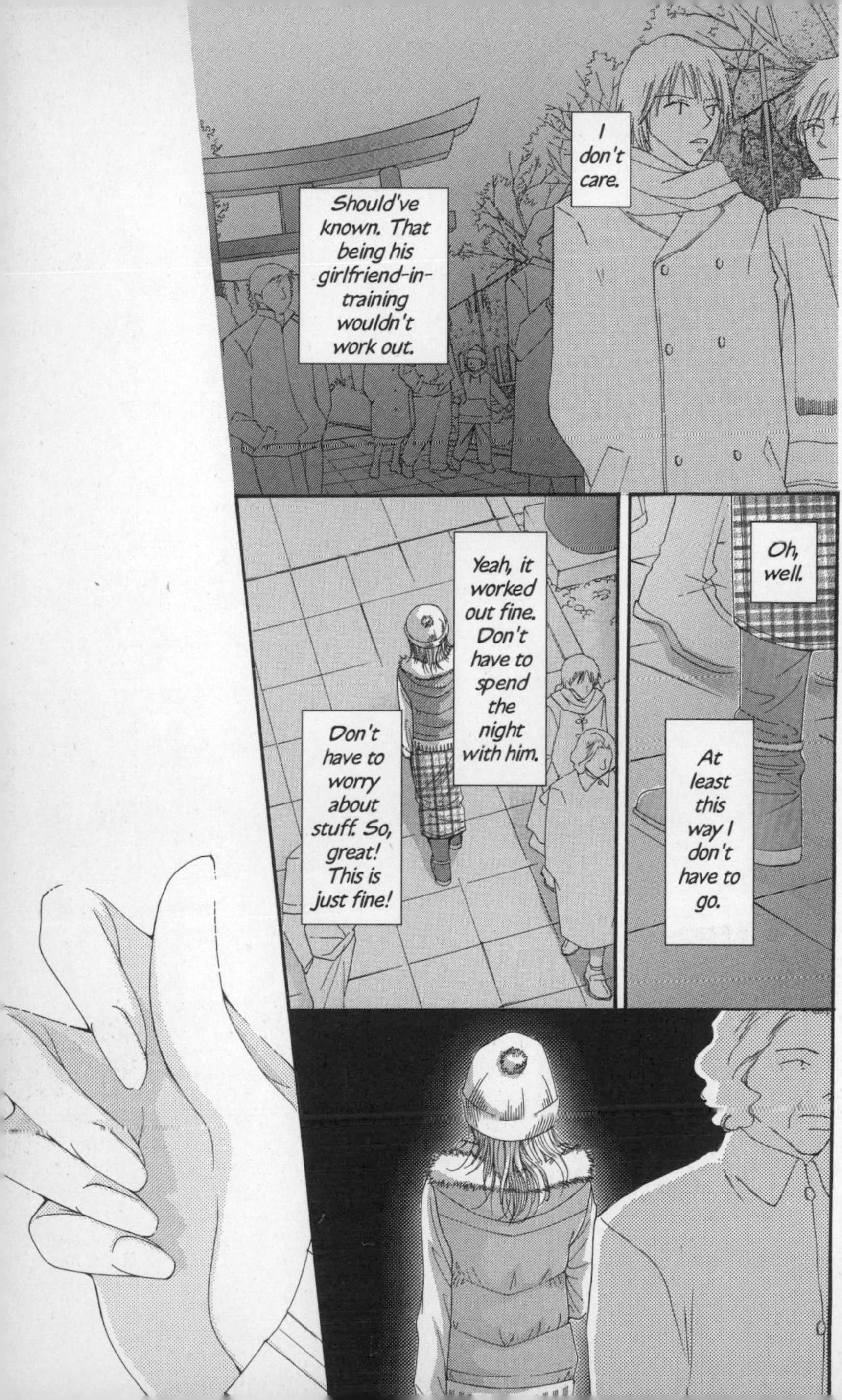
I don't care.
Should've known. That being his girlfriend-in-training wouldn't work out.
Oh, well.
At least this way I don't have to go.
Yeah, it worked out fine. Don't have to spend the night with him.
Don't have to worry about stuff. So, great! This is just fine!

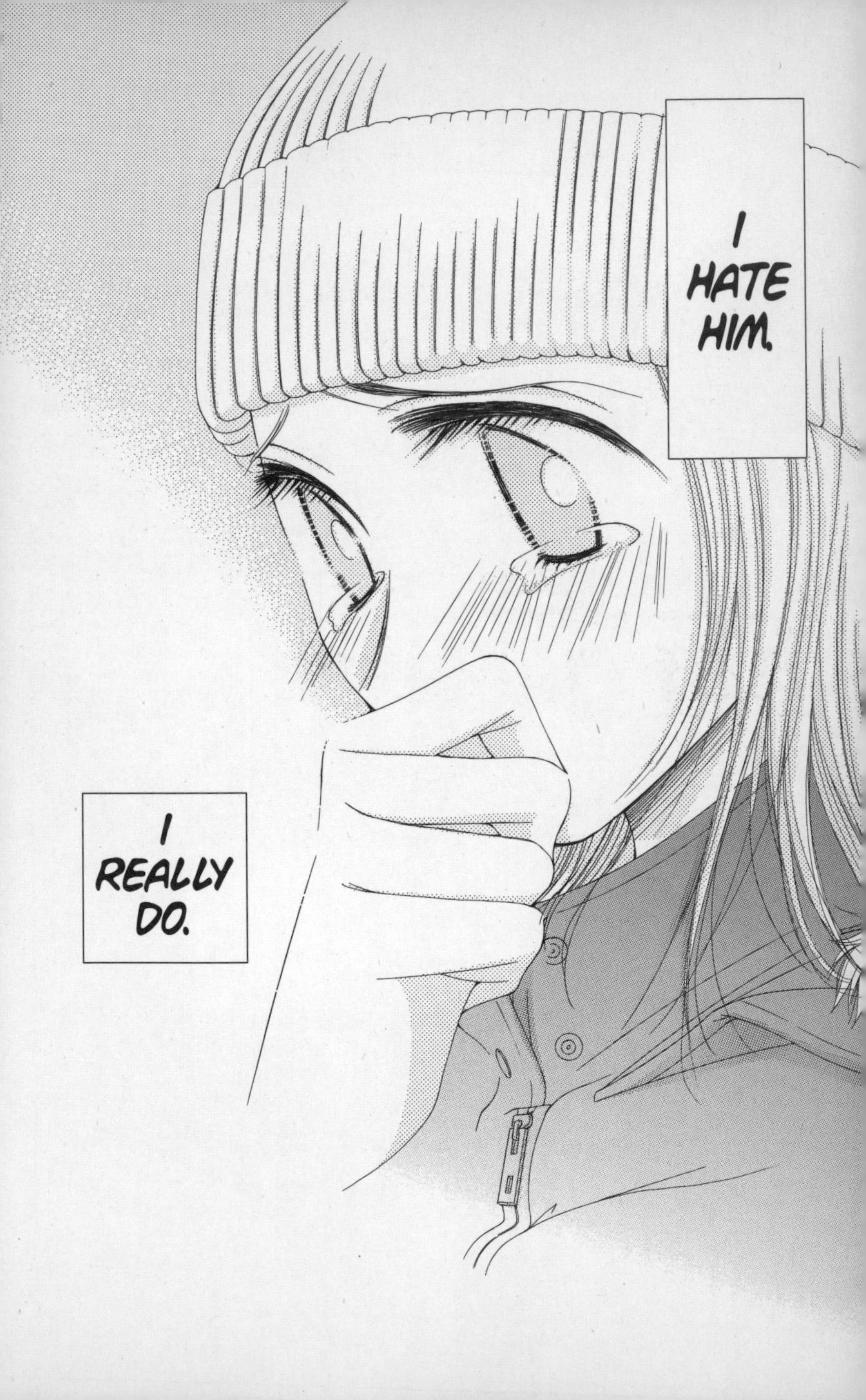
I HATE HIM.
I REALLY DO.

hotgimmick

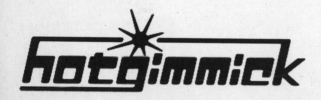

PART 2
OF CHAPTER 26
PRESENTS
RYOKI'S POINT
OF VIEW...

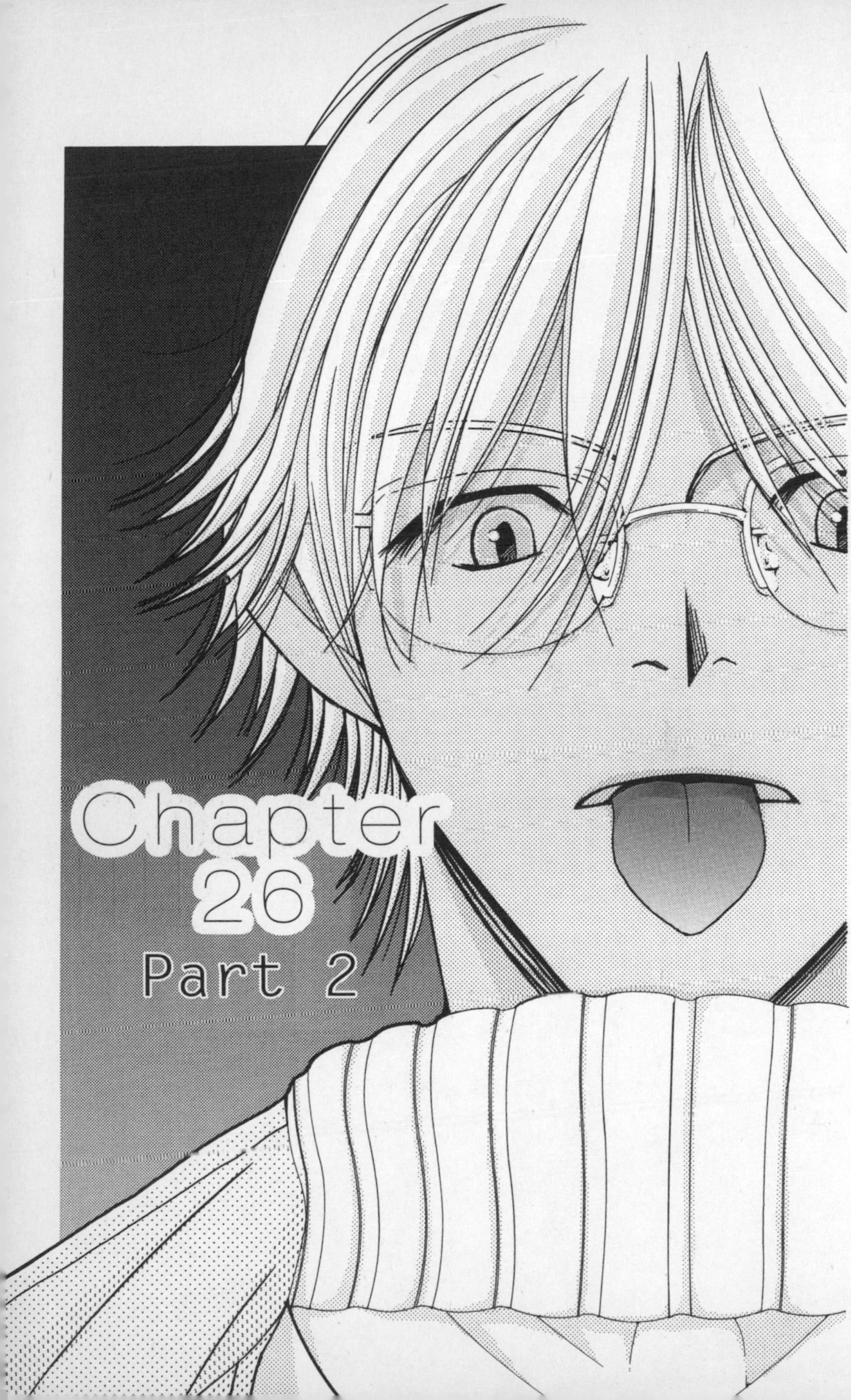
Chapter
26
Part 2

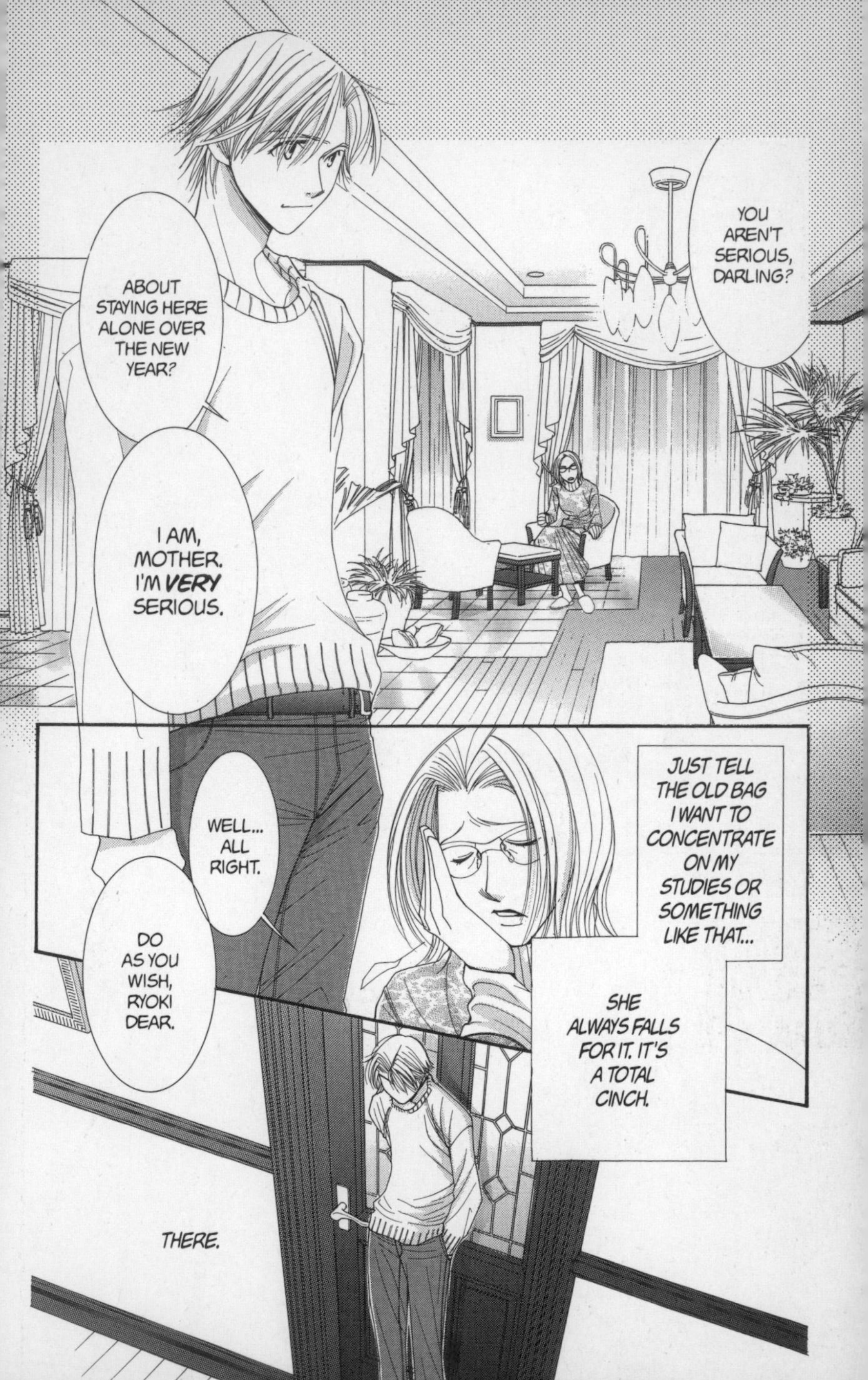
YOU AREN'T SERIOUS, DARLING?
ABOUT STAYING HERE ALONE OVER THE NEW YEAR?
I AM, MOTHER. I'M **VERY** SERIOUS.
JUST TELL THE OLD BAG I WANT TO CONCENTRATE ON MY STUDIES OR SOMETHING LIKE THAT...
WELL... ALL RIGHT.
DO AS YOU WISH, RYOKI DEAR.
SHE ALWAYS FALLS FOR IT. IT'S A TOTAL CINCH.
THERE.

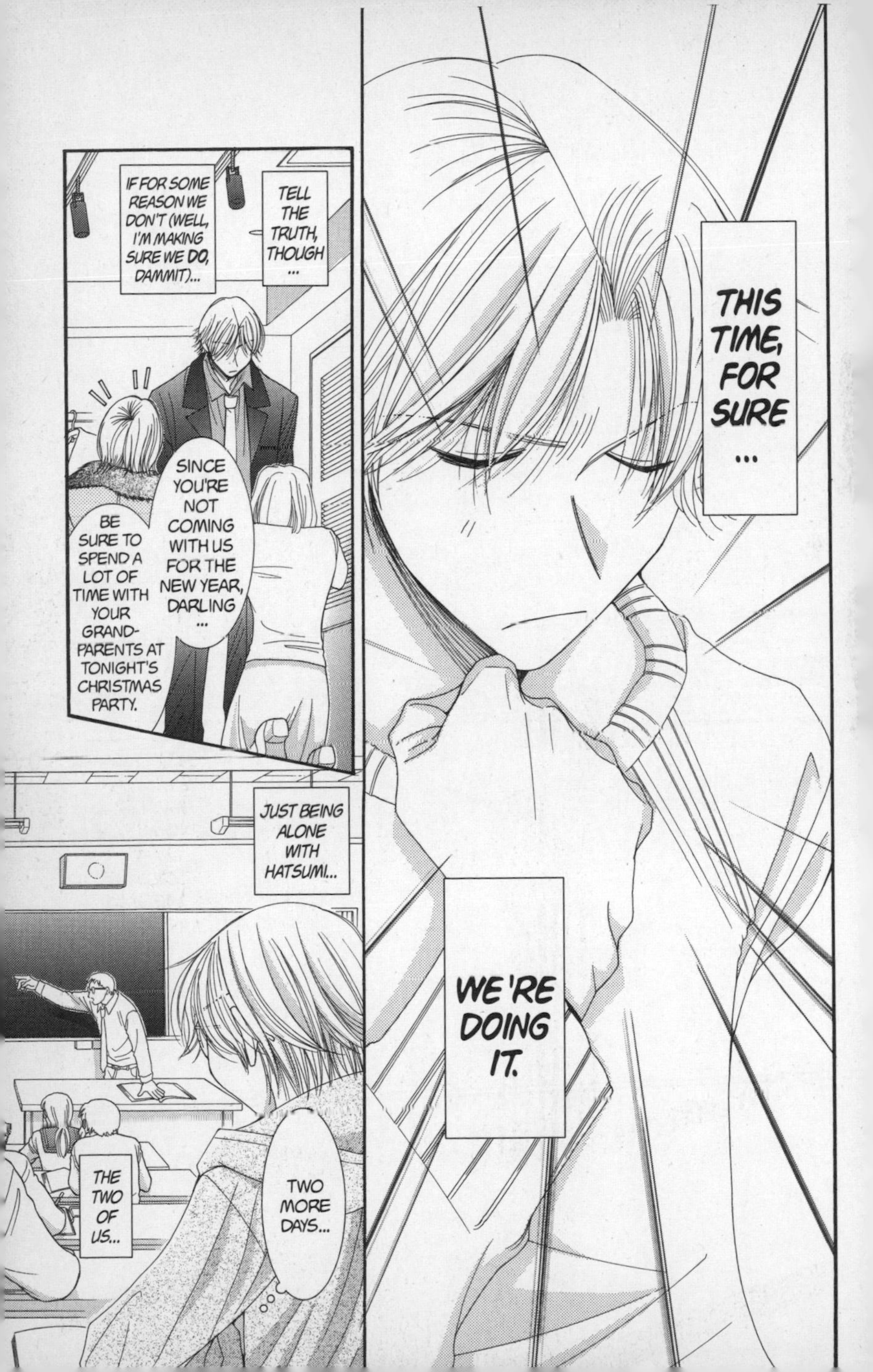
THIS TIME, FOR SURE ...
WE'RE DOING IT.
TELL THE TRUTH, THOUGH ...
IF FOR SOME REASON WE DON'T (WELL, I'M MAKING SURE WE DO, DAMMIT)...
SINCE YOU'RE NOT COMING WITH US FOR THE NEW YEAR, DARLING ...
BE SURE TO SPEND A LOT OF TIME WITH YOUR GRAND-PARENTS AT TONIGHT'S CHRISTMAS PARTY.
JUST BEING ALONE WITH HATSUMI...
TWO MORE DAYS...
THE TWO OF US...

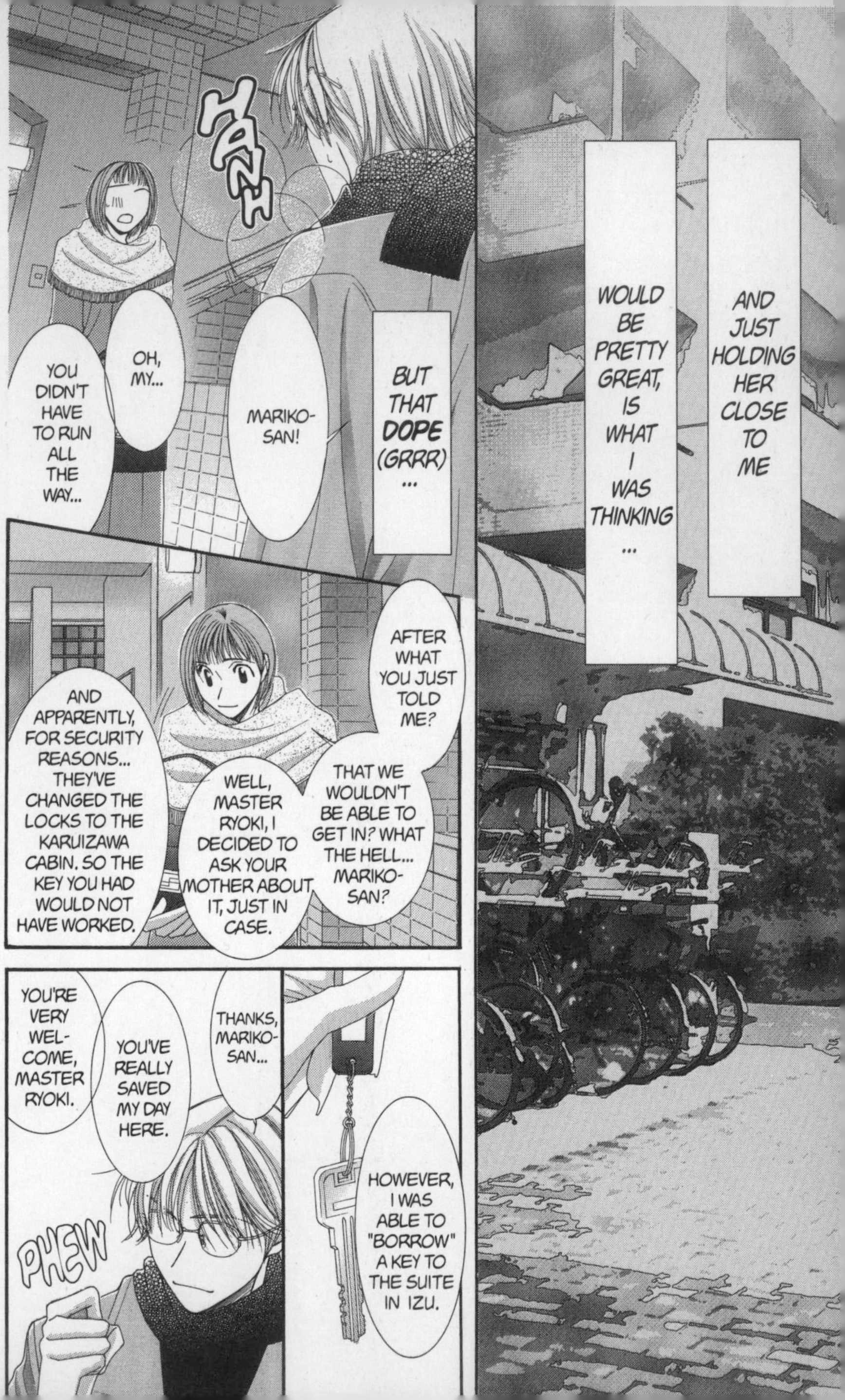
AND JUST HOLDING HER CLOSE TO ME
WOULD BE PRETTY GREAT, IS WHAT I WAS THINKING...
BUT THAT DOPE (GRRR)...
HANH
MARIKO-SAN!
OH, MY...
YOU DIDN'T HAVE TO RUN ALL THE WAY...
AFTER WHAT YOU JUST TOLD ME?
THAT WE WOULDN'T BE ABLE TO GET IN? WHAT THE HELL... MARIKO-SAN?
WELL, MASTER RYOKI, I DECIDED TO ASK YOUR MOTHER ABOUT IT, JUST IN CASE.
AND APPARENTLY, FOR SECURITY REASONS... THEY'VE CHANGED THE LOCKS TO THE KARUIZAWA CABIN. SO THE KEY YOU HAD WOULD NOT HAVE WORKED.
HOWEVER, I WAS ABLE TO "BORROW" A KEY TO THE SUITE IN IZU.
THANKS, MARIKO-SAN...
YOU'VE REALLY SAVED MY DAY HERE.
YOU'RE VERY WEL-COME, MASTER RYOKI.
PHEW

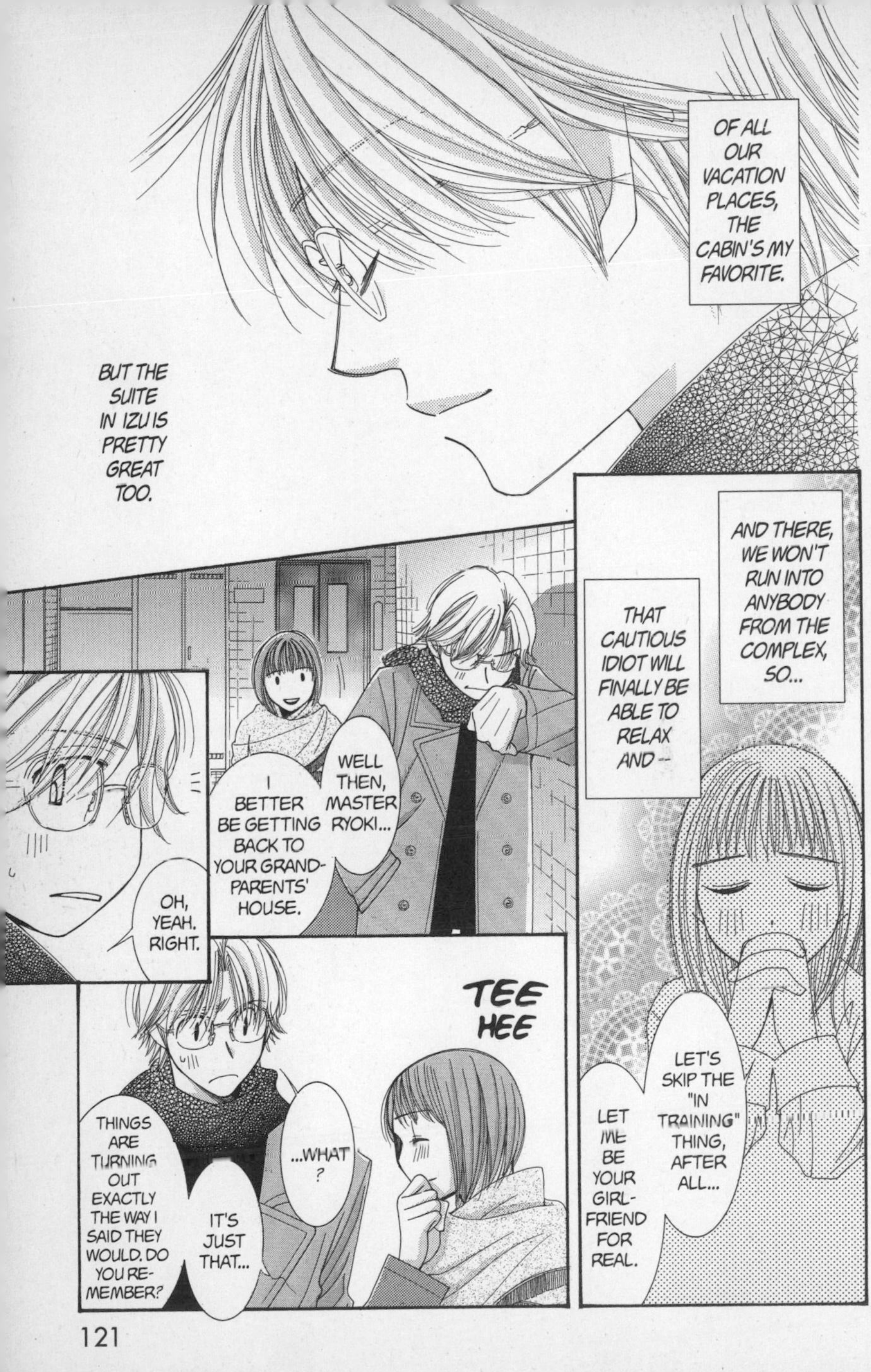
OF ALL OUR VACATION PLACES, THE CABIN'S MY FAVORITE.
BUT THE SUITE IN IZU IS PRETTY GREAT TOO.
AND THERE, WE WON'T RUN INTO ANYBODY FROM THE COMPLEX, SO...
THAT CAUTIOUS IDIOT WILL FINALLY BE ABLE TO RELAX AND--
LET'S SKIP THE "IN TRAINING" THING, AFTER ALL...
LET ME BE YOUR GIRL-FRIEND FOR REAL.
WELL THEN, MASTER RYOKI...
I BETTER BE GETTING BACK TO YOUR GRAND-PARENTS' HOUSE.
OH, YEAH. RIGHT.
TEE HEE
...WHAT?
IT'S JUST THAT...
THINGS ARE TURNING OUT EXACTLY THE WAY I SAID THEY WOULD. DO YOU RE-MEMBER?

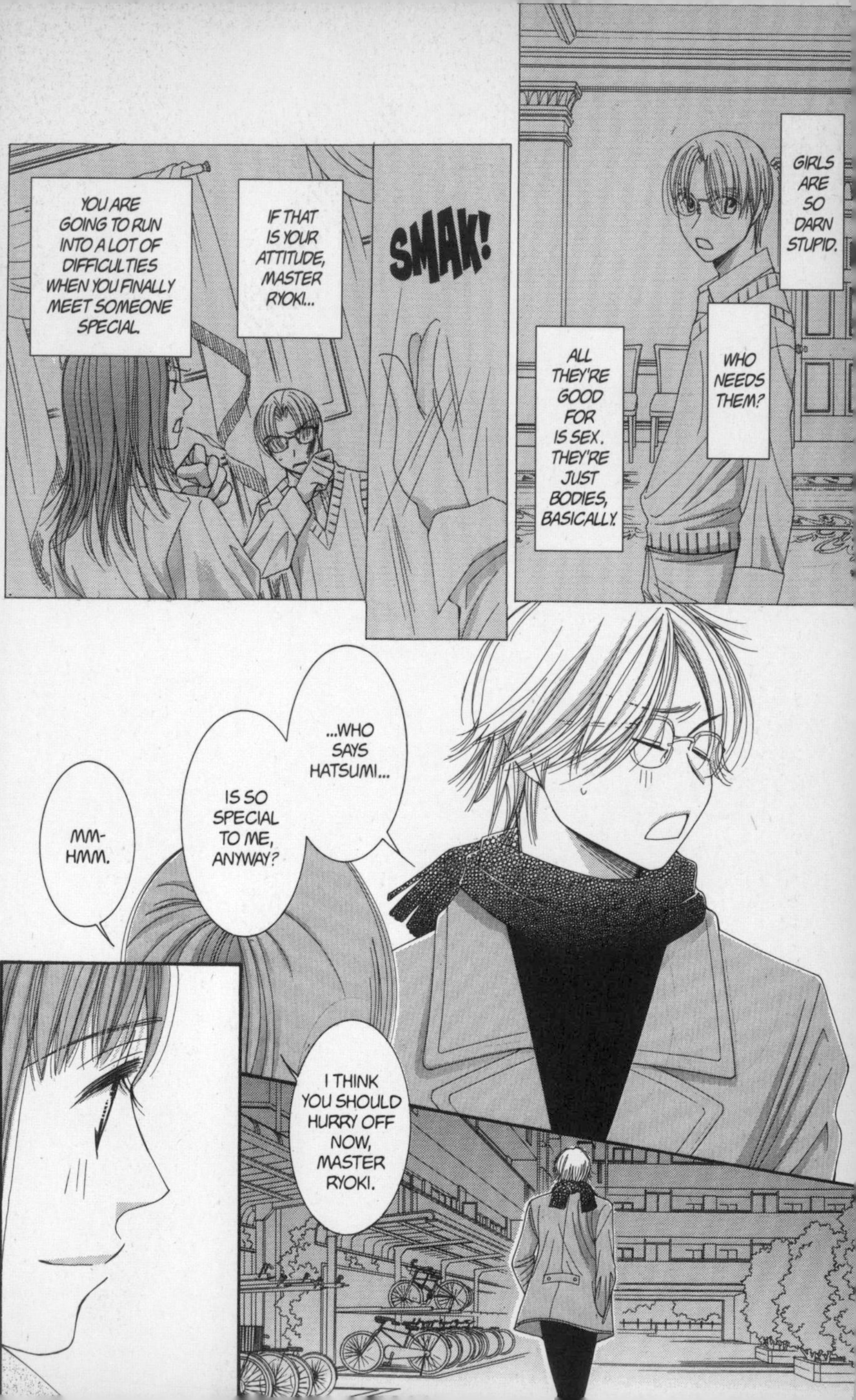
GIRLS ARE SO DARN STUPID.
WHO NEEDS THEM?
ALL THEY'RE GOOD FOR IS SEX. THEY'RE JUST BODIES, BASICALLY.
SMAK!
IF THAT IS YOUR ATTITUDE, MASTER RYOKI...
YOU ARE GOING TO RUN INTO A LOT OF DIFFICULTIES WHEN YOU FINALLY MEET SOMEONE SPECIAL.
...WHO SAYS HATSUMI...
IS SO SPECIAL TO ME, ANYWAY?
MM-HMM.
I THINK YOU SHOULD HURRY OFF NOW, MASTER RYOKI.

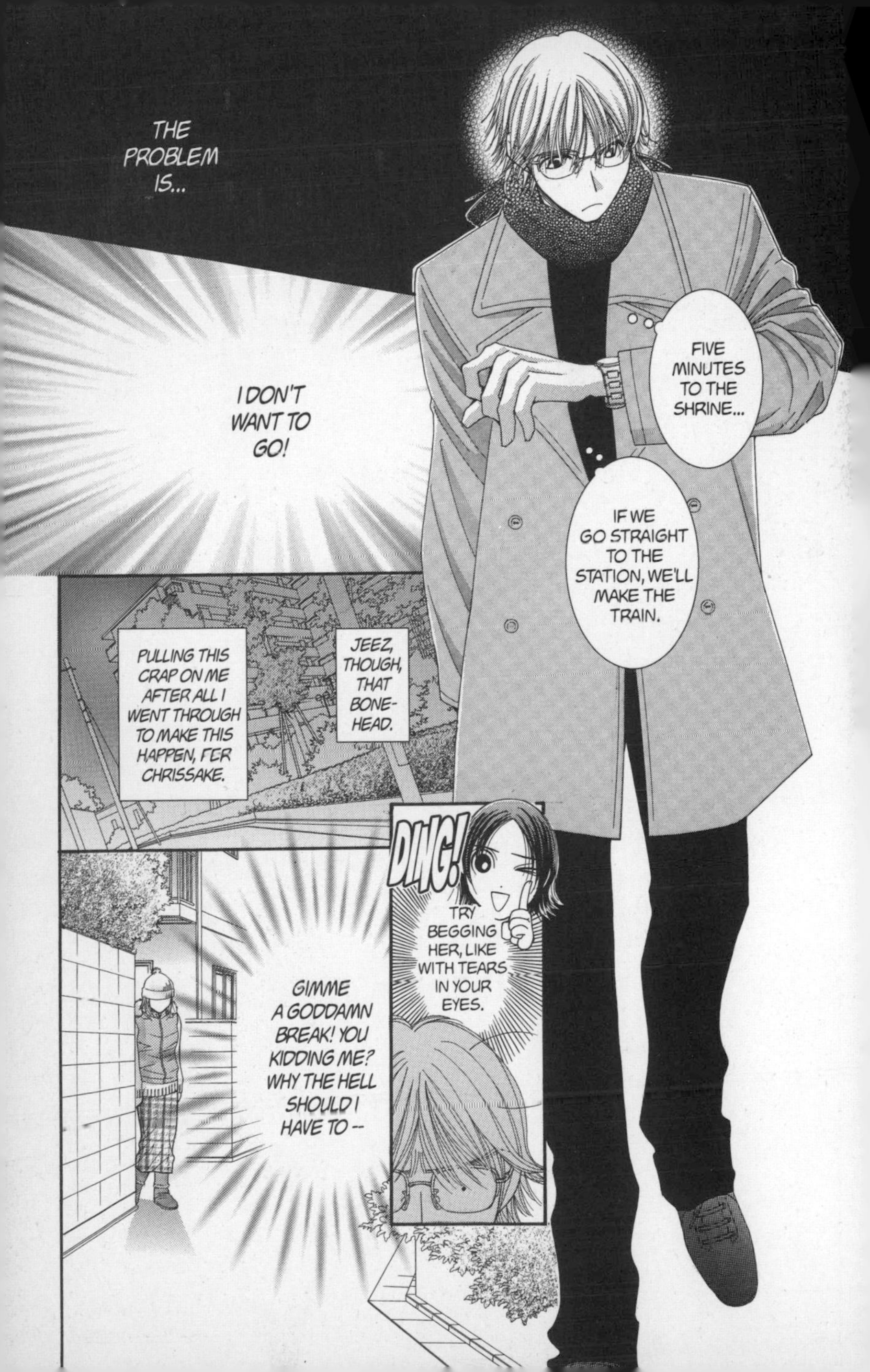
FIVE MINUTES TO THE SHRINE...
IF WE GO STRAIGHT TO THE STATION, WE'LL MAKE THE TRAIN.
THE PROBLEM IS...
I DON'T WANT TO GO!
JEEZ, THOUGH, THAT BONE-HEAD.
PULLING THIS CRAP ON ME AFTER ALL I WENT THROUGH TO MAKE THIS HAPPEN, FER CHRISSAKE.
DING!
TRY BEGGING HER, LIKE WITH TEARS IN YOUR EYES.
GIMME A GODDAMN BREAK! YOU KIDDING ME? WHY THE HELL SHOULD I HAVE TO --

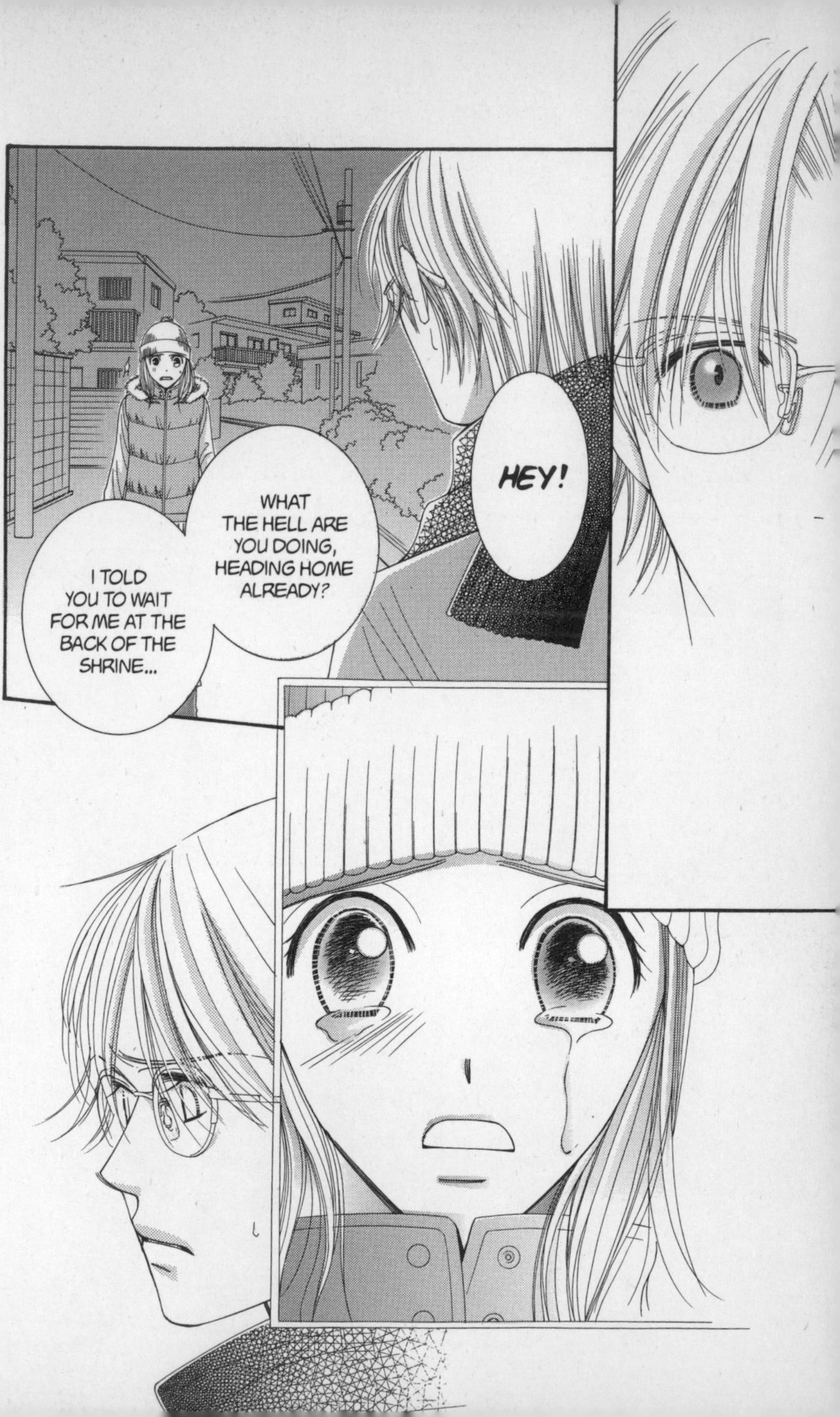
HEY!
WHAT THE HELL ARE YOU DOING, HEADING HOME ALREADY?
I TOLD YOU TO WAIT FOR ME AT THE BACK OF THE SHRINE...

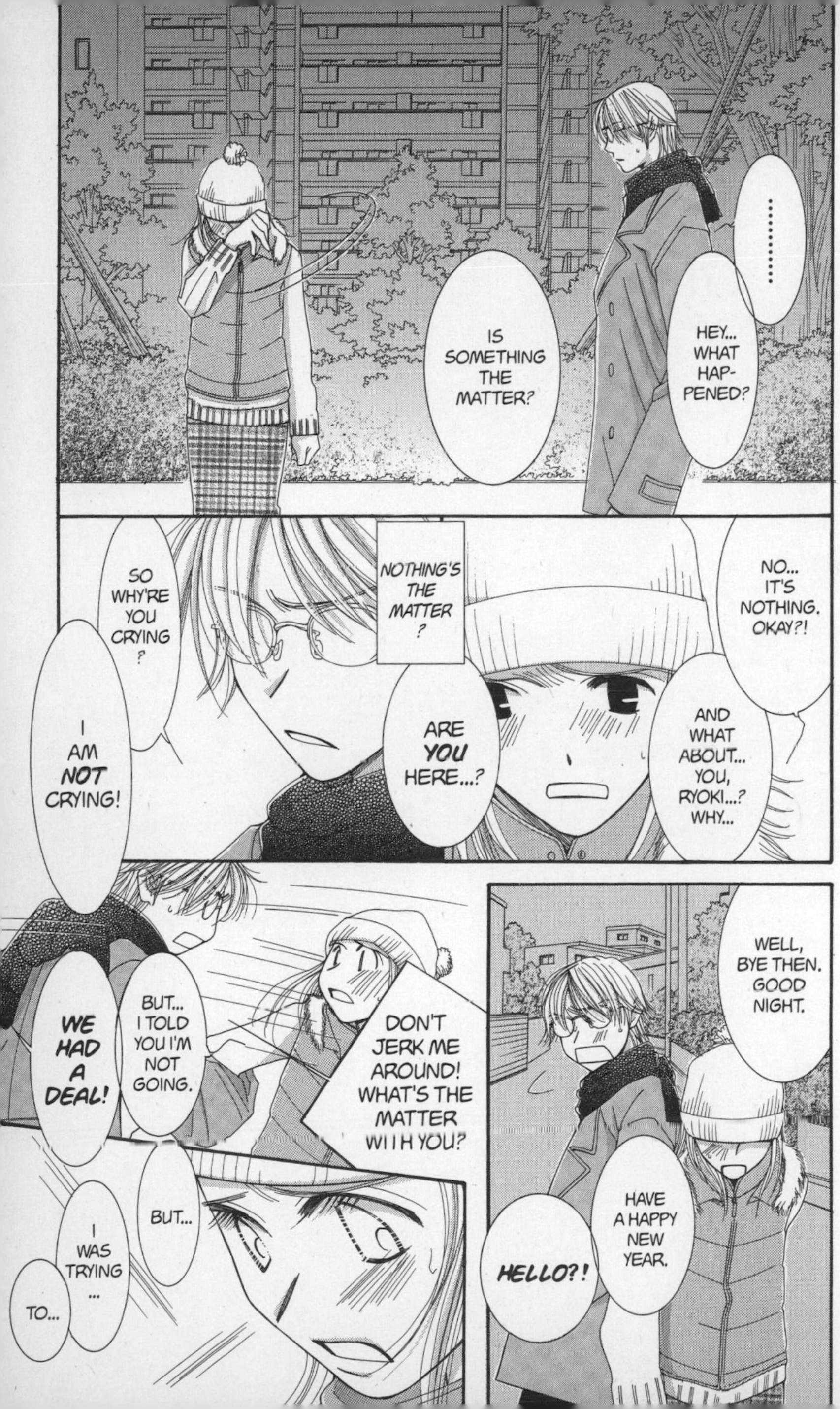
......
HEY... WHAT HAP-PENED?
IS SOMETHING THE MATTER?
NO... IT'S NOTHING. OKAY?!
AND WHAT ABOUT... YOU, RYOKI...? WHY...
ARE YOU HERE...?
NOTHING'S THE MATTER?
SO WHY'RE YOU CRYING?
I AM NOT CRYING!
WELL, BYE THEN. GOOD NIGHT.
HAVE A HAPPY NEW YEAR.
HELLO?!
DON'T JERK ME AROUND! WHAT'S THE MATTER WITH YOU?
BUT... I TOLD YOU I'M NOT GOING.
WE HAD A DEAL!
BUT...
I WAS TRYING...
TO...

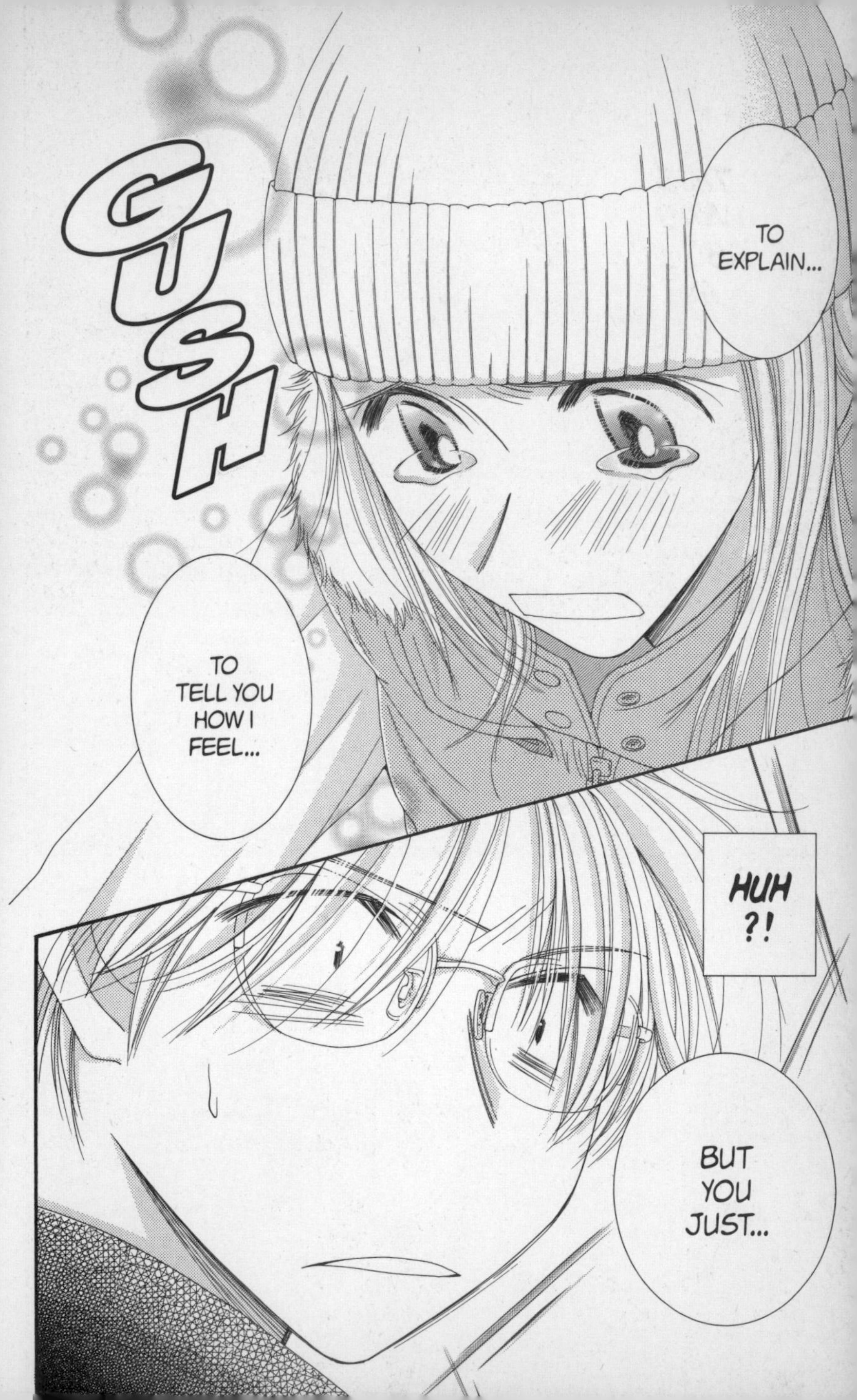
TO EXPLAIN...
GUSH
TO TELL YOU HOW I FEEL...
HUH ?!
BUT YOU JUST...

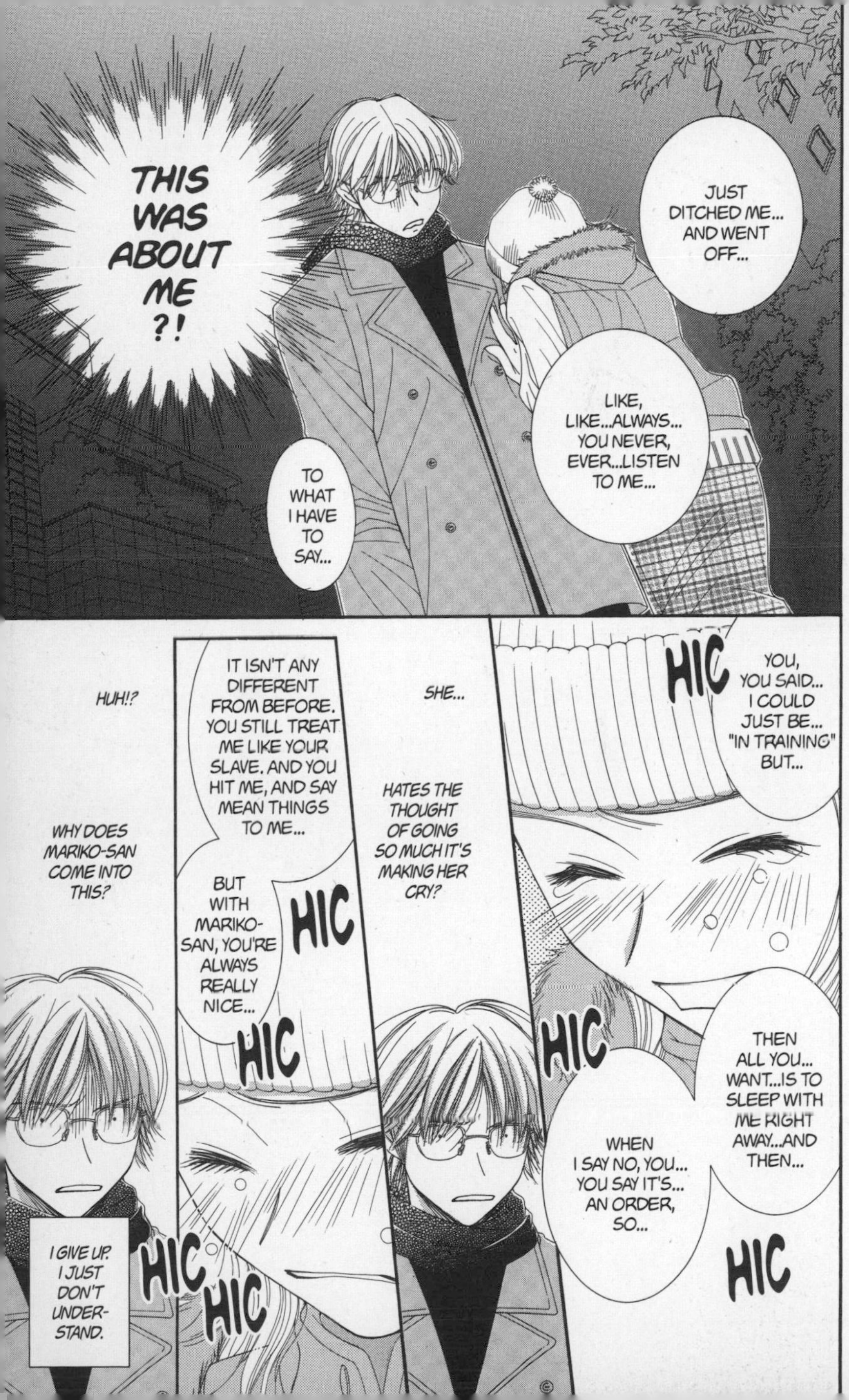
JUST DITCHED ME... AND WENT OFF...
LIKE, LIKE...ALWAYS... YOU NEVER, EVER...LISTEN TO ME...
TO WHAT I HAVE TO SAY...
THIS WAS ABOUT ME?!
HIC
YOU, YOU SAID... I COULD JUST BE... "IN TRAINING" BUT...
HIC
THEN ALL YOU... WANT...IS TO SLEEP WITH ME RIGHT AWAY...AND THEN...
WHEN I SAY NO, YOU... YOU SAY IT'S... AN ORDER, SO...
HIC
SHE...
HATES THE THOUGHT OF GOING SO MUCH IT'S MAKING HER CRY?
IT ISN'T ANY DIFFERENT FROM BEFORE. YOU STILL TREAT ME LIKE YOUR SLAVE. AND YOU HIT ME, AND SAY MEAN THINGS TO ME...
HIC
BUT WITH MARIKO-SAN, YOU'RE ALWAYS REALLY NICE...
HIC
HIC
HIC
HUH!?
WHY DOES MARIKO-SAN COME INTO THIS?
I GIVE UP. I JUST DON'T UNDER-STAND.

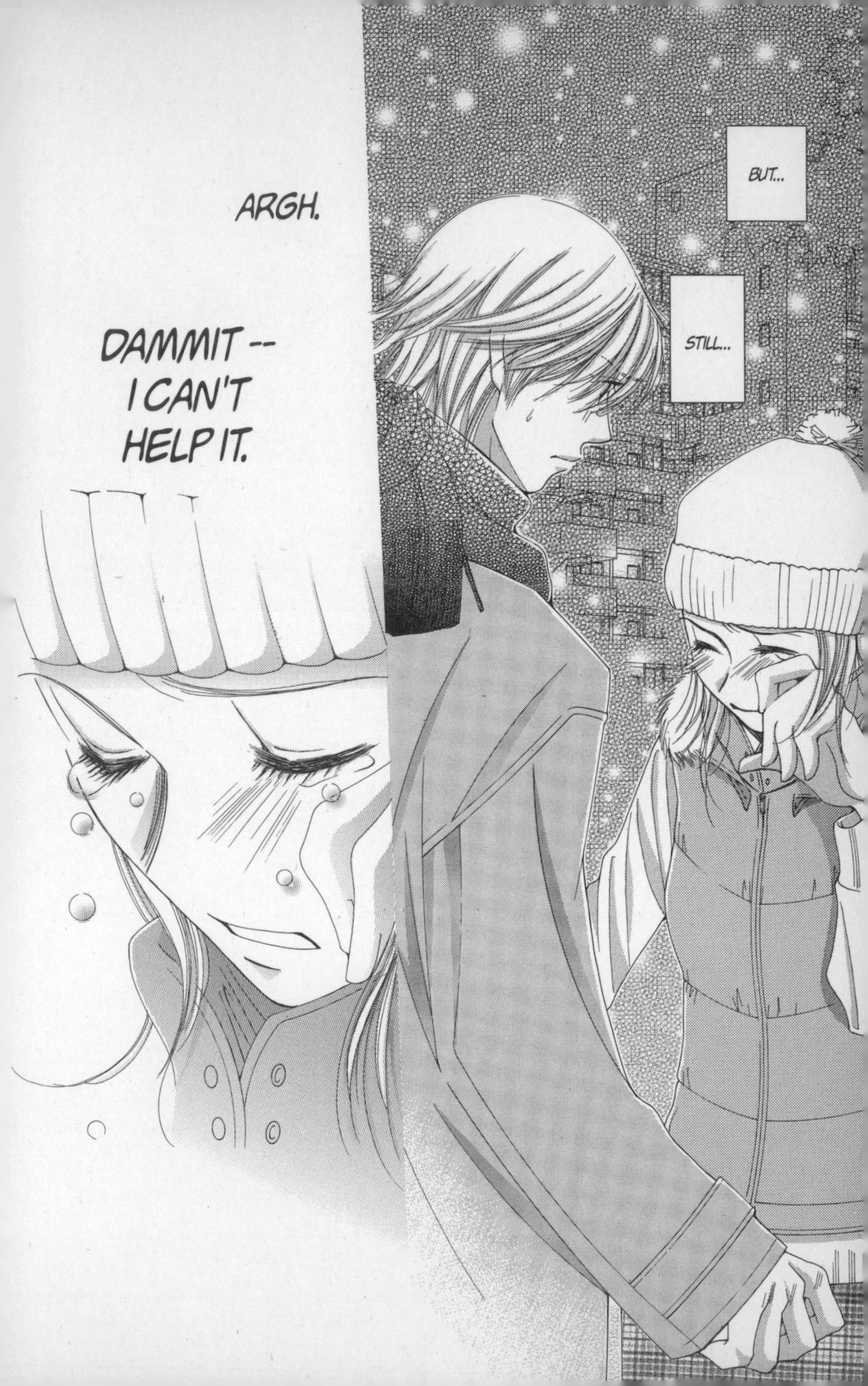
BUT...
STILL...
ARGH.
DAMMIT -- I CAN'T HELP IT.

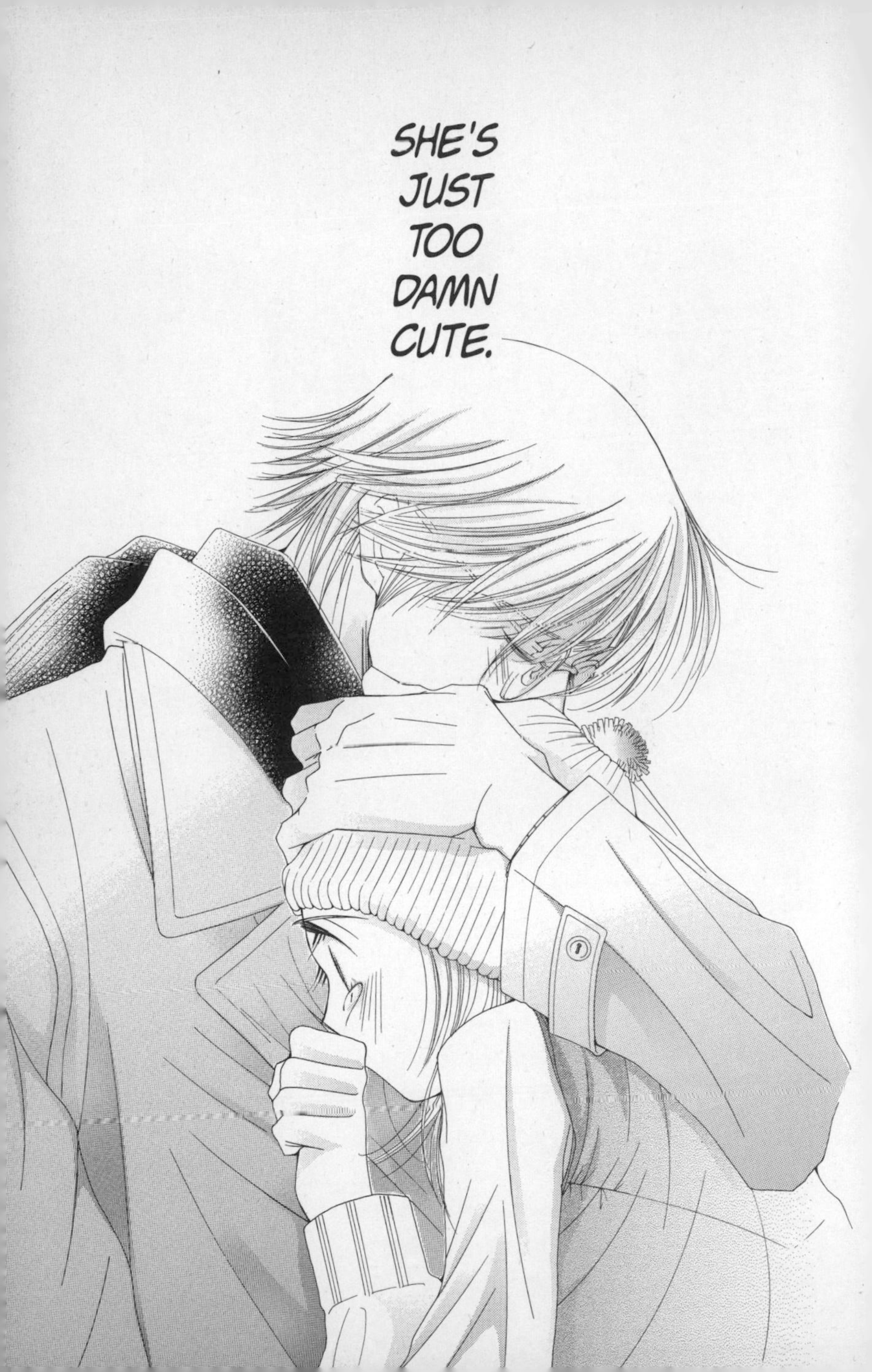
SHE'S JUST TOO DAMN CUTE.

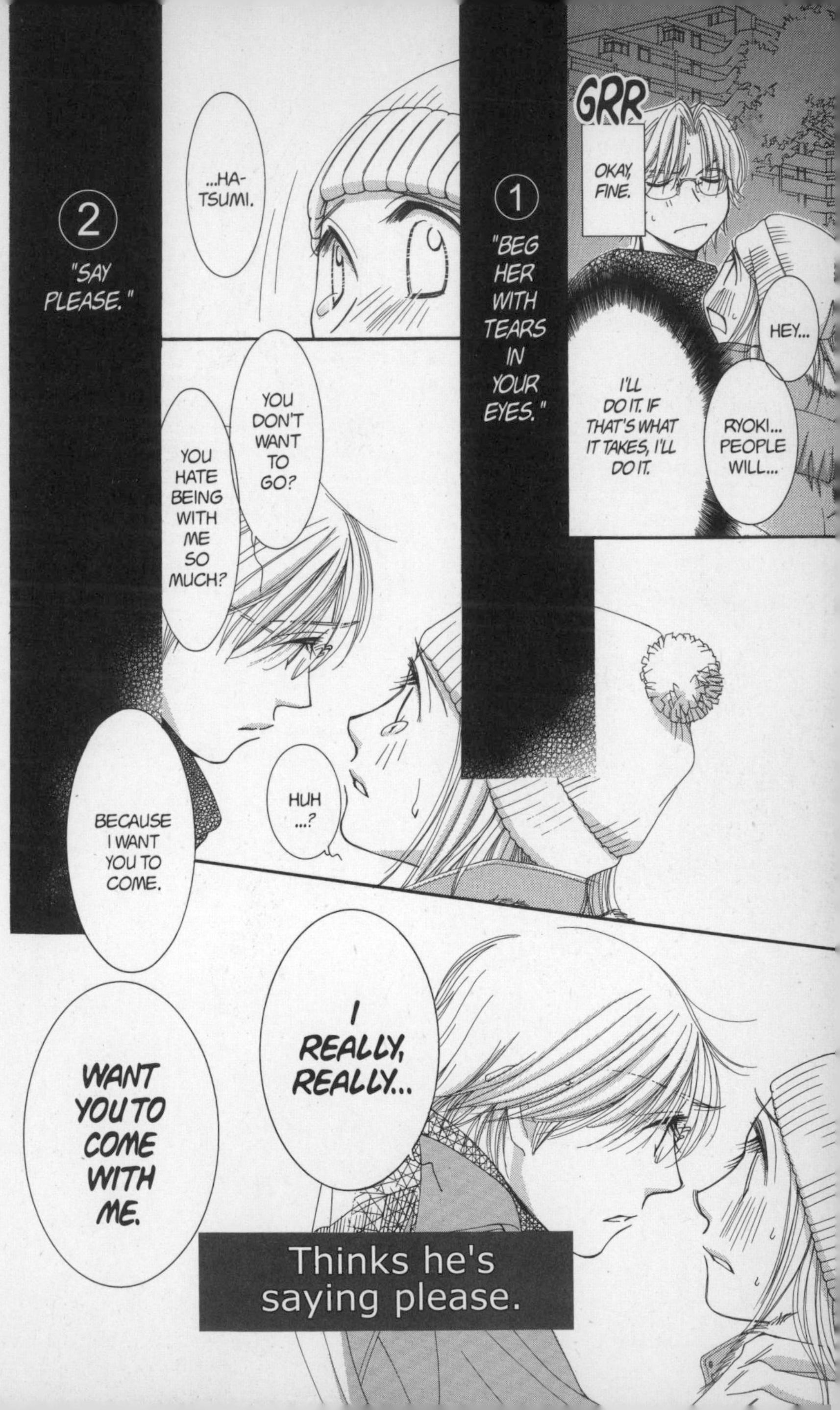
GRR
OKAY, FINE.
HEY...
RYOKI... PEOPLE WILL...
I'LL DO IT. IF THAT'S WHAT IT TAKES, I'LL DO IT.
1
"BEG HER WITH TEARS IN YOUR EYES."
...HA-TSUMI.
2
"SAY PLEASE."
YOU DON'T WANT TO GO?
YOU HATE BEING WITH ME SO MUCH?
HUH ...?
BECAUSE I WANT YOU TO COME.
I REALLY, REALLY...
WANT YOU TO COME WITH ME.
Thinks he's saying please.

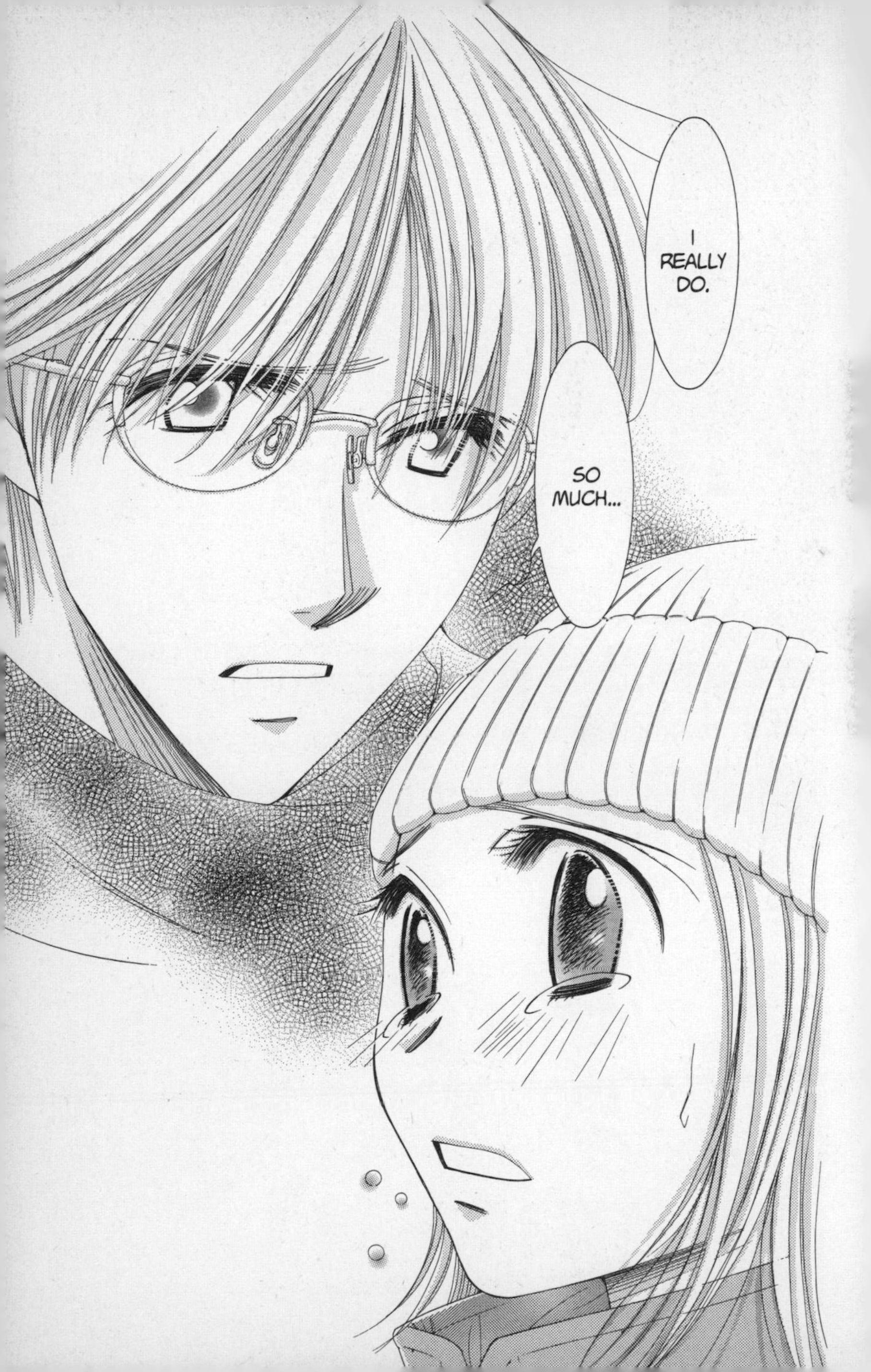
I REALLY DO.
SO MUCH...

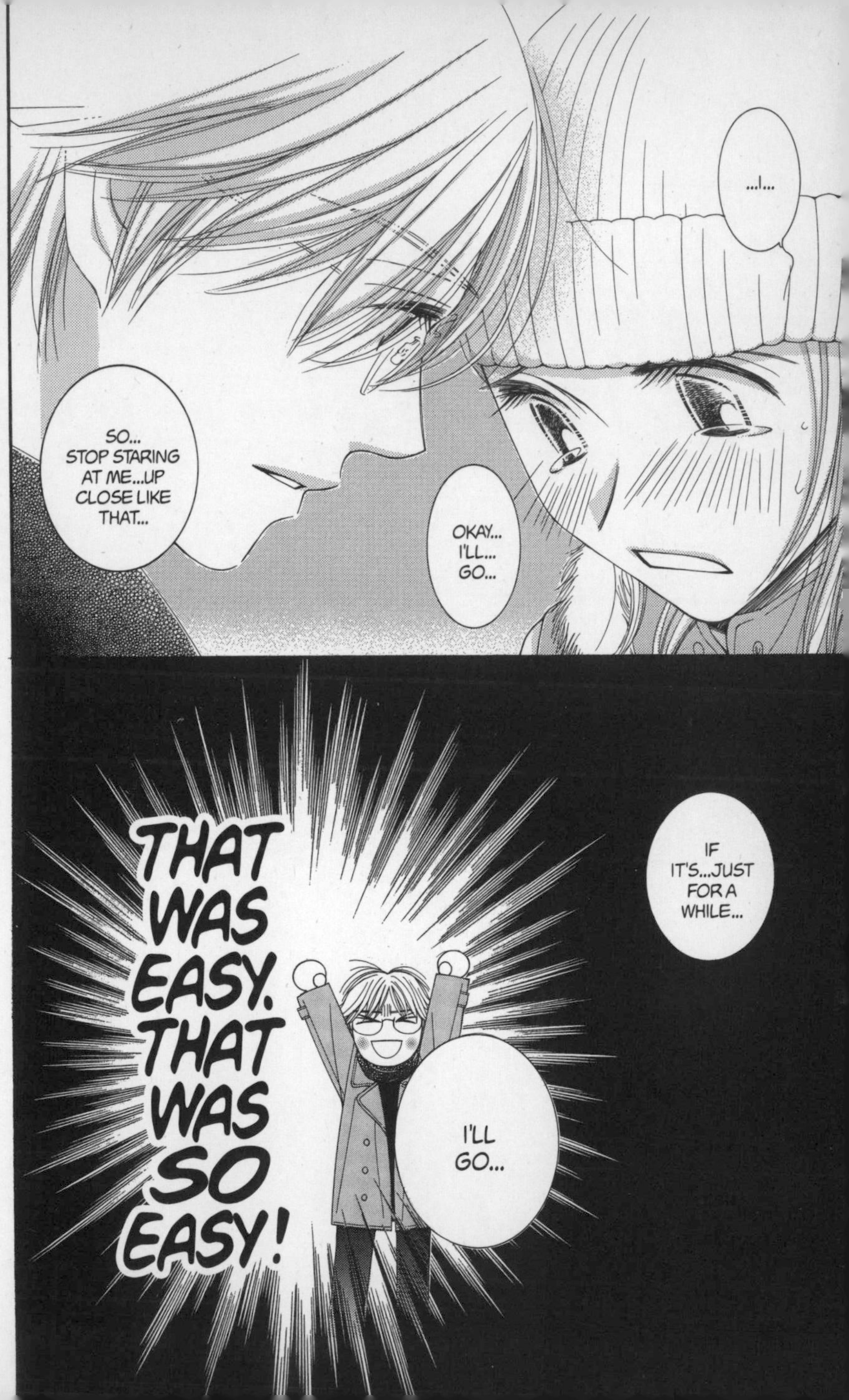
...I...
SO... STOP STARING AT ME...UP CLOSE LIKE THAT...
OKAY... I'LL... GO...
IF IT'S...JUST FOR A WHILE...
I'LL GO...
THAT WAS EASY. THAT WAS SO EASY!

hotgimmick

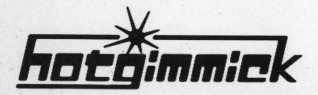

When he was thinking how easy it was:

(Surface expression)

How Ryoki looked to Hatsumi ...

By the way, Ryoki's tuxedo look in Chapter 26 was referred to as "mafia don-chic" by the staff... while readers writing to Betsucomi's "Gimmick Cafe" thought he looked like a male escort...

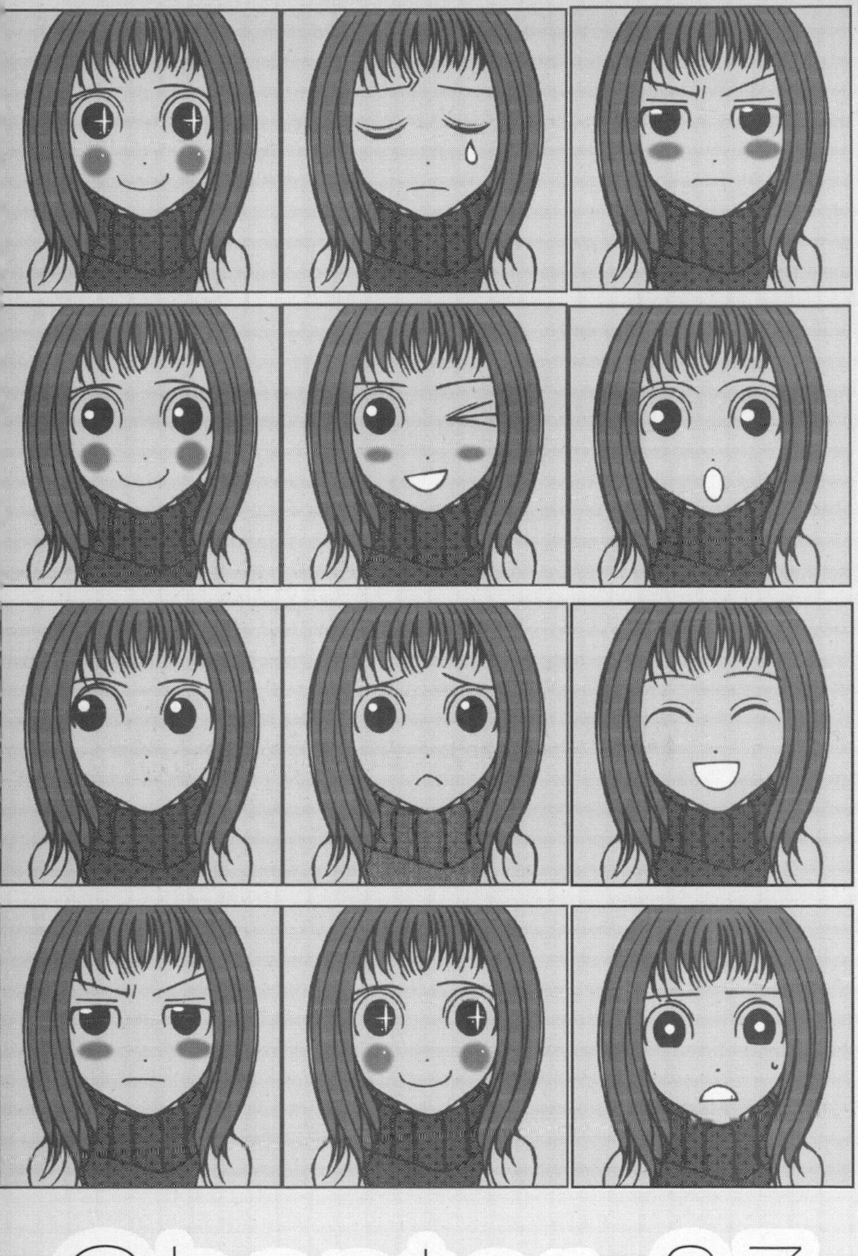

Chapter 27

hotgimmick

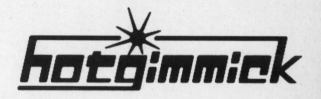

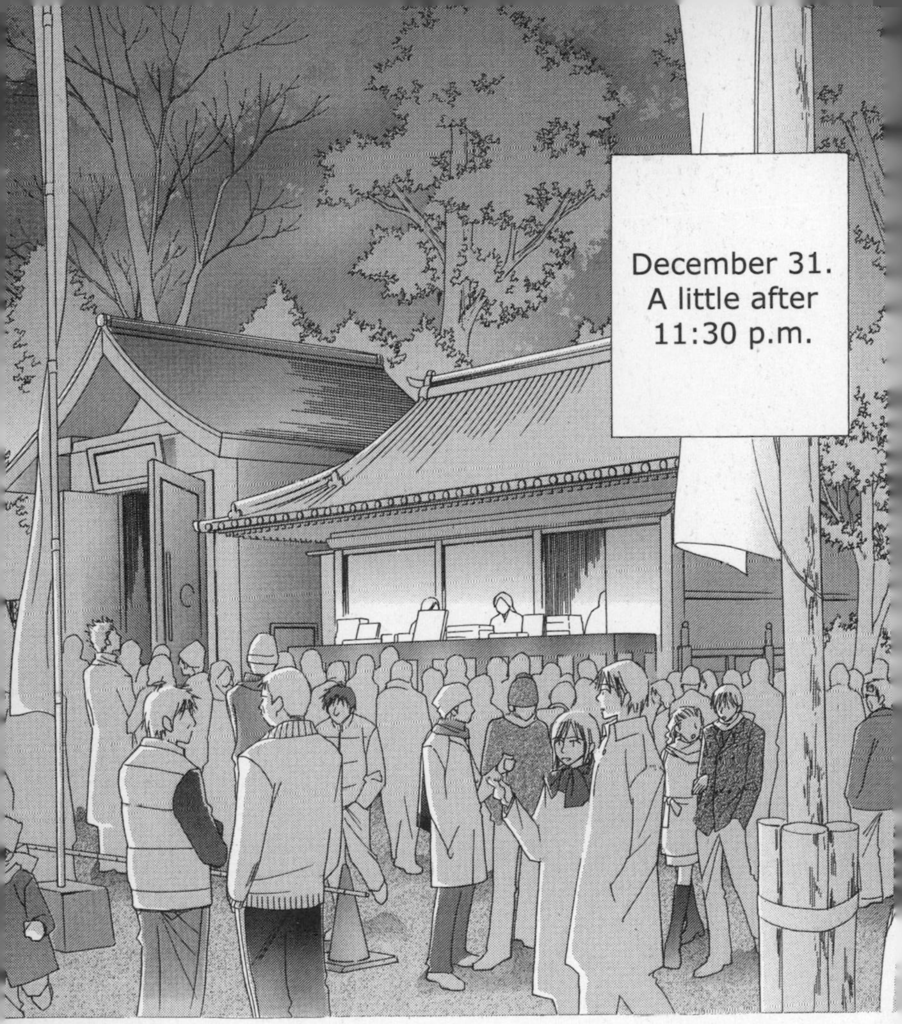
December 31. A little after 11:30 p.m.

hot gimmick

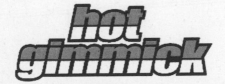

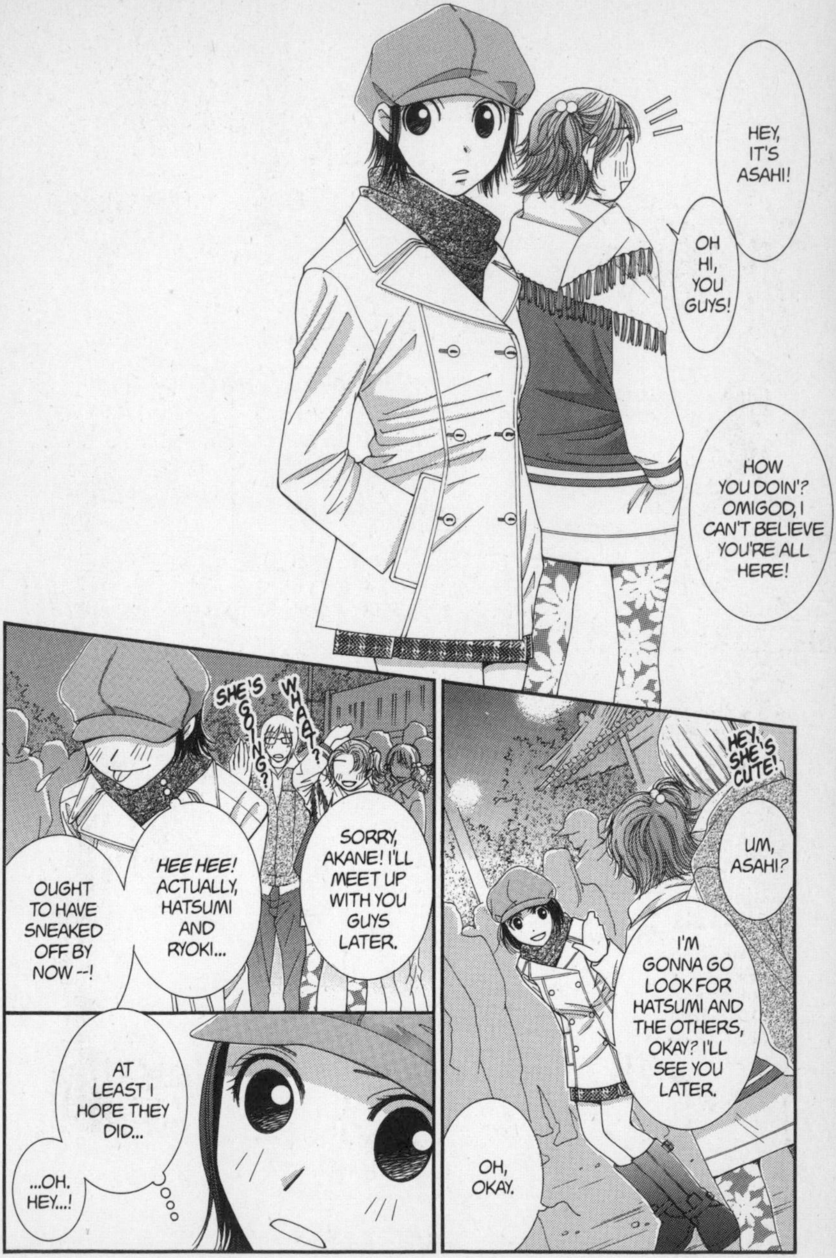
HEY, IT'S ASAHI!
OH HI, YOU GUYS!
HOW YOU DOIN'? OMIGOD, I CAN'T BELIEVE YOU'RE ALL HERE!
HEY, SHE'S CUTE!
UM, ASAHI?
I'M GONNA GO LOOK FOR HATSUMI AND THE OTHERS, OKAY? I'LL SEE YOU LATER.
OH, OKAY.
WHAAT?
SHE'S GOING?
SORRY, AKANE! I'LL MEET UP WITH YOU GUYS LATER.
HEE HEE! ACTUALLY, HATSUMI AND RYOKI...
OUGHT TO HAVE SNEAKED OFF BY NOW --!
AT LEAST I HOPE THEY DID...
...OH. HEY...!

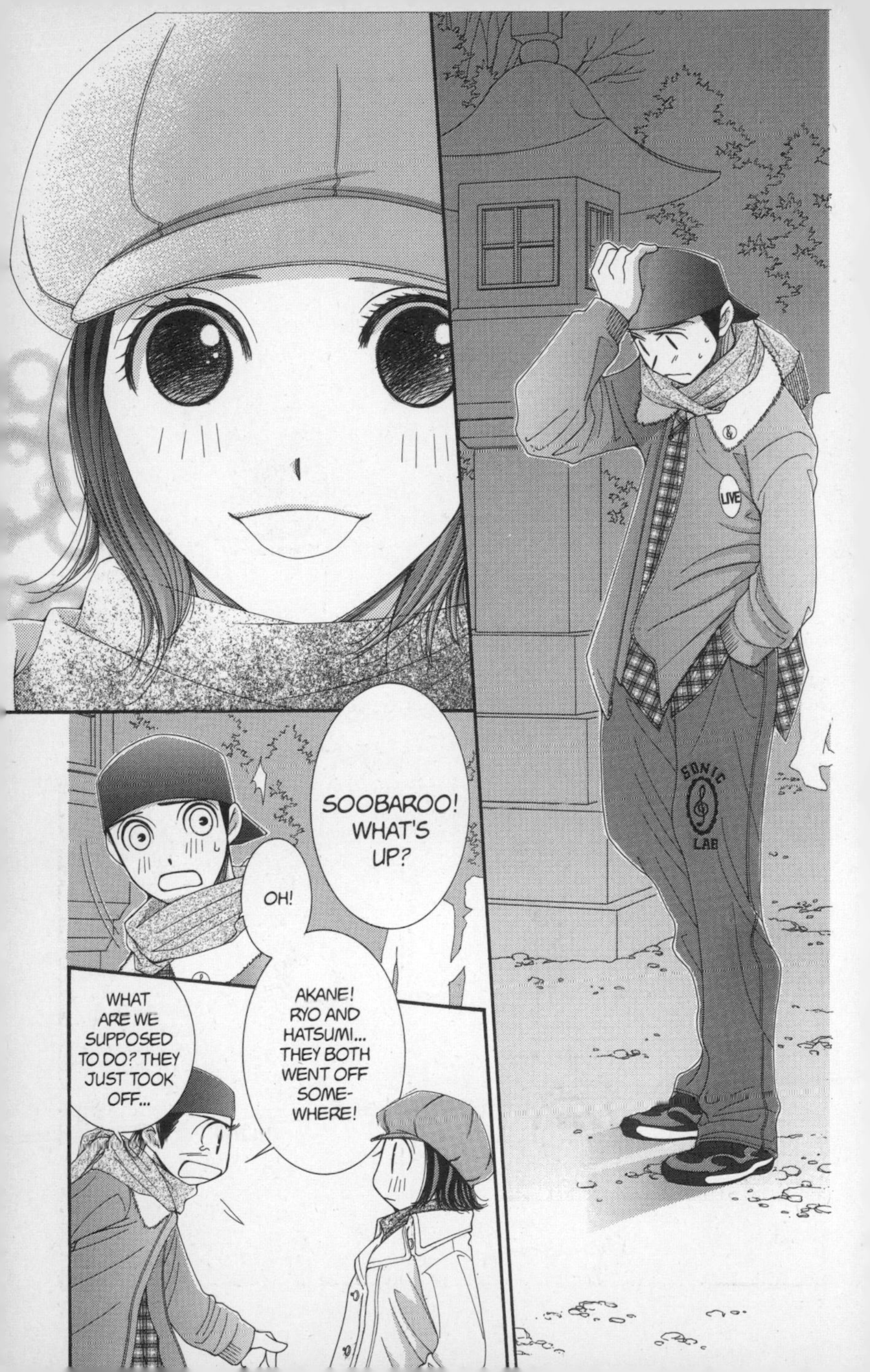
LIVE
SONIC LAB
SOOBAROO! WHAT'S UP?
OH!
AKANE! RYO AND HATSUMI... THEY BOTH WENT OFF SOME-WHERE!
WHAT ARE WE SUPPOSED TO DO? THEY JUST TOOK OFF...

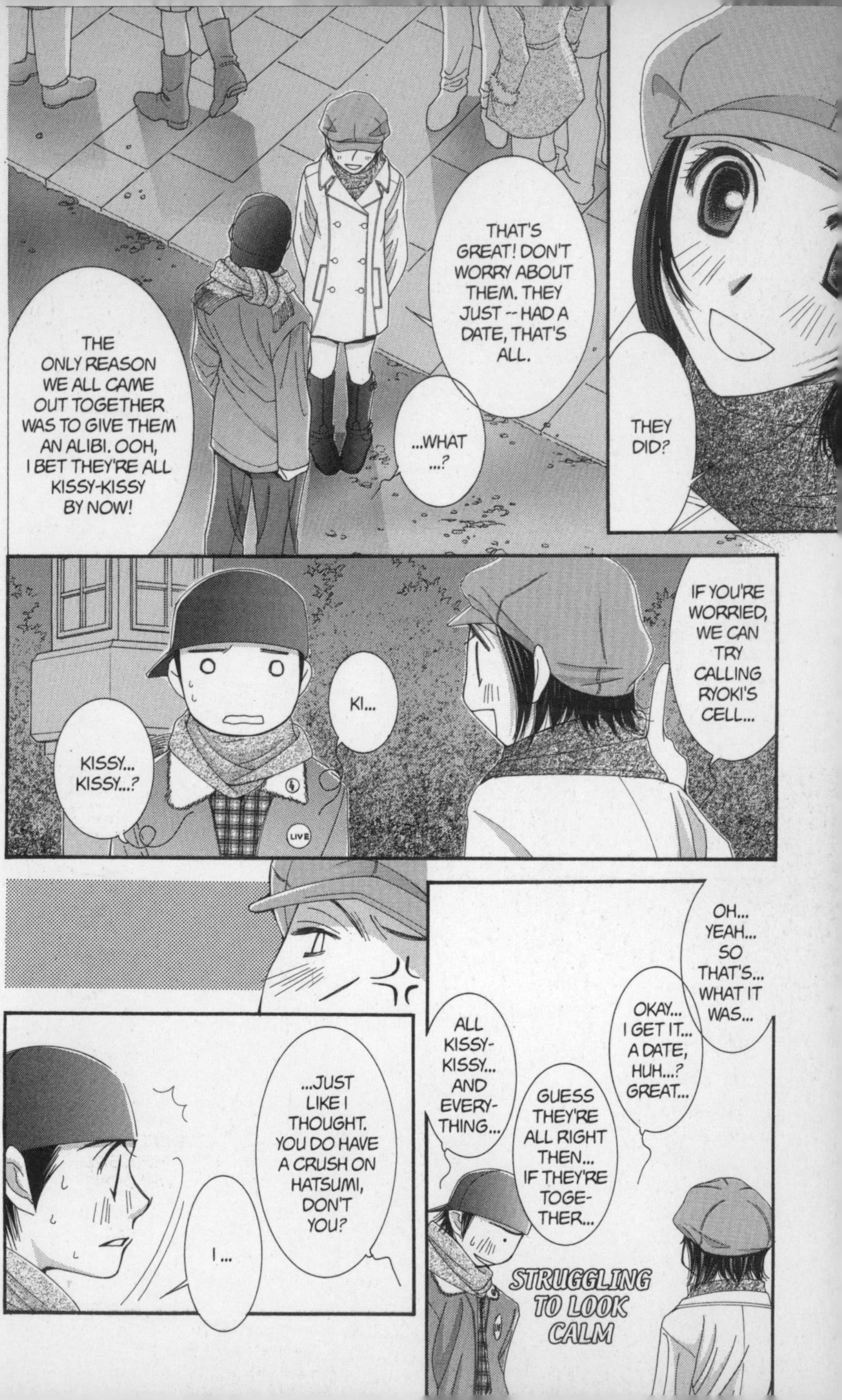
THEY DID?
THAT'S GREAT! DON'T WORRY ABOUT THEM. THEY JUST -- HAD A DATE, THAT'S ALL.
...WHAT ...?
THE ONLY REASON WE ALL CAME OUT TOGETHER WAS TO GIVE THEM AN ALIBI. OOH, I BET THEY'RE ALL KISSY-KISSY BY NOW!
IF YOU'RE WORRIED, WE CAN TRY CALLING RYOKI'S CELL...
KI...
KISSY... KISSY...?
LIVE
OH... YEAH... SO THAT'S... WHAT IT WAS...
OKAY... I GET IT... A DATE, HUH...? GREAT...
ALL KISSY-KISSY... AND EVERYTHING...
GUESS THEY'RE ALL RIGHT THEN... IF THEY'RE TOGE-THER...
STRUGGLING TO LOOK CALM
...JUST LIKE I THOUGHT. YOU DO HAVE A CRUSH ON HATSUMI, DON'T YOU?
I...

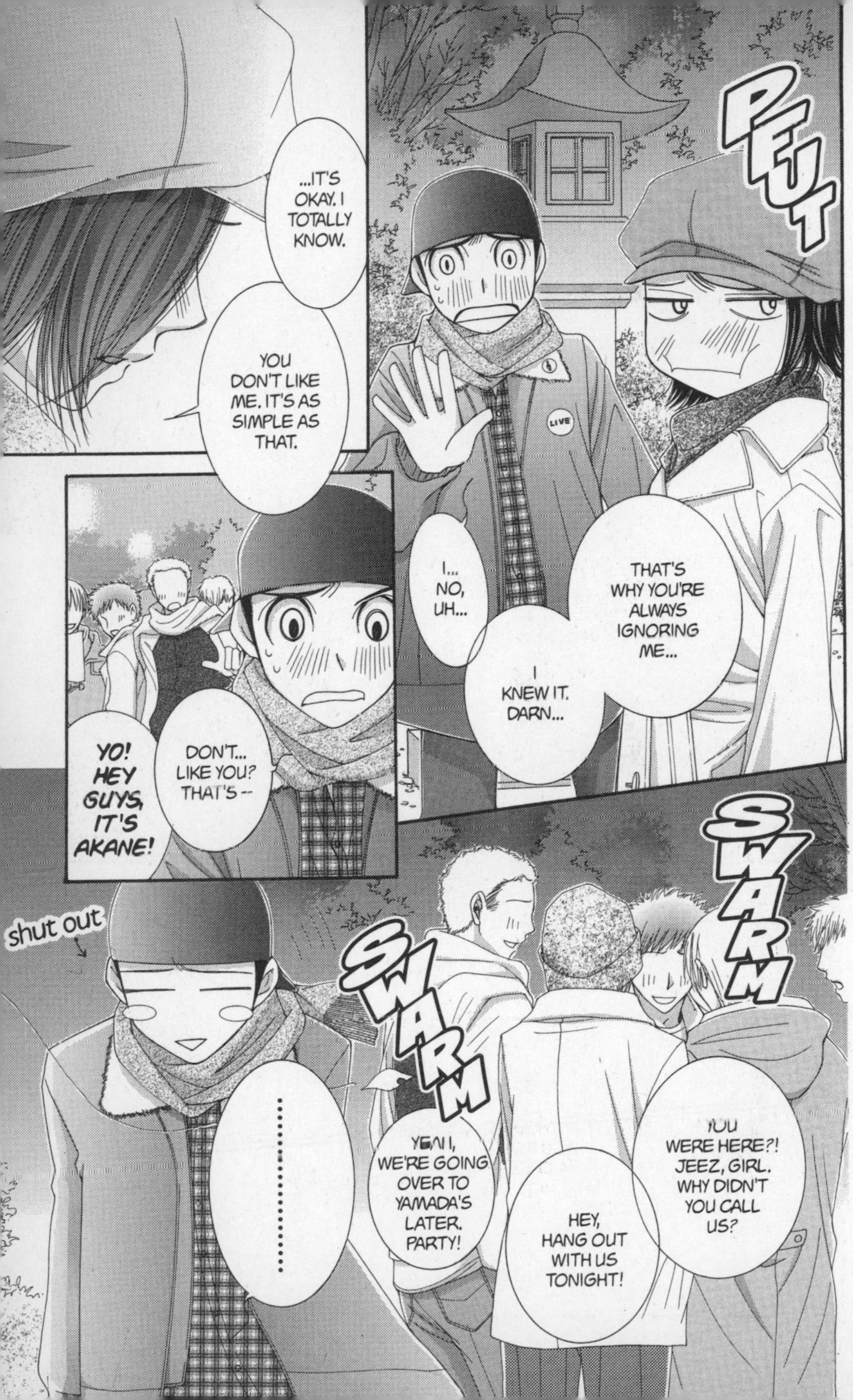
PFUT
THAT'S WHY YOU'RE ALWAYS IGNORING ME...
I... NO, UH...
I KNEW IT. DARN...
...IT'S OKAY. I TOTALLY KNOW.
YOU DON'T LIKE ME. IT'S AS SIMPLE AS THAT.
DON'T... LIKE YOU? THAT'S --
YO! HEY GUYS, IT'S AKANE!
SWARM
SWARM
YOU WERE HERE?! JEEZ, GIRL. WHY DIDN'T YOU CALL US?
HEY, HANG OUT WITH US TONIGHT!
YEAH, WE'RE GOING OVER TO YAMADA'S LATER. PARTY!
......
shut out

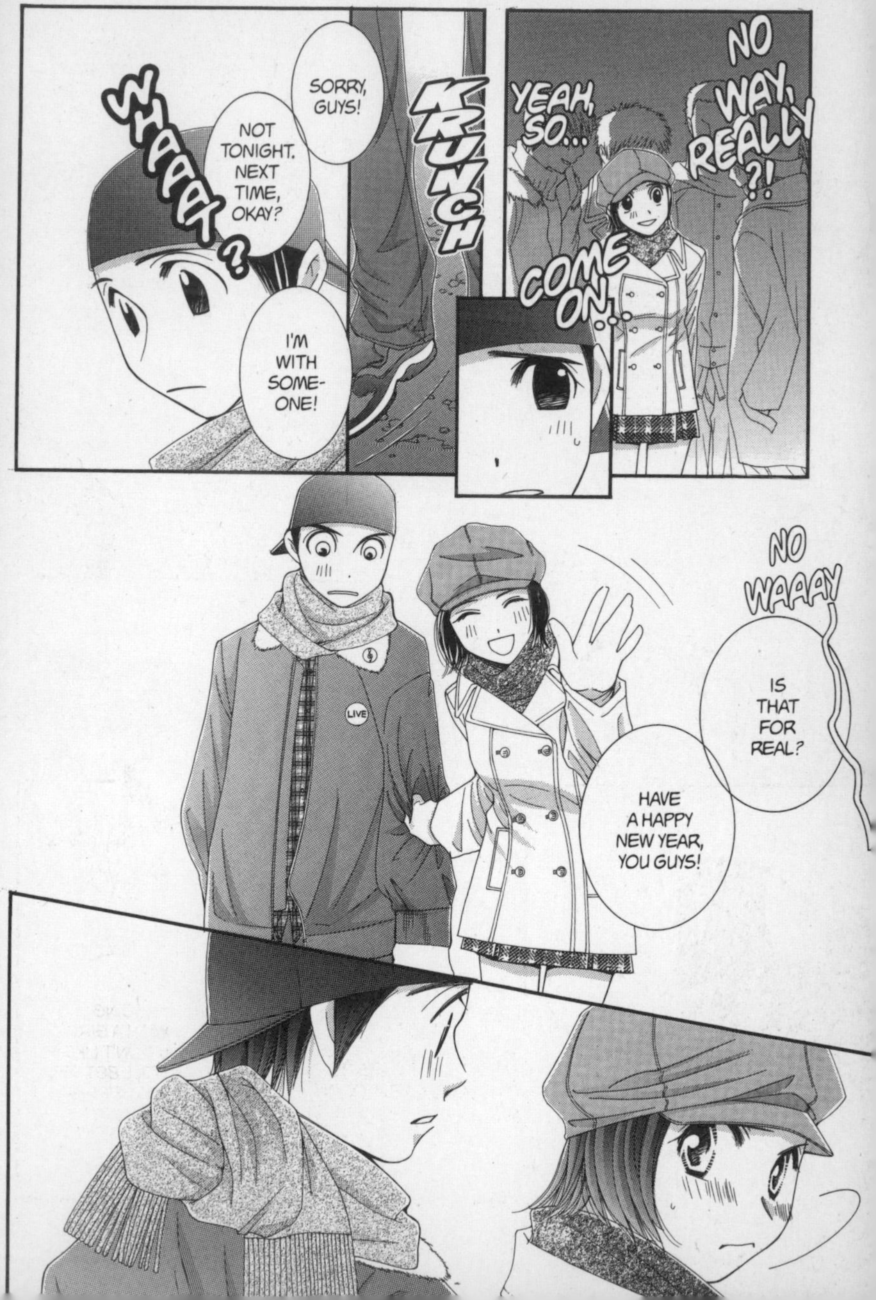
NO WAY, REALLY?!
YEAH, SO...
COME ON...
KRUNCH
SORRY, GUYS!
NOT TONIGHT. NEXT TIME, OKAY?
I'M WITH SOME-ONE!
WHAAAT?
NO WAAAY
IS THAT FOR REAL?
HAVE A HAPPY NEW YEAR, YOU GUYS!
LIVE

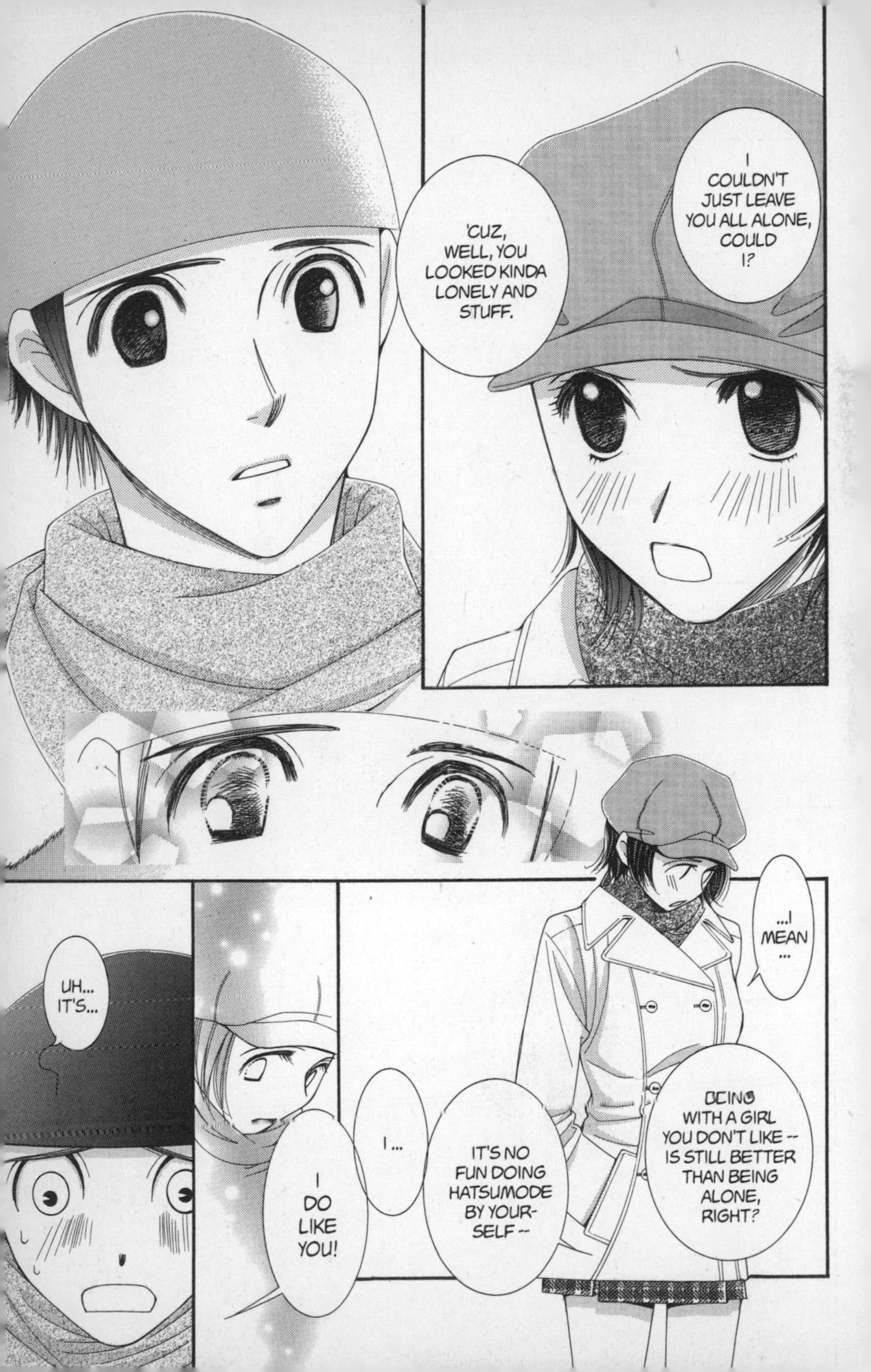
I COULDN'T JUST LEAVE YOU ALL ALONE, COULD I?
'CUZ, WELL, YOU LOOKED KINDA LONELY AND STUFF.
...I MEAN ...
BEING WITH A GIRL YOU DON'T LIKE -- IS STILL BETTER THAN BEING ALONE, RIGHT?
IT'S NO FUN DOING HATSUMODE BY YOUR-SELF --
I ...
I DO LIKE YOU!
UH... IT'S...

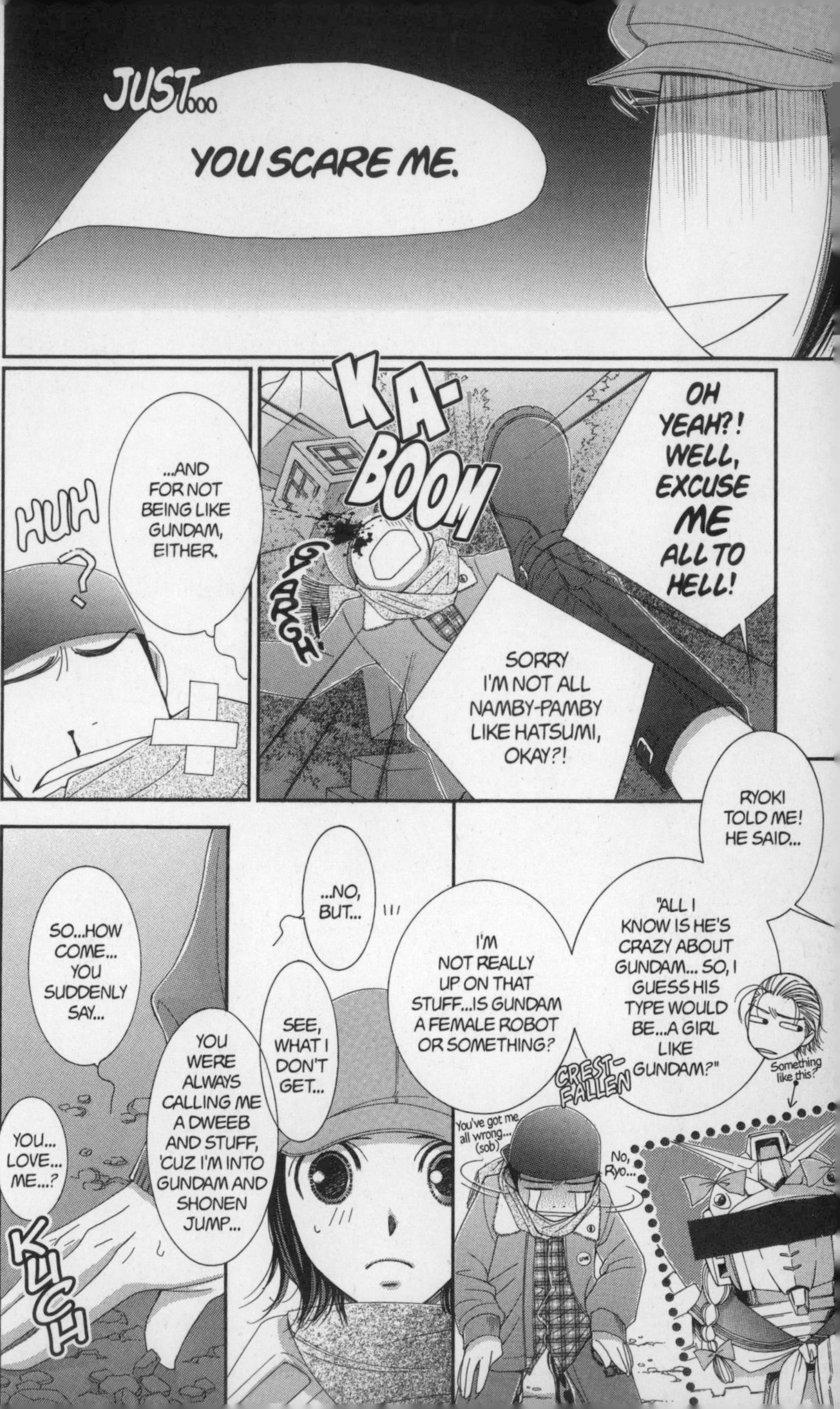
JUST...
YOU SCARE ME.
KA-BOOM
OH YEAH?! WELL, EXCUSE ME ALL TO HELL!
GAARGH!
SORRY I'M NOT ALL NAMBY-PAMBY LIKE HATSUMI, OKAY?!
...AND FOR NOT BEING LIKE GUNDAM, EITHER.
HUH
?
RYOKI TOLD ME! HE SAID...
"ALL I KNOW IS HE'S CRAZY ABOUT GUNDAM... SO, I GUESS HIS TYPE WOULD BE...A GIRL LIKE GUNDAM?"
Something like this?
I'M NOT REALLY UP ON THAT STUFF...IS GUNDAM A FEMALE ROBOT OR SOMETHING?
CREST-FALLEN
You've got me all wrong... (sob)
No, Ryo...
...NO, BUT...
SEE, WHAT I DON'T GET...
YOU WERE ALWAYS CALLING ME A DWEEB AND STUFF, 'CUZ I'M INTO GUNDAM AND SHONEN JUMP...
SO...HOW COME... YOU SUDDENLY SAY...
YOU... LOVE... ME...?
KUCH

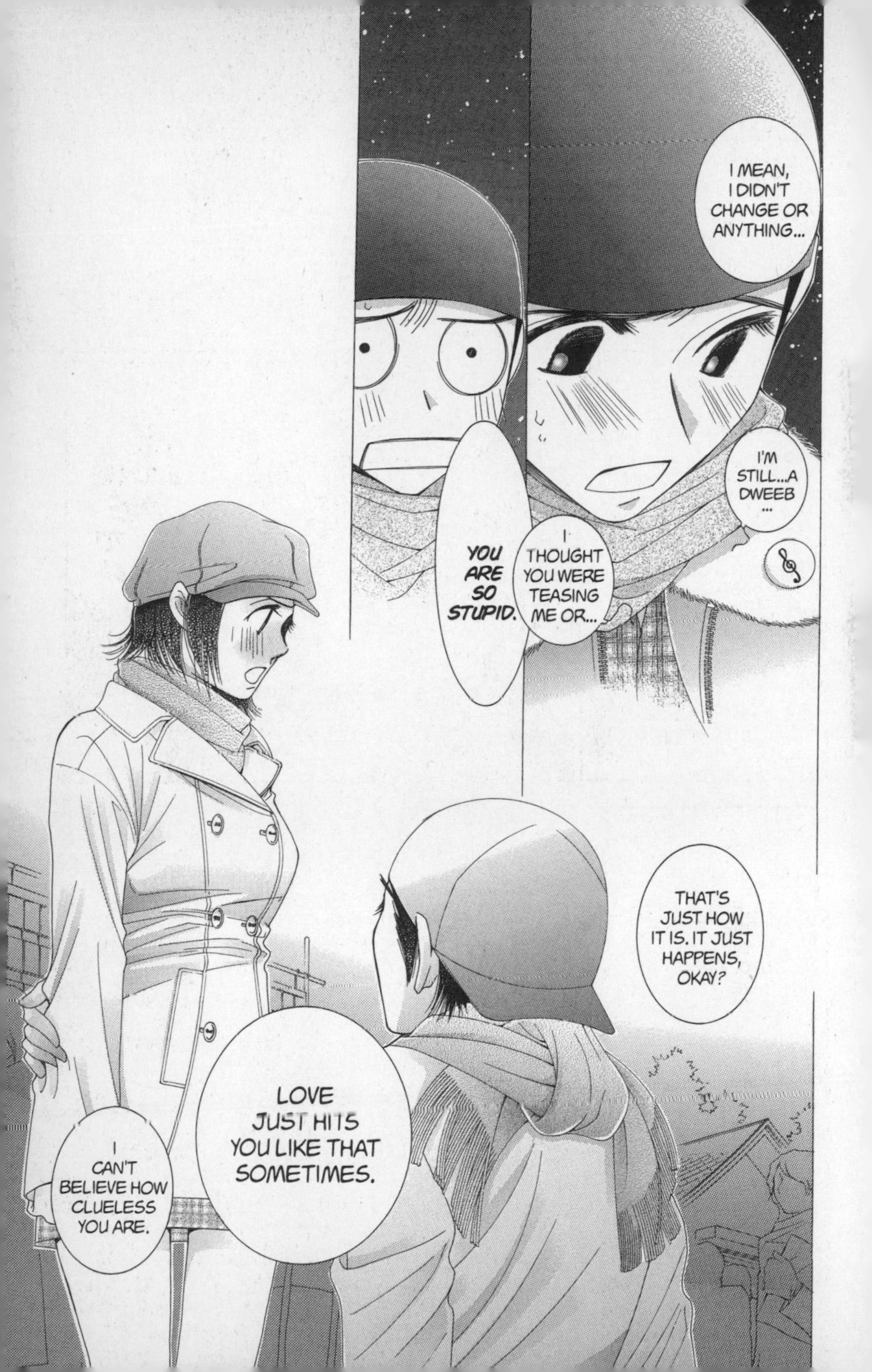
I MEAN, I DIDN'T CHANGE OR ANYTHING...
I'M STILL...A DWEEB ...
I THOUGHT YOU WERE TEASING ME OR...
YOU ARE SO STUPID.
THAT'S JUST HOW IT IS. IT JUST HAPPENS, OKAY?
LOVE JUST HITS YOU LIKE THAT SOMETIMES.
I CAN'T BELIEVE HOW CLUELESS YOU ARE.

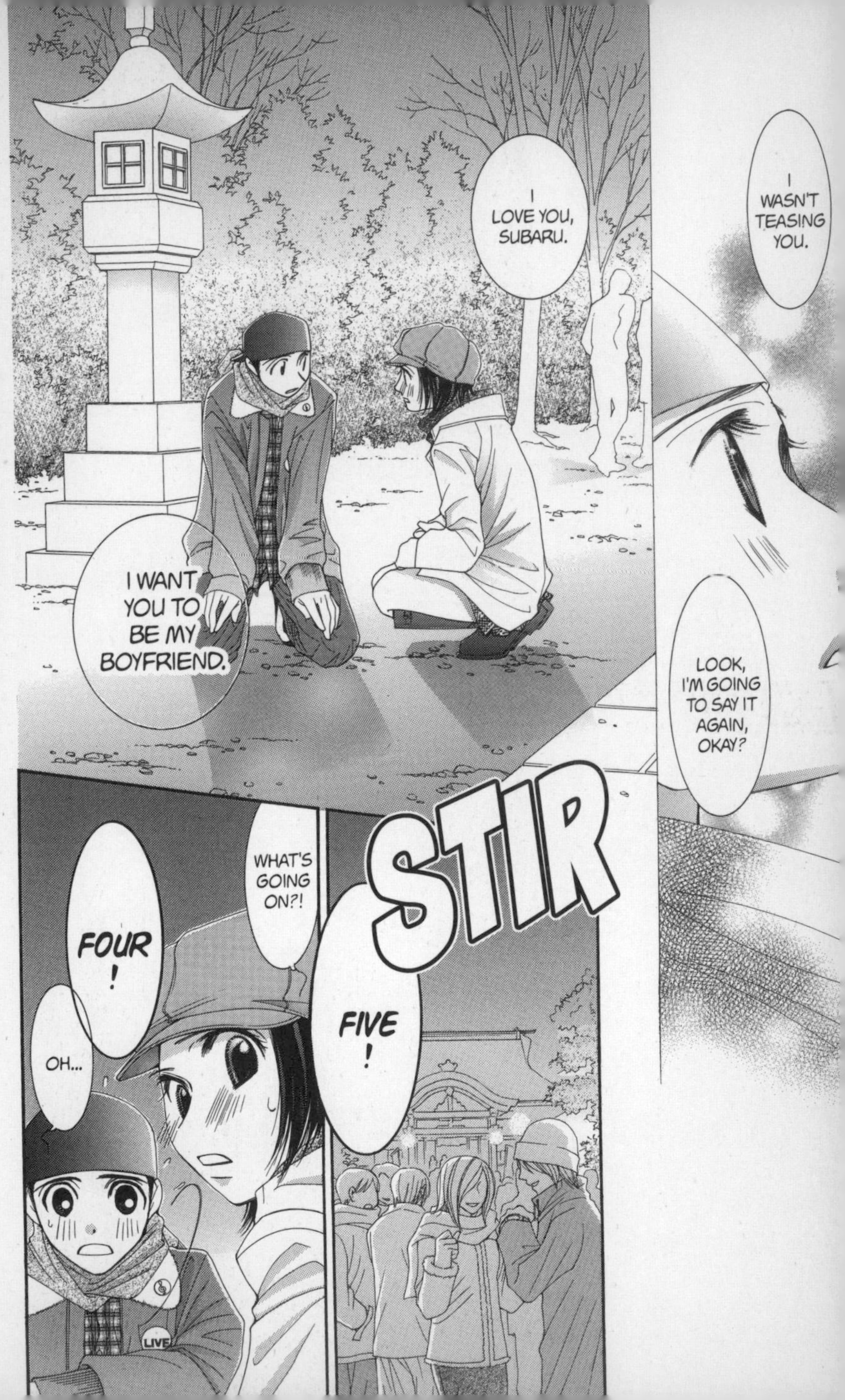
I WASN'T TEASING YOU.
LOOK, I'M GOING TO SAY IT AGAIN, OKAY?
I LOVE YOU, SUBARU.
I WANT YOU TO BE MY BOYFRIEND.
STIR
FIVE!
WHAT'S GOING ON?!
FOUR!
OH...
LIVE

hotgimmick

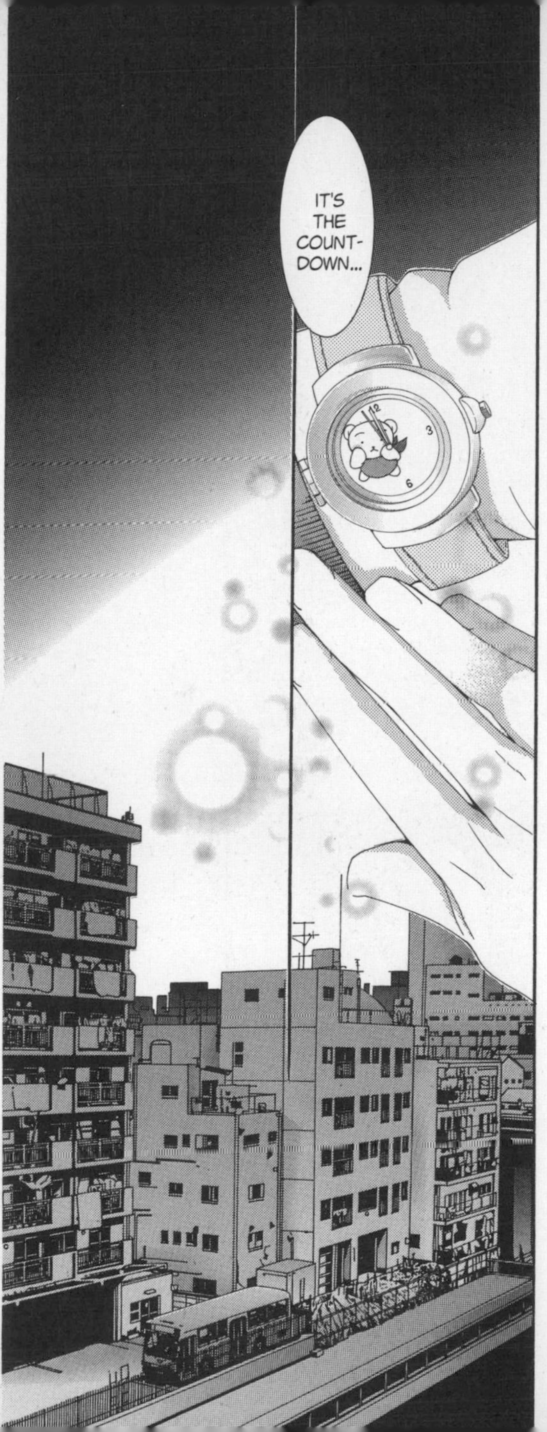
IT'S THE COUNT-DOWN...

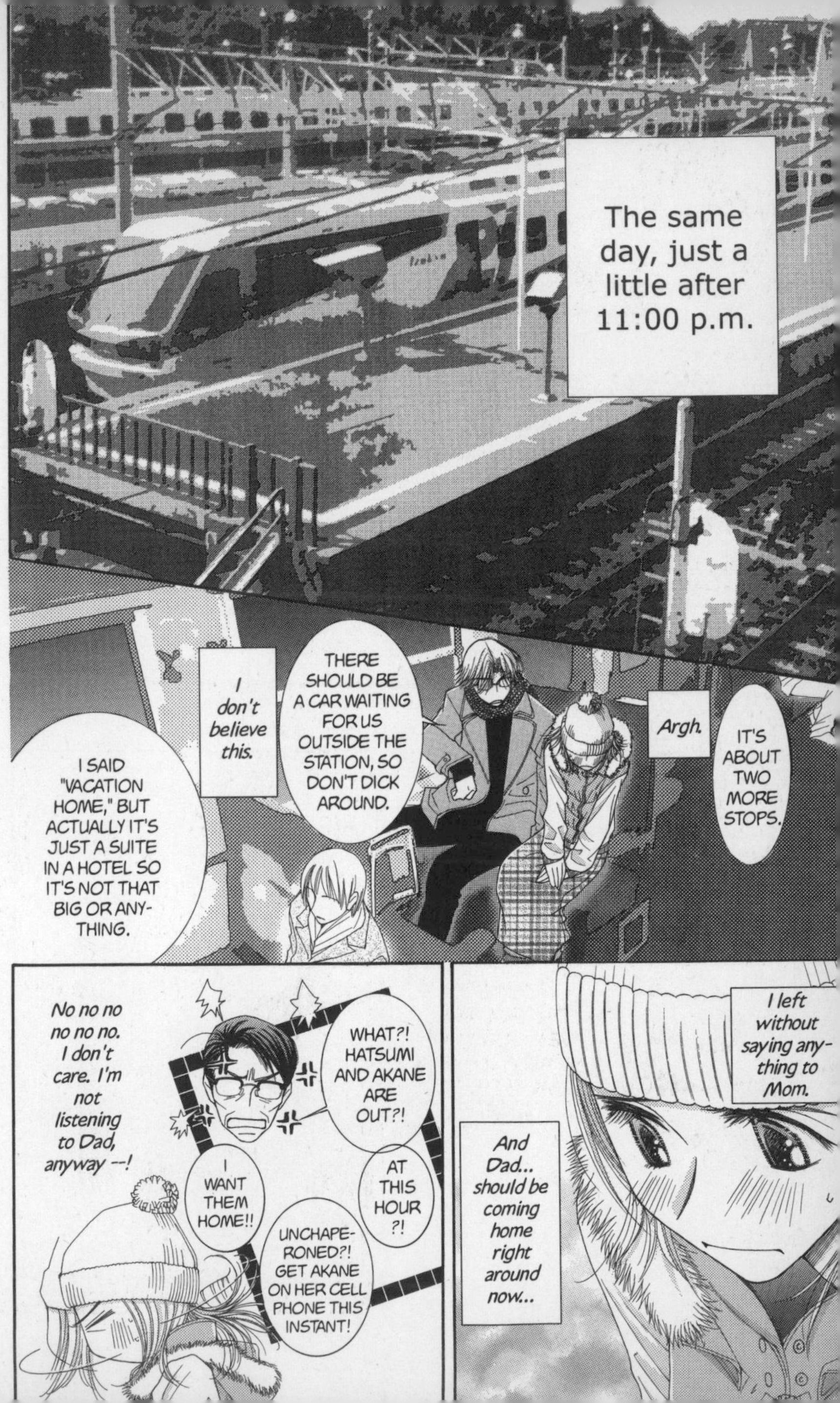
The same day, just a little after 11:00 p.m.
Argh.
IT'S ABOUT TWO MORE STOPS.
THERE SHOULD BE A CAR WAITING FOR US OUTSIDE THE STATION, SO DON'T DICK AROUND.
I don't believe this.
I SAID "VACATION HOME," BUT ACTUALLY IT'S JUST A SUITE IN A HOTEL SO IT'S NOT THAT BIG OR ANYTHING.
I left without saying anything to Mom.
And Dad... should be coming home right around now...
WHAT?! HATSUMI AND AKANE ARE OUT?!
No no no no no no. I don't care. I'm not listening to Dad, anyway --!
AT THIS HOUR?!
I WANT THEM HOME!!
UNCHAPERONED?! GET AKANE ON HER CELL PHONE THIS INSTANT!

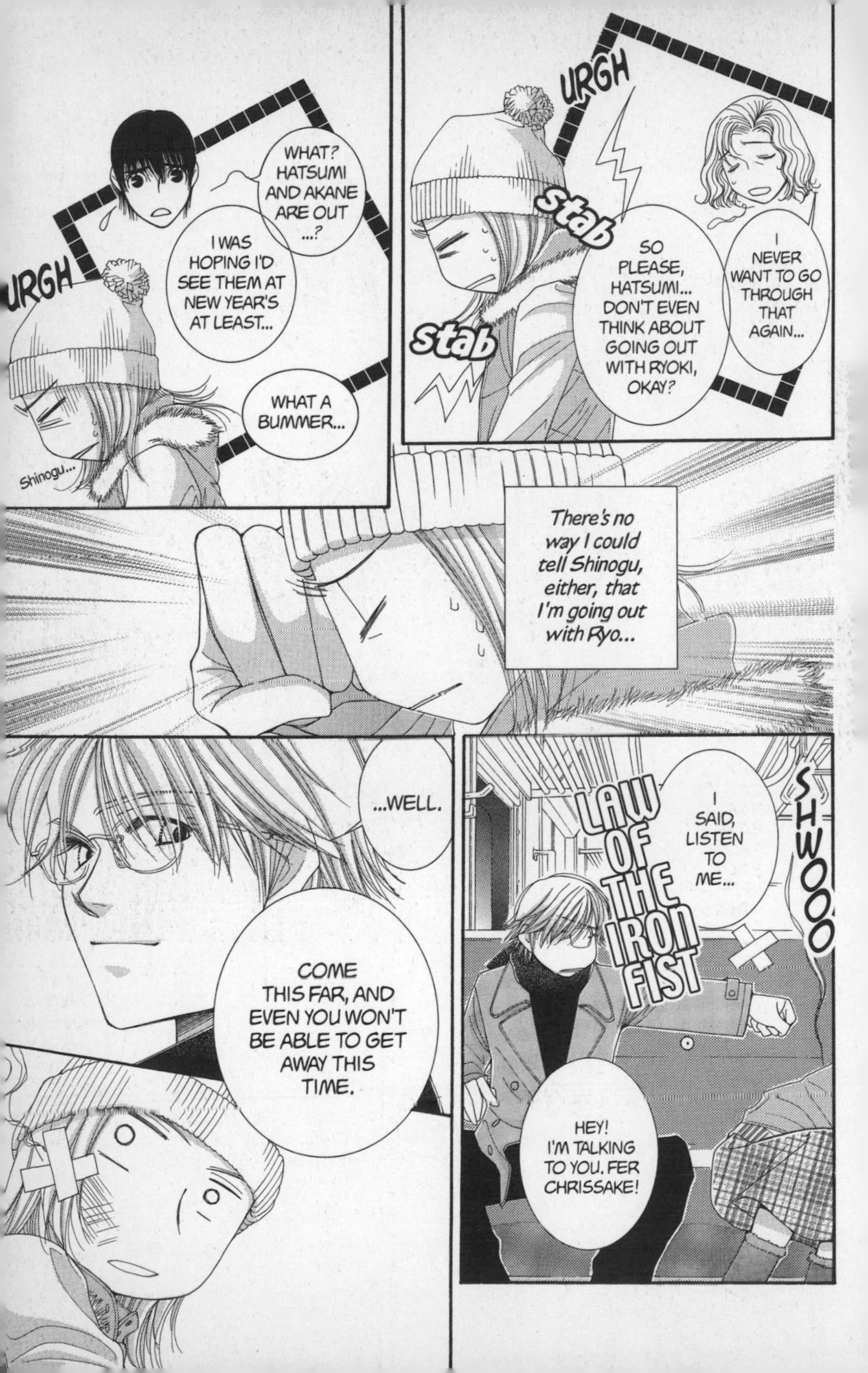
URGH
I NEVER WANT TO GO THROUGH THAT AGAIN...
stab
SO PLEASE, HATSUMI... DON'T EVEN THINK ABOUT GOING OUT WITH RYOKI, OKAY?
stab
WHAT? HATSUMI AND AKANE ARE OUT ...?
I WAS HOPING I'D SEE THEM AT NEW YEAR'S AT LEAST...
URGH
WHAT A BUMMER...
Shinogu...
There's no way I could tell Shinogu, either, that I'm going out with Ryo...
SHWOOO
I SAID, LISTEN TO ME...
LAW OF THE IRON FIST
HEY! I'M TALKING TO YOU. FER CHRISSAKE!
...WELL.
COME THIS FAR, AND EVEN YOU WON'T BE ABLE TO GET AWAY THIS TIME.

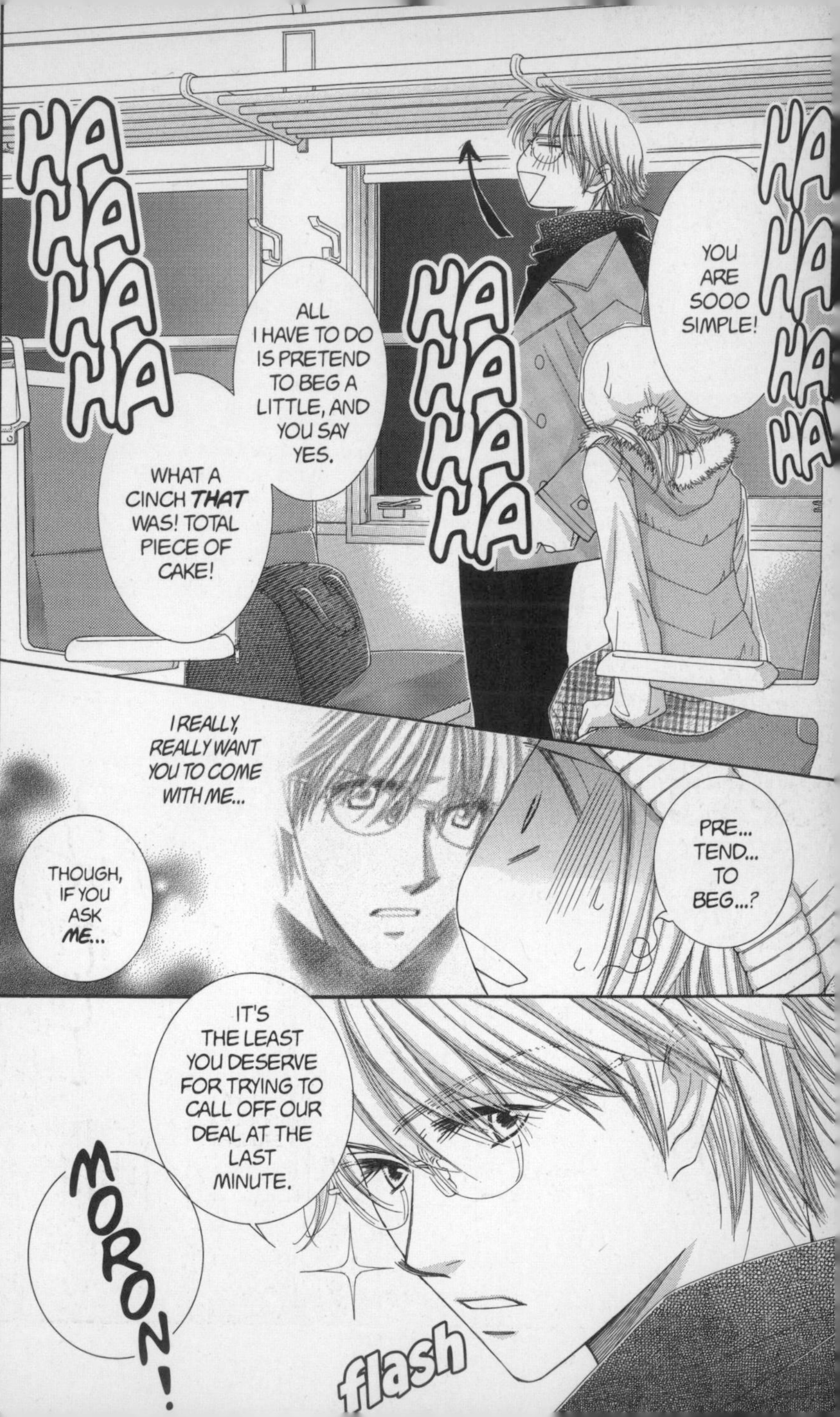
HA HA HA HA
YOU ARE SOOO SIMPLE!
HA HA HA HA HA
ALL I HAVE TO DO IS PRETEND TO BEG A LITTLE, AND YOU SAY YES.
WHAT A CINCH **THAT** WAS! TOTAL PIECE OF CAKE!
HA HA HA HA HA
PRE... TEND... TO BEG...?
I REALLY, REALLY WANT YOU TO COME WITH ME...
THOUGH, IF YOU ASK **ME**...
IT'S THE LEAST YOU DESERVE FOR TRYING TO CALL OFF OUR DEAL AT THE LAST MINUTE.
MORON!
flash

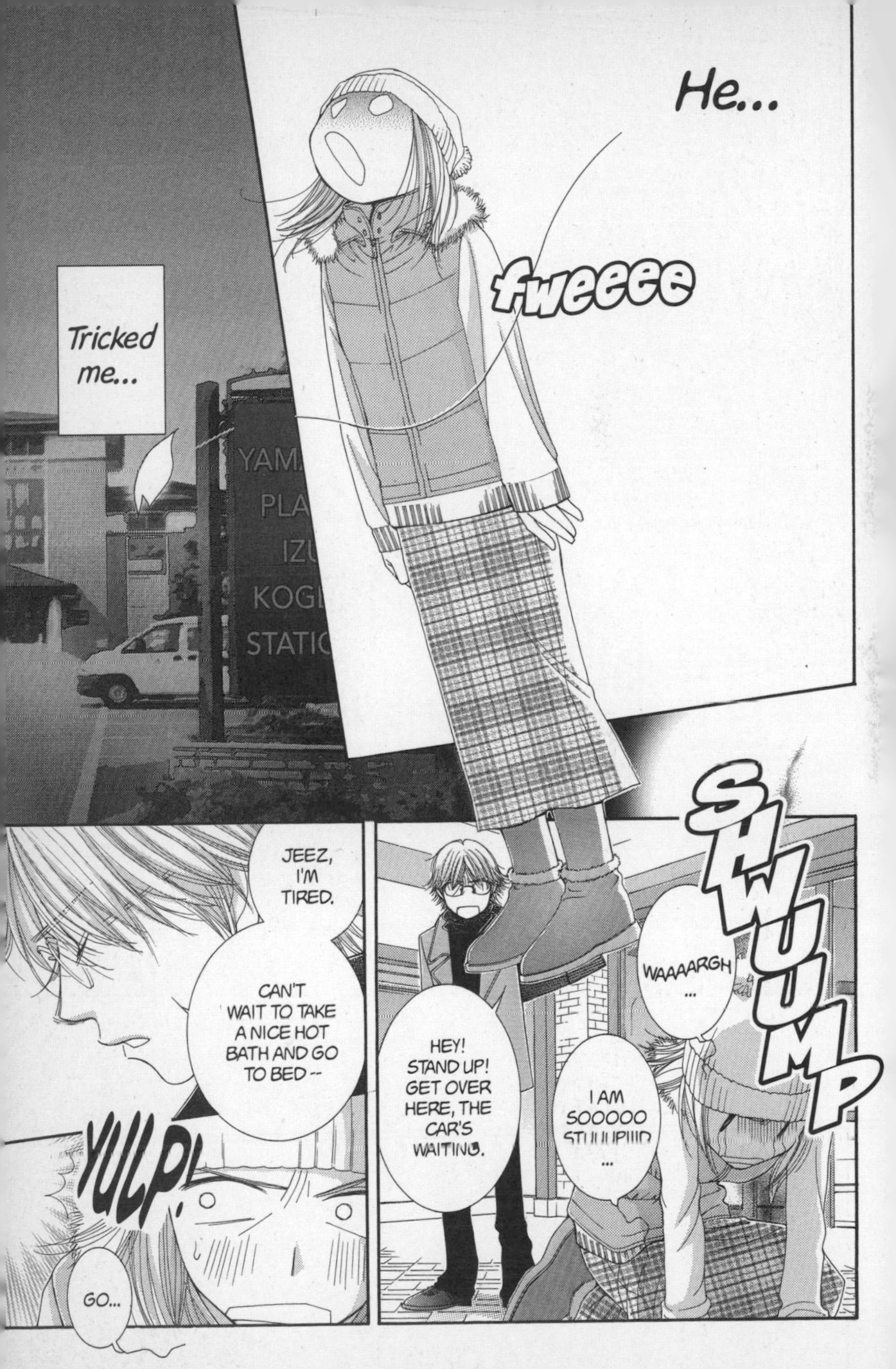
He...
fweeee
Tricked me...
SHWUMP
WAAAARGH ...
I AM SOOOOO STUUUPIIID ...
HEY! STAND UP! GET OVER HERE, THE CAR'S WAITING.
JEEZ, I'M TIRED.
CAN'T WAIT TO TAKE A NICE HOT BATH AND GO TO BED --
YULP!
GO...

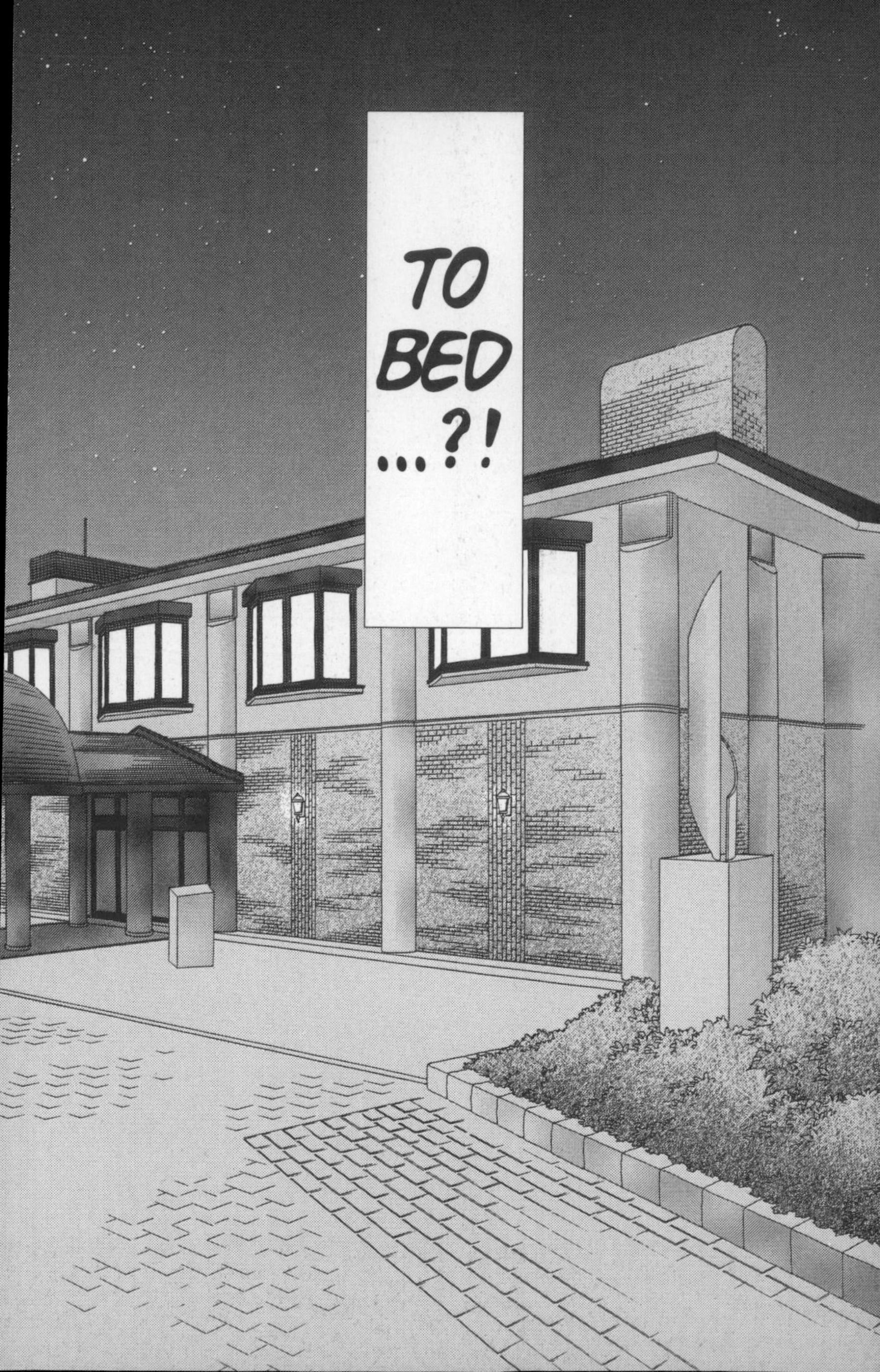
TO BED ...?!

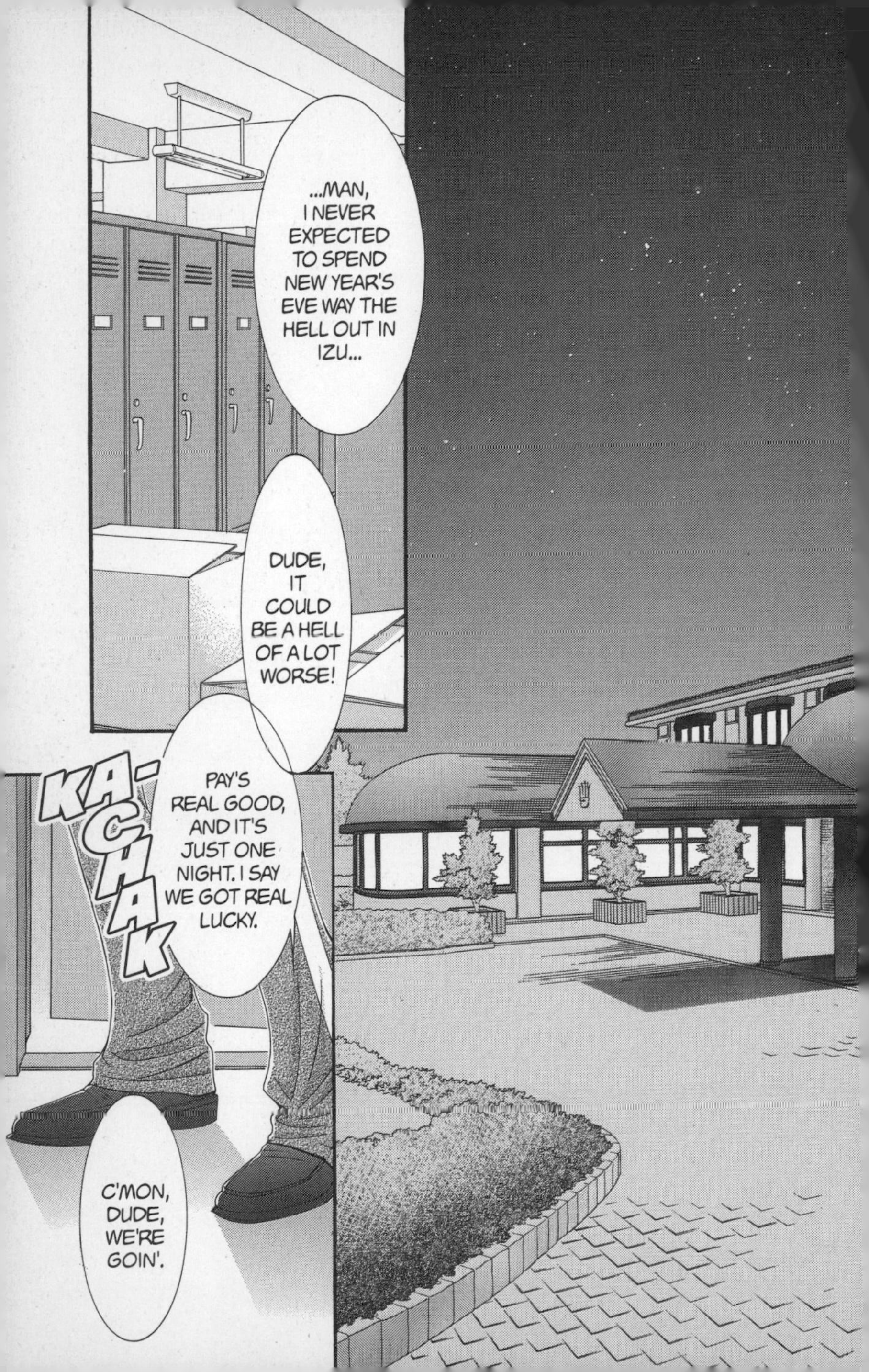
...MAN, I NEVER EXPECTED TO SPEND NEW YEAR'S EVE WAY THE HELL OUT IN IZU...
DUDE, IT COULD BE A HELL OF A LOT WORSE!
PAY'S REAL GOOD, AND IT'S JUST ONE NIGHT. I SAY WE GOT REAL LUCKY.
KA-CHAK
C'MON, DUDE, WE'RE GOIN'.

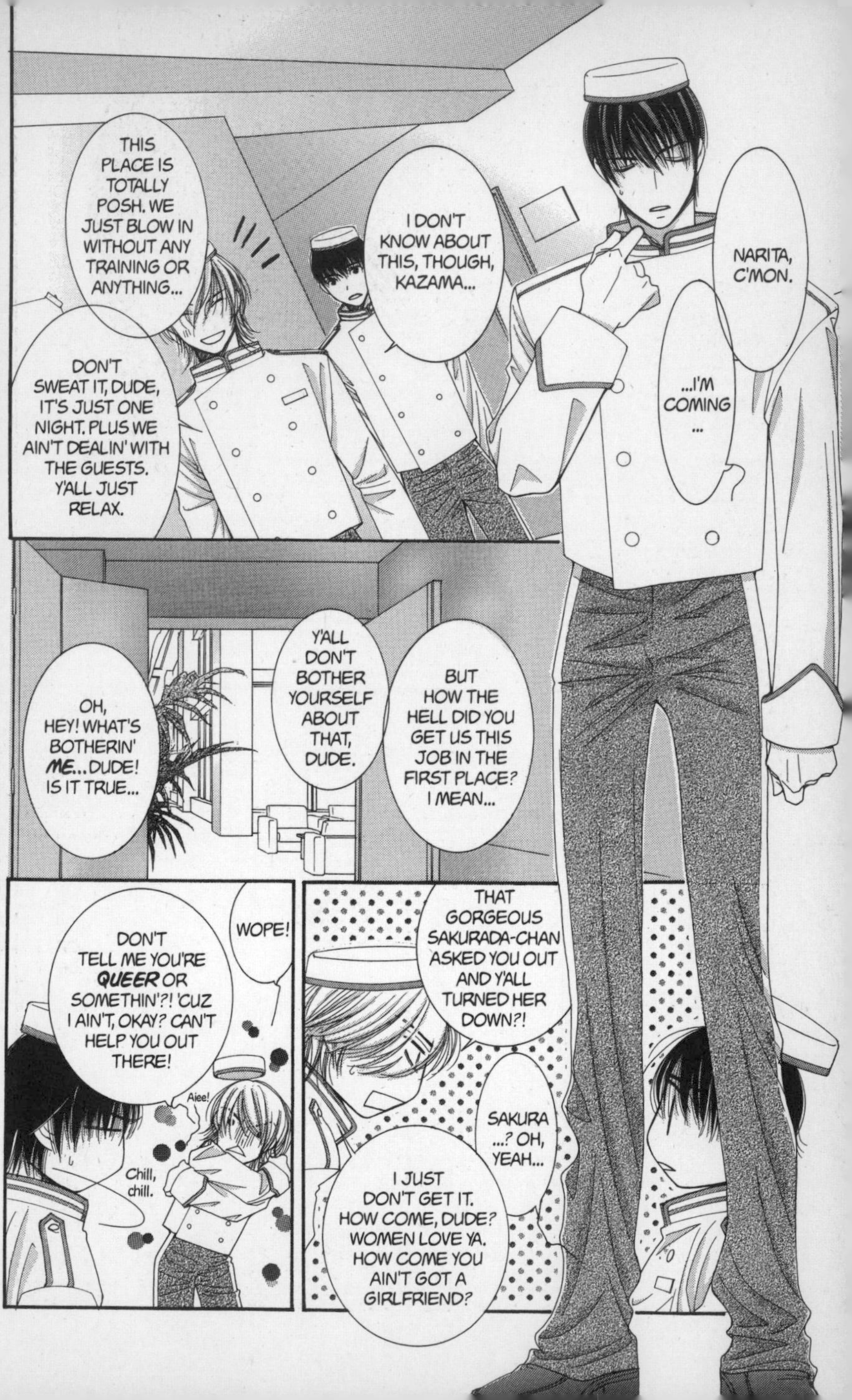
NARITA, C'MON.
...I'M COMING ...
THIS PLACE IS TOTALLY POSH. WE JUST BLOW IN WITHOUT ANY TRAINING OR ANYTHING...
I DON'T KNOW ABOUT THIS, THOUGH, KAZAMA...
DON'T SWEAT IT, DUDE, IT'S JUST ONE NIGHT. PLUS WE AIN'T DEALIN' WITH THE GUESTS. Y'ALL JUST RELAX.
BUT HOW THE HELL DID YOU GET US THIS JOB IN THE FIRST PLACE? I MEAN...
Y'ALL DON'T BOTHER YOURSELF ABOUT THAT, DUDE.
OH, HEY! WHAT'S BOTHERIN' *ME*...DUDE! IS IT TRUE...
THAT GORGEOUS SAKURADA-CHAN ASKED YOU OUT AND Y'ALL TURNED HER DOWN?!
SAKURA ...? OH, YEAH...
I JUST DON'T GET IT. HOW COME, DUDE? WOMEN LOVE YA. HOW COME YOU AIN'T GOT A GIRLFRIEND?
WOPE!
DON'T TELL ME YOU'RE ***QUEER*** OR SOMETHIN'?! 'CUZ I AIN'T, OKAY? CAN'T HELP YOU OUT THERE!
Aiee!
Chill, chill.

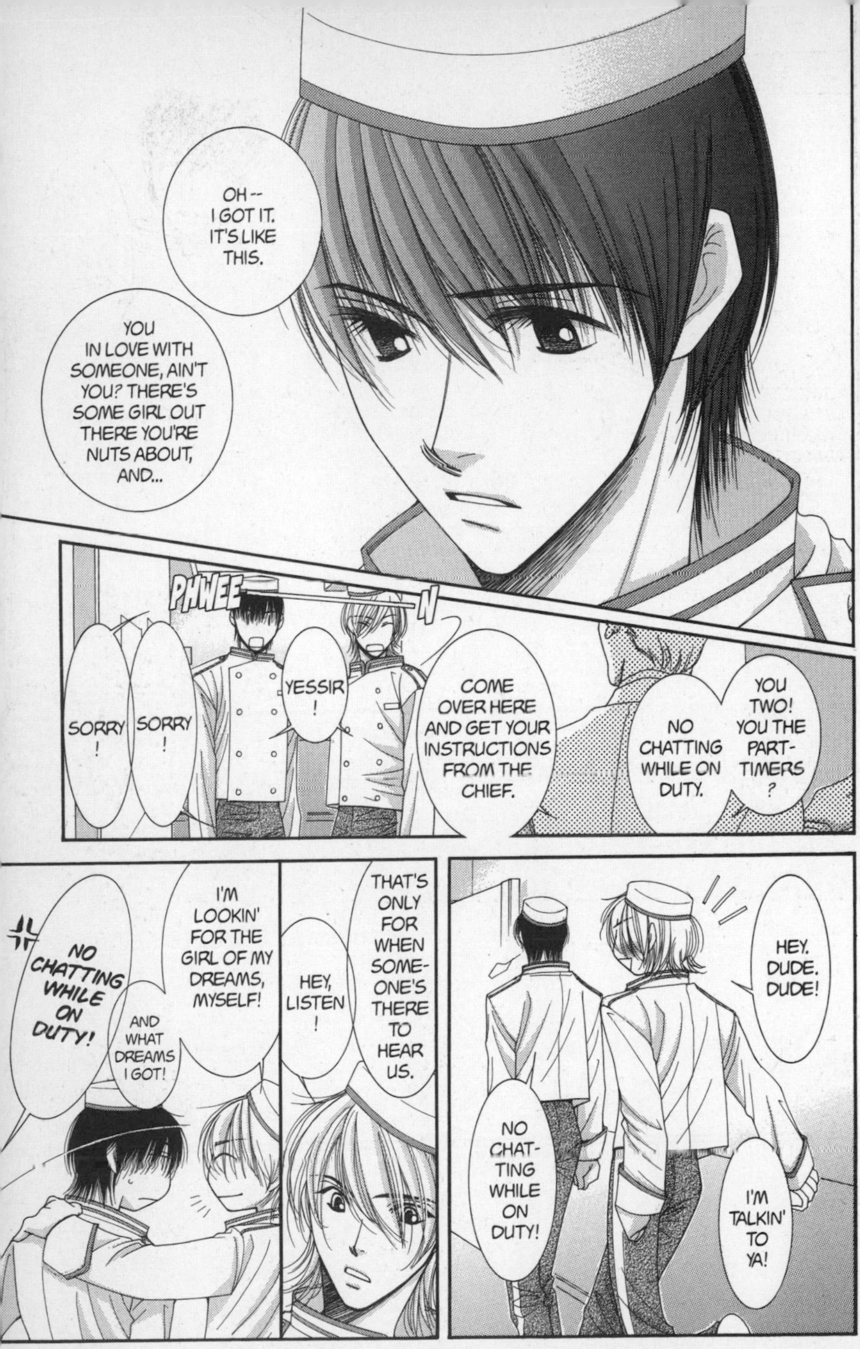
OH -- I GOT IT. IT'S LIKE THIS.
YOU IN LOVE WITH SOMEONE, AIN'T YOU? THERE'S SOME GIRL OUT THERE YOU'RE NUTS ABOUT, AND...
PHWEEN
YOU TWO! YOU THE PART-TIMERS?
NO CHATTING WHILE ON DUTY.
COME OVER HERE AND GET YOUR INSTRUCTIONS FROM THE CHIEF.
YESSIR!
SORRY!
SORRY!
HEY. DUDE. DUDE!
I'M TALKIN' TO YA!
NO CHATTING WHILE ON DUTY!
THAT'S ONLY FOR WHEN SOMEONE'S THERE TO HEAR US.
HEY, LISTEN!
I'M LOOKIN' FOR THE GIRL OF MY DREAMS, MYSELF!
NO CHATTING WHILE ON DUTY!
AND WHAT DREAMS I GOT!

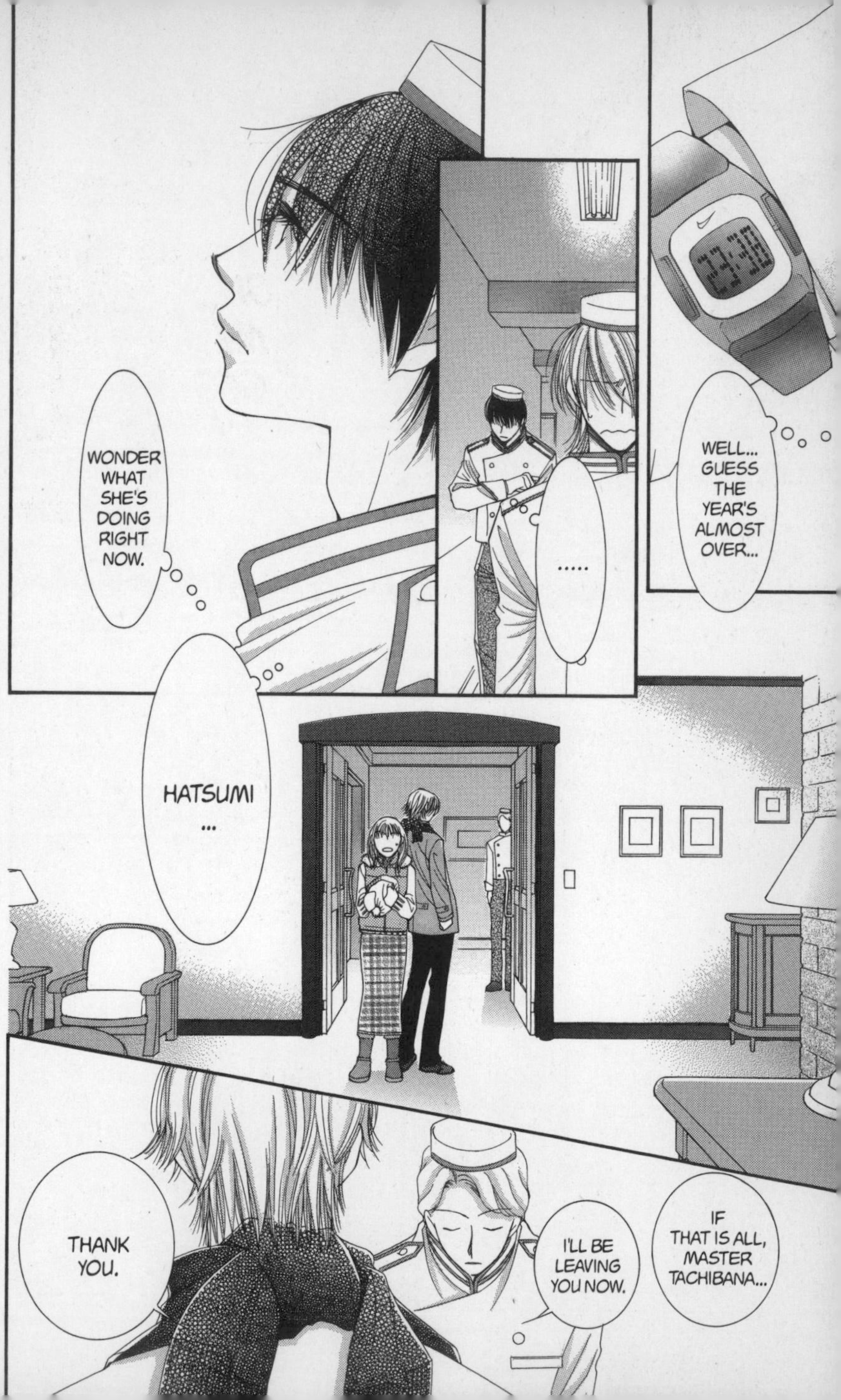
WELL... GUESS THE YEAR'S ALMOST OVER...
.....
WONDER WHAT SHE'S DOING RIGHT NOW.
HATSUMI ...
IF THAT IS ALL, MASTER TACHIBANA...
I'LL BE LEAVING YOU NOW.
THANK YOU.

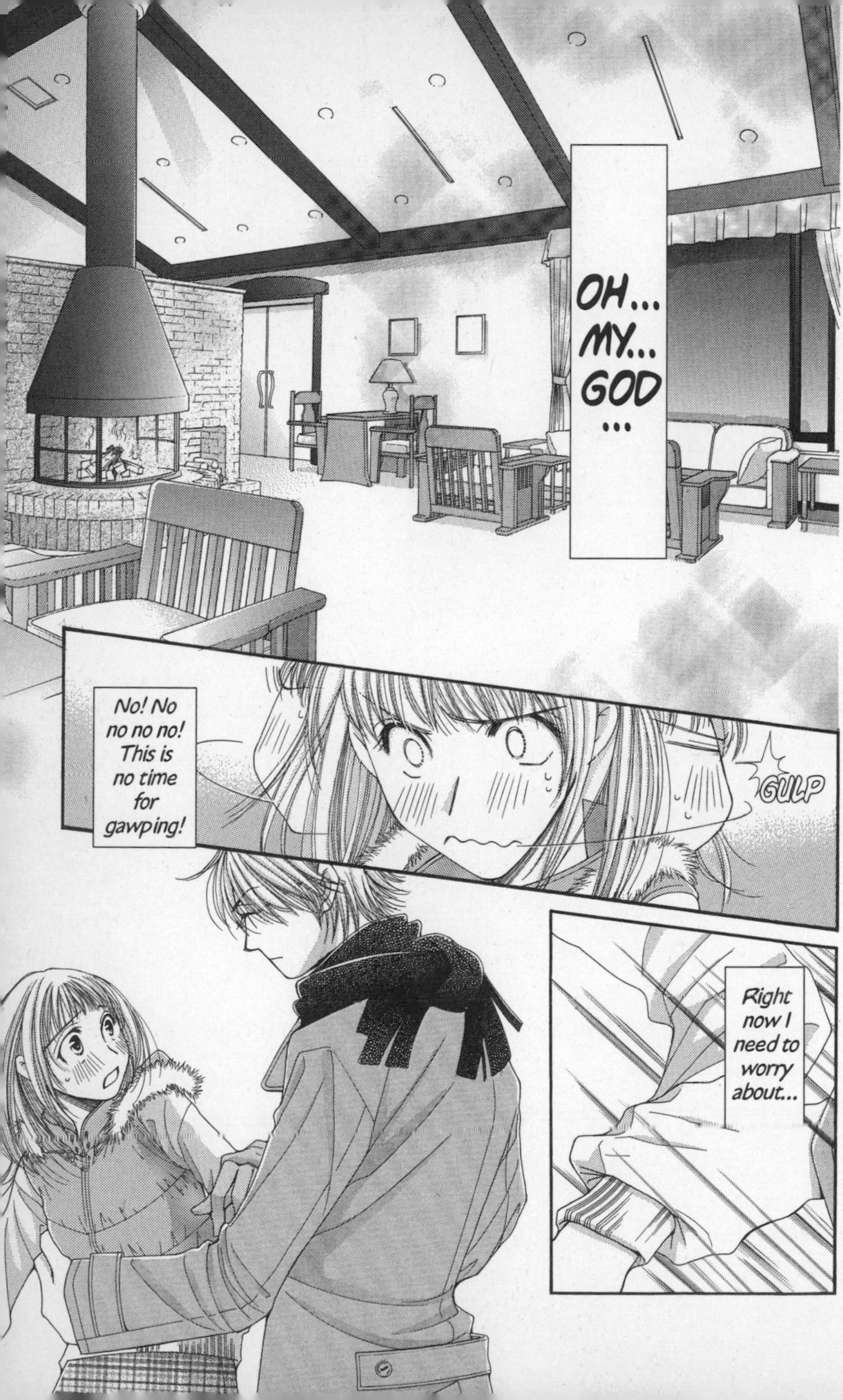
OH... MY... GOD ...
GULP
No! No no no no! This is no time for gawping!
Right now I need to worry about...

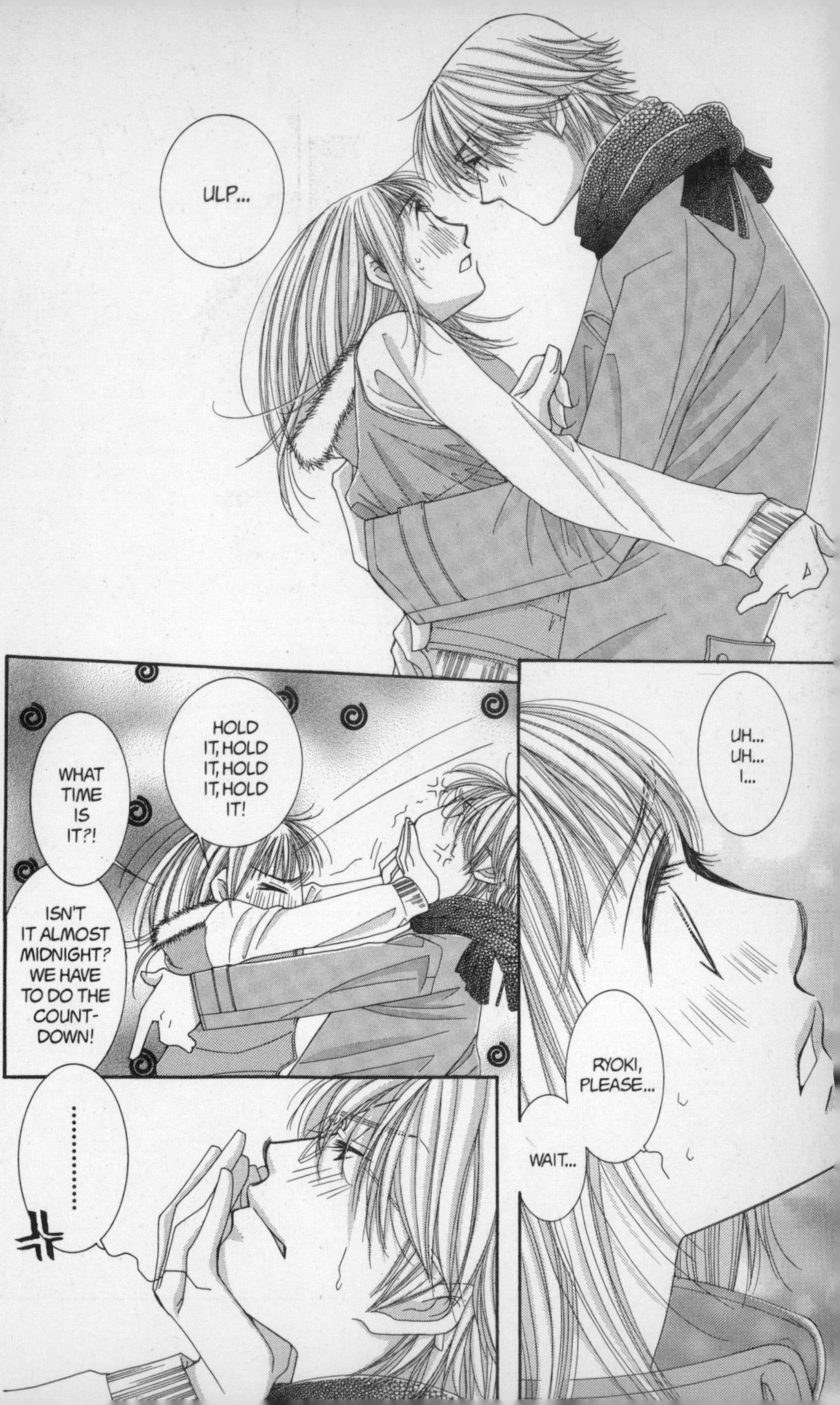
ULP...
UH... UH... I...
RYOKI, PLEASE...
WAIT...
HOLD IT, HOLD IT, HOLD IT, HOLD IT!
WHAT TIME IS IT?!
ISN'T IT ALMOST MIDNIGHT? WE HAVE TO DO THE COUNT-DOWN!
....

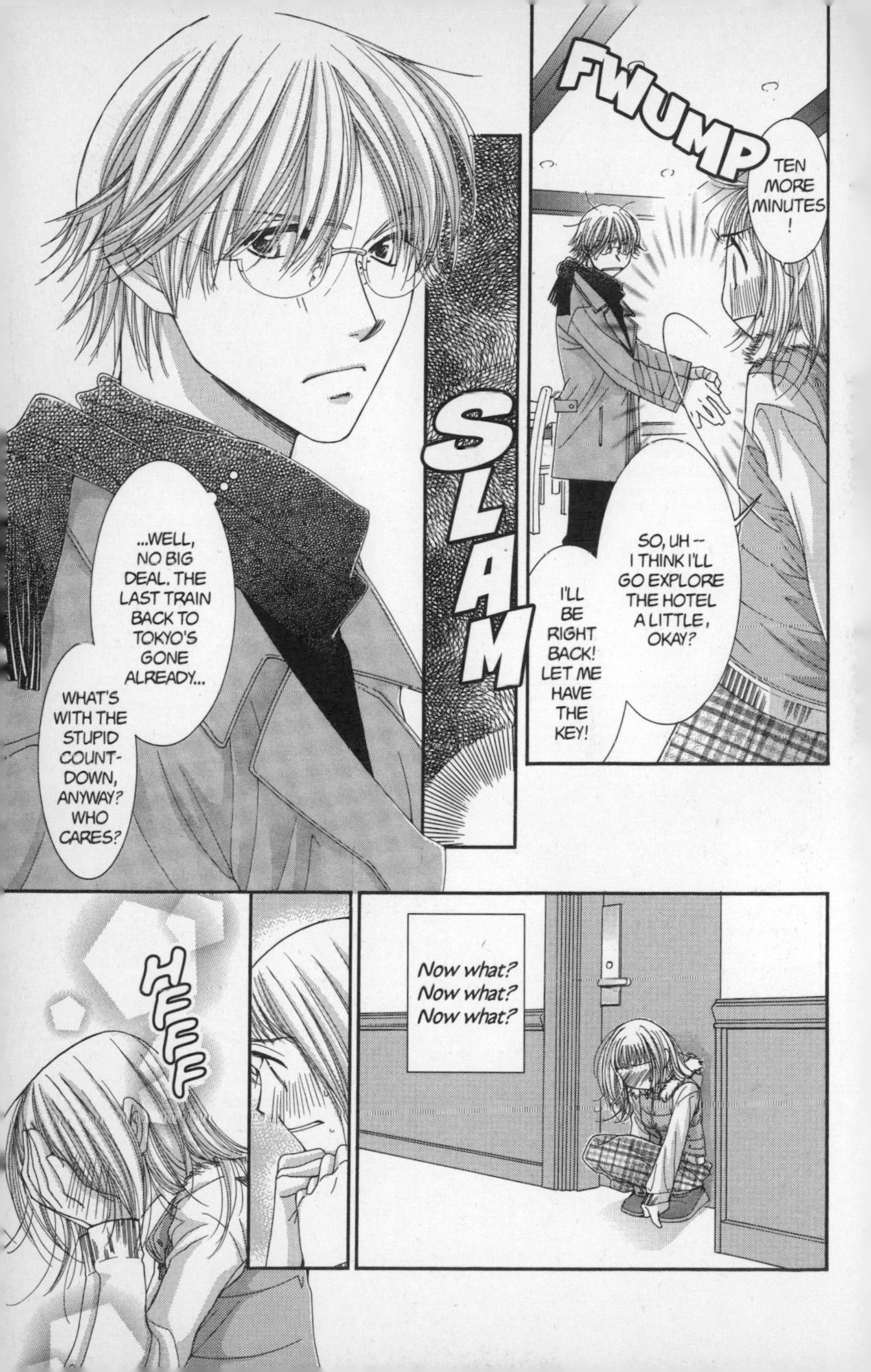
FWUMP
TEN MORE MINUTES!
SO, UH -- I THINK I'LL GO EXPLORE THE HOTEL A LITTLE, OKAY?
I'LL BE RIGHT BACK! LET ME HAVE THE KEY!
SLAM
...WELL, NO BIG DEAL. THE LAST TRAIN BACK TO TOKYO'S GONE ALREADY...
WHAT'S WITH THE STUPID COUNT-DOWN, ANYWAY? WHO CARES?
Now what? Now what? Now what?
HEFF

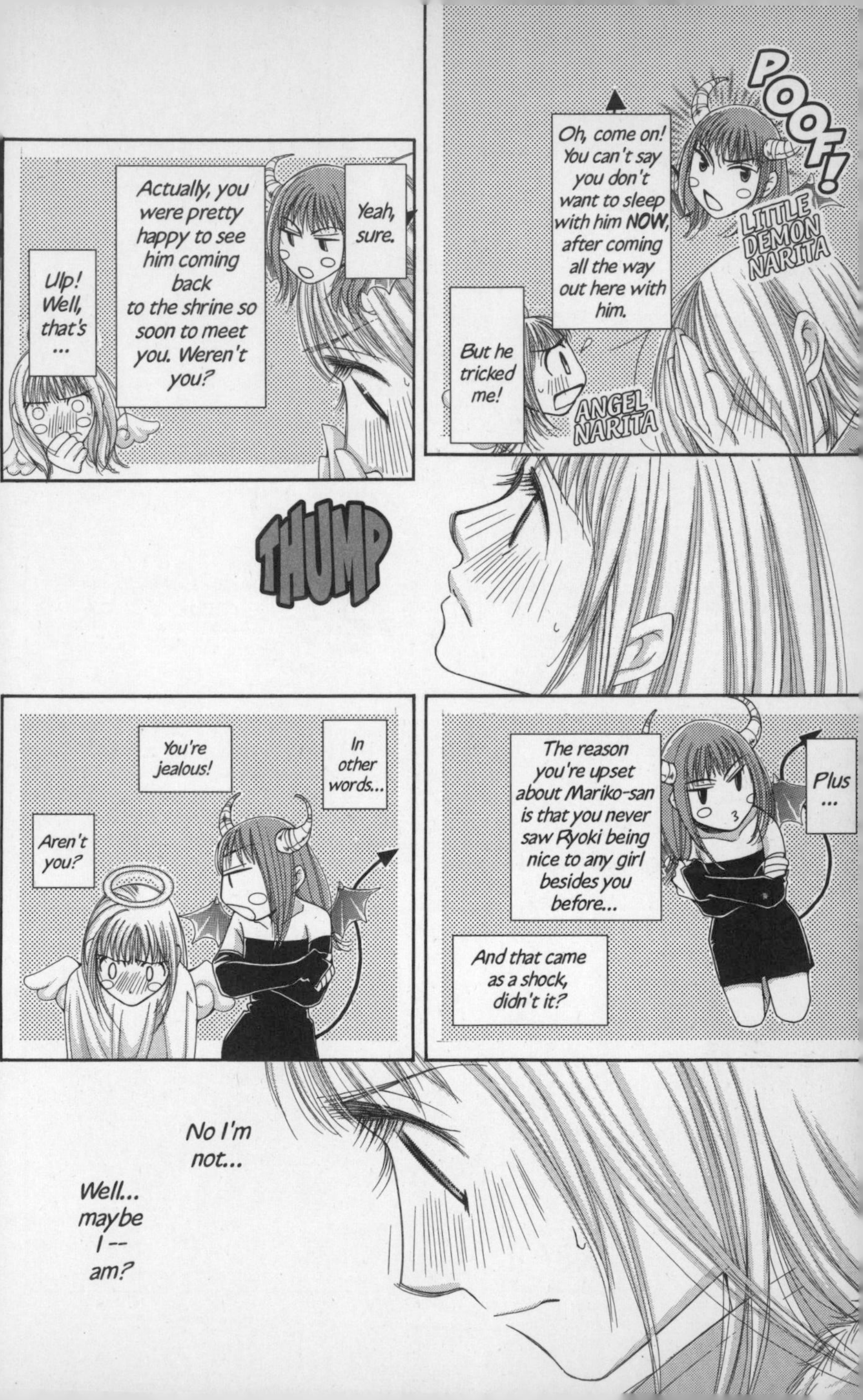
POOF!
LITTLE DEMON NARITA
Oh, come on! You can't say you don't want to sleep with him NOW, after coming all the way out here with him.
ANGEL NARITA
But he tricked me!
Yeah, sure.
Actually, you were pretty happy to see him coming back to the shrine so soon to meet you. Weren't you?
Ulp! Well, that's ...
THUMP
Plus ...
The reason you're upset about Mariko-san is that you never saw Ryoki being nice to any girl besides you before...
And that came as a shock, didn't it?
In other words...
You're jealous!
Aren't you?
No I'm not...
Well... maybe I -- am?

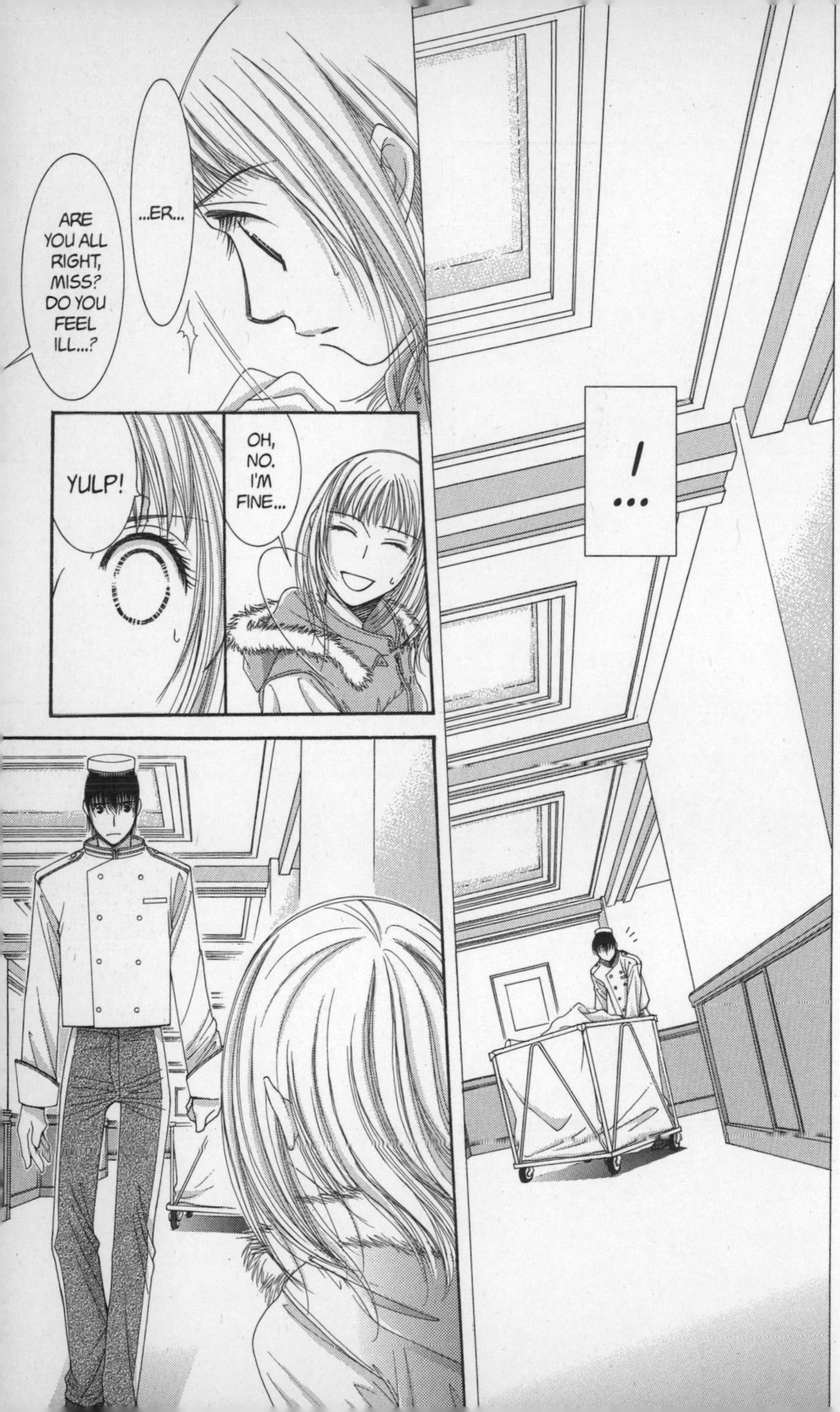
!...
...ER...
ARE YOU ALL RIGHT, MISS? DO YOU FEEL ILL...?
OH, NO. I'M FINE...
YULP!

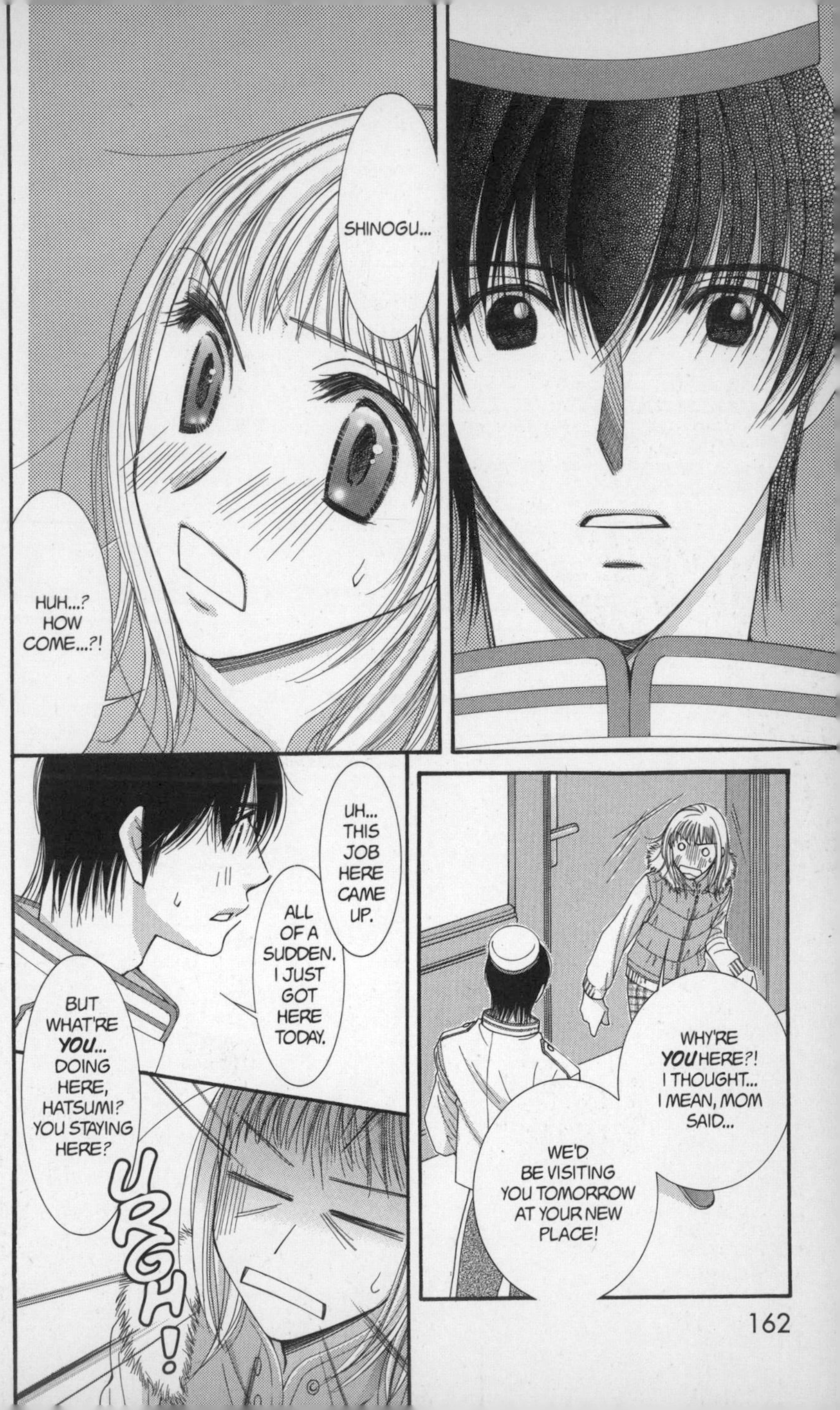
SHINOGU...
HUH...? HOW COME...?!
WHY'RE YOU HERE?! I THOUGHT... I MEAN, MOM SAID...
WE'D BE VISITING YOU TOMORROW AT YOUR NEW PLACE!
UH... THIS JOB HERE CAME UP.
ALL OF A SUDDEN. I JUST GOT HERE TODAY.
BUT WHAT'RE YOU... DOING HERE, HATSUMI? YOU STAYING HERE?
URGH!

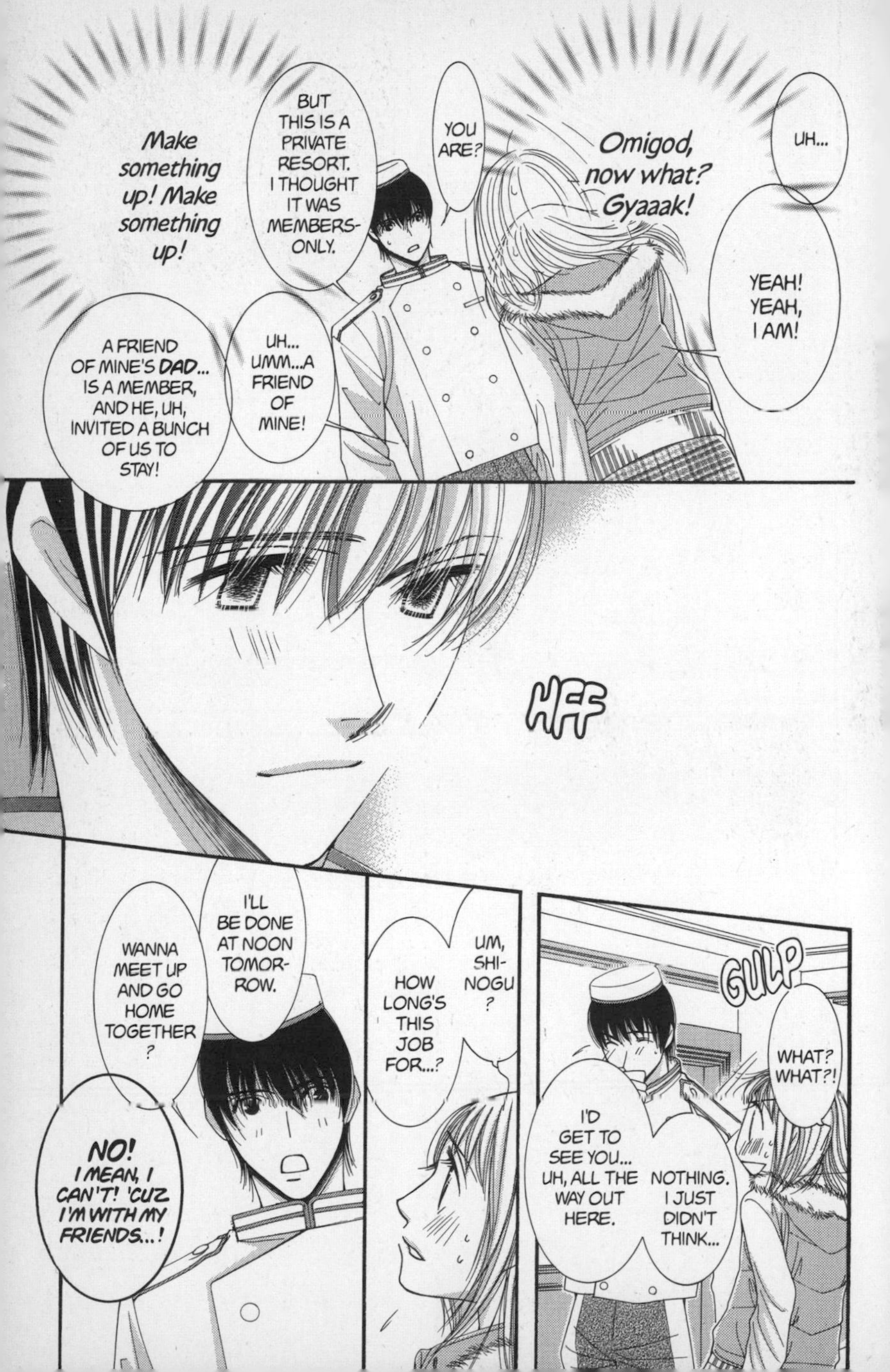
UH...
Omigod, now what? Gyaaak!
YEAH! YEAH, I AM!
YOU ARE?
BUT THIS IS A PRIVATE RESORT. I THOUGHT IT WAS MEMBERS-ONLY.
Make something up! Make something up!
UH... UMM...A FRIEND OF MINE!
A FRIEND OF MINE'S DAD... IS A MEMBER, AND HE, UH, INVITED A BUNCH OF US TO STAY!
HFF
GULP
WHAT? WHAT?!
NOTHING. I JUST DIDN'T THINK...
I'D GET TO SEE YOU... UH, ALL THE WAY OUT HERE.
UM, SHI-NOGU?
HOW LONG'S THIS JOB FOR...?
I'LL BE DONE AT NOON TOMOR-ROW.
WANNA MEET UP AND GO HOME TOGETHER?
NO! I MEAN, I CAN'T! 'CUZ I'M WITH MY FRIENDS...!

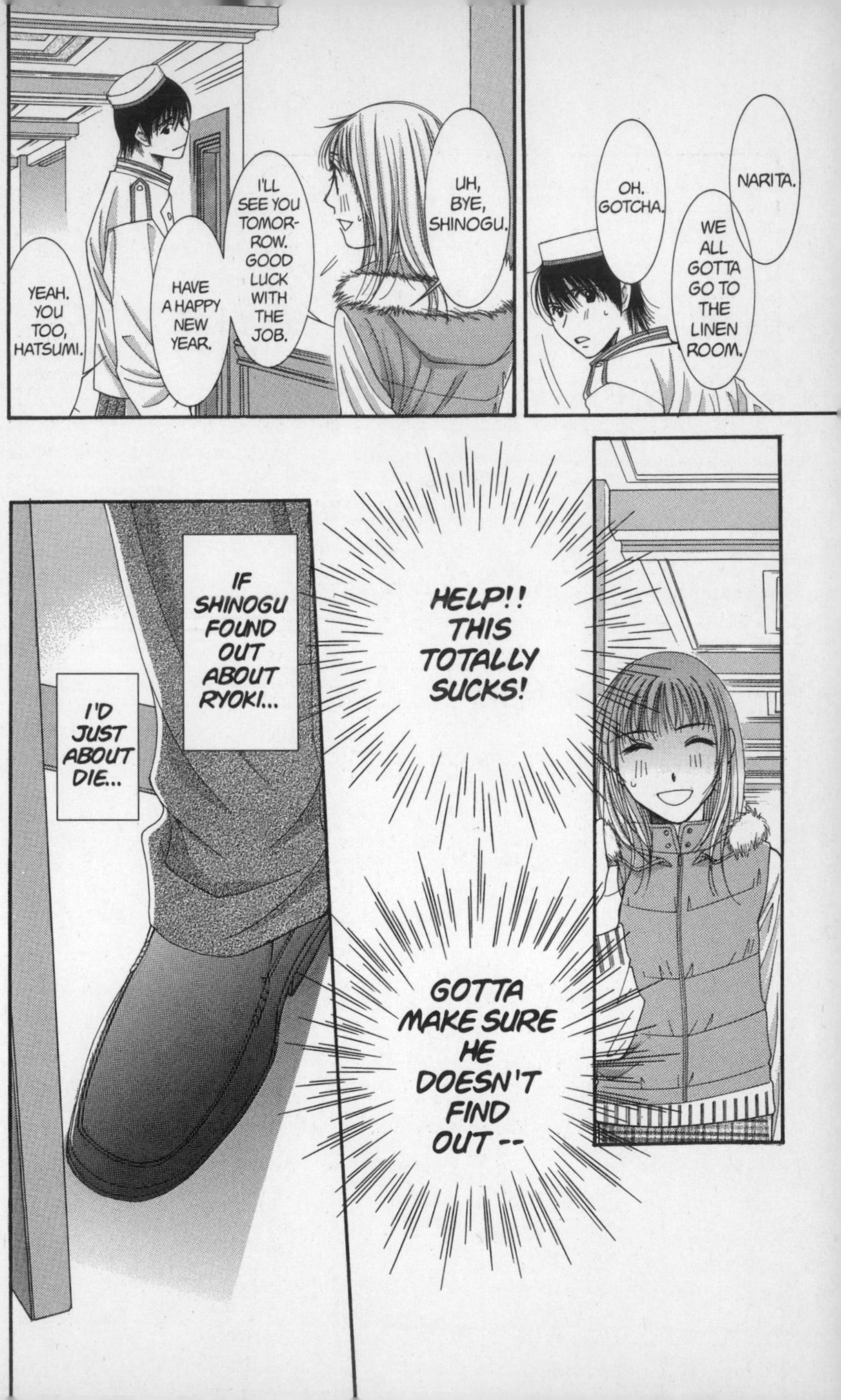
NARITA.
WE ALL GOTTA GO TO THE LINEN ROOM.
OH. GOTCHA.
UH, BYE, SHINOGU.
I'LL SEE YOU TOMOR-ROW. GOOD LUCK WITH THE JOB.
HAVE A HAPPY NEW YEAR.
YEAH. YOU TOO, HATSUMI.
HELP!! THIS TOTALLY SUCKS!
GOTTA MAKE SURE HE DOESN'T FIND OUT --
IF SHINOGU FOUND OUT ABOUT RYOKI...
I'D JUST ABOUT DIE...

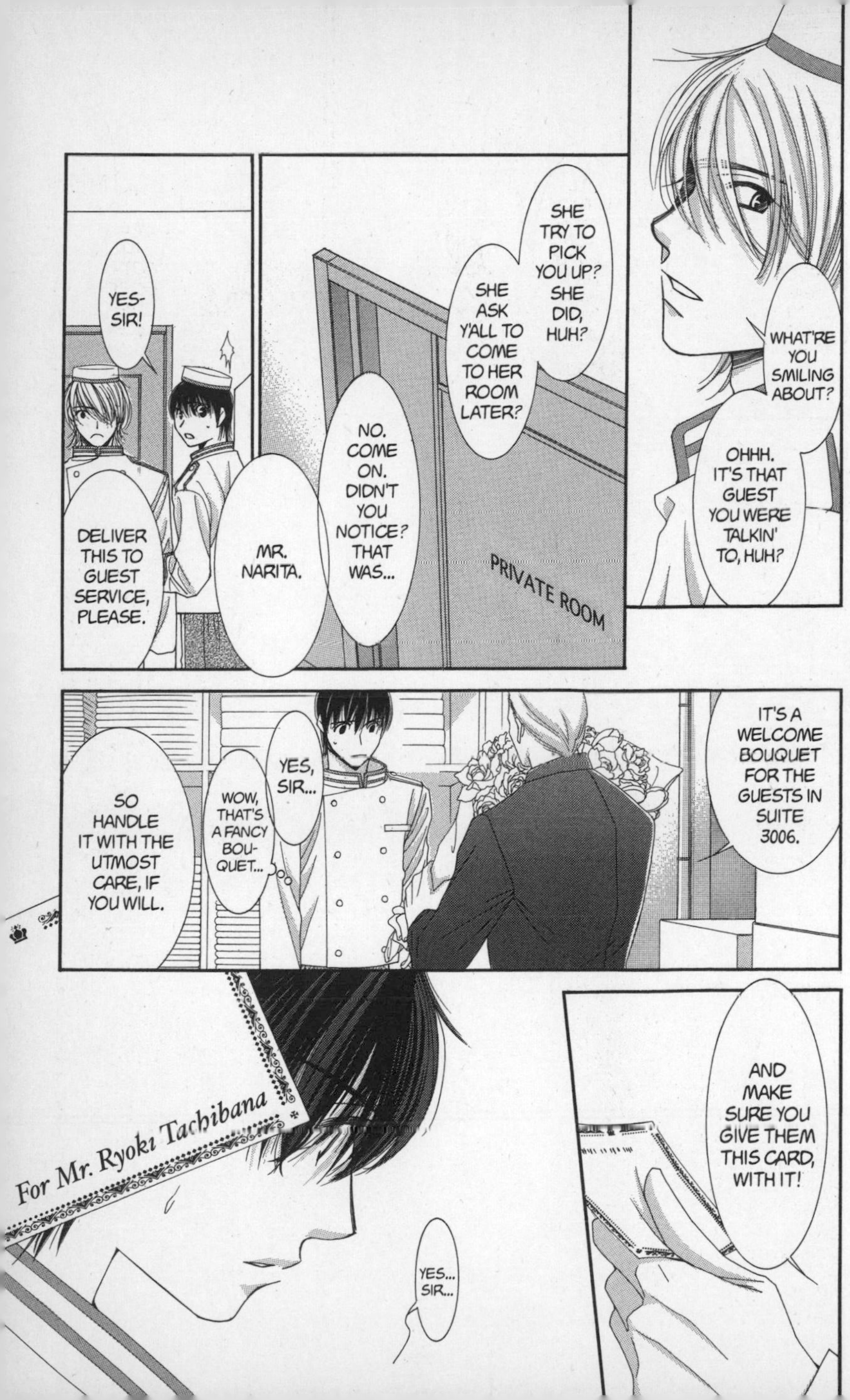
WHAT'RE YOU SMILING ABOUT?
OHHH. IT'S THAT GUEST YOU WERE TALKIN' TO, HUH?
SHE TRY TO PICK YOU UP? SHE DID, HUH?
SHE ASK Y'ALL TO COME TO HER ROOM LATER?
NO. COME ON. DIDN'T YOU NOTICE? THAT WAS...
PRIVATE ROOM
MR. NARITA.
YES-SIR!
DELIVER THIS TO GUEST SERVICE, PLEASE.
IT'S A WELCOME BOUQUET FOR THE GUESTS IN SUITE 3006.
YES, SIR...
WOW, THAT'S A FANCY BOUQUET...
SO HANDLE IT WITH THE UTMOST CARE, IF YOU WILL.
AND MAKE SURE YOU GIVE THEM THIS CARD, WITH IT!
For Mr. Ryoki Tachibana
YES... SIR...

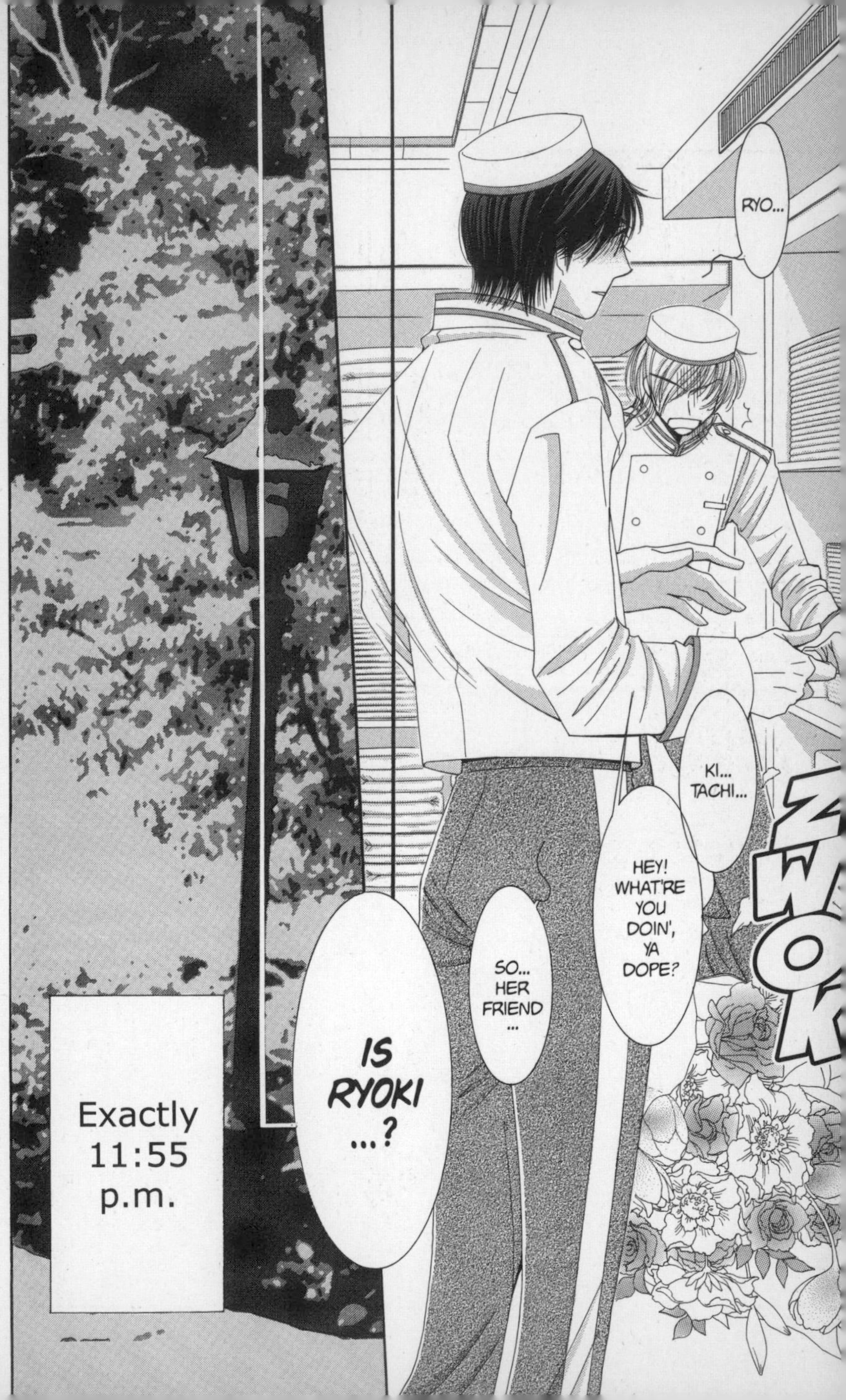
RYO...
KI... TACHI...
HEY! WHAT'RE YOU DOIN', YA DOPE?
ZWOK
SO... HER FRIEND...
IS RYOKI ...?
Exactly 11:55 p.m.

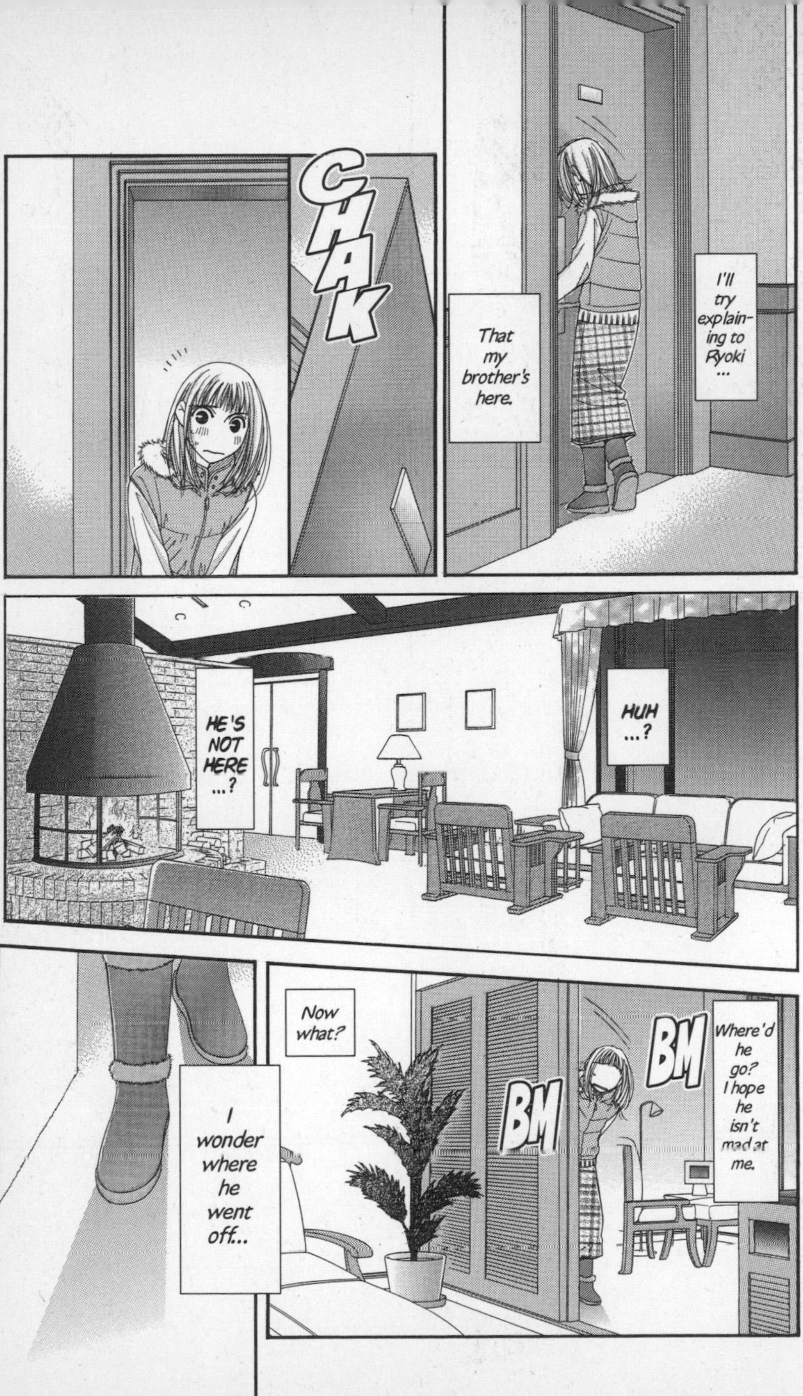
I'll try explaining to Ryoki...
That my brother's here.
CHAK
HUH...?
HE'S NOT HERE...?
Where'd he go? I hope he isn't mad at me.
BM
BM
Now what?
I wonder where he went off...

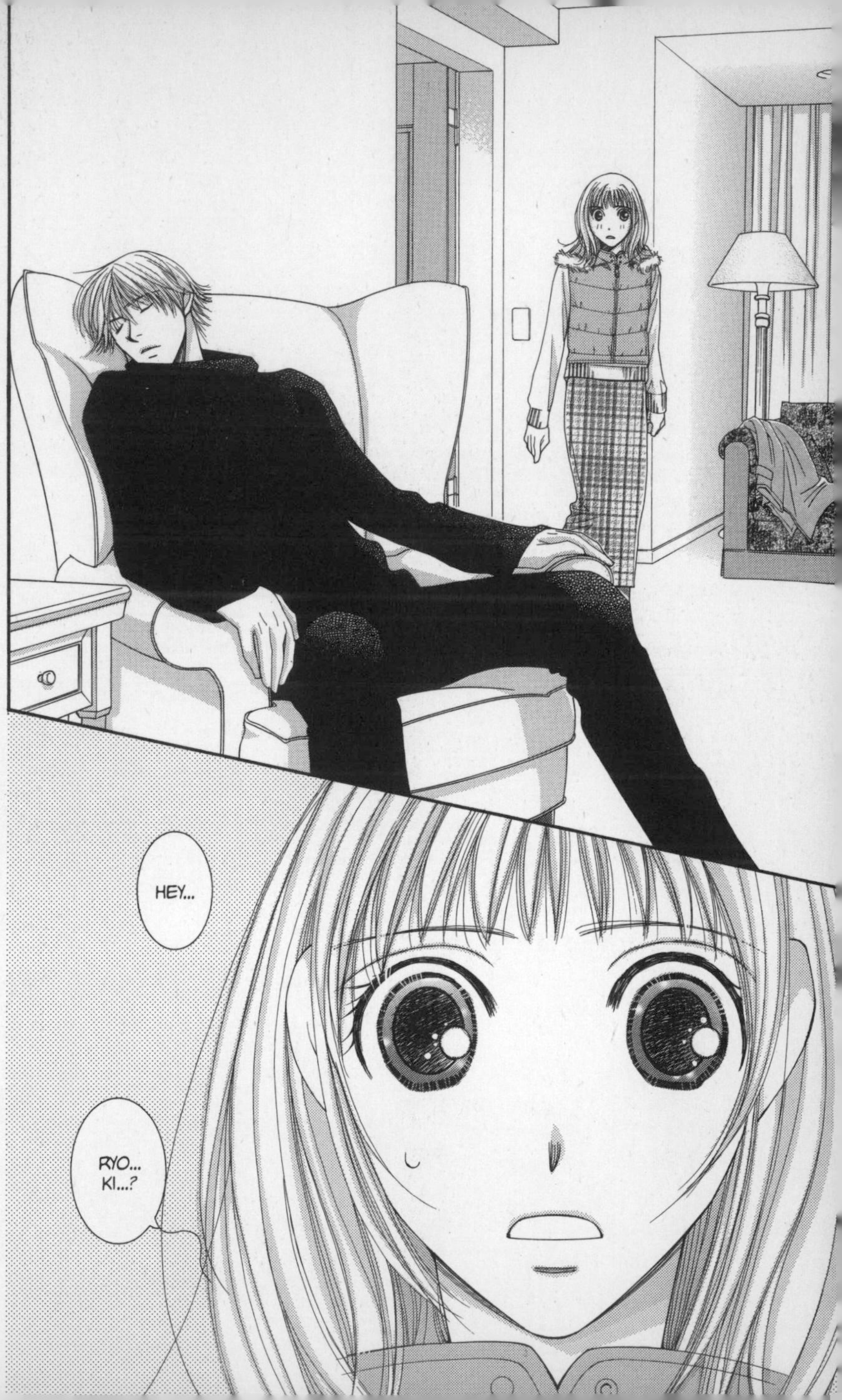
HEY...
RYO... KI...?

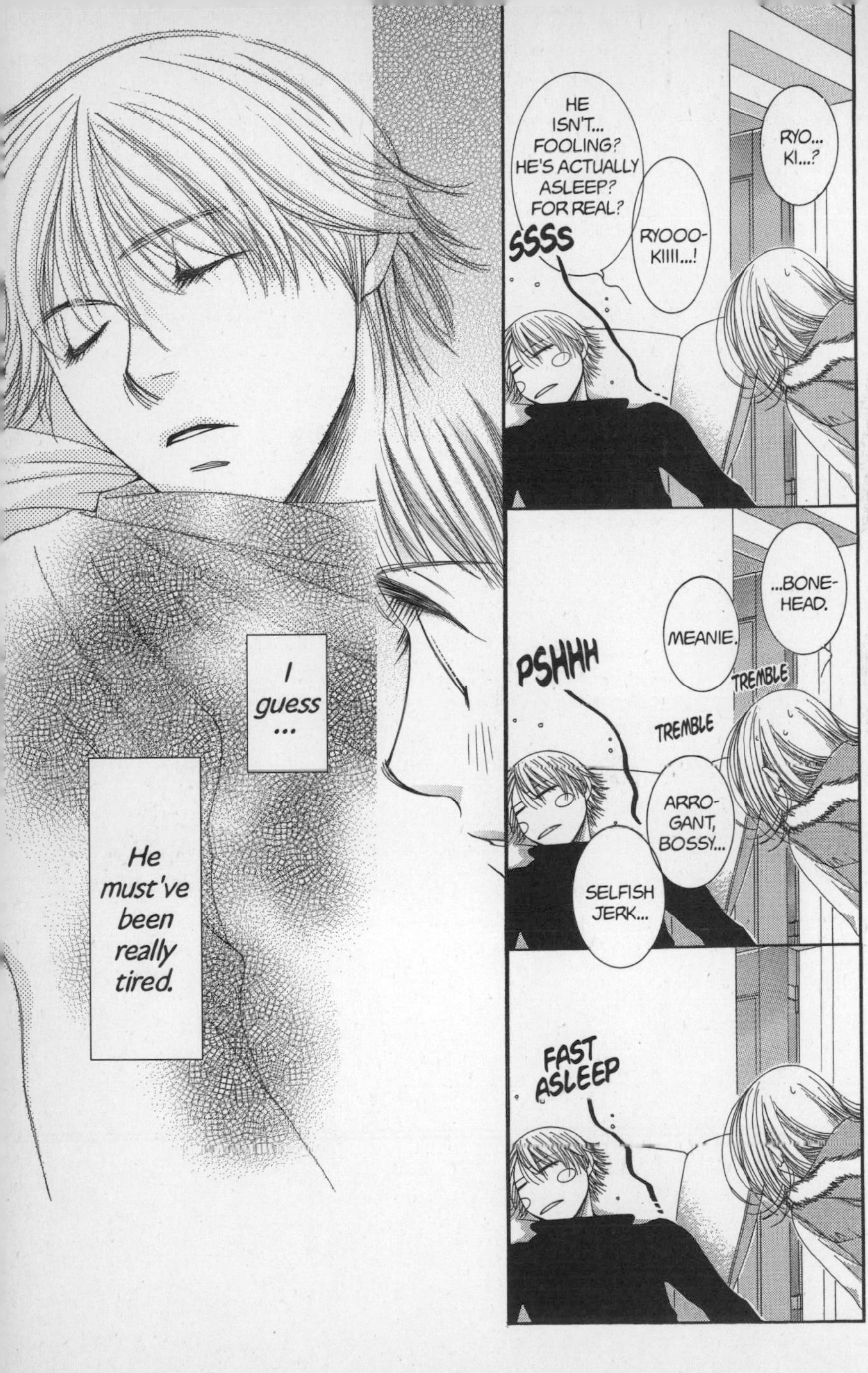

RYO... KI...?
HE ISN'T... FOOLING? HE'S ACTUALLY ASLEEP? FOR REAL?
RYOOO-KIIII...!
SSSS
...BONE-HEAD.
MEANIE.
TREMBLE
PSHHH
TREMBLE
ARRO-GANT, BOSSY...
SELFISH JERK...
FAST ASLEEP
I guess...
He must've been really tired.

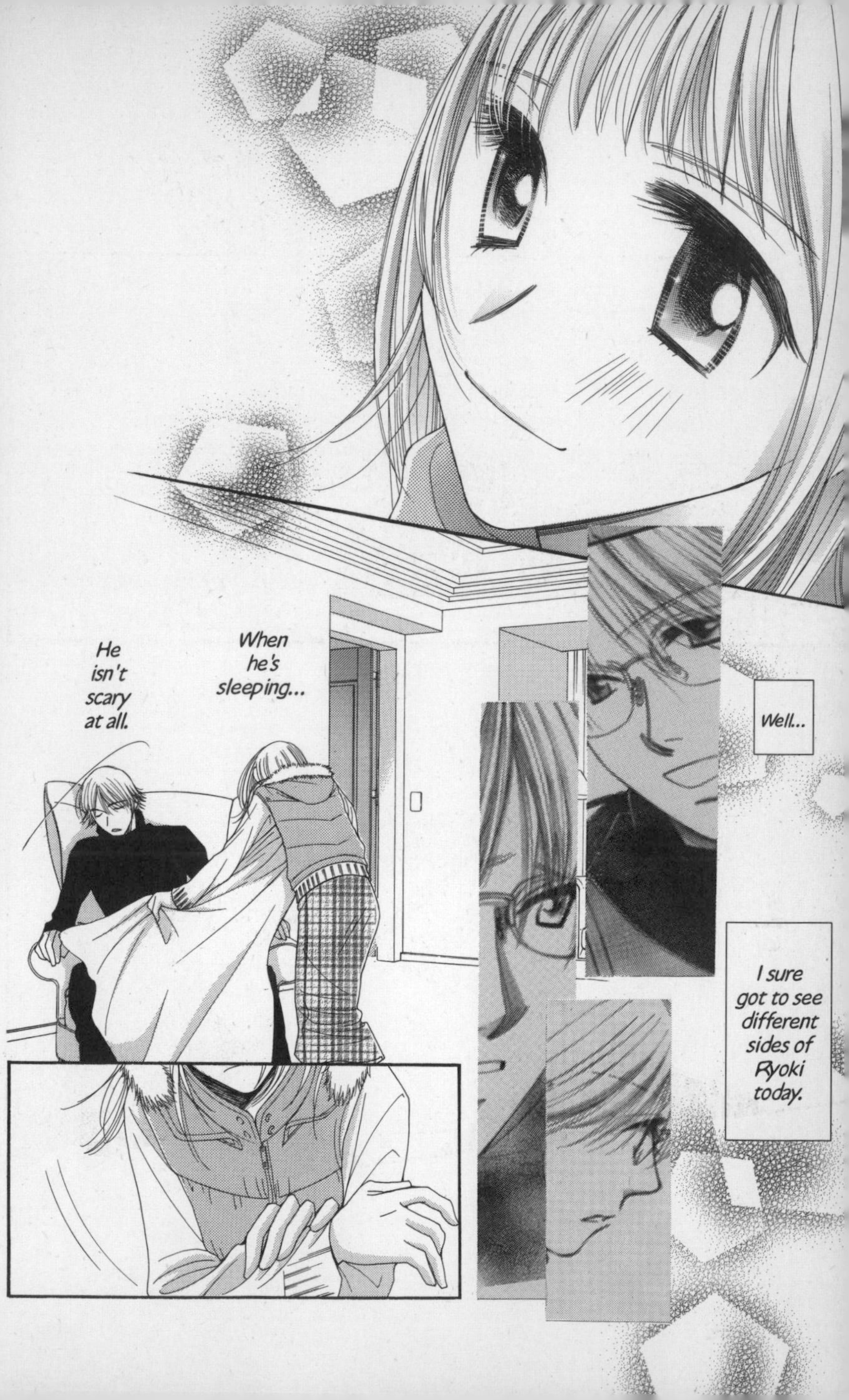
Well...
I sure got to see different sides of Ryoki today.
When he's sleeping...
He isn't scary at all.

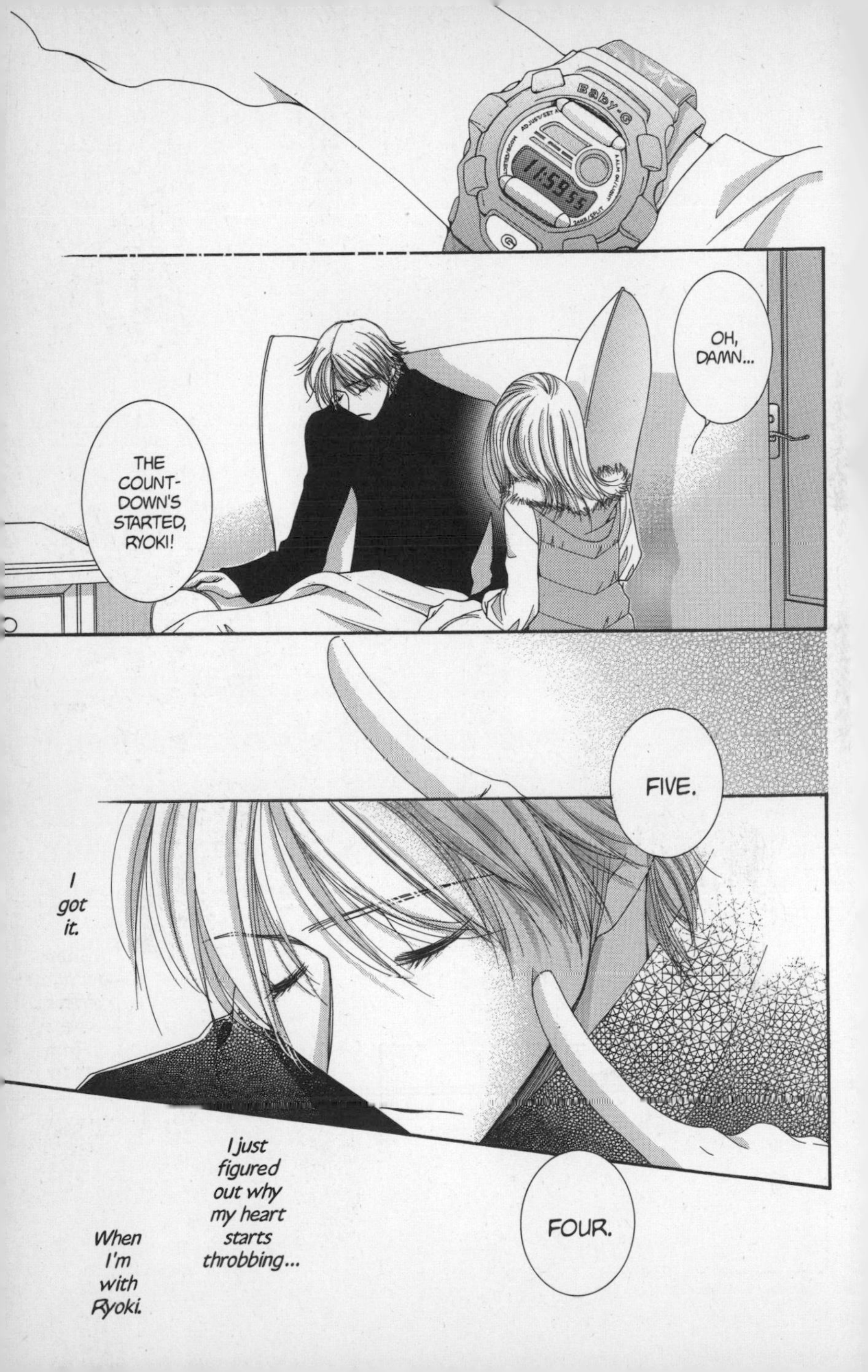
Baby-G
OH, DAMN...
THE COUNT-DOWN'S STARTED, RYOKI!
FIVE.
I got it.
FOUR.
I just figured out why my heart starts throbbing...
When I'm with Ryoki.

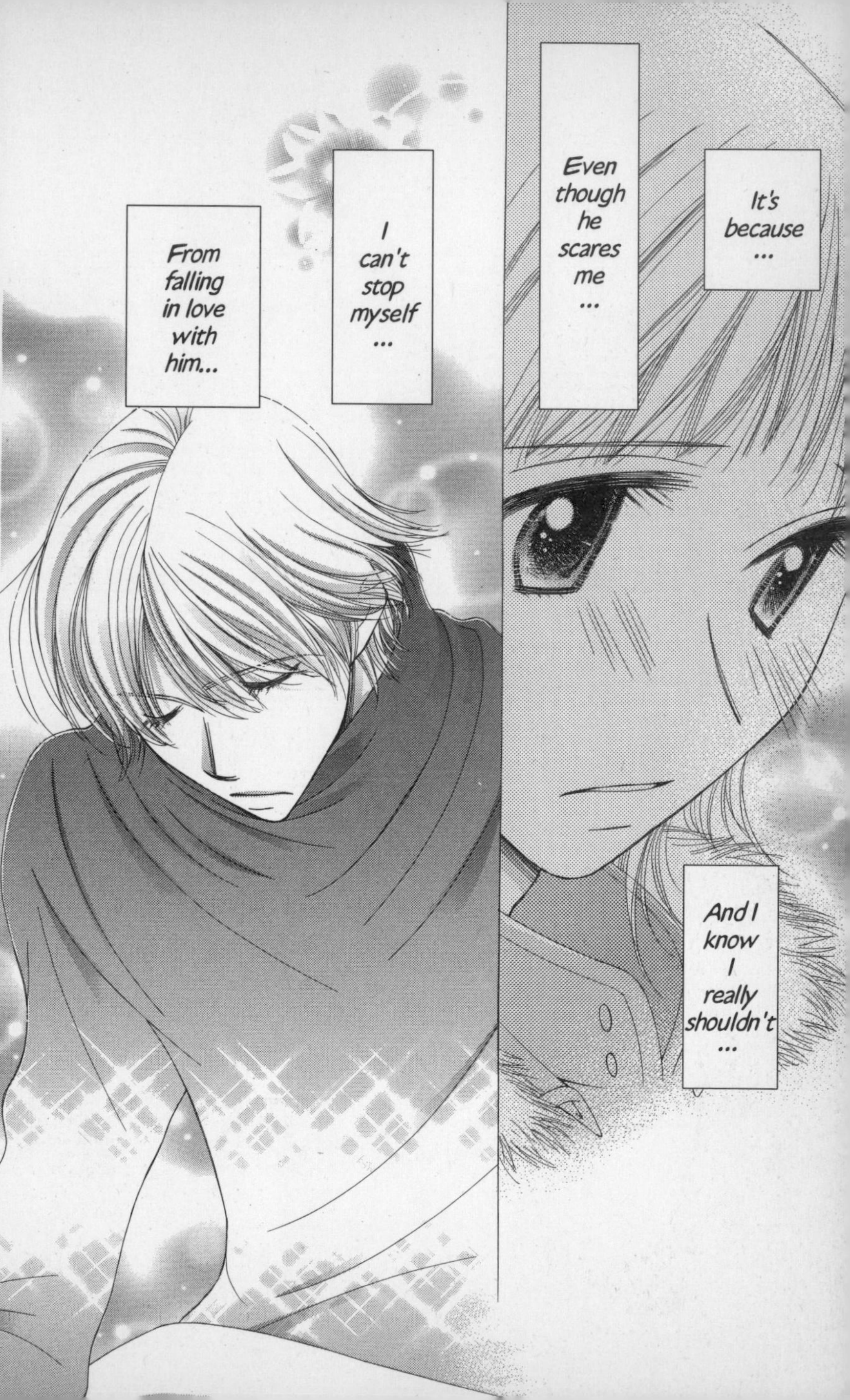
It's because ...
Even though he scares me ...
And I know I really shouldn't ...
I can't stop myself ...
From falling in love with him...

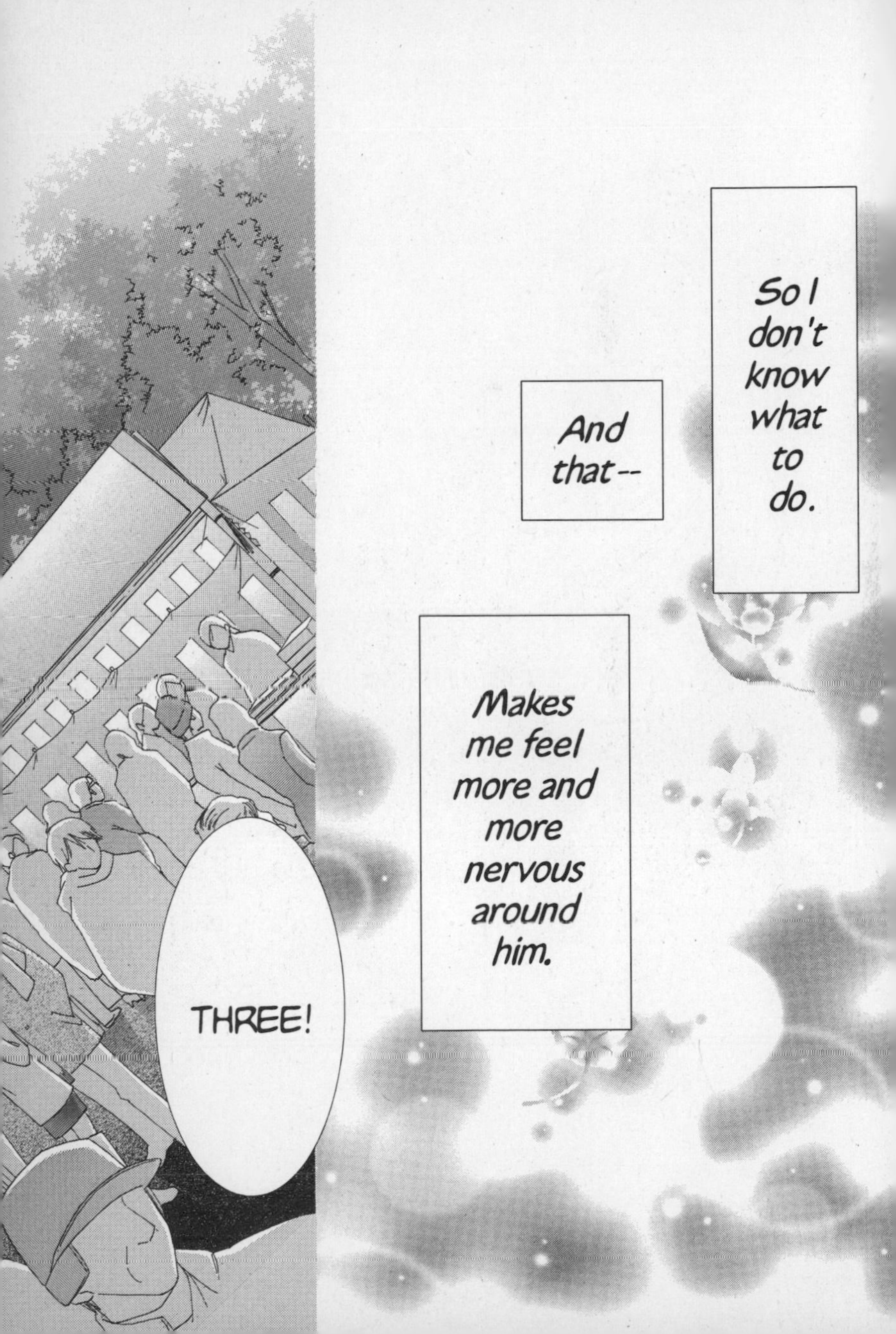
So I don't know what to do.
And that--
Makes me feel more and more nervous around him.
THREE!

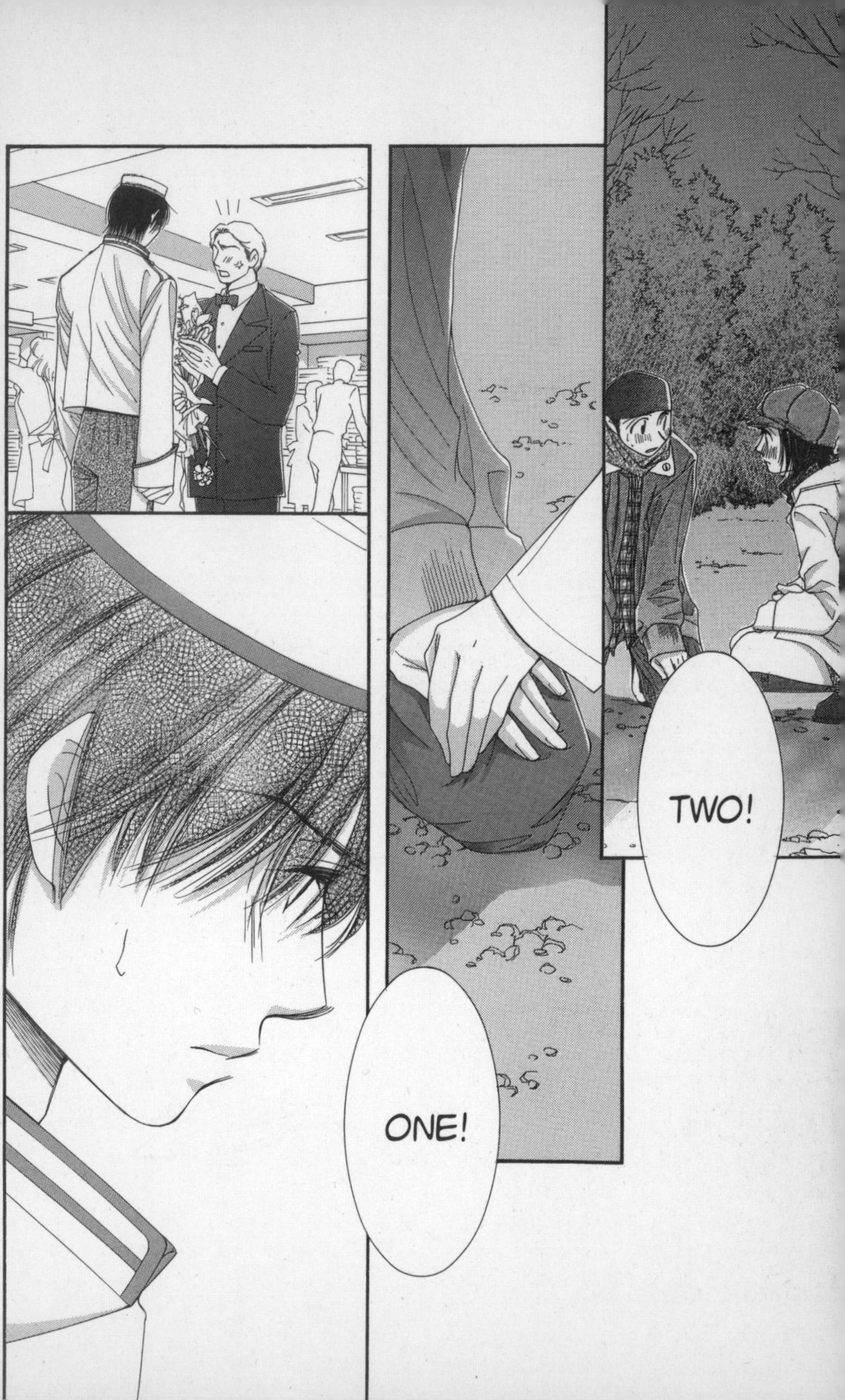
TWO!
ONE!

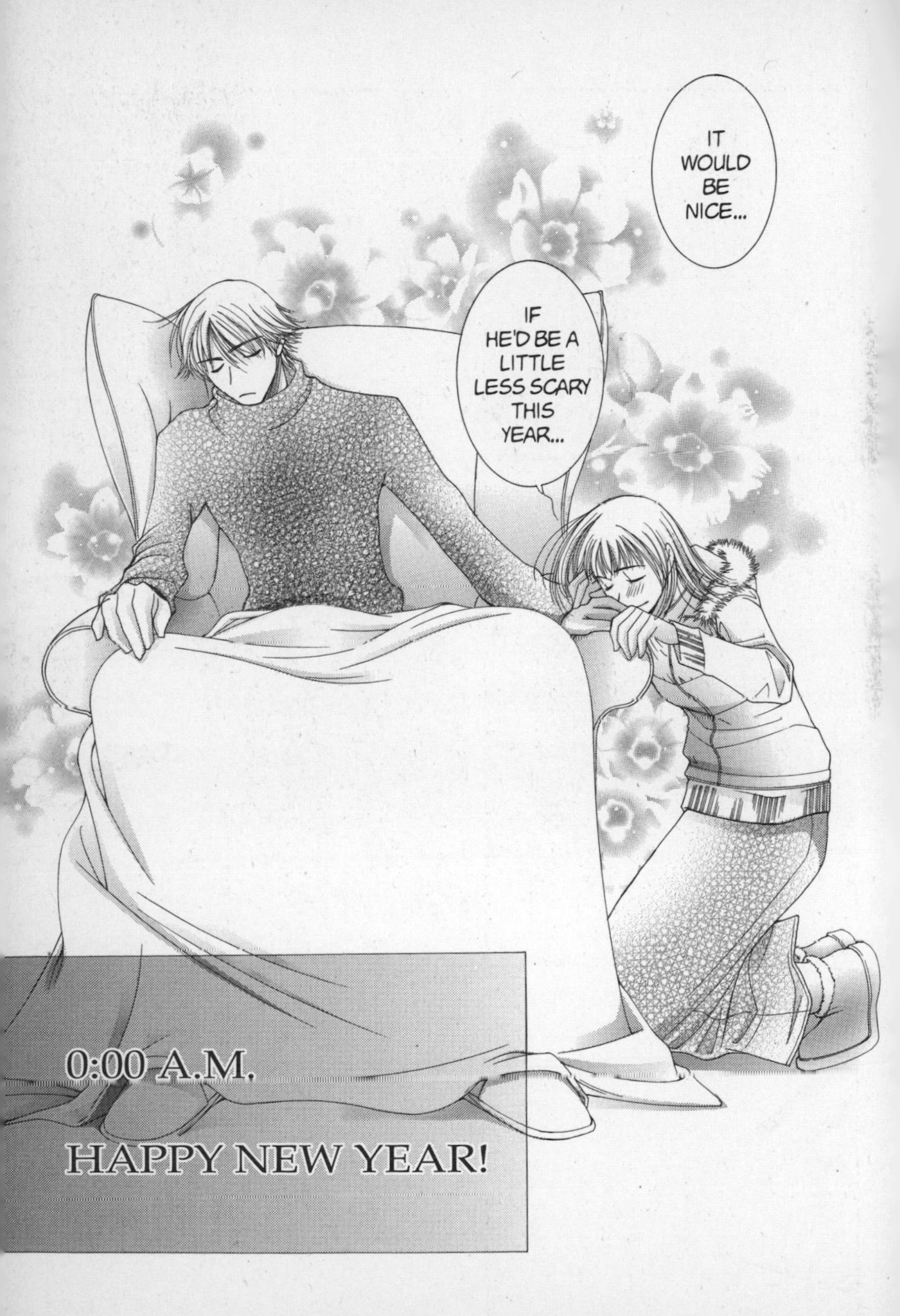
IT WOULD BE NICE...
IF HE'D BE A LITTLE LESS SCARY THIS YEAR...
0:00 A.M.
HAPPY NEW YEAR!

To be continued

EXTRA!!

GIMMICK

Thank you for buying Hot Gimmick Vol. 6.
My name is Miki Aihara.
Here, just for you graphic novel readers, is
more of that extra information that's so hard
to put into the actual story.
Read on!

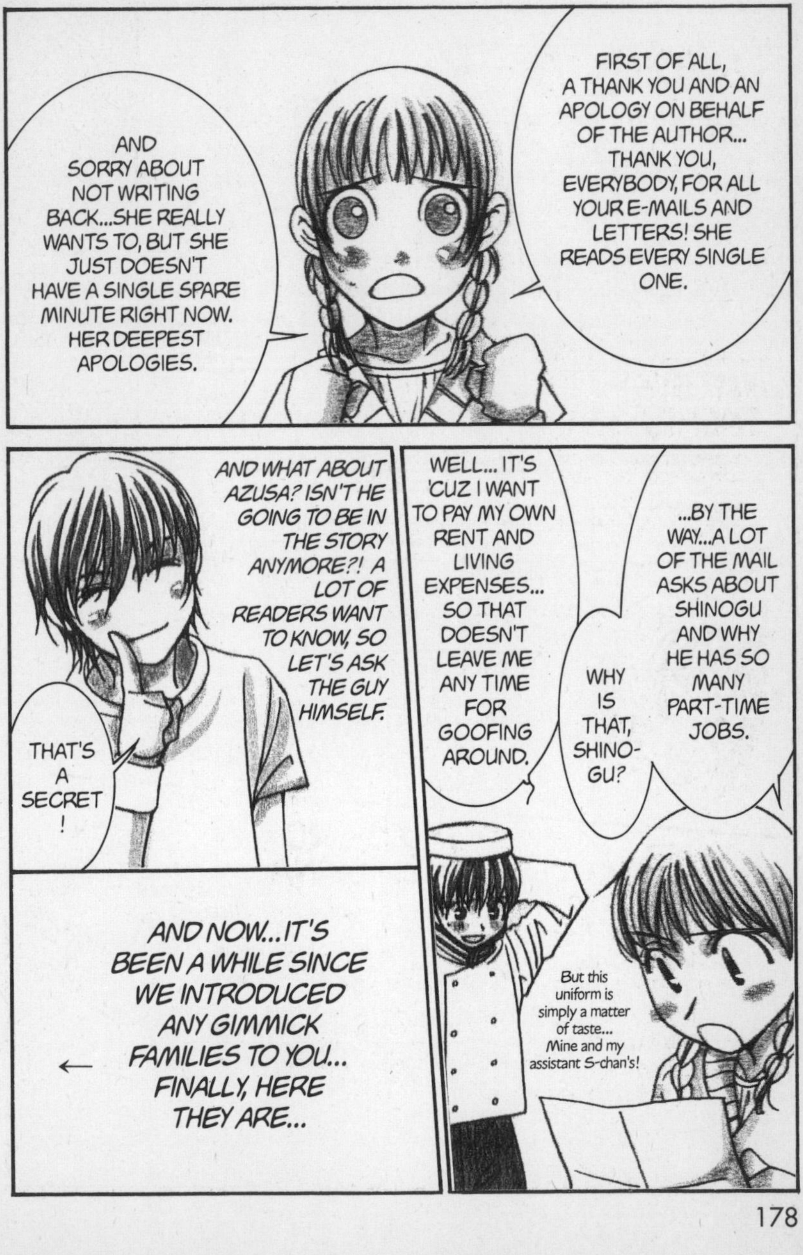
FIRST OF ALL, A THANK YOU AND AN APOLOGY ON BEHALF OF THE AUTHOR... THANK YOU, EVERYBODY, FOR ALL YOUR E-MAILS AND LETTERS! SHE READS EVERY SINGLE ONE.
AND SORRY ABOUT NOT WRITING BACK...SHE REALLY WANTS TO, BUT SHE JUST DOESN'T HAVE A SINGLE SPARE MINUTE RIGHT NOW. HER DEEPEST APOLOGIES.
...BY THE WAY...A LOT OF THE MAIL ASKS ABOUT SHINOGU AND WHY HE HAS SO MANY PART-TIME JOBS.
WHY IS THAT, SHINO-GU?
WELL... IT'S 'CUZ I WANT TO PAY MY OWN RENT AND LIVING EXPENSES... SO THAT DOESN'T LEAVE ME ANY TIME FOR GOOFING AROUND.
But this uniform is simply a matter of taste... Mine and my assistant S-chan's!
AND WHAT ABOUT AZUSA? ISN'T HE GOING TO BE IN THE STORY ANYMORE?! A LOT OF READERS WANT TO KNOW, SO LET'S ASK THE GUY HIMSELF.
THAT'S A SECRET!
AND NOW...IT'S BEEN A WHILE SINCE WE INTRODUCED ANY GIMMICK FAMILIES TO YOU... FINALLY, HERE THEY ARE...
←

The Tachibana Family and Someone Who Works For Them

RYOKI (17)

- SECOND-YEAR STUDENT AT THE PRESTIGIOUS PRIVATE KAISEI ACADEMY.
- 177 cm TALL, 61 kg. (BUT STILL GROWING. A LOT TO GO.)
- WAS SICK DURING ENTRANCE EXAMS FOR PRIVATE ELEMENTARY SCHOOLS, SO FORCED TO GO TO PUBLIC SCHOOL THROUGH SIXTH GRADE. (MAJOR SOURCE OF SHAME TO MRS. T.) SPENT ALL JUNIOR HIGH VACATIONS ABROAD, SO SPEAKS PERFECT ENGLISH.

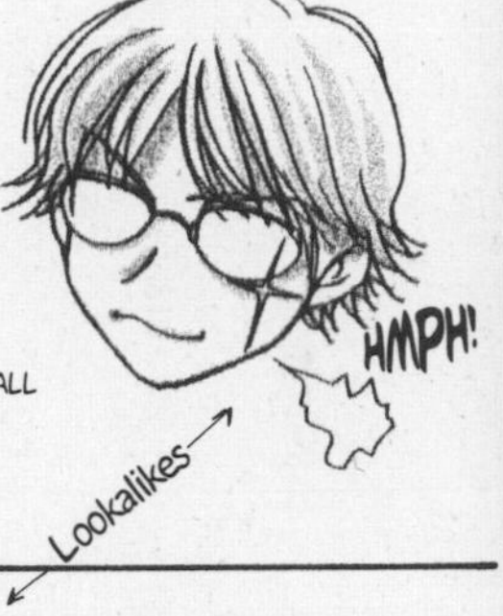
HMPH!
Lookalikes

NATSUE TACHIBANA

- UNDISPUTED QUEEN OF THE COMPANY HOUSING COMPLEX.
- FORMER BEAUTY WHO WAS ONCE CROWNED MISS KOBE.

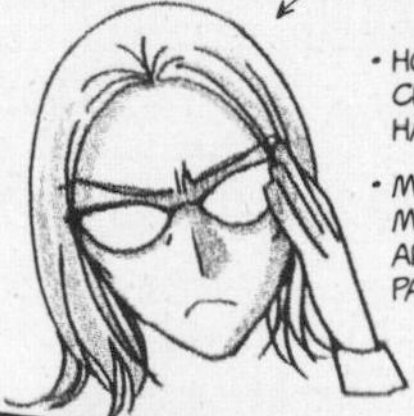

- HOBBIES INCLUDE THE TEA CEREMONY, IKEBANA AND HAIKU.
- MARRIAGE TO MR. TACHIBANA WAS ARRANGED BY THEIR PARENTS.

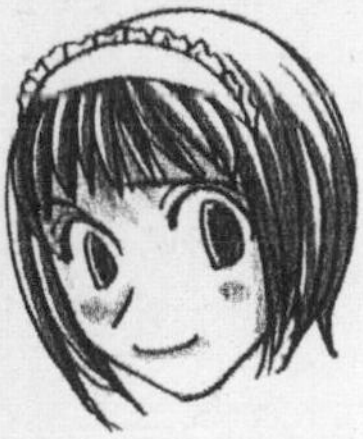

MARIKO TAKATUO (23)

- SERVED IN THE TACHIBANA HOUSEHOLD (RYOKI'S GRANDPARENTS) FROM A YOUNG AGE, DUE TO HER PARENTS' WORK SITUATION.
- HAS KNOWN RYOKI SINCE HE WAS IN ELEMENTARY SCHOOL.

SHUICHIRO TACHIBANA

- AT LAST HE MAKES AN APPEARANCE!
- WENT TO SAME UNIVERSITY AS THE OTHER DADS, BUT A FEW YEARS AHEAD OF THEM.
- MOSTLY STAYS AT A HOTEL NEAR THE COMPANY, SO HARDLY EVER RETURNS TO THE COMPLEX. (UNLIKE HIS WIFE, HAS ABSOLUTELY NO INTEREST IN THE GOINGS-ON THERE.)

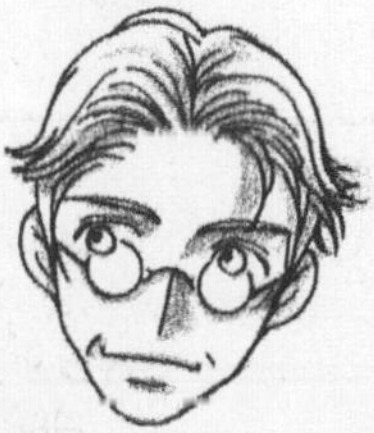

THERE'S A LOT MORE TO TELL ABOUT THE TACHIBANAS, BUT LET'S LEAVE IT AT THIS FOR NOW! AND THAT'S ALL THE EXTRA FOR TODAY, FOLKS.

HOT GIMMICK
Vol. 6

Shôjo Edition

STORY & ART BY MIKI AIHARA

ENGLISH ADAPTATION BY POOKIE ROLF

Touch-Up Art & Lettering/Rina Mapa
Cover Design/Izumi Evers
Interior Design/Judi Roubideaux
Editor/Kit Fox

Managing Editor/Annette Roman
Editorial Director/Alvin Lu
Director of Production/Noboru Watanabe
Sr. Director of Licensing & Acquisitions/Rika Inouye
Vice President of Marketing/Liza Coppola
Vice President of Sales/Joe Morici
Executive Vice President/Hyoe Narita
Publisher/Seiji Horibuchi

Printed in Canada.

Published by VIZ, LLC, P.O. Box 77010, San Francisco, CA 94107

Shôjo Edition
10 9 8 7 6 5 4 3 2 1
First printing, August 2004

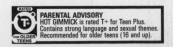

Hot Gimmick

EDITOR'S RECOMMENDATIONS

More manga!
More manga!

Did you like *Hot Gimmick*? Here's what VIZ recommends you try next:

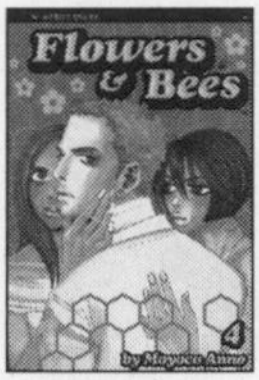
Flowers & Bees
4
by Moyoco Anno

© 2001 Moyoco Anno/
Kodansha Ltd.

FLOWERS & BEES Moyoco Anno's painfully hilarious chronicle of a normal guy attempting to unleash his inner metrosexual is as funny as it is incisive. Hoping to spruce up his image (and at the same time, increase his chances of "gettin' some"), Komatsu becomes a regular at the World of Beautiful Men salon. The salon's proprietresses, a pair of sexy fashionistas, adopt Komatsu as their own private slave and shadow his myriad failed attempts at scoring some points with the opposite sex. Will this equally hapless hero ever get some lovin'? More importantly, will he ever get his act together?

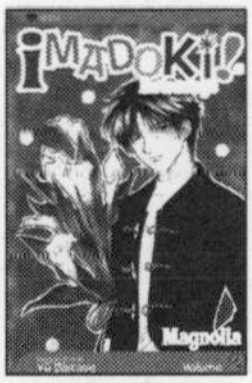
Magnolia

© 2000 Yuu Watase/
Shogakukan, Inc.

IMADOKI! [NOWADAYS] Tanpopo Yamazaki has come a long way from her native Hokkaido to attend prestigious Meio Academy and Yû Watase's *IMADOKI! [NOWADAYS]* follows this tenacious horticulturist as she tries to make friends, influence people, and plant flowers. Trouble is, real flowers are strictly verboten at Meio (the posh student-body suffers from allergies). Tanpopo will have to do a lot more than plant petunias to win over these prudes.

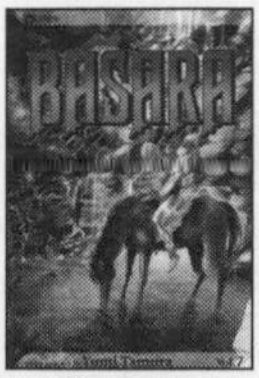
BASARA

© 1991 Yumi Tamura/
Shogakukan, Inc.

BASARA Yumi Tamura's sprawling epic *BASARA* is one of the most gripping shôjo stories around. A young girl must battle despotic warlords, unearth hidden treasures, and unite a nation, all while impersonating her fallen brother. Is Sarasa truly the child of destiny? Or is her quest doomed to fail? *BASARA* has action, romance, and heart-wrenching drama, all on a grand scale. Not to be missed.